GOING DUTCH

A Visitor's Guide to the
Pennsylvania Dutch Country

William N. Hoffman

GOING DUTCH:
A Visitor's Guide to the Pennsylvania Dutch Country

Copyright © 1989 by William N. Hoffman

Published by:
Spring Garden Publications Co.
P.O. Box 1770
New Rochelle, New York 10802-1770

Printed and bound in the United States of America

Library of Congress Catalog Card Number: 89-90965

ISBN: 0-9612050-5-9

First Edition, First Printing: May, 1989

ACKNOWLEDGEMENTS

I would like to acknowledge the valuable assistance of the following people in the research and production of this book: George Beyer, M. Susan Breen, Mary Ann Bungerz, Anne Case, Bill di Scipio, Robert Dryden, Susan Etkind, Linda Exman, Harry L. Flick, Jr., Mildred Forrester, Barnet Frommer, Howard Geisinger, Barbara Groce, John Hickernell, Deb Hickok, Karen Hurwitz, Susan Kenny, John Kremer, Tom Kugle, Melanie Landis, Phil Magaldi, Ruth Mock, Pat Redmond, Sheila Romirowsky, Louis Satz, Mary Ann White, Martina Witmer.

Base map credits: Pennsylvania Department of General Services: all county maps; Lancaster and Environs; Northern, Eastern, Southern, and Western Lancaster County; Allentown-Bethlehem Area; Harrisburg Area and West Shore; Reading Area; York Area; Hershey; Gettysburg. Joint Planning Commission of Lehigh-Northampton Counties: Downtown Allentown, Downtown Bethlehem, Downtown Easton. Tri-County Planning Commission: Downtown Carlisle, Downtown Harrisburg, Shipoke, Capitol District. Lancaster County Planning Commission: Downtown Lancaster. York City Planning Commission: Downtown York. Borough of West Chester: Downtown West Chester.

Author photo: Joel Elkins. Cover and inside photos by the author.

Cover design: Robin DaFano

GOING DUTCH is sold at many bookstores throughout the Northeastern United States and elsewhere, and at many business establishments within the Pennsylvania Dutch Country. If unavailable, you may order directly from the publisher:

Spring Garden Publications Co.
P.O. Box 1770
New Rochelle, New York 10802-1770

Please enclose check or money order, in U.S. funds, for $12.95 per book, plus shipping and handling charge of $1.55 for the first book, and 50¢ for the second and third books. Thus, the total cost is $14.50 for one book, $27.95 for two, and $41.40 for three. Quantity discounts are available for four or more copies; please write for the discount schedule.

TABLE OF CONTENTS

FOREWORD   7

INTRODUCTION   9
    What Is the Pennsylvania Dutch Country   9
    Boundaries of the PDC   10
    Using This Book   11
    Using the Maps   12
    The Ratings   12
    Obtaining Tourist Information   14

BACKGROUND   15
    History   15
    Geography   22
    Climate   22
    Economy   24
    The People   25
    Regional Cooking   35
    Regional Speech   36

USEFUL INFORMATION   39
    Getting to the PDC   39
    Traveling Within the PDC   41
    About Pennsylvania   45
    Recreation Facilities   46
    Shopping   55
    Calendar of Events   57

SPECIAL FEATURES   71
    Farmers' Markets   71
    Covered Bridges   72
    Historic Places and Districts   73
    Walking Tours   74
    Wineries   74
    Caves   75
    Antiquing   75

THE COUNTIES   **76**
    Adams   76
    Berks   90
    Bucks   108
    Chester   120
    Cumberland   134
    Dauphin   142
    Franklin   162
    Lancaster   172
    Lebanon   200
    Lehigh Valley (Lehigh & Northampton)   208
    Montgomery   230
    York   240

APPENDIX   **255**
    A State Parks   256
    B Bed and Breakfast Inns   258
    C Farm Vacation Homes   270
    D Hotels and Motels   274
    E Campgrounds   290
    F Restaurants   298

GENERAL INDEX   **307**
SUBJECT INDEX   **310**

FOREWORD

The Pennsylvania Dutch Country (PDC for short) is one of America's most popular tourist areas. The beautiful countryside and the presence of hundreds of historic, cultural, and recreation attractions make this a delightful vacation spot. I was fortunate to have been born and raised in this area, and I would like to introduce you to the place I still call "home."

Many travel books cover the PDC, but always as part of a larger work—for example, a guide to Philadelphia, or the mid-Atlantic region, or excursions from nearby large cities. Consequently, they devote, at most, a chapter or two to the PDC, usually highlighting the Amish area, paying scant attention to the rest of the region if they mention it at all. This book is different—it covers the entire PDC, and therefore, is the most comprehensive travel guide ever written about this special corner of America.

Here you will find listings and descriptions of all the historic, cultural, and recreational attractions in the PDC, along with evaluations, time needed to visit, and driving directions, to help you make the most of your time. Lodging accommodations (hotels, motels, bed and breakfast inns, campgrounds, farm vacation homes) and a selection of restaurants are included to aid in your planning. In short, whether you're spending just a weekend or several weeks, everything you need to plan and enjoy your PDC vacation is here.

THE PENNSYLVANIA DUTCH COUNTRY (PDC)

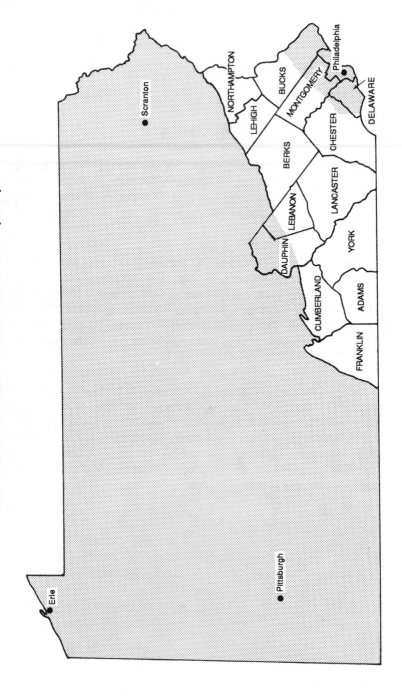

INTRODUCTION

WHAT IS THE PENNSYLVANIA DUTCH COUNTRY?

Most people, when they hear the term "Pennsylvania Dutch Country", probably think of the area of Lancaster County that contains settlements of Amish people. Most advertising directed at tourists perpetuates this belief. Although the Amish are the best known of the numerous ethnic and religious groups living in this region, and are most heavily concentrated in Lancaster County, they are by no means the only "Pennsylvania Dutch" people, nor does their homeland represent the entire "Pennsylvania Dutch Country".

The term "Pennsylvania Dutch" itself is a misnomer; its origins lie in a corruption of the word *Deutsch*, which is German for "German". But that's a story for another chapter. The purpose here is to better define the Pennsylvania Dutch Country as it really is (I've referred to it throughout the book as "PDC" for short), and as it's covered in this book.

The PDC is the area of southeastern Pennsylvania that was settled predominantly by Germans seeking religious freedom in William Penn's new colony Pennsylvania. This is the area where their influence in all aspects of life remains strong to this day. Primarily a farming people (the PDC had fertile soil and bore a physical resemblance to their native land), they resumed their former way of life here, but, in the absence of persecution, at a higher economic level than in Europe.

The PDC is a unique part of America and has much to offer visitors of all ages. There are beautiful rolling hills and farmlands, historic towns, majestic old homes and churches, museums commemorating the lives and culture of early settlers, hundreds of historic places and districts, numerous recreation facilities, and many one-of-a-kind attractions. It's no wonder that the area has become such a popular vacation spot. Moreover, it's within one day's travel of one-fourth of the country's population, and no more than a few hours from most of the major East Coast metropolitan areas, making it an ideal place for weekend getaways as well as for longer trips.

What you will see here is not a region living in its past, but one where the business of making and growing things for America and the world at large goes on amid aspects of its history that have been maintained, preserved, and restored, in recognition of the region's place in the development of America. Thus, visiting the PDC is not the same as visiting Williamsburg, Virginia, where, in effect, time is frozen. The PDC is a sort of "open air museum", where the old co-exists with the new.

The PDC is much more than the Amish area of Lancaster County. The region has scores of worthwhile attractions that most visitors overlook. I wanted to introduce you to the many unheralded places—the excellent historical museums in Allentown, Carlisle, West Chester, and York; the Moravian settlement in Bethlehem; the unspoiled charm of Mercersburg; the fascinating transportation museums of Berks County—to name just a few examples. Experience the beauty of towns such as Chambersburg, Doylestown, Lititz, Maytown, Nazareth, and Stouchsburg—communities that have largely retained their original appearance through preservation, not renovation. If you can't take time this trip to visit some or all of the unsung attractions, I hope I've encouraged you to come back another time (or times) and see what you (and most everyone else) have missed.

BOUNDARIES OF THE PDC

The PDC includes all or parts of 14 of Pennsylvania's 67 counties, and encompasses an area of some 7,100 square miles, or about 16% of the State's land area. This is slightly smaller than the state of New Jersey. The map on page 8 shows the PDC in relation to the rest of Pennsylvania, with the major cities indicated for reference.

Blue Mountain, the southernmost ridge of the Appalachian Mountains, forms the northern and western limit of the PDC, except for the southernmost twenty miles south of the point in Franklin County where the mountain ends; the boundary there shifts several miles west to the next ridge, Tuscarora Mountain. Not only did Blue Mountain constitute a major travel barrier in colonial times (and still does today in many areas), it is also the dividing line between two very different geographic, topographic, geological, and to a lesser extent, climate zones. The Delaware River, separating Pennsylvania from New Jersey, is the eastern PDC boundary. In early times it was an important physical as well as political border. Moreover, New Jersey was settled before Pennsylvania and had different development patterns in its early history. On the south, the PDC ends at the Mason-Dixon line that forms the boundary between Pennsylvania and Maryland. The southeastern border of the PDC, connecting the Delaware River with the Mason-Dixon line, is the least readily identifiable. US Route 202, which traverses southeastern

Pennsylvania in an arc about 25 miles from downtown Philadelphia, is approximately the point where the PDC ends and the Philadelphia metropolitan area begins. It's not a precise demarcation, but is the most easily identified.

USING THIS BOOK

The book is divided into four sections. The first sets the stage with background information about the PDC—its history, geography, climate, economy, people, and regional cooking and speech patterns.

Next is a "nuts and bolts" section, with facts and figures you may need or find informative about getting to and traveling within the PDC, traffic laws, telephones, liquor laws, sales tax, and the types and sources of maps available for the region. This section also describes recreation facilities, amusements, and shopping, including the increasingly popular outlet stores, and contains a classified calendar of events.

The third section describes the special features for which the PDC is famous—its farmers' markets, covered bridges, historic districts, walking tours, wineries, caves, and antique shops.

Each of the fourteen counties is fully described in individual chapters in part four. Places of interest are organized alphabetically by town. The largest and most important towns also have listings of "Community Resources" (tourist information centers, public buildings, and emergency information). Maps of the counties head their respective chapters, and there are detailed maps of downtown and metropolitan areas of the major cities. See USING THE MAPS for complete explanations. The county's covered bridges (if any), recreation facilities, and a chronological calendar of events are listed at the end of each chapter.

The appendix contains listings of state parks, hotels, motels, bed and breakfast inns, farm vacation homes (in the three counties where these exist), campgrounds, and restaurants.

There are two indexes at the end of the book—a general index, and a subject index to help you quickly locate all places of interest in the same general category (art galleries or transportation-oriented museums, for example).

The factual information (hours of operation, admission charges, contents of museum exhibits, room rates, restaurant prices, etc.) was correct at press time, but is subject to change. Therefore, you may wish to call to confirm before visiting.

USING THE MAPS

There are three types of maps in this book. County maps at the beginning of each county chapter show the communities referred to in the text, a few major roads, and state parks. Note that they are oriented in different ways in order to fit on the page. Metropolitan area maps for Allentown-Bethlehem, Harrisburg, Lancaster, Reading, and York are sufficiently detailed to enable you to travel the main roads in and around these cities, but you may need a more detailed street map if you expect to use side streets. Downtown area maps of the cities having walking tours or a large number of places of interest appear with the respective community. These maps are detailed enough to use without supplementation.

See the facing page for map symbols.

THE RATINGS

There are more than 200 places of interest in the PDC, and nearly all have been rated on a scale of one to four stars. The only ones not rated are those that were closed for renovations or that observe very limited hours or a short season and were not open while this book was researched and written. I felt it unfair to rate places I had not visited. In addition, most locations on walking tour routes that can be viewed only from the outside are not rated. So, the absence of a rating is not an indication of an unworthy attraction. The stars have the following meanings:

★★★★ Outstanding, don't miss
★★★ Well worth a visit
★★ Good
★ See it if you have time

The evaluations and ratings are my own and no attempt to influence them was made by operators of any of the enterprises. The ratings reflect whether each museum, historic site, etc. has offered something of value to the visitor, how well it accomplishes its purpose, and how it compares to other attractions of similar type, if any. Your comments and suggestions, not only about individual ratings but about any aspect of this book, are most welcome and will be considered for future editions.

MAP SYMBOLS

◯ Interstate highway

◯ State highway

◯ Federal (US) highway

▭ State-owned
secondary highway

City, borough, unincorporated community, by population category:

- ● Under 1,000
- ● 10,000-24,999

- ● 1,000-9,999
- ● 25,000 and over

---

[1] Place of interest described in text

● County seat   ▲ State park

+——+——+— Railroad (shown only where important as landmark)

→ One-way street   ⊢→ Start
                       —→| End

PUBLIC BUILDINGS AND FACILITIES
(Downtown & Metropolitan maps only)

[?] Visitor center

[CC] Chamber of commerce

[CO] Court House

[H] Hospital

[B] Bus station

[PO] Post office

[CH] City hall or borough offices

[L] Public library

[SP] State Police

Ⓣ Amtrak station
(Harrisburg, Lancaster)

✈ Airport (Allentown-Bethlehem-Easton, Harrisburg)

OBTAINING TOURIST INFORMATION

The Pennsylvania Department of Commerce aggressively promotes tourism, both through its own Division of Travel Marketing and throught its support of a network of Tourist Promotion Agencies covering all 67 counties. Here are the names, addresses, and phone numbers of the Agencies covering the PDC (they are also listed under Community Resources for the cities where they are located):

Statewide: Department of Commerce, Division of Travel Marketing, 453 Forum Bldg., Harrisburg, PA 17120; (800) VISIT-PA (847-4872), ext. 370, or (717) 787-5453.

Adams Co.: Gettysburg Travel Council, 35 Carlisle St., Gettysburg, PA 17325; (717) 334-6274.

Berks Co.: Berks County Pennsylvania Dutch Travel Association, Sheraton-Berkshire Inn, US 422 & Paper Mill Rd., Wyomissing, PA 19610; (215) 375-4085.

Bucks Co.: Bucks County Tourist Commission, 152 Swamp Rd., Doylestown, PA 18901; (215) 345-4552.

Chester Co.: Chester County Tourist Promotion Bureau, 117 W. Gay St., West Chester, PA 19380; (215) 344-6365, (800) 228-9933 (Brandywine Valley Tourist Information Center).

Cumberland and Dauphin Cos.: Harrisburg-Hershey-Carlisle Tourism & Convention Bureau, 114 Walnut St., PO Box 969, Harrisburg, PA 17108; (717) 232-1377.

Franklin Co.: Cumberland Valley Visitors Council, 75 S. 2nd St., Chambersburg, PA 17201; (717) 264-7101.

Lancaster Co.: Pennsylvania Dutch Convention & Visitors Bureau, 501 Greenfield Rd., Lancaster, PA 17601; (717) 299-8901.

Lebanon Co.: Lebanon Valley Tourist & Visitors Bureau, PO Box 626, Lebanon, PA 17042; (717) 272-8555.

Lehigh & Northampton Cos.: Lehigh Valley Convention & Visitors Bureau, Inc., PO Box 2605, Lehigh Valley, PA 18001; (215) 266-0560.

Montgomery Co.: Valley Forge Convention & Visitors Bureau, PO Box 311, Norristown, PA 19404; (215) 278-3558, (800) 441-3549.

York Co.: York County Convention & Visitors Bureau, 1 Marketway East, PO Box 1229, York, PA 17405; (717) 848-4000.

BACKGROUND

HISTORY

Since so many of the PDC's attractions date directly from, or are based on, the region's history, a summary of the most significant events and trends from several perspectives—early settlement, the Colonial period, transportation development, and cultural development—is included in order to provide some essential background information.

Early Settlement

Three tribes of native Americans (Indians) inhabited the PDC before and up to about 100 years after the first white settlers arrived from Europe. The Delawares, also called the Lenni-Lenape, lived in the easternmost counties in the region (Bucks, Lehigh, Montgomery, and Northampton) and belonged to the Algonquin nation, one of two major Indian groups in Pennsylvania. The Delawares had three sub-groups: the Munsees (Wolf Clan), Unami (Turtle Clan), and Unalachtigo (Turkey Clan).

The Shawnees, a nomadic tribe and also members of the Algonquin nation, lived in the Susquehanna valley and also among the Munsees near Easton. They came to Pennsylvania from the southwest in the 1690s.

The Iroquois Confederacy, the other major Indian alliance, consisted of the famous "Five Nations" who lived mostly in New York State and extreme northern Pennsylvania. The only Iroquoian group in the PDC were the Susquehannocks, also known as Conestogas, for the creek valley in Lancaster County where they settled.

It appears that although there were a number of tribes, the total Indian population in all of Pennsylvania probably never exceeded 20,000.

While the Indians enjoyed good relations with the Swedes, Dutch, and English under William Penn, the rapid growth of the white population in the early 1700s effectively drove them out of the region, and most of those who remained were massacred in the French and Indian War.

15

The Indians' most lasting legacy is the many colorful (and hard to pronounce and spell!) names given to creeks and rivers in the PDC and throughout Pennsylvania.

Pennsylvania, the only one of the thirteen original colonies not located on the Atlantic coast, was the last to be settled by Europeans. The first white settlers were Dutch, who arrived beginning in 1616. Because they were more interested in trading with the Indians than in forming settlements, the earliest Dutch left no permanent community or fortification other than Fort Beversrede at the mouth of the Schuylkill, which was established in 1647.

The Swedes were the first to form settlements in Pennsylvania; the first permanent white settlement in the state, therefore, was that of Governor Johan Printz at Tinicum Island, about 20 miles south of Philadelphia, in 1643. The Swedes remained the largest nationality in Pennsylvania (then still part of New York) until the English came under the aegis of William Penn.

The title to what became Pennsylvania was granted to William Penn's father by King Charles II in repayment for war loans (the English had captured this land from the Dutch in 1644). William Penn, Jr., who had been disinherited because of his adoption of the Quaker church, was nonetheless able to exert the political influence in England that his wealthy family background commanded. Before his father died in 1670, he reconciled with his son and restored his inheritance. The younger Penn wanted the Quakers to have their own colony, and petitioned Charles to give him land in America in exchange for cancelling his father's claims against the Crown. Charles agreed, and in 1681 granted Penn the land from the Delaware River westward for five degrees longitude, bounded on the north by the "beginning of the three and fortieth degree of northern latitude, and on the south by a circle drawn at twelve miles distant from New Castle", and then by a straight line westward for the remainder of the five degrees of longitude. Precise boundaries were not firmly established until the late 1700s, but as the population was quite sparse throughout the colonies, it wasn't an important issue.

The King wanted the colony named "Pennsilvania"; William Penn objected on Quaker principles to having a place named for himself, but the King said the name was in honor of Admiral Penn, William's father, so Pennsylvania it remained. At first the colony included the "Lower Counties", which became the state of Delaware, but these separated from Pennsylvania in 1703. Penn quickly moved to establish local governments; Philadelphia, Chester, and Bucks Counties were set up in Pennsylvania, and New Castle, Kent, and Sussex in Delaware.

All religions were permitted under the Great Law, which formed the basis for government for 94 years, until 1776. Quaker ideals of law and morality were reflected in the colony's laws. Parcels of land began to be sold. The Welsh and Germans were early purchasers, the Welsh settling along the Schuylkill River northwest of Philadelphia, and the Germans initially establishing a settlement in the part of Philadelphia that came to be called Germantown, a community name that remains today as a Philadelphia neighborhood.

Germans came originally for political and religious freedom, but they soon found the fertile limestone soil of southeastern Pennsylvania ideal for maintaining their agrarian life. The first Germans came shortly after the founding of the colony, but German immigration rose sharply toward the middle of the 1700s. These people settled first in Northampton and Berks Counties, and later moved south and west into Lancaster, Lebanon, and York Counties, where their influence is still the strongest of any nationality living in these areas today. This wave of German immigration brought the Mennonites, and their offspring, the Amish, to Pennsylvania.

Scotch-Irish Presbyterians, who had experienced poor relations with the Church of England as well as with Irish Catholics, came to Pennsylvania about the same time as the Germans. Rather individualistic, they moved to the frontier, which was then west of the Susquehanna River, presumably to be farther from the Quaker-dominated government, but possibly also by Penn's design. He feared that the Scotch-Irish would not get along with the Germans, and used his land distribution policy to try to keep them separate. The Scotch-Irish ignored treaties that Penn had made with the Indians, which contributed to friction, and later to war, in which the Indians were permanently driven out of Pennsylvania.

Small numbers of French Protestants (Huguenots), English from Maryland, and Jews from Portugal, and perhaps Spain, also came to Pennsylvania.

The Colonial Period

The existence of a stable and open government in Pennsylvania aided Philadelphia's development as the cultural, financial, political, and social capital of colonial America, and in turn promoted development of the rural areas of the colony. Pennsylvania had an abundance of natural resources, so the economy flourished. The colony enjoyed a prosperity that was unmatched elsewhere in America at the time.

Philadelphia, in addition to being a port city, was also the largest market for the farm products and other goods that were produced in the interior counties.

Numerous flour mills developed along the inland creeks and rivers. In addition to the commonly produced flour and corn meal, the mills ground rags to produce paper and stone to make plaster. Germans in Lancaster County produced rifles, developed from those they used in Europe, which were called Pennsylvania long rifles. Iron furnaces originated in Berks County but soon spread to all the counties. They first produced tools, wagon parts, and cooking utensils, and later, during the Revolution, ammunition for the colonial army. Conestoga wagons, named for the Conestoga Creek valley in Lancaster County, were built prior to 1750 to haul crops to market. These wagons were huge—16 feet long, 4 feet high, and 4 feet deep—but of a size necessary to make the long trip to market worthwhile. These covered wagons gained later fame during America's westward expansion in the mid-1800s.

Art and music flourished, as did education. Most music of the period was religious in origin; the Moravians of Bethlehem and Lititz developed an extensive repertory of hymns, and used brass bands in their services.

By the time the Revolutionary War broke out, Pennsylvania's reputation as the "keystone state" had become well established. If anything, the Revolution strengthened Pennsylvania's and the PDC's economies. Pennsylvania was relatively unscathed by the war; the largest battles were fought in other colonies even though the seat of colonial government remained in Pennsylvania throughout the war.

After the new national government was established and peace returned, cultural development resumed. Several colleges were established, road building began in earnest, and the interior sections (mainly the PDC) boomed.

Transportation Development

In order to have a full picture of the PDC's development, it is necessary to look at the role transportation played in the region's growth.

Public roads in early Pennsylvania, usually called "King's Highways", converged on Philadelphia. There was the "York Road" which ran from Philadelphia to New York via Bucks County; the Great Conestoga Road, later called the Pennsylvania Road, to Lancaster, and eventually to Pittsburgh; and numerous others. Many followed old Indian paths, which by this time were in disuse because of the dispersal and decline of the Indian population. However, the Indians had developed an intricate path network; their trails were unusually direct, yet managed to avoid both wet lowlands and steep ridges, except where they descended to cross streams.

Roads were established pushing into the western part of the region by the 1750s, several of which played important roles in shipping troops and equipment over the Appalachians during the French and Indian War in 1755-60.

After the Revolutionary War, the state's General Assembly began to appropriate funds, collected mainly from import duties, for highway construction. Although roads were rather heavily used, they were impassible under certain weather conditions. In 1792 the legislature chartered a turnpike company to build a paved road from Philadelphia to Lancaster, a distance of 65 miles. This was the first macadamized road in America, having a base of heavy stone and a top surface of gravel or mixed fine stone and dirt. The road cost about $7,100 a mile and was completed in 1794. This turnpike was a financial success as a toll road, encouraging others to be built in a similar manner. Early turnpikes were named for the towns at one or both ends or for geographical features they followed. Many names remain today: Gap and Newport, Ridge, Bethlehem, and other (Turn)Pikes.

While the early turnpikes represented great advances in transportation, travel was by no means easy or fast. As western parts of the Commonwealth developed, the need for improved transportation became greater, particularly because of the numerous ridges of the Appalachians that had to be crossed. Several major rivers and tributaries penetrated the interior from Delaware and Chesapeake Bays, but they were navigable only so far inland, beyond which portages had to be made to reach the next navigable stream. In dry seasons, however, the rivers became too shallow for navigation, but towpath canals, introduced in England in the late 1700s, had proved feasible. Originally in Pennsylvania, canals were viewed only as connectors between rivers, and in fact, a survey for such a canal between the Schuylkill and Susquehanna had been made as early as 1762. This later became the Union Canal, completed in 1828, linking Reading on the Schuylkill with Portsmouth (now Middletown) on the Susquehanna. Actually, the first true canal in the state, the Conewago, opened in 1797 to bypass the Conewago Falls on the Susquehanna at the present site of York Haven. It remained in use until 1894.

Pennsylvania's canal system, the most extensive of any state, was built mainly to serve the growing inland area, but also to compete with New York's Erie Canal, which was completed in 1825, and with the Chesapeake and Ohio Canal along the Potomac in Maryland. During the 1820s and 1830s, numerous canals operated in the PDC and elsewhere in Pennsylvania. The longest in this region were the Schuylkill, the Lehigh, the Union mentioned above, and the Delaware. These canals were all state-operated, and some remained in use until as late as 1931, although most ceased operations by the 1890s.

To some extent the canals competed with the turnpikes which often paralleled them, and except in winter when they were drained to prevent freeze damage, the canals diverted business from the toll roads. However, the next transportation development, the railroad, brought an eventual end to both the canals and the state-franchised toll road system.

Railroads were initially used as an adjunct to the highway system: carriages pulled by horses rode on the rails. Such a railroad existed in Delaware County in 1809. Later, gravity railroads were used in the coal mining region of northeastern Pennsylvania to transport coal from the mines downhill to the rivers. During the 1830s numerous railroad companies were chartered in the state; the oldest of these, the Philadelphia and Reading, survives today as the Reading Railroad. Despite problems such as inadequate construction, lack of standardized track gauge, and opposition from farmers who feared a loss of their markets, the railroads survived and prospered. By 1860 there were nearly 2,600 miles of track in the state, more than in any other. The Industrial Age had arrived in America.

Highway development remained at a virtual standstill from the inception of railroads until the invention of the bicycle in the late 1800s, but even then did not proceed rapidly until automobile mass production began. The Pennsylvania Department of Highways (now the Department of Transportation—PennDOT) was established in 1905 to oversee road construction and maintenance and vehicle registration. What Pennsylvania in general, and the PDC in particular, should be most remembered for is being a major center of automobile production before the industry consolidated in Detroit and elsewhere in the Midwest. Some 131 different makes of cars and trucks were manufactured in Pennsylvania starting in 1895. The largest manufacturing centers were Philadelphia, with 37 makes; Pittsburgh, 16; Reading, 15; and York, 8. Other PDC communities with automobile manufacturing plants included Lebanon, Pottstown, Allentown, Carlisle, Harrisburg, Bethlehem, Hanover, Fleetwood, Cherryville, Oxford, Strasburg, and Valley Forge. Few of the auto makers became profitable, but this may have been due to the infant stage of the industry. Among the few names that achieved more than local notoriety were Duryea, Bantam, Autocar, and Pullman.

Pennsylvania's present-day state and local highway system dates from the 1920s and 1930s. The second-term election in 1930 of Governor Gifford Pinchot, made possible largely because of his promise to "get the farmer out of the mud", initiated a massive road improvement effort by the State. Over 20,000 miles of dirt roads were widened and paved, and by 1934 less than 30% of the state's highway mileage was unimproved.

America's first true "superhighway", the Pennsylvania Turnpike, was opened in 1940, running 160 miles from Carlisle, Cumberland County, to Irwin, Westmoreland County, following the route of the defunct South Penn Railroad. Extensions east and west to the New Jersey and Ohio boundaries, respectively, and the Northeastern Extention to Scranton opened by 1957. A total of 186 of the Turnpike's 470 miles, and 14 of its 38 interchanges, are in the PDC.

Cultural Development

Being predominantly a farming region, the PDC did not develop in the arts, music, and science, to the extent that cities such as Philadelphia did. The rural areas lacked the population concentrations and leisure time necessary to nurture such "accoutrements" of life. However, the settlers brought from Europe aspects of their culture that flourished here. Religion was the underlying characteristic in most of the cultural contributions made by early PDC inhabitants.

Moravian immigrants from Saxony in Germany brought a tradition of use of brass instruments in their services in the 1740s. Nearly every town had its own band starting about 1830, some of which are still in existence, such as the Allentown Band and the Spring Garden Band in York.

Universities were established prior to the Revolution, with the College of Philadelphia, later called the University of Pennsylvania (1740) the oldest. Other colleges in the PDC founded before 1800 were Moravian in Bethlehem (1742), Dickinson in Carlisle (1773), and Franklin and Marshall in Lancaster (1787). Free public schools began in 1834, although many private and church-run schools existed before that time.

Pennsylvania German art was noted for the use of bright colors and fanciful designs, even though the religious training of many of the people forbade the same kind of adornment in their dress. In rural areas, virtually the only places where art could be displayed was in the home and barn. Thus, we have the origin of so-called "hex signs" and *frakturs*. The term "hex sign" comes from "hexefiess", or witches' feet. It has never been satisfactorily proven whether the barn signs were intended to ward off evil spirits or were simply heathen symbols. Frakturs were family records—births, baptisms, and marriages—and therefore are as valued for the historical facts they reveal as for their artistic content. They were invariably written in the German language and script, with similar designs and symbols that were used in hex signs—doves, distelfinks (goldfinches), lions, and unicorns were among those used most frequently. Fraktur painting developed in the Middle Ages and continued in America until about 1850.

21

Pennsylvania Germans produced pottery and furniture, both rooted in utility rather than luxury, taking advantage of raw materials that existed in abundance in the land around them. Early Pennsylvania furniture probably remains in existence because most Pennsylvania Germans lived on farms where they had barns in which to store old furniture once it had outlived its usefulness (throwing anything away was abhorrent to them!). Stiegel glass and pewterware were also produced by the Germans, and their handcrafts are still recognized today for their high degree of workmanship.

GEOGRAPHY

The PDC lies within the Piedmont region, a transition zone between the coastal plain and Appalachian mountains. This is an area of gently rolling terrain with a few well-defined ridges. The region is underlaid by limestone, which combined with the favorable terrain, creates an ideal farming environment. Elevations range from about 100 feet above sea level along the Susquehanna, Schuylkill, and Delaware Rivers at their southernmost points in the region, to 2,400 feet at the top of Tuscarora Mountain in Franklin County. The valleys range from about 300 feet above sea level in the southeast to about 600 feet in the northeastern and southwestern sections. Some ridges rise as much as 800 feet above the valleys, but generally the elevation difference is not as great as this. Hills are mainly 200 to 300 feet high, and tend to have rounded tops rather than sharp peaks. This is sufficient to provide many pleasant vistas from the summits but not formidable enough to create travel barriers.

The PDC is drained almost entirely by the Delaware and Susquehanna Rivers and their tributaries. The only areas not in these rivers' watersheds are Franklin and the southern part of Adams Counties, which are drained by the Potomac. The region's other major streams are the Lehigh and Schuylkill Rivers and Brandywine, Perkiomen, Tulpehocken, Swatara, Conestoga, Conewago, and Conodoguinet Creeks.

CLIMATE

The PDC has a humid continental climate, like most of the northeastern United States. Summers are warm to occasionally hot, with relatively high humidity, and winters are comparatively mild for the region's latitude.

Summer temperatures in the region generally average in the low- to mid-80s during the day and the 60s at night. Readings above 90 occur on about 15-20 days a year, and fall below 55 at night about 10-15 times during June, July, and August. 100-degree readings are rare, and occur on average less than once a year.

The mildest parts of the PDC are the extreme southeast and the Susquehanna valley, while the coolest are usually the western and northeastern portions. However, there is not usually a substantial daytime temperature difference throughout the region; the greatest local variations occur at night.

Precipitation in the region averages 40-45 inches a year, which falls fairly uniformly throughout the year and is ample to sustain the agriculture industry. During the summer months, rainfall is more likely to come in afternoon and evening thundershowers than in day-long soakings.

The growing season ranges from about 177 days at Allentown to 192 at Harrisburg and 210 at Philadelphia. The first frost usually occurs in mid-October, although late September frosts are not uncommon, and the last frost is usually in late April, but freezing temperatures have been recorded into mid-May. Annual snowfall over the past thirty years has averaged 32 inches at Allentown, 36 at Harrisburg, and 22 at Philadelphia.

Prevailing summer winds are westerly and southwesterly; winter winds are west and west-northwest. Velocities average under 10 mph most of the year but are slightly stronger during the winter.

If you have a weather radio, you can receive National Weather Service broadcasts 24 hours a day on the following stations serving the PDC:

Allentown	162.40 mH
Harrisburg	162.55 mH
Philadelphia	162.475 mH

The PDC's primary tourist "season" extends from about Easter to Thanksgiving, with June through Labor Day being the busiest time. Optimum temperatures and humidity for visiting are from about May 1 to June 15 and from early September through October. Crowds are also smaller, and some prices lower, than in the peak summer months. However, while many museums and attractions are open all year, some have reduced hours outside the summer season. Many outdoor-based attractions close during the winter (usually after Thanksgiving weekend until mid-March).

ECONOMY

While the PDC is a prime vacation area, with tourism increasing each year, its economy does not depend on the tourist business alone. Farming, light and heavy manufacturing, food processing, and in recent years, high tech research, all play important roles. The region's economy is highly diversified, which contributes greatly to its prosperity and insulates it from the effects of recessions.

The PDC has always enjoyed a prosperous economy relative to the rest of Pennsylvania and many other states. This stems from the abundance of natural resources, hard-working people, and proximity to large East Coast markets.

Manufacturing Industry

PDC factories produce a wide variety of products, from steel to microchips. One of the region's strengths has been its ability to adapt to changes in national and world economic conditions. As some industries went into long-term declines, others were attracted to replace them. For example, in the Lehigh Valley, where the steel and truck manufacturing industries had been dominant, high-tech companies are now booming. Twelve "Fortune 500" companies are headquartered in the PDC.

Agriculture

Farming is one of the PDC's most important industries, and its farms are among the most productive in the nation. The fourteen PDC counties, with less than 18% of the state's land area, account for 55% of the total value of farm products sold; Lancaster County alone produces nearly 20% of the total. PDC farms produce corn, wheat, tobacco, and a variety of vegetables for local consumption and processing. Dairy farming and fruit growing are also important.

Population growth, and the subsequent need for more highways, shopping facilities, and places of employment have made farmland more valuable for non-agricultural uses. However, despite the reduction in farm acreage, production is increasing.

Perhaps the most significant impact of the loss of farmland is a social one. Persons who have made farming their way of life are displaced from their homes and lifestyle, an adjustment that some are never fully able to make. The strong economy in the PDC is usually able to absorb farmers who must make a career change, but this is by no means guaranteed. For the Amish, this is a particular hardship because their entire lifestyle is based on small-scale farming.

The Service Economy

The service economy in the PDC is increasing rapidly, with tourism one of the fastest growing segments. It is estimated that 3-5 million persons visit Lancaster County each year, Gettysburg attracts about 1 million, and the outlet stores in Reading draw some 6 million persons annually.

A number of large hospitals in the region are the major employers in their communities. The many colleges throughout the region are not only employment centers but also focal points for local cultural activities. Penn State University maintains branch campuses at Allentown (Fogelsville), King of Prussia, Middletown, Mont Alto, Reading, and York, and a medical school at Hershey. The state-run university system, which originated in 1854 to set up and maintain teacher-training colleges has campuses at Kutztown, Millersville, Shippensburg, and West Chester, in addition to ten others throughout the state.

THE PEOPLE

The PDC today is home to nearly 3 million people of many national, ethnic, and racial backgrounds. The mix has become more cosmpolitan in the past generation. This chapter does not attempt to mention all the groups present in the PDC, or even to present a complete discussion of those that are noted. Its purpose is to introduce you to those you may want information about or perhaps did not realize are here.

Amish

The group that generates the most attention is, of course, the Amish. The Amish, and their culture, are unique. The term "Amish" is popularly used to refer to a group of people who live on farms without electricity, ride in horse-drawn buggies, and wear plain dark-colored clothing. In fact, there are differences among the Amish as to religious practices, social customs, and use of modern conveniences, as there are in degree of observance among other religions. These differences vary geographically as well as socially. Most references to the Amish in this chapter are to the "Old Order", the strictest of the sects. Other groups, such as the Beachy Amish and New Amish, are more liberal in certain aspects of their society.

The largest concentration of Amish by far is in Lancaster County, mainly in a wedge-shaped area east of the city of Lancaster. Other smaller communities are in southern Lancaster County, western Chester County, the Schaefferstown-Newmanstown area of Lebanon County, Berks County, western Cumberland and adjacent northern Franklin Counties, and southeastern York County.

The Amish are an offspring of the Anabaptist movement of the 16th century. Their name is taken from their original leader, Jacob Ammann, a member of the Swiss Brethren, one of three German Anabaptist groups that broke away from the Roman Catholic church at the time of the Reformation. The Anabaptists were so named because they rejected the idea of infant baptism. To this day, the Amish baptize only adults, whom they consider to have the mental and emotional maturity to decide for themselves if they wish to follow the teachings of the Amish religion. Infants cannot make these judgments, and the Amish believe one's choice of religion should be an informed one, not solely determined by parentage.

The Amish were originally Mennonites, but, led by Ammann, they split from the latter group in 1693 over the principle of shunning, the practice of avoiding an expelled member of the church at communion. Ammann felt the Mennonites were too liberal in their interpretation of this practice, and he and his followers formed a more conservative sect.

Like most heretic (according to the established church) groups, the Amish suffered persecution in their homeland, Switzerland. They eventually fled to the Jura and Vosges Mountains of Alsace, then part of Germany. It was the promise of religious freedom that later brought the Amish to Pennsylvania.

The first wave of emigration lasted from 1727 to about 1770, and the Amish were not alone among Germans who came to Penn's colony. Actually, the first Mennonite groups, with whom the Amish are often mistakenly associated, arrived in 1683, settling in Germantown (as their community in Philadelphia came to be named). The date of the first Amish arrivals is not precisely known because they did not keep formal records, partly as a protection against state persecution in Europe. Moreover, the Amish are not a "literary" people, in that they view writing and literature as worldly and inimical to their agrarian-rooted lifestyle.

The first Amish settlements in America were in the areas of the present-day towns of Shartlesville, Womelsdorf, and Leesport, all in Berks County, Elverson and Malvern in Chester County, and Churchtown and in the Conestoga valley of Lancaster County. The Shartlesville community was known as Northkill, dating from about 1738, and is believed to be the oldest.

Nineteenth-century emigration, lasting from about 1815 to 1860, saw most Amish going to Ohio, Indiana, Illinois, with smaller numbers settling in Iowa, upstate New York, Maryland, and Ontario, Canada.

Today the Amish population in North America totals about 85-90,000. Although the PDC settlements are the oldest and best known, the largest Amish population is in Ohio, with about 30,000 residents. Pennsylvania has about 25,000, and there are approximately 16,000 Amish in Indiana. These three states account for about 80% of all Amish, but there are settlements today in 20 states and the province of Ontario.

Amish religious tenets include a strict interpretation of the New Testament, adult rather than infant baptism, pacifism, and a belief that they are a "chosen" people who, in order to do God's work on earth, must keep themselves umblemished by secular influences. This explains the Amish desire for remaining separate from the outside world and its corrupting influences. The needs of the community (*Gemeinde* in German) take precedence over those of the individual.

The basic social unit of Amish society is the church district, or congregation, which generally includes about 30 to 40 households. The Old Order Amish actually have no churches—they conduct their services in members' homes. Church buildings are unnecessary to them. Other groups do have churches, and also permit automobiles and some concessions toward the use of power-driven machinery on farms.

Old Order church services are held every other Sunday and last about four hours. For several days in advance, women in the district assist the family in whose home the service will be held in setting up the living room or barn where the service takes place, and preparing food for the meal that follows. Preaching is done by a minister who is knowledgeable about Scriptures and who can speak without books or notes, since very little of Amish religion, aside from the Bible, is written. The church service is the occasion for relaying community news, for example, the announcement of an upcoming wedding or barn-raising, a member's illness, or an auction sale in the neighborhood.

One pervasive characteristic of the Amish is their emphasis on smallness of scale. This is seen in the size of their farms and communities. It enables them to keep life simple and to maintain the inter-personal relationships that help them preserve their faith and way of life. The Amish, today as in the 18th century in the Rhine valley of Europe, are an agrarian people. They believe that everything necessary and worthwhile in life comes from the land, and see themselves as custodians of God's earth. Therefore, farming is the vocation that is closest to God. Their dependence on and respect for the land led the Amish to develop the efficient farming practices for which they are renowned. These techniques originated in Europe, when the Anabaptists were forced to flee to previously unproductive agricultural regions, and had to devise new methods in order to survive.

While self-reliance and individual responsibility are stressed in terms of being a productive member of society, the community readily helps any Amish family faced with a hardship. If a family member is ill, others assume his or her responsibilities until the person is recovered. The legend of the barn-raising is an outstanding example of how the Amish help their neighbors. Should an Amish farmer's barn burn down, the entire community turns out a few days later to rebuild it. While the men and boys do the carpentry work, the women and girls prepare the food that the horde of workmen will eat in enormous quantities.

The Amish have their own form of "social security", without government support. The elderly, after retiring from farming, usually move into a separate house on the farm, or into their own apartment in the home of one of their children. In this manner they remain physically as part of the family, and while they're free to lead their own lives, they maintain their "roots". The elderly are highly respected in Amish society; they are responsible for passing on the largely unwritten customs and values to younger generations. Retirement communities or old-age homes are not part of the Amish way of life.

Accumulation of wealth for its own sake is forbidden, but acquiring sufficient means to enable a farmer to set up each of his sons on his own farm is a highly valued and visible measure of a man's success. Given the prohibition against using mechanized equipment, Amish farms must remain small in order to be effectively managed by one family. The Amish believe that bigness, advanced technology, and wealth are enemies of the society because they lead to impersonality and alienation from God.

Despite their aversion to technology and the worldly way of life of the "English" (anyone outside Amish society is referred to as English, regardless of their nationality), the Amish do insist that their children learn the "three R's" so that they can function within their own community and in necessary dealings with the outside world. However, knowledge beyond this level is discouraged because it engenders worldliness and feelings of superiority over others in the community. Amish schools also serve an important socialization function; children are taught to get along with others, and to place the needs of the community above those of the self. Amish children, as a result of a Supreme Court decision in 1972, are permitted to leave school after the eighth grade, which occurs at an age when they are mature enough, physically to do strenuous work on the family farm, and mentally to understand the responsibilities that will be theirs in a few years when they marry and set up their own farms.

The Amish prefer their own schools rather than the public schools. Control over the curriculum, isolation from unwanted "English" influences, and nearness to the home are the main reasons Amish operate their own schools. Tests have shown that Amish children do at least as well as public school children in the rote skills of arithmetic, spelling, and reading that both systems teach in the early grades.

Amish society is controlled by men. Women have more involvement in the running of the house and the rearing of children, and are respected and valued for their contributions, but when decisions affecting the husband and wife jointly, or the entire family, are made, the husband has the final say. However, circumstancess vary within individual families.

Children are a valued asset in Amish society, and families of six or seven children are about average size. Children are needed for domestic and farm work and are reared to perpetuate the society. Although there is some attrition to the "English" world, the Amish population overall is increasing. The absence of divorce and avoidance of birth control combine to produce large families.

The Amish lose a small percentage of their members to the outside world. This can happen in two ways. The most serious is through the excommunication or "shunning" of a member who committed a serious sin against the church. In such a case, the member is forbidden to have contact with any Amish, including his family, and they likewise may not associate with him, even involuntarily. Excommunication can occur only to an adult who had previously been baptized in the faith. The strong social order of Amish society acts as a deterrent to disruptive behavior at all ages.

Probably a more frequent loss of members occurs when an Amish person decides to leave the church. Such a move could be the result of an inability to find acceptable work within the Amish community, and the social disgrace it brings, or it could occur upon marrying out of the religion, or the decision of a young person to further his education. Most of those who leave join a Mennonite church.

One apparently growing reason for a loss of members is the difficulty in buying farms in an Amish district due to a combination of escalating prices and decrease in the amount of farm land remaining. This problem is most acute in Lancaster County, and the situation has caused some Amish to relocate into adjacent counties, or farther away, sometimes to other states. The breakup of families creates many hardships, even if the person who moves away remains with the Amish church. However, the Amish themselves may be partly the cause of the problem: their tradition of setting up each son on his own farm has diminished the number of farms available for purchase. Lancaster County farms are already the smallest, on average, of any county in Pennsylvania, so further subdivision is not a long-term solution.

It is important to examine the effects of tourism on the Amish. They are unwilling victims of an industry that has mushroomed in the past thirty or so years. Ironically, it is because the Amish are so widely admired for their productive farms and ascetic lifestyle that they have become objects of curiosity to outsiders.

The most serious impact of tourism on the Amish is the traffic jams it creates on their farm roads, although the congestion, of course, does not affect the Amish alone. This in turn leads to a loss of privacy, as long queues of cars and tour buses pause at Amish farms so visitors can get a glimpse of the people "in action." While the Amish generally resent these intrusions, there is little they can do to stop them, as their religion discourages confrontations. The typical reaction to all this unwanted attention is to ignore it, or to respond coolly. The Amish thus may appear unfriendly, but it's merely a defensive response. If they stopped to chat with every curious tourist, even those who approach them in a friendly, pleasant manner, they'd never get their chores finished.

The Amish object most strongly to the intrusion of the camera. Not only does their religion forbid "graven images", but posing for photographs is a form of worldly pride and vanity. The Amish will usually decline a request, however polite, to be photographed, but will not take strong measures to stop a determined photographer, as this contravenes their pacifism. This dilemma between the religious principles of the Amish and the honest and admiring curiosity of most tourists can probably never be resolved to the satisfaction of both parties. Discretion on the part of visitors is the best compromise.

It must be said that tourism does not have a totally negative impact on the Amish. Many farmers sell their produce, eggs, ice cream, and handmade quilts to visitors passing by their roadside stands, thereby supplementing income earned from farm product sales through normal markets. Very recently, some Amish men have taken up carpentry on a full-time basis, forsaking farming. They work for construction companies or for themselves making storage barns, gazebos, and furniture. Much of their production is sold outside Lancaster County where the demand far exceeds the level of production that the Amish are able or willing to meet.

Despite what the Amish consider the adverse effects of tourism on their way of life, and the threat of government intervention in the form of consolidation of rural schools and compulsory welfare and retirement programs, they are maintaining their productive society. Their population is increasing, and everywhere Amish families settle they have a positive influence in the local community. The key to their survival, however, is more internal than external: they must continue to inculcate the values and virtues of simple, agrarian living to their children, and the sense of community and self-fulfillment that it provides.

Mennonites

Mennonites have often been linked with the Amish, but the association really should be viewed the other way around. The Mennonites preceded, and originally encompassed, the more conservative sect that, in the late 17th century in Europe, broke away and became the Amish. The split was the result of a difference in interpretation of the principle of shunning, as described in the preceding chapter.

The Mennonites' origin is tied to Menno Simons, a Catholic priest in the Netherlands. Because of their common Anabaptist roots, many Mennonite precepts are similar to those of the Amish, but they are clearly a more world-oriented people and today vary widely in their way of living. Still, Mennonites must be considered one of the more conservative branches of Christianity. Mennonites do not adhere solely to agrarian life as do the Amish, although until this century this was also the norm for them. Today farming is the occupation of only about 20% of American Mennonite families.

Mennonites, like the Amish, follow the New Testament. The major differences between the two groups occur in the interpretation of the Bible as a prescription for daily living: Mennonites are more liberal in concessions to modern life than the Amish. Mennonites have adopted modern conveniences such as cars, telephones, and electricity, and place a high value on education. In fact, they operate several high schools in Lancaster County, and a number of colleges, among them Eastern Mennonite College in Harrisonburg, Virginia, and Goshen College in Indiana. Unlike the Amish, Mennonites are active evangelists, and have established ministries in many foreign countries.

Mennonites do not dress in the austere, plain manner that the Amish do, although most dress conservatively. Many women wear white skull caps at all times, others wear them only in church or in public; the wearing of caps is derived from Scriptures (1 Corinthians 11:3-15).

31

Mennonites, because of their relatively gregarious nature, have a more benign view of the tourist industry than do the Amish. While they too are often inconvenienced by heavy tourist traffic on the roads, the Mennonites see the presence of millions of visitors to Lancaster County as an opportunity to explain their mission. In the earliest days of tourism development, they established the Mennonite Information Center as an outlet to describe their philosophy and tell the story of Mennonite and Amish life (refer to the chapter on Lancaster County for a full description of The Mennonite Information Center). Also, many tourist-oriented businesses are owned by Mennonites.

Mennonite communities are scattered throughout the United States and Canada and in over 40 countries. The largest concentration in North America is in the PDC, mainly Lancaster, Montgomery, and Bucks Counties. There are about 235,000 Mennonites in the United States and 90,000 in Canada today. However, these two countries comprise less than half the world Mennonite population. Some related denominations in North America include the Mennonite Brethren Church, Brethren in Christ, Old Order Amish, Old Order Mennonites, Beachy Amish, and Old Order River Brethren. The Mennonites are clearly a diverse group.

Moravians

The Moravians came to America originally to bring Christianity to the Indians, and their missionary work continues today in such diverse places as the West Indies, Central America, Africa, and Asia. The world Moravian population is about half a million, but only 60,000 are in the United States. Their largest communities in this country are Bethlehem, and Winston-Salem, North Carolina.

The Moravian Church originated in 1457 in Bohemia, now a province of Czechoslovakia, and was the first to break away from Roman Catholicism. The Thirty Years War (1618-48) nearly obliterated the church. Protestantism had been outlawed in Bohemia and Moravia, but the church members continued to meet secretly for many years. In 1722 some of the remaining members fled to Saxony, where a Lutheran nobleman, Count Zinzendorf, provided them a sanctuary. The renewed church, now named Moravian for the province where most of its members came from, was born in 1727 at Zinzendorf's estate in Saxony.

Missions soon began; the first permanent settlement in America, originally intended to be at Savannah, Georgia, occurred instead in Northampton County, Pennsylvania, in 1740. A few Moravians did go to Savannah, but a war between England and Spain was in progress. The Moravians there were called on to fight for the English but refused, which caused them to be viewed with suspicion. Thus, their colony at Savannah was abandoned, although it might have died anyway because of natural attrition. Meanwhile, Pennsylvania had been selected by the Moravian Bishop Augustus Spangenberg for a settlement, after his visit there revealed an opportunity for missionary work among the numerous persecuted religious minorities from Europe.

Thus, the first lasting Moravian settlement occurred at Nazareth, where the English evangelist, George Whitefield proposed to build a village for English debtors. The following year, 1741, Bishop David Nitschmann, designated to be the Moravian leader in Pennsylvania, obtained property at the present location of Bethlehem, and the first house was built. This was on the frontier of the colony, but the site fit in well with the Moravians' plans to bring Christianity to the Indians. Churches were established at Nazareth and at Lititz, Lancaster County. Within a few years boarding schools for girls were opened in Bethlehem and Lititz, both of which are still operating, although the Bethlehem school was later merged with a boys' school to become Moravian Academy.

The Moravian doctrine is that of the Old and New Testaments. They are a "mainstream" Protestant denomination and practice infant baptism and Holy Communion. They are known, however, for the early use of music in their services, dating from John Hus's time. Their first hymnal was published in 1501 and contained some hymns written by Hus. The Bethlehem church's trombone choir (1754) may be the oldest instrumental music organization in continuous existence in the country. Passion Week, the name given by Moravians to Holy Week, the week before Easter, is a time of reading the stories of Christ's suffering and death and singing appropriate hymns.

Their most significant contributions in the PDC are the historic and cultural value of their settlements and written records, which have been beautifully preserved in places such as Bethlehem, Lititz, and Nazareth.

Schwenkfelders

The Schwenkfelders are one of the smallest denominations of Protestant-ism, with only five churches and about 3,000 members. The churches are in Palm, Lansdale, Center Point (Worcester), and Norristown, all in Montgomery County, and Philadelphia. The church takes its name from Caspar Schwenckfeld von Ossig, a Silesian nobleman, scholar, and preacher who lived from 1489 to 1561. Trying to aid the Reformation, Schwenckfeld did not attempt to establish his own church, but instead worked for a united, ecumenical, Christian church. This movement was known popularly as the "Reformation by the Middle Way", but was viewed as heretical by established churches. Persecution of Schwenckfeld's followers ensued, and they emigrated to Pennsylvania, arriving in Philadelphia on September 22,

1734. Two days later they held a service of thanksgiving for their safe arrival, and that date has been marked as a Memorial Day ever since.

Schwenkfelders believe in the supremacy of individual conscience in matters of faith, work and service in public office and the military. They practice adult baptism and open Communion, and emphasize the spirit over the letter in all matters.

The Schwenkfelders, perhaps in keeping with the practices of their founder, did not organize as a society until 1782, and the Schwenkfelder Church was not incorporated until 1909. Today the church operates the Perkiomen School, a college preparatory institution founded by the society in 1892 in Pennsburg, Montgomery County. A museum and library of Schwenckfeld's publications and 18th and 19th century artifacts are located on the school grounds.

Jews

Like persecuted Christian minorities, Jews found refuge in early Pennsylvania. Jews were, and still are, primarily city dwellers; in Europe they had been tradesmen, shopkeepers, and professionals, and retained those occupations here. The earliest Jewish immigrants were from Germany and adjacent countries in central Europe, who arrived by the 1730s. They settled in Easton, Lancaster, and Schaefferstown, Lebanon County, as well as Philadelphia. Today there are congregations in all the largest PDC cities, and in some of the smaller towns closest to Philadelphia.

Other Religious Denominations

Among the most prevalent denominations in the PDC are Lutheran, United Methodist, Presbyterian, Baptist, and Roman Catholic, though not necessarily in that order of predominance. Many smaller denominations exist, such as Brethren, Brethren in Christ, Episcopal, Latter Day Saints (Mormons), Society of Friends (Quakers), and Universalist Unitarian, as well as ethnically oriented groups such as the Islamic and African Methodist Episcopal. There are also numerous nondenominational and fundamentalist Christian churches.

REGIONAL COOKING

The Pennsylvania Dutch are famous for their cooking; culinary talents are highly valued among Amish and non-Amish alike. Owing to their agrarian background, the "Dutch" diet is one of common, filling foods, not "gourmet" type cooking. Their diet consists largely of foods that are or can be produced locally—beef, pork, poultry, vegetables, and dairy products. Fish and seafood do not figure heavily in a typical Dutchman's diet, although they are readily available in food markets and restaurants.

The Pennsylvania Dutch diet typically is high in fats and starches. Sugar is used liberally in cooking, and fried foods are common. Vegetables, which should be near perfection in flavor in this extremely fertile area, are often overcooked and oversweetened, robbing them of much of their natural taste and nutrition. In short, while Dutch cooking is tasty and filling, it would not win many awards for its health value by today's standards. Remember that Dutch cooking originated among farmers, who needed to replace the many calories burned in hard physical labor. Cholesterol, hypertension, and other modern maladies were unknown then, and most additives and preservatives hadn't been invented. While food growing methods have changed over the years, the Dutch diet and food preparation have largely stuck to tradition.

Recipes for Pennsylvania Dutch standbys vary slightly from one cook to another, as cooking is an art, not an exact science. Measurements are often given in these terms: "as large as an apple", "butter the size of a walnut", and so on. The Dutch have many unique dishes with Deitsch names, such as *schnitz un knepp* (dried apples and dumplings, often served with ham), *tzitterle* (souse, or pickled pigs' feet), and hexel and mummix, which are any leftover meats, potatoes, and vegetables ground into hash. In the farmers' markets you can buy *ponhaws* (scrapple), *hog maw* (pig's stomach, which is usually stuffed with ground meat, potatoes, and onions), apple butter, and *chow chow* (similar to piccalilli).

The area is renowned for its baked goods. The pies, cakes, puddings, and cookies are legendary, and occupy a large amount of space in many Dutch cookbooks. Shoo-fly pie, a molasses mixture topped with crumbs, is probably the best known specialty, made famous by the 1940s song "Shoo-fly Pie and Apple Pan Dowdy." There are (at least) two varieties—dry bottom and wet bottom. Other favorites include schnitz (dried apples) pie, "funeral" (raisin) pie, and funnel cakes (a mixture of eggs, milk, sugar, flour, salt, and baking powder mixed into a batter thin enough to flow through a funnel, which is then deep fried and served with powdered sugar, molasses, or jelly).

Many restaurants catering to tourists feature Pennsylvania Dutch cooking. Some offer a fixed menu of popular favorites served "family style", where diners are seated at long tables and food is served on platters from which everyone helps themselves. Unlimited quantities of each course are brought out until everyone has had enough and is ready to move on to the next course. Rarely does anyone complain of being hungry after such a meal.

The legend of the "seven sweets and seven sours" is a long-standing tradition of the Pennsylvania Dutch, but nobody can verify its origin or authenticity. It definitely does not come from the Amish, according to one highly respected Amish authority.

No visit to the PDC can be complete without at least one traditional Pennsylvania Dutch meal. If you're on a restricted diet, you hopefully will be able to enjoy at least some, if not all, of the local specialties.

REGIONAL SPEECH

Nearly all Pennsylvania Germans a few generations ago spoke a cross between German and English known as *Deitsch*. It is still the mainstay of Amish conversation within their own community (but the Amish speak English when talking with non-Amish and use formal German in their religious services). Deitsch is heard only occasionally today outside the Amish community, mainly among older people with limited formal education. However, many more PDC residents, while not speaking Deitsch, possess many of the speech patterns stemming from it and from its forerunner German. This results in what outsiders often find to be very humorous expressions. They originate primarily from German word order and sentence structure, which when translated directly to English, sound stilted.

Some of the more common expressions you may hear in your travels include:

"Make the light out" or "Outen the light." (Turn off the light.)
"The cake is all." (all gone)
"Is it making anything down?" (Is it raining (snowing)?)
"What for soup have you today?" (What kind of soup....?)
"It'll make when those two get together." (There'll be a fight....)
"I take my coffee so." (I drink my coffee black with no sugar.)
"The school bell went." (rang)
"Just you don't make no never-mind." (Mind your own business.)

"I'll give you that." (I'll concede that.)
"The factory leaves out at 4 o'clock." (stops work at...)
"John was played out (exhausted) after working hard all day."

In addition to colloquialisms such as these (and there are hundreds more), the Pennsylvania Dutch often use other words and idioms as part of their normal speech. "Yet", "still", "once" (often pronounced with a "T" sound at the end, as "onc't"), and "now mind" can appear almost anywhere in a Dutch person's conversation. There are many unique "non-word" words that the Dutch use as part of their normal speech that are so obvious as to their meaning that even outsiders know instinctively what is being said (a similar situation exists with some Yiddish terms). For example, when a Dutchman says to his child, "Don't *reutsch* around so!", it's immediately clear to all that he means "Stop squirming!" Or consider these: "His hair is *streubly*" (unkempt); "I'm all *faheudelt*" (confused); "Don't *spritz* the furniture" (splash).

Pennsylvania Dutch speech has a distinctive lilt and sound. Changes in voice inflection give it a singing tone. Certain vowels and diphthongs have unusual sounds, as they do in other regional accents. The "ou" sound, as in "house", comes out "aah" from the Dutch, and a "j" sound is usually "ch" ("chust", rather than "just"). A "v" is often pronounced like a "w", and "th" like "s".

USEFUL INFORMATION

GETTING TO THE PDC

Most PDC visitors who come alone, with their families, or in small groups, travel by car, since once in the PDC, some form of motor vehicle is almost a necessity for getting around (although the bicycle is an ideal vehicle for leisurely travel—refer to page 47 for information about bicycle touring).

By car. The PDC is easily accessible by car, as a network of superhighways linking all the major East Coast metropolitan centers serve the region. The PDC is within a two-hour drive (about 100 miles) of Philadelphia, Baltimore, Washington, and New York, and six hours or less (300 miles) from Boston, Buffalo, Cleveland, Pittsburgh, and Norfolk. The proximity to such a large population (one-quarter of the nation's population lives within 300 miles of the PDC) is one reason for its popularity. The table below shows driving distances from selected major cities to the largest towns in the PDC.

ROAD MILEAGES FROM MAJOR CITIES TO PDC CITIES

To From	ALLENTOWN	GETTYSBURG	HARRISBURG	LANCASTER	READING	YORK
ALBANY	220	338	302	288	256	328
BALTIMORE	160	54	78	76	108	52
BWI AIRPORT	170	62	88	86	118	62
BOSTON	311	429	393	378	347	419
BUFFALO	351	341	305	341	349	331
CHICAGO	743	675	661	697	716	678
CINCINNATI	570	502	488	524	543	505
CLEVELAND	426	358	344	380	399	363
COLUMBUS	467	399	385	421	440	402
DETROIT	599	531	517	553	572	536
NEW YORK	85	223	187	166	121	190
NEWARK AIRPORT	72	210	174	153	108	177
PHILADELPHIA	56	146	107	70	62	94
PHILA. AIRPORT	66	156	117	80	72	104
PITTSBURGH	285	216	203	233	257	214
RICHMOND	312	189	230	228	260	204
WASHINGTON, DC	202	79	120	118	150	94
DULLES AIRPORT	207	84	125	123	155	99

By bus. Greyhound and Capital Trailways Bus Companies provide intra-regional service as well as service to and from Philadelphia, New York, Baltimore, Washington, Pittsburgh, and Buffalo. Schedules and fare information are available from Greyhound at 901 Main St., Suite 2500, Dallas, TX 75202, and from Capital Trailways at 1061 S. Cameron St., P.O. Box 3353, Harrisburg, PA 17105, (717) 233-7673 or (800) 444-BUSS (2877). Additionally, Bieber Bus Company, Vine and Baldy Sts., Kutztown, PA 19530, serves Reading and Kutztown from the Port Authority Bus Terminal in New York City, and Reading, Kutztown, Allentown, Bethlehem, and intermediate points from the Greyhound Terminal in Philadelphia. Bieber's phone numbers are (215) 683-7333, (212) 971-6363 in New York, and (215) 931-4001 in Philadelphia. Trans-Bridge Lines, 2012 Industrial Dr., Bethlehem, PA 18017, serves Allentown, Bethlehem, Easton, and Wind Gap from the Port Authority and Newark Airport, with intermediate stops at several towns in western New Jersey. Their phone number is (215) 868-6001. See city and metropolitan area maps in the individual county chapters for locations of bus depots in the PDC.

Charter bus operators bring thousands of visitors a year in guided tour groups. Some come for general tours of the area while others come to visit one or just a few points of interest or to attend one special event such as a fair or festival.

By train. Amtrak serves the PDC on its New York-Philadelphia-Pittsburgh-Chicago runs; trains stop at Lancaster and Harrisburg. Frequent daily commuter service is provided by SEPTA (Southeastern Pennsylvania Transportation Authority) on branches of the former Pennsylvania and Reading Railroads from Philadelphia's 30th Street Station to Doylestown, Norristown, and Downingtown. Connections can be made at 30th Street with long-distance Amtrak trains from the Midwest, Northeast, and South. However, SEPTA trains, and some Amtrak trains, do not provide checked baggage service, so travelers on these trains are limited to the luggage they can reasonably handle themselves. Checked baggage service on Amtrak is available only at Philadelphia and Harrisburg. For Amtrak information call (800) USA-RAIL (872-7245). SEPTA's phone number in Philadelphia is (215) 574-7800.

By air. Philadelphia International Airport is probably the most convenient destination for visitors flying in from distant locations, although Baltimore-Washington, Dulles, and Newark International Airports should not be ruled out, depending on your ultimate PDC destination. The part of the PDC west of the Susquehanna River is closer to Baltimore and Washington than to Philadelphia, and the driving time to Easton, for example, is less from Newark than from Philadelphia. The driving distances from these four major airports to PDC cities appear in the table on page 39.

Bus service to various PDC cities is available as follows from several of these airports:

From Newark: Trans-Bridge Lines (address above) serves Easton, Bethlehem, and Allentown. Capitol Bus Company, a division of Capitol Trailways (address above), serves Ephrata, Lancaster, York, and Harrisburg.

From Baltimore-Washington International: Capitol Bus serves York and Harrisburg.

From Philadelphia: bus (and train) connections to the PDC can be made, although using them requires getting to center city via either the SEPTA high-speed rail line or SEPTA- or privately-operated buses. This is, at best, time-consuming, and may not be worth the inconvenience if you're traveling with your family or have lots of luggage. Moreover, if you plan to rent a car for traveling within the PDC, you'll find it most practical and probably no more expensive to pick it up at the airport.

Harrisburg International and Allentown-Bethlehem-Easton (A-B-E) Airports have major airline service from some hub cities as well as short-hop commuter service; Lancaster and Reading are served only by commuter airlines. Car rentals are available at all airports mentioned above, although the choice of rental companies is much wider at Philadelphia, Baltimore, Washington, and Newark.

TRAVELING WITHIN THE PDC

Finding your way around the PDC is not difficult if you understand the various forms of road identification that are used.

Virtually all roads in Pennsylvania outside of incorporated cities and boroughs are named and numbered. The touring route network includes Interstate, federal, and state numbered roads. The identifying signs are the standard red, white, and blue shield for Interstate highways, and the black-on-white federal marker for US highways that are used in all states. State touring routes are marked with black numbers inside a white keystone. These three levels in the hierarchy are common to all states in the continental U.S., and these routes are shown on all the state maps.

Pennsylvania has an extensive network of paved, well maintained secondary roads serving the rural areas, but most are not shown on state maps because the scale is too small to maintain readability. These include state and township roads and a small number of county-owned roads that were formerly in the state system but in recent years have been turned over to county control.

ROAD MILEAGES WITHIN PDC

	ALLENTOWN	BETHLEHEM	CARLISLE	CHAMBERSBURG	DOYLESTOWN	EASTON	EPHRATA	GETTYSBURG	HARRISBURG	HERSHEY	KUTZTOWN	LANCASTER	LEBANON	READING	VALLEY FORGE	YORK
ALLENTOWN	-	4	102	135	27	13	55	119	82	72	18	68	58	36	50	108
BETHLEHEM	4	-	106	139	26	9	59	123	86	76	22	72	62	40	54	112
CARLISLE	102	106	-	33	129	115	69	28	20	34	90	56	47	75	104	35
CHAMBERSBURG	135	139	33	-	154	148	104	25	53	67	123	89	80	108	137	54
DOYLESTOWN	27	26	129	154	-	30	72	135	111	103	42	85	95	55	27	109
EASTON	13	9	115	148	30	-	68	132	95	85	31	81	71	49	63	121
EPHRATA	55	59	69	104	72	68	-	66	40	30	35	13	22	19	46	37
GETTYSBURG	119	123	28	25	135	132	66	-	37	51	107	53	64	93	121	29
HARRISBURG	82	86	20	53	111	95	40	37	-	14	70	38	27	55	86	26
HERSHEY	72	76	34	67	103	85	30	51	14	-	55	29	13	41	77	40
KUTZTOWN	18	22	90	123	42	31	35	107	70	55	-	48	42	16	49	72
LANCASTER	68	72	56	89	85	81	13	53	38	29	48	-	24	32	59	24
LEBANON	58	62	47	80	95	71	22	64	27	13	42	24	-	28	69	53
READING	36	40	75	108	55	49	19	93	55	41	16	32	28	-	37	56
VALLEY FORGE	50	54	104	137	27	63	46	121	86	77	49	59	69	37	-	83
YORK	108	112	35	54	109	121	37	29	26	40	72	24	53	56	83	-

State touring routes and state-owned secondary roads form the State Route number system adopted by PennDOT in 1986. Touring route numbers are the same as those shown on the roadside signs, and have 1, 2, or 3 digits; for example, US 30 is SR 30, PA 309 is SR 309. Secondary roads have 4-digit numbers, such as SR 1001, 2042, etc., and numbers repeat from one county to another. Intersections of two or more State routes are marked, as shown here, by 12-by-18 inch white signs with black numbers. However, intersections of State routes with city, township, or borough roads are not signed in this manner.

Township routes have 3-digit numbers preceded by "T". In some townships the route number appears with the road name on the street sign, while in others it does not. Commercially made maps usually show township roads by name but not by number, while official PennDOT county maps (described later) show numbers but no names.

While traveling on state routes you will notice small square white signs at intervals of about 0.45 miles. These are segment numbers used by PennDOT in its information management system. While normally of no interest to travelers, the segment number could be useful if you have to call the State Police in an emergency. Segment numbers start with 10 and increase in increments of 10 until the end of the road or the county line is reached. Segment numbers often change at a readily identifiable feature such as a bridge or intersection. Segment numbers increase as you travel north and east and decrease as you go south and west. A somewhat different method of segment numbering is used on Interstates, but these roads have distance markers every mile which are much more visible, so they are more useful as location descriptions in case of emergency. Interstate mileage also increases in the northbound and eastbound directions and decreases toward the south and west.

The street network in most PDC towns and cities is easy to follow because streets are in a regular gridiron pattern, and many cities have numbered streets. This system originated in Philadelphia and has been copied nationwide. Downtown streets in PDC cities tend to be rather narrow because the population growth and volume of traffic produced by that 20th century invention, the automobile, were not envisioned when the streets were laid out over 200 years ago. Fortunately, the street grid is ideally suited for one-way streets to improve traffic flow, and most cities have adopted them. Street addresses are assigned 100 numbers to the block as they are virtually everywhere in the United States outside of New England. The only exception among sizeable towns in the PDC is Doylestown, which has irregularly numbered streets.

While Pennsylvania has made improvements in its highway system in recent years, many rural roads are still narrow and some are used in excess of capacity. Congestion occurs in and around the urban areas at rush hours, particularly in those with heavy tourist traffic. If you have adequate maps to enable you to confidently negotiate the secondary road network, you can usually save time by bypassing traffic jams on the main highways. Please keep in mind, however, that street signs can be missing, turned around, or hidden by foliage, which is why good detailed maps (and the ability to read them) are a prerequisite for getting off the beaten track.

Obtaining Detailed Maps

A state road map, either the version published by PennDOT or one obtained at your local gas station, is quite adequate to get you to the PDC and to give you the "big picture"—a general orientation of the region—but it may not be detailed enough to enable you to travel the myriad secondary roads that reveal the true beauty of the area. If you want to really see the countryside, particularly covered bridges, unspoiled farmlands, and out-of-the way villages, some kind of detailed map is needed.

There are commercially made maps of most PDC counties that can be bought at bookstores, map or sporting goods stores, chambers of commerce, tourist

43

information centers, supermarkets, and gas stations. These usually show all roads with names and numbers (if the road carries a state touring route number), a street and town index, as well as major points of interest. Some are in typical folded map format, while others are in atlas form, with each section of the county or region on a separate page. The atlas type maps are usually more complete and of a larger scale than the folded maps, but can be somewhat harder to use because of the necessity of turning pages frequently and the inability to view the entire county in detail at once.

Some of the better maps include the atlases made by ADC and the locally produced "Map of Lancaster County" which is available at many tourist businesses in that county. The latter has an enlargement of Lancaster city and the heart of the "Amish country" to the east. ADC's address is 6440 General Green Way, Alexandria, VA 22312, phone (703) 750-0510 or (800) ADC-MAPS (232-6277); their maps currently available cover Bucks, Chester, Lancaster, Montgomery, and York Counties, and the greater Harrisburg area.

The only way to obtain maps for the entire PDC in the same format, scale, and typography is to buy PennDOT's county maps. The most useful PennDOT county map is the "Type 10", which is at a scale of one inch to the mile, on a 36"x49" sheet, printed in black on white. Type 10s cost $1.50 per county and can be ordered from PennDOT, Distribution Services Unit, P.O. Box 2028, Harrisburg, PA 17105. PennDOT maintains a publications sales office in Room G-125 of the Transportation and Safety Building at Commonwealth Avenue and Forster Street in Harrisburg, which is open 8:00 AM to 4:00 PM Monday through Friday except Commonwealth holidays. Checks are accepted for map purchases by mail or in person and should be made payable to Pennsylvania Department of Transportation. The 6% state sales tax applies to all purchases except those mailed out of state.

Street maps of the region's largest cities are readily available locally, most often in the same places where county maps are sold. The PennDOT official state transportation map contains enlargements of the dozen largest metropolitan areas plus a few heavily visited smaller communities such as Gettysburg and Hershey, but the enlargements show only the major streets. If you need more detail than this, then a street map is a necessity. Some street maps can be obtained free, so check with the chamber of commerce first. If the map contains advertising, the businesses whose ads appear may give copies away.

This book contains an orientation map of each county at the beginning of the respective chapter, detailed street maps of the downtown areas of the most important towns, and metropolitan area maps for the largest cities. The orientation maps heading each county's chapter are designed only to show the locations of places referred to in the text or in the Calendar of Events; they are not intended as road maps because there is insufficient space to provide the necessary detail.

ABOUT PENNSYLVANIA

Traffic Laws

Pennsylvania's rules of the road are largely in conformance with the Uniform Vehicle Code, which is the model for traffic law in all 50 states. Therefore, there are few unique laws that drivers and pedestrians need be concerned with. One traffic rule that is rigidly applied is the yield sign law. If you pass a yield sign when entering a road and are involved in an accident, the law automatically presumes you to be at fault.

The minimum driving age in Pennsylvania is 16; the state has reciprocity with most other states and Canadian provinces in recognizing the validity of driver's licenses.

Bicyclists are considered vehicle operators for purposes of traffic law, so they must obey the same rules that apply to motorists, and have essentially the same rights to use the roads.

Liquor Laws

The minimum legal age for buying and drinking alcoholic beverages is 21. All wines and liquors are sold in state-operated stores, but beer is sold by licensed private distributors; in both cases, never on Sunday. Credit cards may be used in State stores, and any of the following forms of identification that have photos attached may be used as proof of age: driver's license, passport or visa, military ID, and non-driver's ID issued by any state driver licensing agency.

Up to 144 ounces of beer (the equivalent of two 12-ounce six-packs) can be bought at bars. Establishments where food and non-alcoholic beverages account for at least 40% of sales are permitted to serve alcoholic beverages on Sundays from 11 AM to 2 AM Monday. Normal bar hours are 7 AM to 2 AM Monday through Saturday.

Sales Tax

Pennsylvania's sales tax is 6% and it applies uniformly throughout the state. Food bought in stores and "everyday" clothing are exempt. However, restaurant meals, take-out food, and "special purpose" clothing (such as swimwear, uniforms, and furs) are taxed. Wine and liquor bought in State stores are taxed; the tax is built into the price. A few counties have imposed a hotel occupancy tax in addition to the sales tax as a way of increasing revenue without directly taxing local residents (and voters).

Telephones

The PDC lies within the 215 and 717 area codes. Generally, Berks, Bucks, Chester, Lehigh, Montgomery, and Northampton Counties are in the 215 zone, while Adams, Cumberland, Dauphin, Franklin, Lancaster, and York are in 717. The boundary between the two zones does not follow county lines precisely, and the exceptions are listed in the counties where they exist. Each county's area code is given at the beginning of its chapter, and is not repeated with phone numbers elsewhere in the chapter except for those numbers in the small portion with a different area code from the rest of the county. For example, in the Lancaster County chapter, the area code appears only with (215) numbers, but not with (717) which covers the bulk of the county. You must dial "1" before the number when making a long-distance call, whether within the same or a different area code. Most local calls cost 25 cents and are timed. Some pay phones require you to dial first, and when the party answers, quickly put the coin in the slot, so be sure to read the instructions on the phone before dialing.

RECREATION FACILITIES

Amusements

There are three notable **amusement parks** in the PDC that you may wish or need to include in your plans if traveling with children: Hersheypark (Dauphin Co.), Dorney Park in Allentown (Lehigh), and Dutch Wonderland outside Lancaster (Lancaster). These parks operate seasonally. Opening is around Easter or late April (depending when Easter falls) for weekends only until Memorial Day. From Memorial Day through Labor Day weekends the parks operate seven days a week, and resume a weekends only schedule after Labor Day until the end of September or Columbus Day weekend; Dorney Park closes for the season on Labor Day.

The PDC features two **zoos**, one in Norristown (Montgomery) and the other at Hersheypark (Dauphin), which are described in their respective county chapters.

Bicycling

A bicycle is an ideal vehicle for touring the PDC. Whether you participate in an organized group tour or travel on your own, you'll be able to absorb the region's natural beauty in a way motor tourists cannot.

With a labyrinth of well-maintained secondary roads throughout the area, it's possible to reach virtually all of the attractions that automobile and bus tourists go to without encountering heavy motor traffic. Yet you're never more than a few miles from a town where food, and often lodging and other services, are available.

Before starting on an extended tour, or even just a day ride, you should make sure your equipment is in safe operating condition and be aware of the basic rules of the road. Even though bicycles are not defined as vehicles in the Pennsylvania Vehicle Code, bicyclists are recognized as vehicle drivers and, with minor exceptions, have the same rights and responsibilities as motorists.

Bicyclists are the only vehicle drivers who are permitted to use the shoulder of a roadway, but riding on the shoulder is not required unless it is signed as a bike route. Bicyclists are prohibited from limited-access highways if a "Motor Vehicles Only" sign is posted at the entrance; if the sign isn't posted, you may use that road, although it probably won't afford very pleasurable cycling. Bicycling on the sidewalk is not allowed in business districts, and is usually permitted in residential zones only by children. A white headlight and red rear reflector are required for nighttime cycling.

It's a good idea to wear a hard-shell helmet, preferably one that meets both Snell and ANSI (American National Standards Institute) standards, a bright-colored shirt or jacket, and stiff-soled shoes, and to always carry a pump, spare inner tube and/or patch kit, water bottle, and identification including medical emergency information.

Most of the larger PDC towns have bicycle clubs, and several commercial bike tour operators are headquartered in or run tours in the region. A good place to get information on these organizations is from the League of American Wheelmen, 6707 Whitestone Road, Baltimore, MD 21207, (301) 944-3399. Ask for their

Tourfinder. The League is a national organization of individuals, families, and bicycle clubs.

American Youth Hostels, a non-profit membership organization promoting self-propelled travel, whether by bicycle, canoe, skis, or on foot, has eight hostels in the PDC. Hostels are simple overnight accommodations where travelers share housekeeping duties. Sleeping is dormitory-style and there is a communal kitchen. Hostels provide an opportunity for cheap travel and the chance to meet other travelers. Typically, hostelers are high-school and college age men and women, but AYH membership is by no means limited to young people. Strict discipline is enforced at the hostels by the houseparents who own the property and operate it under an agreement with AYH.

Two AYH hostels are in state parks and are leased from the Pennsylvania Department of Environmental Protection, and a third is operated by the Bucks County Parks and Recreation Department, but all others are privately owned. AYH membership is normally required in order to use hostels, and advance reservations are usually necessary. Contact AYH at P.O. Box 37613, Washington, DC 20013, (202) 783-6161, for information.

To find the most pleasant cycling environment, detailed maps are essential. PennDOT publishes a Bicycling Guide consisting of a statewide map and four quadrant maps. The statewide map highlights a network of linear routes prepared with the cooperation of the Bicycling Federation of Pennsylvania. The quadrant maps also show nearly all state-maintained highways, names and addresses of local bike clubs, bike shops, tourist information offices, campgrounds, youth hostels, and State Police phone numbers. The quadrant maps also have relief maps to give you an approximate idea of the terrain that each of the linear routes encounters, making them much more useful for bicycling than the state map alone. The entire PDC, with the exceptions of most of Franklin County and the extreme northeastern corner of Northampton County, is contained on the southeastern quadrant map. The excluded areas are on the southwestern and northeastern quadrants, respectively.

The state map is free, and the quadrants cost $1.25 each, or $4.50 for the entire set including the state map. The Pennsylvania Bicycling Guide can be ordered from PennDOT, Distribution Services Unit, P.O. Box 2028, Harrisburg, PA 17105. Orders shipped within Pennsylvania are subject to the 6% sales tax.

You will probably find that even the quadrant maps are not detailed enough, as they do not show the thousands of miles of city, borough, and township roads. Only a county map will give you this complete coverage, and although some county maps tend to be awkward to use and carry on a bicycle, you'll probably find them worth the cost and bother. Refer to **Obtaining Detailed Maps** for map sources and recommendations.

A publication that's useful for planning short loop trips is <u>25 Bicycle Tours in Eastern Pennsylvania</u> by Dale Adams and Dale Speicher (Backcountry Publications, P.O. Box 175, Woodstock, VT 05091: 1986 (rev.), $6.95). The book includes maps and descriptions of tours ranging from 25 to 55 miles long, although some are outside the PDC.

Boating

All motor boats used in Pennsylvania waters, regardless of the power source, must be registered in the owner's home state or state in which the boat is primarily used. The registration fee in Pennsylvania is $4.00 for boats under 16 feet, and $6.00 for those 16 feet or longer. Registrations expire annually on March 31. Out-of-state boats are allowed up to 60 days a year of use in Pennsylvania waters. Boat registrations are handled by the Pennsylvania Fish Commission, 3517 Walnut Street, Harrisburg, PA 17109, (717) 657-4551.

No registration is required for sailboats, canoes, kayaks, or other non-powered boats, but when used in state parks or on the Susquehanna River, the operator(s) must have a launching permit obtainable at the state park ranger's office.

Camping

There are numerous private and public campgrounds throughout the PDC; they are listed in Appendix E.

The Bureau of State Parks, P.O. Box 1467, Harrisburg, PA 17120, (717) 787-8800, is in charge of all state parks and state forest picnic areas. Brochures and information relating to these facilities are available from the above address or on-site.

Four state parks in the PDC have overnight cabins as well as tent facilities, but due to demand, a lottery system has been instituted to apportion the cabins fairly. There are modern cabins at Gifford Pinchot (York Co.) and Nockamixon State Parks (Bucks), and rustic cabins at Cowans Gap (Franklin) and Ralph Stover (Bucks). Rentals are for one-week periods only during the summer season, but half-week rentals are also available during the other three seasons. Ask for the brochure "Cabins in Pennsylvania State Parks" for complete lottery details and rates.

The Bureau offers a program of reduced campsite fees for Pennsylvania residents who are age 65 or over or who are physically or mentally handicapped. The program offers reduced fees at campgrounds operated by the Bureau and applies to Sunday through Thursday nights. No discount is offered on Friday or Saturday nights or on the night before one of the major summer holidays. Registration for the program is required and one form of supporting identification must be presented when applying. Enrollment in the program is permanent and free of charge.

The Bureau also publishes a guide for handicapped visitors entitled "Access Pennsylvania State Parks" listing facilities in each state park that are wheelchair accessible.

Canoeing, Kayaking, Rafting, Tubing

Point Pleasant Canoeing and Bucks County River Tubing offer canoeing, rafting, kayaking, and tubing at three locations on the Delaware River: six miles north, and 17 and 30 miles south of Easton. Phone numbers are (all (215)) 258-2606, 982-9282, and 297-TUBE (8823). Trips operate daily from May to September, but are subject to change due to river conditions.

Generally, PDC rivers have shallow stream gradients, and frequently low water levels, and that is the major reason why there is not more activity of this type in the region. A long-standing tale has it that in dry weather, it's possible in many places to walk across the Susquehanna and not get your feet wet. That adage is very close to the truth at times.

Fairs and Festivals

Fairs and festivals of various types take place throughout the year. From county fairs to crafts festivals to antique car shows to ethnic festivals, there is always something interesting to enjoy, regardless of the season. The major events are listed in each county's **Calendar of Events**. These Calendars are arranged chronologically so you can save time by having to read only the portion of the calendar that matches the time of your visit. There is a Calendar arranged by subject in this section so that you won't overlook any events concerning the types of activities that interest you, regardless of when and where they occur. But do eventually read the entire calendar—you may find other events that you'll want to attend, or return for at a later time.

If you're planning to spend several days taking in any of the better-known happenings, such as the Kutztown Folk Festival, Musikfest in Bethlehem, the Fall Meet of the Antique Auto Club of America in Hershey, or the Allentown and York Fairs, it's best to make lodging reservations well in advance, and to allow extra time getting there and finding a parking space. Events such as these have generated widespread acclaim and crowds number in the tens of thousands.

Hiking

There are five established trails in the PDC, and all state parks in the region except one have hiking facilities. The most famous trail of all, the **Appalachian Trail**, crosses the PDC in Franklin and Cumberland Counties and then follows the summit of Blue Mountain along the northern border of Berks, Lehigh, and Northampton Counties to the Delaware Water Gap. A total of 222 miles of the AT are in Pennsylvania. A guide to the AT in Pennsylvania ($4.50), and a set of twelve maps covering this portion of the Trail, are available from Keystone Trails Association, P.O. Box 251, Cogan Station, PA 17728. Additional information on the AT can be obtained from the headquarters of the Appalachian Trail Conference, P.O. Box 807, Dept. SD, Harpers Ferry, WV 25425.

Four regional trails criss-cross the PDC; they are described briefly below, and the sources for information and guides are given.

Horse-Shoe—130 miles. Begins at the AT in northern Dauphin County and runs southeast across the Lebanon Valley to the Furnace Hills of northern Lancaster County, then generally eastwardly via French Creek State Park to Valley Forge. Information and guidebooks are available from the Horse-Shoe Trail Club, c/o Mrs. Robert Chalfant, 509 Cheltena Avenue, Jenkintown, PA 19046. Guidebooks cost $5.00 and include detailed trail directions, maps, lists of overnight accommodations, and information of historical interest.

Tuscarora—105 miles. Runs west from the AT atop Blue Mountain, crosses Path Valley in northern Franklin County, and ascends Tuscarora Mountain, continuing southwest to Hancock, Maryland. Information, a guidebook ($2.40), and a set of two maps ($5.35), from Keystone Trails Association, P.O. Box 251, Cogan Station, PA 17728.

Mason-Dixon—204 miles, some of which are in Maryland and Delaware. Leaves the AT near Mount Holly Springs in Cumberland County and runs east to the Susquehanna near York Haven, then follows the river to its mouth at Chesapeake Bay in Maryland. Continues east and then north in Maryland and Delaware and re-enters Pennsylvania near Chadds Ford, Delaware County, and generally follows Brandywine Creek, ending at the Horse-Shoe Trail near Ludwigs Corner, Chester County. Thus, there are two separate segments in the PDC. Information, and a guidebook ($4.50), are available from Mason-Dixon Trail System, 1225 Rosedale Avenue, Bellefonte, Wilmington, DE 19809.

Conestoga—65 miles, connecting the Mason-Dixon and Horse-Shoe Trails. The entire trail is in Lancaster County except for the Mason-Dixon juncture on the York County side of the Susquehanna. Information, and a guidebook ($4.50), from Lancaster Hiking Club, P.O. Box 6037, Lancaster, PA 17603.

All trails listed above are maintained by local hiking clubs for the benefit of all hikers. A list of clubs that are affiliated with the Keystone Trails Association is available from KTA (see address above). Individuals may also join KTA; write for an application. KTA publishes and sells maps and guides to other trails in Pennsylvania.

Professional Sports

Two professional baseball teams and one each in football, hockey, and soccer, have homes in the PDC. The baseball teams, both members of the Class AA Eastern League, are the **Harrisburg Senators** and **Reading Phillies.** The Eastern League plays a 140-game season starting around April 10 and ending on Labor Day.

The Continental Interstate Football League is represented by the **Harrisburg Patriots**; their season extends from August to early December. The American Hockey League **Hershey Bears** play a 70-game schedule beginning in early October and extending through the end of March. Home games are played Wednesday and Saturday evenings at Hershey Arena. The **Hershey Impact** of the American Indoor Soccer League also plays at the Arena; their season of approximately 40 games runs from early November through March. See Berks and Dauphin Counties for details about schedules and stadium locations.

Philadelphia has a full range of professional sports, and its teams' games are broadcast on radio and TV stations throughout the PDC. Baltimore teams are covered by some stations in the western part of the region, and fans' loyalties in this area are split between the two cities.

Skiing

Downhill and cross-country skiing can be enjoyed in the PDC, although good conditions for the latter are chancy because the region does not normally receive enough snow to support nordic skiing throughout the winter.

These are the **downhill** ski areas in the region:

Doe Mountain, SR 1010 near Mertztown (Berks Co.), (215) 682-7109; for ski report 682-7107.

Ski Liberty, PA 116, 1 mi. south of Fairfield (Adams), (717) 642-8282; for snow conditions (800) 382-1390 in PA, and (800) 233-1134 in DC, DE, MD, NJ, NY, VA.

Ski Roundtop, 925 Roundtop Road, Lewisberry (York), (717) 432-9631; for snow conditions (800) 382-1390 in PA, and (800) 233-1134 in DC, DE, MD, NJ, NY, VA.

Spring Mountain Ski Area, Spring Mount Road, Spring Mount (Montgomery), (215) 287-7900.

Cross-country skiing, usually on hiking trails, is available at the following state parks: Caledonia (Franklin & Adams), Codorus and Gifford Pinchot (York), Colonel Denning and Pine Grove Furnace (Cumberland), Cowans Gap (Franklin), Evansburg (Montgomery), French Creek (Chester), Jacobsburg (Northampton), Memorial Lake (Lebanon), and Nockamixon and Roosevelt (Bucks). At Roosevelt, skiing is done on the Delaware Canal towpath, which means that no loop trails are possible. Codorus State Park, with 15 miles of trails, has the most mileage among these parks.

There is one cross-country touring center in the region: Apple Valley X-C Ski, located on PA 29/100 about 2 miles south of Old Zionsville (Lehigh), (215) 996-5525. It has 7 miles of trails, 4 of them maintained, and instruction and rentals are available.

State Parks

There are twenty state parks in the PDC; three of these are Environmental Education Centers, which offer educational programs rather than recreation facilities. The parks are listed in Appendix A on pages 256 and 257 as to types of facilities available. A more detailed list of facilities is available in the Pennsylvania Recreational Guide published by the Bureau of State Parks, PO Box 1467, Harrisburg, PA 17120, (717) 787-8800. The guide is free and also includes an official state highway map showing the locations of all parks. State parks are also listed as to location in their respective county chapters.

Train Rides

If you're a steam locomotive fancier, there are six railroads where you can ride steam-powered trains through the picturesque countryside:

The Gettysburg RR, Gettysburg (Adams Co.)—to Biglerville or Mount Holly Springs;

The Wanamaker, Kempton & Southern RR, Kempton (Berks)—to Wanamakers;

Blue Mountain & Reading RR (Berks)—Temple to South Hamburg (board at either station);

New Hope Steam Railway (Bucks)—New Hope to Buckingham Valley;

Middletown & Hummelstown RR, Middletown (Dauphin)—to Hummelstown;

Strasburg RR, Strasburg (Lancaster)—to Paradise.

One railroad, the Stewartstown (York), uses gasoline and diesel locomotives on its runs from Stewartstown to New Freedom and York.

The Strasburg and Stewartstown Railroads are true short-line roads, while all the other trains operate on former Reading Railroad tracks. Most trains operate during the warm weather months only, and some only on weekends. See the county chapters for full details on these railroad excursions.

SHOPPING

Major Shopping Areas

Stores to suit a wide range of tastes and budgets are found in the PDC. While each city has its traditional downtown shopping district, in most cases it has been surpassed by outlying malls and strip shopping centers in terms of variety of stores, quality of merchandise, and availability of parking. The downtown districts in the smaller towns have fared better than those in the cities, probably because there is less competition from shopping centers there.

Many cities have made an effort to upgrade their downtowns by building pedestrian malls, planting trees to create a park-like effect, and refurbishing storefronts to highlight historic architectural features. While the outward appearance may have been improved, the quality of the stores often has not. Had these steps been taken before shopping centers became dominant, the results might have been different, but for most cities the effort has been too late.

All of the largest cities in the PDC have enclosed regional shopping malls in the suburbs, and several have more than one. The region's, and state's, largest shopping complex is at King of Prussia (Montgomery Co.). Located at the interchanges of the Turnpike, Schuylkill Expressway, and US 202, the combined Plaza and Court contain about 2.5 million square feet of space and feature such famous stores as Macy's, Bloomingdale's, and Abraham & Straus. Other large malls (1/2 million square feet or more) in the region, and their locations, are:

City	Name
Allentown/Bethlehem	Lehigh Valley Mall
	Whitehall Mall
Harrisburg	Camp Hill Shopping Mall
	Capital City Mall
	Colonial Park Plaza
	Harrisburg East Mall
Lancaster	Park City Mall
Lansdale	Montgomery Mall
Reading	Berkshire Mall
York	Galleria (to open 1989)
	West Manchester Mall
	York Mall

Regional malls have, in effect, become the new "downtown" shopping district for most cities. Like the former downtowns, they emphasize "shoppers' goods" stores, or those primarily selling items of infrequent purchase. "Convenience goods" stores, such as supermarkets and drug stores, are usually not found in regional malls, although some malls have "convenience centers" adjacent to them where stores of this type are located. There are many smaller shopping centers in the region—too many to list—that contain a variety of convenience goods stores. If you need to make any purchases of this type, you're likely to find them faster in one of the smaller local shopping centers. Also, parking and accessibility are usually easier in such shopping centers.

Outlets

A new kind of shopping has become quite popular in recent years—factory outlets. These stores feature name-brand merchandise, sometimes store quality, sometimes seconds, at greatly reduced prices. Reading is the outlet capital of the PDC, and much of the East Coast as well, but there are also major outlet shopping centers in Lancaster, York, Hanover (York Co.), Morgantown (Berks), and Waynesboro (Franklin). Bus charters are organized from major East Coast cities to the outlets, bringing in thousands of people a year. The Reading outlets count six million patrons annually, although some are undoubtedly repeat visitors as well as local residents.

Some outlets are in newly built shopping centers, but those in Reading are in old factory buildings. The VF Outlet, for example, occupies the former Vanity Fair hosiery factory.

CALENDAR OF EVENTS

This is a classified calendar of the major annual events that take place in the PDC. Use it as you would the yellow pages of the telephone directory: look up the subject(s) of interest to you, then go through the alphabetical listing of events to find the name, date, place, and contact for further information. Please remember that dates of annual events sometimes change from year to year because of the shifts in the calendar or for other reasons. So be sure to check with the sponsors for precise dates of the events you want to attend.

Antiques Shows, Sales, and Flea Markets

Antique Show. Late May, Chadds Ford. c/o Brandywine River Museum, P.O. Box 141, Chadds Ford, PA 19317, (215) 459-1900.

Antique & Craft Fair. Late June, Columbia. c/o Columbia Area Chamber of Commerce, 40 N. 3rd St., Columbia, PA 17512, (717) 684-5249.

Antique Show and Sale. Early May and Early October, Pottstown. Sunnybrook Ballroom, Sunnybrook Rd. c/o Edna Smith, Box 164, Huntingdon Valley, PA 19006, (215) 947-1254.

Antique Show & Sale. Early July, Lititz. Warwick Middle School. c/o Lititz Historical Foundation, 431 W. Orange St., Lititz, PA 17543, (717) 626-8427.

Buckingham Antiques Show. Mid-June, Buckingham. Tyro Grange Hall. (215) 275-4148 (Norristown).

Chester Co. Historical Society Antiques Show. Late May, West Chester. Hollinger Field House, West Chester Univ. c/o Chester Co. Historical Society, 225 N. High St., West Chester, PA 19380, (215) 692-4800.

Civil War Collectors Show. 1st weekend in July, Gettysburg. Sheraton Inn. c/o Gettysburg Travel Council, 35 Carlisle St., Gettysburg, PA 17325, (717) 334-6274.

Eastern National Antique Show and Sale. Late April, Harrisburg. Farm Show Complex. (215) 437-5534 (Allentown).

Gettysburg Outdoor Antiques Show. 3rd Sat. in May and 4th Sat. in September, Gettysburg. Lincoln Sq. and adjacent streets. c/o Gettysburg Travel Council, 35 Carlisle St., Gettysburg, PA 17325, (717) 334-6274.

Greater York Antiques Show and Sale. Late May, York. Memorial Hall, York Fairgrounds. c/o George Sheets, P.O. Box 1388, York, PA 17405, (717) 741-0911 or 854-5907.

Historical Society Antiques Show & Sale. Late November, New Hope. Eagle Fire Co. c/o New Hope Historical Society, S. Main St., New Hope, PA 18938, (215) 862-5652.

Moravian College Antique Show. Early June, Bethlehem. c/o Patricia Helfrich, Alumni House, Moravian College, Bethlehem, PA 18018, (215) 861-1366.

New Oxford Outdoor Antiques Show. 3rd Sat. in June, Lincolnway, New Oxford. c/o Gettysburg Travel Council, 35 Carlisle St., Gettysburg, PA 17325, (717) 334-6274.

Old House Fair and Antiques Show. Late May, Downtown Carlisle. c/o Carlisle Economic Development Center, 114 N. Hanover St., Carlisle, PA 17013, (717) 245-2648.

Tinicum Antique Show. Early June, Tinicum Park. c/o Bruce Davidson, P.O. Box 234, Erwinna, PA 18920, (215) 294-9601.

Up-Country Flea Market. Third Saturday in May, June, July, and August, Cedars. c/o Cedars Village Shops, P.O. Box 173, Cedars, PA 19423, (215) 584-1490.

World's Greatest Yard Sale. Mid-June, York. York Fairgrounds. c/o Sherry Ehrhart, 226 E. Market St., York, PA 17403, (717) 848-1841.

Arts and Crafts Exhibitions and Fairs

Art Competition. Mid-April, York. Cora Miller Art Gallery, York College of PA. c/o York College, Country Club Rd., York, PA 17403 (717) 846-7788, ext. 257.

Art Day at Fonthill. Early August, Doylestown. Fonthill Museum. (215) 343-6760.

Arts Festival. Early October, Downtown Carlisle. c/o Carlisle Economic Development Center, 114 N. Hanover St., Carlisle, PA 17013, (717) 245-2648.

Arts Festival. Late May, Harrisburg. State Museum of Pa., 3rd & North Sts. c/o Nick Feher, P.O. Box 770, Harrisburg, PA 17108, (717) 238-5180.

Arts Festival. Mid-June, Lahaska. Peddlers Village. c/o Peddlers Village, Box 218, Lahaska, PA 18931, (215) 794-7055.

Arts Festival. Early September, New Hope. c/o New Hope Borough Information Center, 1 W. Mechanic St., New Hope, PA 18938, (215) 862-5880.

Autumn Arts Festival. Late September, Mt. Bethel. Slate Belt Museum. (717) 897-6181.

Children's Art Festival. Mid-September, Doylestown. Fonthill and Moravian Tile Works. (215) 348-6114.

Country Crossroads Show and Sale. Mid-April and Early October, York. Memorial Hall, York Fairgrounds. c/o Robert Goodrich, P.O. Box 236, Carlisle, PA 17013, (717) 243-7890.

Deep Run Festival of the Arts. Late June, Bedminster. Deep Run Presbyterian Church. c/o Mrs. Schmidt, RD 2, Box 370, Perkasie, PA 18944, (215) 249-3689.

Doll and Teddy Bear Celebration. Early March, Skippack. Skippack Village. (215) 584-6397 or -1438.

Family Oktoberfest. Mid-September thru mid-October, weekends only, Strasburg. Mill Bridge Village, S. Ronks Rd., (717) 687-6521.

Fantasy of Flowers. Late May, Dublin. Green Hill Farm. c/o Pearl S. Buck Foundation, Dublin Rd., Perkasie, PA 18944, (215) 249-0100.

Fine Arts Festival. Late July, Sinking Spring. Gring's Mill Recreation Area. c/o Berks Co. Parks & Recreation Dept., RD 5, Box 272, Sinking Spring, PA 19608, (215) 372-8939.

Hershey Arts Festival. Late June, Hershey. Hershey Botanical Gardens. c/o Hershey Gardens, (717) 534-3492.

Historic Yellow Springs Art Show and Sale. Late April, Chester Springs. Village of Yellow Springs. c/o Sandy Momyer, P.O. Box 627, Art School Rd., Chester Springs, PA 19425, (215) 827-7414.

Historical Society Colonial Arts and Crafts Fair. Mid-June, Middletown. Hoffer Park. c/o Leon Daily, P.O. Box 248, Middletown, PA 17057, (717) 944-3420.

Juried Exhibition of Contemporary Crafts. October, Bethlehem. Luckenbach Mill Gallery. c/o Bethlehem Visitor Center, 459 Old York Rd., Bethlehem, PA 18018, (215) 691-0603.

Juried Holiday Craft Show. Early November, Reading. Penn State University, Berks Co. Campus. (215) 779-4488.

Outdoor Art Show. Late August, Mt. Gretna. Chautauqua Grounds. c/o Mt. Gretna Art Show, P.O. Box 419, Mt. Gretna, PA 17064, (717) 964-2028.

Outdoor Woodcarving Show. Early June, Intercourse. Kitchen Kettle Village, (717) 768-8261.

Pennsylvania Crafts Day. Late April and Early September, Chadds Ford. c/o Brandywine River Museum, P.O. Box 141, Chadds Ford, PA 19317, (215) 459-1900.

Pennsylvania National Arts and Crafts Show. Late March, Harrisburg. Farm Show Complex, (717) 763-1254.

Pennsylvania Relief Show and Sale of Mennonite Crafts. Early April, Harrisburg. Farm Show Complex. (717) 944-0293 (Middletown).

Pennsylvania State Craft Fair. Late July, Lancaster. Franklin & Marshall College. c/o Pennsylvania Designer Craftsmen, P.O. Box 718, Richboro, PA 18954, (215) 860-0731.

Plain and Fancy Craft Fair. Mid-September, Bird-in-Hand. Plain and Fancy Farm. c/o Plain and Fancy Farm, PA 340, Bird-in-Hand, PA 17505, (717) 768-8281.

Quilt Show. Late April, Boyertown. c/o Boyertown Area Historical Society, 43 S. Chestnut St., Boyertown, PA 19512, (215) 367-9843.

Quilters Heritage Celebration. Early April, Lancaster. Host Farm Resort, 2300 Lincoln Hwy. E. c/o Rita Barber, Rt. 3, Box 119, Lancaster, PA 17601, (717) 854-9323 (York).

Riverwalk Art Festival. Late August, York. Codorus Creek Boat Basin, downtown. c/o York Area Chamber of Commerce, 1 Marketway East, York, PA 17401, (717) 848-4000

Spring Craft Show. Late May, Lancaster. Central Park. c/o Pennsylvania Dutch Convention & Visitors Bureau, 501 Greenfield Rd., Lancaster, PA 17601, (717) 295-1500.

Tinicum Art Festival. Early July, Tinicum. Tinicum Park. c/o Civic Association, Erwinna, PA 18920, (215) 294-9309.

Victorian Tyme Arts & Crafts Show. Late June, Skippack. Skippack Village. (215) 584-6397 or -1438.

Visiting Artists Festival. Mid-July, Mont Alto. c/o A Little Gallery, P.O. Box 397, Mont Alto, PA 17237, (717) 749-3831.

Yellow Springs State Craft Festival. Mid-June, Chester Springs. c/o Sandra Momyer, P.O. Box 627, Chester Springs, PA 19425, (215) 827-7414.

Antique Vehicle Shows and Rallies

Antique Auto Show and Flea Market. Early July, York. York Fairgrounds.

Antique Car & Truck Show. Late August, Skippack. Skippack Village. (215) 584-6397 or -1438.

Antique Fire Apparatus Show and Muster. Mid-July, Harrisburg. Riverfront Park. c/o Dave Buskey, 7210 Chambers Hill Rd., Harrisburg, PA 17111, (717) 564-6935.

Auto Show. Mid-August, New Hope. New Hope-Solebury High School. c/o New Hope Borough Information Center, 1 W. Mechanic St., New Hope, PA 18938, (215) 862-5880.

Car Show and Flea Market. Late May, Exton. c/o Chester County Antique Car Club, 580 Pine Dr., Phoenixville, PA 19460, (215) 933-0381.

Collector Auto Auction. Late September, Lancaster. Dutch Wonderland, 2249 Lincoln Hwy. E., (717) 291-1888.

Duryea Day. Early September, Boyertown. Community Park. c/o Boyertown Museum of Historic Vehicles, 28 Warwick St., Boyertown, PA 19512, (215) 367-2090.

Fall Collector Car Flea Market and Corral. Late September, Carlisle. Carlisle Fairgrounds. c/o Flea Marketeers, 1000 Bryn Mawr Rd., Carlisle, PA 17013, (717) 243-7855.

Fall Meet of the Antique Auto Club of America. Early October, Hershey. Hersheypark Stadium, (717) 534-3829.

Grand Finale Collector Car Auction. Early October, Carlisle. Carlisle Fairgrounds. c/o Flea Marketeers, 1000 Bryn Mawr Rd., Carlisle, PA 17013, (717) 243-7855.

National Street Rod Association East Meet. Early June, York. York Fairgrounds. c/o York Area Chamber of Commerce, 1 Marketway East, York, PA 17401, (717) 848-4000.

Pennsylvania International Auto Show. Late January, Harrisburg. Farm Show Complex, (717) 657-1310.

RV Expo. Mid-September, Harrisburg. Farm Show Complex, (717) 774-3470.

Spring Collector Car Flea Market and Corral. Late April, Carlisle. Carlisle Fairgrounds. c/o Flea Marketeers, 1000 Bryn Mawr Rd., Carlisle, PA 17013, (717) 243-7855.

Spring Steam-Up. Mid-May, Kinzers. Rough and Tumble Museum, US 30, (717) 442-4249.

World of Wheels Custom Car Show. Mid-November, Allentown. (215) 394-8365.

Ethnic Festivals

Chesterland International Three-Day Event. Late October, Unionville. PA 82, (215) 347-2333 or (215) 933-2712 (Phoenixville).

Folk Fest. Mid-May, Doylestown. Mercer Museum. c/o Bucks County Historical Society, Pine & Ashland Sts., Doylestown, PA 18901, (215) 345-0210.

Pennsylvania German Day. Mid-June, Sinking Spring. Gring's Mill Recreation Area. c/o Berks Co. Parks & Recreation Dept., RD 5, Box 272, Sinking Spring, PA 19608, (215) 372-8939.

Polish Festival. Early September, Doylestown. Shrine of Czestochowa. c/o Our Lady of Czestochowa, Ferry Rd., Doylestown, PA 18901, (215) 345-0600.

Pulaski Festival. Late April, Bethlehem. (215) 838-6858 (Hellertown)

Scottish Festival. Mid-September, Pipersville. c/o Bucks County Tourist Commission, 152 Swamp Rd., Doylestown, PA 18901, (215) 345-4552.

Fairs, Circuses, and Carnivals

A-Day Fair. Late April, Doylestown. Delaware Valley College. c/o Delaware Valley College, US 202, Doylestown, PA 18901, (215) 345-1500.

Apple Blossom Festival. 1st weekend in May, Arendtsville. South Mountain Fairgrounds, PA 234. c/o Gettysburg Area Chamber of Commerce, 33 York St., Gettysburg, PA 17325, (717) 334-8151.

Apple Harvest Festival. 1st two weekends in October, Arendtsville. South Mountain Fairgrounds, PA 234. c/o Gettysburg Travel Council, 35 Carlisle St., Gettysburg, PA 17325, (717) 334-6274.

Das Awkscht Fescht (August Festival). Early August, Macungie. (215) 820-3393 (Allentown).

Blue Valley Farm Show. Late August, Bangor. (215) 588-3693.

The Great Allentown Fair. Late August-Early September, Allentown. Fairgrounds, 17th & Chew Sts. (215) 433-7541.

Carlisle Fair. Mid-August, Carlisle. Carlisle Fairgrounds, Carlisle Springs Rd.

Chadds Ford Days and Country Fair. Mid-September, Chadds Ford. (215) 388-7376.

Christmas City Fair. Mid-July, Bethlehem. Christmas City Fairgrounds. c/o Richard Szulborski, 669 Atlantic St., Bethlehem, PA 18015, (215) 865-3751.
Cornwall Country Fair. Mid-July, Cornwall. Cornwall Iron Furnace. c/o Manager, Cornwall Iron Furnace, P. O. Box 251, Cornwall, PA 17016, (717) 272-9711.
Denver Community Fair. Mid-September, Denver. Denver Memorial Park, (215) 267-2831.
Elizabethtown Fair. Late August, Elizabethtown. Fairgrounds, E. High St. c/o Sally K. Nolt, 25 Iris Cir., Elizabethtown, PA 17022, (717) 367-7256.
Ephrata Fair. Late September, Ephrata. (717) 733-8132.
Fall Festival. Late September, Wernersville. Old Dry Run Farm. (215) 693-6000.
Farmers Fair. Mid-October, Dillsburg. Baltimore St. (717) 432-5228.
Franklin County Fair. Late August, Chambersburg. Chambersburg Rod & Gun Club, 3725 Warm Spring Rd. (PA 995). c/o Franklin Co. Fair, P.O. Box 49, Chambersburg, PA 17201, (717) 264-6359.
Goschenhoppen Folk Festival. Mid-August, East Greenville. New Goschenhoppen Park. c/o Goschenhoppen Historians, Box 476, Green Lane, PA 18054, (215) 754-6013 (Sassamansville).
Hanover Dutch Festival. Late July, Hanover. Wirt Park, 100-block of High St. c/o Hanover Area Chamber of Commerce, 146 Broadway, Hanover, PA 17331, (717) 637-6130.
Kimberton Fair. Late July, Kimberton. (215) 933-9715.
Kutztown Folk Festival. Late June-Early July, Kutztown. c/o Kutztown Folk Festival, 461 Vine La., Kutztown, PA 19530, (215) 683-8707.
Kutztown Fair. Early August, Kutztown. Kutztown Fairgrounds. c/o Marvin I. Beltzner, P.O. Box 177, Kutztown, PA 19530, (215) 683-3324.
Lebanon Area Fair. Late July-early August, Lebanon. Lebanon Area Fairgrounds, Rocherty Rd. c/o Ben Bow, RD 1, Box 829, Annville, PA 17003, (717) 867-1305.
Manheim Community Fair. Early October, Manheim. Memorial Park, (717) 665-7480.
Mayfair. Late May, Allentown. Allentown Parks System. c/o Marie Conway, 2020 Hamilton St., Allentown, PA 18104, (215) 437-6900.
New Holland Farmers Fair. Late September, New Holland. (717) 354-0423.
Landis Valley Fair. Early June, Landis Valley. Pennsylvania Farm Museum, 2451 Kissel Hill Rd., Lancaster, PA 17601, (717) 569-0401.
Olde York Street Fair. May (Mother's Day), York. Market Street, downtown. c/o York Area Chamber of Commerce, 1 Marketway East, York, PA 17401, (717) 848-4000.
Oley Valley Community Fair. Mid-September, Oley. (215) 929-0488 or (215) 375-4085 (Reading).

Pennsylvania Renaissance Faire. Early July thru early October, every weekend, Manheim. Mt. Hope Estate and Winery. c/o Mt. Hope Estate & Winery, P.O. Box 685, Cornwall, PA 17016, (717) 665-7021.

Philadelphia Folk Festival. Late August, Schwenksville. Old Poole Farm. c/o Philadelphia Folk Song Society, 7113 Emlen St., Philadelphia, PA 19119, (215) 242-0150.

Reading Fair. Mid-September, Reading. Fairgrounds Square Mall, 5th St. Hwy. (US 222 north). (215) 921-9223 or (215) 370-3473.

Schaefferstown Folk Festival. Mid-July, Schaefferstown. c/o Historic Schaefferstown, Inc. P.O. Box 307, Schaefferstown, PA 17088, (717) 949-3795.

Sherwood Hall Country Festival. Late June, Grantville. Harrison School Rd. c/o Sherwood Hall Country Festival, P.O. Box 288, Grantville, PA 17028, (717) 865-3911 (Annville) or (717) 469-7486.

Shippensburg Community Fair. Late July, Shippensburg. Shippensburg Fairgrounds. c/o Shippensburg Area Chamber of Commerce, 75 W. King St., Shippensburg, PA 17257, (717) 532-5509.

Shrine Circus. Early April, Harrisburg. Farm Show Complex. (717) 236-4591.

South Mountain Fair. End of August or beginning of September, Arendtsville. South Mountain Fairgrounds, PA 234. c/o Gettysburg Travel Council, 35 Carlisle St., Gettysburg, PA 17325, (717) 334-6274.

Southern Lancaster County Fair. Late September, Quarryville. (717) 786-1054.

Unionville Community Fair. Early October, Unionville. Unionville High School. (215) 347-2087.

Village Fair. Mid-June, Doylestown. War Memorial Field. c/o Mary Ann Garton, P.O. Box 182, Doylestown, PA 18901, (215) 345-0597.

Warwick Summer Festival. Late June, Knauertown. Warwick Park. c/o Chester Co. Parks & Recreation Dept., 235 W. Market St., West Chester, PA 19382, (215) 431-6415.

York Interstate Fair. Early September, York. York Fairgrounds. c/o York Co. Agricultural Society, 334 Carlisle Ave., York, PA 17404, (717) 848-2596.

Food and Harvest Festivals

All-American Dairy Show. Late September, Harrisburg. Farm Show Complex, (717) 787-2905.

Apple Blossom Festival. 1st weekend in May, Arendtsville. South Mountain Fairgrounds, PA 234. c/o Gettysburg Area Chamber of Commerce, 33 York St., Gettysburg, PA 17325, (717) 334-8151.

Apple Butter Frolic. Early October, Harleysville. Indian Creek Farm. c/o Mennonite Heritage Center, 24 Main St., Souderton, PA 18964, (215) 723-1700.

Apple Fest and Town Fair. Late September, Mercersburg. E. Seminary St. c/o Tuscarora Tourist Council, (717) 328-5701.

Apple Festival. Early November, Lahaska. Peddlers Village. c/o Peddlers Village, Box 218, Lahaska, PA 18931, (215) 794-7055.

Apple Harvest Festival. 1st two weekends in October, Arendtsville. South Mountain Fairgrounds, PA 234. c/o Gettysburg Travel Council, 35 Carlisle St., Gettysburg, PA 17325, (717) 334-6274.

"At the Sign of the Plough" Oyster Festival. Mid-October, York. Golden Plough Tavern, 157 W. Market St. c/o Historical Society of York Co., 250 E. Market St., York, PA 17403, (717) 848-1587.

Bavarian Beer Fest. Late June thru Labor Day, every weekend, Adamstown. Stoudt's Black Angus Brewery Hall, PA 272, (215) 484-4385.

Cherry Fair. Late June, Schaefferstown. c/o Historic Schaefferstown, Inc., P.O. Box 307, Schaefferstown, PA 17088, (717) 949-3795.

Corn Festival. Late August, Shippensburg. King St., Shippensburg. c/o Rose Dillner, Box F, Shippensburg, PA 17257, (717) 532-5509 or -3940.

Corn Planting Ceremony. Early May, Allentown. Lenni Lenape Historical Society. c/o Carla Messinger, Lenni Lenape Historical Society, Fish Hatchery Rd., Allentown RD 2, PA 18103, (215) 797-2121 or (215) 434-6819.

Great American Chocolate Festival. Mid-February, Hershey. Hotel Hershey, (717) 533-2171.

Harvest Days. Early October, Landis Valley. Pennsylvania Farm Museum, 2451 Kissel Hill Rd., Lancaster, PA 17601, (717) 569-0401.

Harvest Festival. Mid-September, Intercourse. Kitchen Kettle Village, (717) 768-8261.

Harvest Festival and Horse Plowing Contest. Mid-September, Schaefferstown. c/o Historic Schaefferstown, Inc., P.O. Box 307, Schaefferstown, PA 17088, (717) 949-3795.

Harvest Home Jubilee. Early September, Lenhartsville. Pennsylvania Dutch Folklife Museum. (215) 682-7432 (Topton).

Herb Festival. Early May, Harleysville. Heckler Plains Farmstead. c/o Joan DiMaria, Morris & Landis Rds., Harleysville, PA 19438, (215) 256-8087 or (215) 822-7422 (Chalfont).

International Food Festival. Mid-September, Chambersburg. Memorial Sq. c/o Chamber of Commerce, 75 S. 2nd St., Chambersburg, PA 17201, (717) 264-7101.

Lebanon Bologna Fest. Late August, Lebanon. Lebanon Area Fairgrounds. c/o Lebanon Valley Tourist & Visitors Bureau, P.O. Box 626, Lebanon, PA 17042, (717) 272-8555.

Maple Sugar Festival. Mid-March, Coatesville. Hibernia Park. c/o Chester Co. Parks & Recreation Dept., 235 W. Market St., West Chester, PA 19382, (215) 431-6415.

Market Day and Festival. Mid-August, Quakertown. Burgess-Foulke House. c/o William Amey, 26 N. Main St., Quakertown, PA 18951, (215) 536-3298.

Martha Washington Strawberry Festival. Mid-June, Bethlehem. Sun Inn. c/o Jeannette MacDonald, Sun Inn Preservation Assn., 564 Main St., Bethlehem, PA 18018, (215) 866-1758.

Mushroom Festival. Late September, Kennett Square. c/o Southeastern Chester County Chamber of Commerce, P.O. Box 395, Kennett Square, PA 19348, (215) 444-0774 or (215) 388-7806.

Rhubarb Festival. Late May, Intercourse. Kitchen Kettle Village, (717) 768-8261.

Strawberry Festival. Late April-Early May, Lahaska. Peddlers Village. c/o Peddlers Village, Box 218, Lahaska, PA 18931, (215) 794-7055.

Time of Harvest. Early October, Kinzers. Rough and Tumble Museum, US 30, (717) 442-4249.

Historical Observances

Brandywine Battlefield Muster. Mid-September, Chadds Ford. c/o Brandywine Battlefield Park, Chadds Ford, PA 19317, (215) 459-3342.

Canal Festival. Early July, Easton. Hugh Moore Park. c/o Hugh Moore Park, P.O. Box 877, Easton, PA 18044, (215) 250-6700.

Chambersfest. Late July, Downtown Chambersburg. c/o Chamber of Commerce, 75 S. 2nd St., Chambersburg, PA 17201, (717) 264-7101. (In 1989 the 125th anniversary of the burning of the town will be commemorated.)

Civil War Heritage Days. Last weekend in June and 1st week in July, Gettysburg. Encampment, outdoor church services, band concerts, lectures by Civil War historians, Battle re-enactment.

Colonial Days. 2nd Sat. in September, East Berlin. c/o Gettysburg Travel Council, 35 Carlisle St., Gettysburg, PA 17325, (717) 334-6274.

Departure of the Continental Army. Mid-June, Valley Forge. c/o Valley Forge National Historical Park, P.O. Box 953, Valley Forge, PA 19481, (215) 783-7700 or -1066.

Easton Area Heritage Day. Downtown Easton. c/o Two Rivers Area Chamber of Commerce, 157 S. 4th St., Easton, PA 18042, (215) 253-4211.

Fort Hunter Day. Mid-September, Fort Hunter. Fort Hunter Mansion, 5300 N. Front St., Harrisburg, PA 17110, (717) 599-5751.

French Alliance Day Celebration. Early May, Valley Forge. c/o Valley Forge National Historical Park, P.O. Box 953, Valley Forge, PA 19481, (717) 783-7700 or -1066.

Foundry Day. Early June, Boiling Springs. c/o Boiling Springs Civic Assn., 619 Lerew Rd., Boiling Springs, PA 17007, (717) 258-3256 or (717) 766-8739.

Hecklerfest. Late September, Harleysville. Heckler Plains Farmstead. (215) 256-8087.

Heritage Celebration. Early October, Reading. Gruber Wagon Works, Berks Co. Heritage Center. c/o Berks Co. Parks & Recreation Dept., RD 5, Box 272, Sinking Spring, PA 19608, (215) 372-8939 or (215) 374-8839.

Historic Days. Late July, Skippack. Skippack Village. (215) 584-6397 or -1438.

Historic Easton House Tour. Late May, Easton. c/o Toni Mitman, P.O. Box 994, Easton, PA 18042, (215) 258-1612.

Laerneswert (Worth Learning). Early October, Center Point. Peter Wentz Farmstead. (215) 584-5104.

Lancaster County Spring Pilgrimage. Early May, Willow Street. Hans Herr House, 1849 Hans Herr Dr. c/o Steve Friesen, (717) 464-4438.

Living History Days. Mid-October, Bethlehem. 18th Century Industrial Area. (215) 868-6311.

May Day. May 1, Fort Hunter. Fort Hunter Mansion. c/o Dauphin Co. Parks & Recreation Dept., 5300 N. Front St., Harrisburg, PA 17110, (717) 599-5751.

Memorial Day Encampment. Memorial Day weekend, Chadds Ford. c/o Brandywine Battlefield Park, Chadds Ford, PA 19317, (215) 459-3342.

Muster Day. Mid-June, Center Point. Peter Wentz Farmstead. c/o Elizabeth Gannon, P.O. Box 240, Worcester, PA 19490, (215) 584-5104.

Neas House Tour. Mid-Late December, Hanover. High & Chestnut Sts. c/o Hanover Area Historical Society, (717) 632-3207.

Red Rose Payment. Mid-June, Manheim. Zion Lutheran Church. c/o Zion Lutheran Church, 2 S. Main St., Manheim, PA 17545, (717) 665-5880.

Re-enactment of Washington's March. Mid-December, Valley Forge. c/o Valley Forge National Historical Park, P.O. Box 953, Valley Forge, PA 19481, (215) 783-7700 or -1066.

Remembrance Day. Sat. closest to November 19, Gettysburg. Gettysburg National Cemetery. c/o Gettysburg Travel Council, 35 Carlisle St., Gettysburg, PA 17325, (717) 334-6274.

Skippack Days. Early October, Skippack. Skippack Village. (215) 584-6397 or -1438.

Washington's Birthday Weekend. c/o Valley Forge Convention & Visitors Bureau, P.O. Box 311, Norristown, PA 19404, (215) 278-3558; (800) 441-3549.

Holiday-Based Events

Brandywine Christmas. Late November thru New Year's weekend, Chadds Ford. c/o Brandywine River Museum, Chadds Ford, PA 19317, (215) 459-1900.

Candlelight Tour. Early December, Center Point. Peter Wentz Farmstead. (215) 584-5104.

Candlelight Tour of Historic Schaefferstown. Mid-December, Schaefferstown. c/o Historic Schaefferstown, Inc., P.O. Box 307, Schaefferstown, PA 17088, (717) 949-3795.

Candlelight Tours. Early December, Coatesville. Hibernia Mansion. c/o Chester Co. Parks & Recreation Dept., 235 W. Market St., West Chester, PA 19382, (215) 431-6415.

Christkindlesmarkt Fair. Early November, Downtown York. c/o York Area Chamber of Commerce, 1 Marketway East, York, PA 17401, (717) 848-4000.

Christmas Celebration. Early December, Chadds Ford. c/o Brandywine Battlefield Park, Chadds Ford, PA 19317, (215) 459-3342.

Christmas City Lighting Ceremony. Late November, Bethlehem. City Center Plaza, 10 E. Church St. (215) 868-1513.

Christmas City Night Light Tours. Late November-Late December, Bethlehem. Lehigh Valley Bank, 52 W. Broad St., (215) 868-1513.

Christmas Festival. Early December, Lahaska. Peddlers Village. c/o Peddlers Village, Box 218, Lahaska, PA 18931, (215) 794-7055.

Christmas House Tour. Late November-Early December, Dublin. Green Hills Farm. c/o Pearl S. Buck Foundation, Dublin Rd., Perkasie, PA 18944, (215) 249-0100.

Christmas Open House. Mid-November, Lahaska. Peddlers Village. c/o Peddlers Village, Box 218, Lahaska, PA 18931, (215) 794-7055.

Doylestown Christmas House Tour. December, Doylestown. James-Lorah House. c/o Junior Women's Club of Doylestown, 132 N. Main St., Doylestown, PA 18901, (215) 348-2187.

Holiday Open House. Late November, Skippack. Skippack Village. (215) 584-6397 or -1438.

Kipona Celebration. Labor Day weekend, Harrisburg. Riverfront Park. c/o Harrisburg Parks & Recreation Dept., (717) 255-3020.

Memorial Day Observance. May 30, Gettysburg. c/o Gettysburg Travel Council, 35 Carlisle St., Gettysburg, PA 17325, (717) 334-6274.

Moravian Christmas Putz. Late November-January 1, Bethlehem. Christian Education Bldg. c/o Moravian Museum, 66 W. Church St., Bethlehem, PA 18018, (215) 866-5661 or (215) 867-0173.

Peace Candle Lighting Ceremony. Late November, Easton. Centre Square. (215) 250-6612.

A Time of Thanksgiving. Early October, Allentown. Lenni Lenape Historical Society. c/o Carla Messinger, Lenni Lenape Historical Society, Fish Hatchery Rd., Allentown RD 2, PA 18103, (215) 797-2121 or (215) 434-6819.

Washington's Birthday Celebration. Mid-February, Valley Forge and Chadds Ford. c/o Valley Forge National Military Park, Valley Forge, PA 19460, (215) 783-7700, or Brandywine Battlefield Park, Chadds Ford, PA 19317, (215) 459-3342.

Musical Events

All American Ragtime Festival and Contest. Early July, Strasburg. Mill Bridge Village, S. Ronks Rd. c/o Karen Reynolds, P.O. Box 86, Strasburg, PA 17579, (717) 687-6521.

Bach Music Festival. Mid-May, Bethlehem. Lehigh University. c/o Bonnie Salventi, Bach Choir of Bethlehem, 423 Heckewelder Pl., Bethlehem, PA 18018, (215) 866-4382.

Central Pennsylvania Jazz Festival. Mid-June, Harrisburg. Sheraton East Hotel, I-83 & Union Deposit Rd. (exit 29). c/o Joe Intreri, P.O. Box 10738, Harrisburg, PA 17105, (717) 257-5441.

Fall Fiddle Festival. Mid-September, Lyons. Community Park. (215) 682-6103.

Fiddle Festival. Early June, Reading. Berks Co. Heritage Center. c/o Berks Co. Parks & Recreation Dept., RD 5, Box 272, Sinking Spring, PA 19608, (215) 372-8939 or (215) 374-8839.

Gettysburg Bluegrass Festival. 1st weekend in May and 2nd weekend after Labor Day, Fairfield. Granite Hill Campground. c/o Granite Hill Campground, 3340 Fairfield Rd., Gettysburg, PA 17325, (717) 642-8749.

Mountain Springs Bluegrass Festival. Early September, Shartlesville. c/o Mountain Springs Camping Resort. Shartlesville, PA 19554, (215) 488-6859.

Musikfest. Late August, Downtown Bethlehem. c/o Margaret Barshine, 556 Main St., Bethlehem, PA 18018, (215) 861-0678.

Newport Jazz Festival All-Stars. Early April, Easton. State Theater. c/o State Theater, 453 Northampton St., Easton, PA 18042, (215) 252-3132.

Old Fiddlers' Picnic. Mid-August, Coatesville. Hibernia Park. c/o Chester Co. Parks & Recreation Dept., 235 W. Market St., West Chester, PA 19382, (215) 431-6415.

Traditional Irish Music and Dance Festival. Early September, Lansdale. Fischer's Pool, 2375 Kriebel Rd., (215) 849-8899 (Philadelphia).

Sporting and Recreational Events

Annual Copperhead Snake Roundup. Late August, Airville. Indian Steps Museum. c/o Conservation Society of York Co., (717) 862-3948 or (717) 741-1527 (York).

Gettysburg Square Dance Round-Up. 4th weekend in May, Gettysburg. Gettysburg College. c/o Gettysburg Travel Council, 35 Carlisle St., Gettysburg, PA 17325, (717) 334-6274.

Harrisburg Historic Canoe Tour. Mid-July, Harrisburg. Susquehanna River, Fort Hunter to City Island. c/o Dauphin Co. Parks & Recreation Dept., (717) 255-1369.

Keystone Nationals. Mid-September, Mohnton. Maple Grove Park. c/o Maple Grove Raceway, RD 3, Box 3420, Mohnton, PA 19540, (215) 856-7612.

Lady Keystone Open Golf Tournament. Mid-June, Hershey. Hershey Country Club. c/o LKO Office, 2101 N. Front St., Harrisburg, PA 17110, (717) 238-9344.
Lehigh Valley Balloon Festival. Late July, Allentown. Queen City Airport. c/o Lehigh County Convention & Visitors Bureau, P.O. Box 2605, Lehigh Valley, PA 18001, (215) 266-0560.
Northbrook Canoe Challenge. Mid-April, Mortonville. Brandywine Creek. c/o Northbrook Canoe Co., 1810 Beagle Rd., West Chester, PA 19382, (215) 793-2279.
Port Indian Regatta. Mid-July, Port Indian. Schuylkill River. c/o Port Indian Civic and Boating Assn., 66 W. Indian Lane, Norristown, PA 19403, (215) 666-9428 or (215) 688-1426 (Wayne).
Scenic River Days. Late July, Reading. Riverfront Park. c/o Robert Kerper, P.O. Box 1442, Reading, PA 19603, (215) 375-6508.
Shad Festival. Mid-May, Bethlehem. 18th Century Industrial Area. c/o Historic Bethlehem, Inc., 459 Old York Rd., Bethlehem, PA 18018, (215) 868-6311.
White Rose Square Dancing Festival. Mid-June, York. York College of PA. c/o York College, Country Club Rd., York, PA 17403, (717) 846-7788.

Miscellaneous Events

Air Show. Reading Airport. Mid-August, Reading. c/o Kent G. George, RD 9, Box 9416, Reading, PA 19605, (215) 372-4666.
Annual Threshermen's Reunion. Mid-August, Kinzers. Rough and Tumble Museum, US 30, (717) 442-4249.
Antiquarian Book Fair. Late June, Carlisle. Holland Union Bldg., Dickinson College. c/o Carlisle Economic Development Center, 114 N. Hanover St., Carlisle, PA 17013, (717) 245-2648.
Buffalo Bill Days. Mid-September, Coatesville. Main St. (215) 383-0584.
Chester County Day. Early October, countywide. c/o Chester Co. Tourist Promotion Bureau, 117 W. Gay St., West Chester, PA 19380, (215) 344-6365.
Civil War Book Fair. 1st weekend in July, Gettysburg. Gettysburg Jr. High School. c/o GBPA, Box 1863, Gettysburg, PA 17325.
Halloween Lantern Tours. Late October, Strasburg. Railroad Museum of Pennsylvania, PA 741 east, (717) 687-8628.
Historic Horse, Steam, and Gas Show. Mid-July, Menges Mills. c/o Betty Staines, 621 E. Rocky Hill Rd., Sparks, MD 21152, (301) 472-2701 or (717) 225-4811 (Spring Grove).
Lost Dutchman Gemboree. Late August, Strasburg. Historic Strasburg Inn. c/o Richard Hasner, 217 Nevin St., Lancaster, PA 17603, (717) 392-6825.
Pennsylvania Farm Show. Mid-January, Harrisburg. Farm Show Complex, (717) 787-5373.
Pennsylvania 4-H Horse Show. Late October, Harrisburg. Farm Show Complex, (814) 863-3657 (State College, PA).

Pennsylvania International Air Show. Late October, Middletown. Harrisburg International Airport, (717) 948-5760.

Pennsylvania National Horse Show. Mid-October, Harrisburg. Farm Show Complex, (717) 236-1600.

Pennsylvania Wild Horse and Burro Days. Late September, Lewisberry. c/o Wild Horse & Burro Adoption Center, Pleasant Hill Rd., Lewisberry, PA 17339, (717) 938-2560.

Rose Display. Mid-June, Hershey. Hershey Gardens, Hotel Rd. (717) 534-3492.

Scarecrow Weekend Festival. Late September, Lahaska. Peddlers Village. c/o Peddlers Village, Box 218, Lahaska, PA 18931, (215) 794-7055.

Train Display. Early January, Lebanon. Stoy Museum, 924 Cumberland St.. c/o Lebanon Valley Tourist & Visitors Bureau, P.O. Box 626, Lebanon, PA 17042, (717) 272-8555.

Tulip Display. Mid-April, Hershey. Hershey Gardens, 621 Park Ave., Hershey, PA 17033, (717) 534-3492.

SPECIAL FEATURES

FARMERS' MARKETS

Among the best-preserved attractions in the PDC are its farmers' markets. The markets maintain a tradition established in early colonial times, although the markethouses themselves date from the late 1800s. Farmers still bring their produce, meats, poultry, baked goods, and fruits to market two or three days a week where they sell them in large shed-like buildings. Markets open early in the morning, usually 6 or 7, and close around 3 PM, but most of the goods are sold by then. Unless you're only planning to browse, it's best to get there early for the widest selection.

It is not uncommon for a family to have "tended" the same market stand for three or four generations. Despite competition from supermarkets, the relative inconvenience of the markets for both vendors and buyers, the farmers' markets prosper. Perhaps it's because they preserve a tradition of featuring high quality products and personal service. The market stand operators know many of their customers personally, since they live in the same community or general area. Their reputation depends on retaining their customers' loyalty. Just as many stands have been operated by several generations of one family, several generations of other families have been their steady customers. For many long-time market-goers, market day is as much a social occasion as a shopping trip.

There have been some changes in markets. Some selling of "hard goods" (notions, used books, "Pennsylvania Dutch" souvenirs) takes place, but for the most part the markethouses carry on their century-old tradition of selling produce, meats, dairy products, and homemade baked goods.

The markethouses feature wide doors that were designed to allow horses and wagons to enter to unload. High ceilings helped keep the building cooler in summer. As much use as possible was made of natural light, since the oldest houses predate electric lights.

The best markethouses are Central in Lancaster, Central and Farmers in York, and Broad Street in Harrisburg. The latter, built in 1860, is the oldest in the state still in use. Columbia and Hanover also have markets, but being smaller

71

communities than Lancaster, York, and Harrisburg, their markets are also smaller. Nearly all PDC cities had at least one farmers' market—York had four—but most have been torn down because of declining trade. The Southern Market in Lancaster operated until 1987, and the building is now a visitors' center and the starting point for downtown walking tours.

There are farmers' markets in the suburbs, and they are often open evenings. Some farm families tend these as well as the downtown markets if their operating hours don't conflict. However, while some of the newer markets feature the same types of goods as the traditional ones, they clearly lack the "atmosphere" of the old-time markethouses, and in a few cases, despite being called "farmers' markets", bear little resemblance to their namesakes.

COVERED BRIDGES

Covered bridges seem to epitomize rural life—simple and slow-paced. They are prized today for aesthetic reasons as well as for their historical value.

Pennsylvania had the first covered bridge built in America, and still has more in existence (over 200) than any other state. Within the PDC there are 61 such bridges in 9 of the 13 counties (Dauphin, Lebanon, Montgomery, and York have none remaining). The roster of counties and the number of bridges is: Adams and Franklin, 2 each; Berks, 5; Bucks, 11; Chester, 11, including 2 shared with Lancaster; Cumberland and Northampton, 1 each; Lancaster, 22; and Lehigh, 6. Several bridges not counted here are reproductions of now-destroyed spans, or have been modernized to the extent that they have no historic value.

Floods have been the greatest enemy of covered bridges, and several were lost during Hurricane Agnes in 1972. Arson has also claimed several bridges, as has general deterioration.

Seven different designs of trusses have been identified on bridges inventoried by the Pennsylvania Historical and Museum Commission in 1980. Perhaps more obvious distinctions can be made by casual observers in rooflines, portals, and sides. Many of the bridges have greater appeal for their bucolic settings than for the design or condition of the structures themselves.

Covered bridges are listed for each county that has them, except in Lehigh and Bucks, where the tourist association has prepared a brochure giving an itinerary that visits all its bridges. In these two counties, reference is to the brochure.

All the bridges are located on (or in a few cases, adjacent to) secondary roads, and most can be driven through. All are one-lane spans, so use caution approaching the bridge in case an oncoming vehicle is already inside. Most of the bridges are perched several feet higher than the road, meaning that visibility may be impaired by the steep slope up to each end of the bridge. All driveable bridges have weight limits posted—some may not be suitable for trailers or motor homes.

HISTORIC PLACES AND DISTRICTS

There are nearly 700 sites and 90 districts within the PDC that are listed on the National Register of Historic Places (referred to throughout the book as NRHP). Most larger PDC cities, and many smaller towns, have Historic Districts, which have been established to preserve important parts of the community's past. They may be noteworthy for historical events or for their architecture or "ambience", and a listing on the NRHP usually brings restrictions on developments that would substantially alter the area's character. The most important districts are described in the book.

The historic sites include primarily homes and churches, but a wide variety of other structures are listed. Some sites are outstanding attractions in their own right, while others are significant for reasons that may not be obvious without background information on the site or general area in question. Still other properties on the NRHP got there because they are within a Historic District and thus got a "free ride", whereas they might not otherwise have qualified for listing. The best known and many of the unusual NRHP sites are mentioned.

WALKING TOURS

The best way to see the sights clustered in the downtown areas of PDC cities is on foot. Therefore, walking tours are described (and prescribed!) in Allentown, Bethlehem, Carlisle, Chambersburg, Doylestown, Easton, Gettysburg,

Lancaster, Lititz, New Hope, Reading, West Chester, and York. Lancaster's walk can be done accompanied by a guide; all the others are self-guided. I've referred you to brochures that supplement the text where they're available, otherwise, use this book and the downtown maps to navigate. None of the walks cover unusually great distances, and the terrain is not excessively strenuous in any of the cities. Be sure to take the usual precautions against street crime; while not common, it can happen.

WINERIES

Commercial winemaking began in Pennsylvania in 1968, although private production, legal or illegal, has been around since William Penn himself, in 1684.

The PDC had never been thought of as having a favorable environment for grape cultivation, yet today nearly two-thirds of all wineries in the state are in this region. The PDC has 20 winemaking establishments where you can tour the production facilities and, usually, taste the results. Lancaster County has five wineries, Bucks, Chester, and York, three each; Adams, two; and Berks, Lehigh, Montgomery, and Northampton, one each. Each winery is listed in its respective county chapter as to the type of facility, location, driving directions, and hours of operation.

Sales of locally produced wines are regulated by the state, which is why you won't find local brands in state liquor stores. Most PDC vineyards have limited production, which is sold exclusively on the premises. Several vineyards have stores in shopping centers in nearby cities that offer tastings as well as sales of wine and wine accessories.

CAVES

Limestone soil, which the PDC has in abundance, is very conducive to the formation of caves and caverns, and there are three caves that are open for public tours: Crystal Cave, near Kutztown (Berks Co.), Indian Echo Caverns at Hummelstown (Dauphin), and Lost Caverns in Hellertown (Northampton). See the county chapters for complete details.

ANTIQUING

The PDC is famous for its antiques shops. Many of the wares originated in the region because the thrifty early families never threw anything out! There are numerous antiques shows and fairs throughout the region, both indoor and outdoor—consult each county's Calendar for dates and locations. The PDC's proximity to major East Coast cities has greatly boosted the antiques business, but this has also induced a rising effect on prices.

Most antiques shops are in the smaller communities. The New Hope-Lahaska area (Bucks Co.), New Oxford and Gettysburg (Adams), and Carlisle (Cumberland) are among the major antiques centers, but there are dealers in many other towns and cities as well.

ADAMS CO.

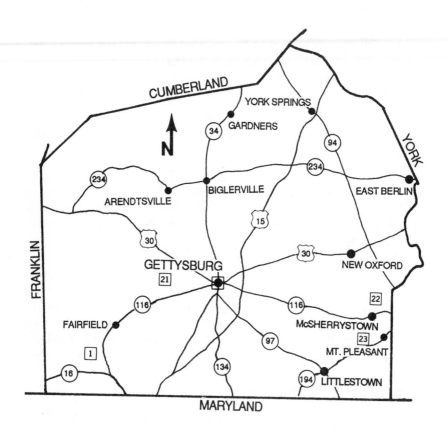

ADAMS

Created: January 22, 1800, as the 26th county, from part of York County
County Seat: Gettysburg
Land Area: 526 square miles
Population (1989 est.): 73,000
Area code: 717

Adams County is named for President John Adams, during whose term in office it was created. Most of its terrain is gently rolling hills, but the northern and western fringes are ringed with mountains. The county is primarily rural and is the least populated of any in the PDC.

Today Adams County is a farming and fruit-growing area; the county leads the state in apple and peach production. Most of the orchards are in the hilly terrain in the northern and western portions. Several of the smaller communities have shoe and textile factories.

Historical Highlights

The fame of the Battle of Gettysburg is so overwhelming that the Civil War obscures all other periods in the county's history.

The land that includes Adams and several adjacent counties was bought from the Indians by William Penn's descendants in 1736, but the first settlements were established about 1734. Several communities existed by the time of the Revolution, and the oldest German church, Christ Reformed, was organized in 1747 just outside of what is now Littlestown. Conewago Chapel, the oldest Jesuit mission west of the Susquehanna, was built about a mile north of McSherrystown, in the southeastern part of the county, in 1740.

The earliest settlers represented several nationalities-Germans, Dutch, and Irish-and there were some English from Maryland in the southern part of the county. It's possible that they thought they were still in Maryland, as the Mason-Dixon line was not surveyed until 1766 in this area. Until 1800 Adams County was part of York County, and it remained a backwoods region for some years thereafter because of the sparse population.

PLACES OF INTEREST

East Berlin, pop. 1,200. Original home of the Studebaker family, noted wagon, and later automobile and truck, manufacturers. Their wagon works was located several miles west of town in the 1830s. David Studebaker, a forebear of the famous later generations, built a house in 1790 at 200 W. King St. (PA 234, one block west of PA 194). The house is now privately owned and is on the NRHP, as is the East Berlin **Historic District** in which it is located. The district includes part of King Street, South and North Avenues, and Locust Street.

Fairfield, pop. 600. Attractive small community in the southwestern part of the county, founded 1801.

Gettysburg Game Park ([1]), 320 Zoo Rd., 642-5229. Open May 1-Nov. 1—10-6. Admission: adults, $4.00; children 2-12, $2.00. 85-acre park with over 250 animals. Petting area with deer, llamas, and sheep. Picnic area. Directions: 1.2 mi. west of center of town, bear right off PA 116 onto Jacks Mountain Rd. (SR 3021) for 0.5 mi. Turn right on Zoo Rd. immediately after passing through covered bridge.

Gettysburg, pop. 8,200. County seat and dominant market center for the county. The town was settled about 1790 and named for James Gettys, a local landowner. It was at the crossroads of the Philadelphia-Pittsburgh and Shippensburg-Baltimore turnpikes. At the time of the Civil War, it was a farming community of about 2,000 people. A very attractive town with typical 19th century Pennsylvania architecture, one wonders if it might be overlooked today if millions did not come to see the Battlefield.

Downtown and Battlefield Area

★★★★ The **Battlefield,** the generic name widely used to encompass **Gettysburg National Military Park** and **Gettysburg National Cemetery.** Many books have told the story of the bloodiest and most famous battle ever fought on American soil, so it is not repeated here. The main part of the Military Park nearly surrounds Gettysburg, and there are isolated small segments scattered within a radius of several miles of town, commemorating the sites of minor skirmishes. Most of the important sites are south of town and are located on Baltimore St., Taneytown Rd. (PA 134), and Steinwehr Ave. (US 15 Business). The best place to begin a tour is at the **Visitor Center** ([2]) located on Taneytown Rd. (entrance also from Steinwehr Ave., 334-1124. Open daily—mid-June to 1st weekend after Labor Day, 8-6; remainder of year, 8-5. Closed Thanksgiving, Christmas, and New Year's Day. There are orientation displays, exhibits, the Rosensteel collection of Civil War artifacts, an electric map presentation using colored lights to show troop movements

GETTYSBURG

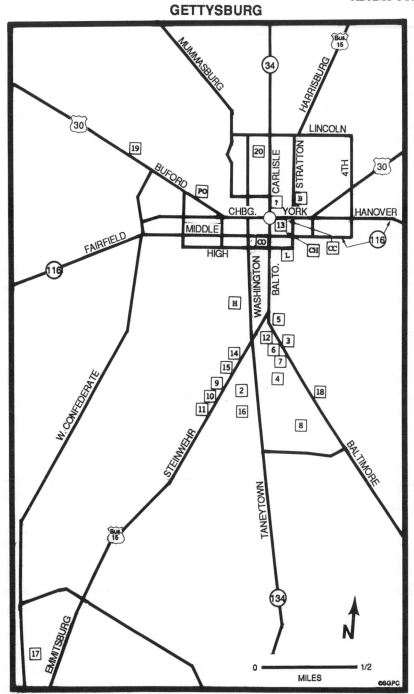

during the battle, and National Park Service rangers on hand to answer questions. There is an admission charge for the **Electric Map Show** (30 min.): adults, $2.00; age 62 and over, $1.50; children 15 and under, free; but none for the V.C. itself or for the brochure outlining the self-guided Battlefield tour.

The Battlefield can be toured three ways: on your own by car, bicycle, or on foot; with a licensed guide in your car; or in a bus operated by one of the commercial tour operators in Gettysburg. Auto tape tours are available for rent for $9.50 per car (includes tape player) at the National Civil War Wax Museum, 297 Steinwehr Ave., 334-6245.

The 15-mile **self-guided tour** starts at the Visitor Center parking lot and takes a minimum of about 2 hours. There are 17 stops on the tour, including the National Cemetery. The entire tour can also be done by bicycle, but there is a shorter route covering Cemetery Ridge, Big and Little Round Tops, the Peach Orchard, and Seminary Ridge. The short route is easier than the full 15-mile loop, but it is not without hills. The tour route is clearly marked and there are plaques identifying and describing the significance of each stop. The best way to get a real sense of the battle is to walk the Battlefield, or at least, parts of it. Park roads are open from 6 AM to 10 PM daily.

Touring with **licensed guides** costs $14.00 for a private car, van, or RV with up to 5 passengers. There is an additional charge for more passengers in vans and RVs. Chartered bus tours cost $30.00 for 16 or more passengers. Shorter or longer private car tours can be arranged with the guide. The guides are licensed by the National Park Service. Guided tours start at the Visitors Center, 334-1124, ext. 31, and at the West End Station, a mile west of town on US 30, 334-9876.

Bus tours begin at the Gettysburg Tour Center (③), 778 Baltimore St., 334-6296, about one block south of the intersection of Steinwehr Ave. Tours take 2 hours; free shuttle service from major motels and campgrounds is provided.

The **Gettysburg National Cemetery** (④) is located between Baltimore St. and Taneytown Rd. directly east of the Visitors Center. It was the first of the 83 military cemeteries in the United States, dedicated by the immortal words of President Lincoln on November 19, 1863. About 3,700 Union soldiers are buried there; an almost equal number of Confederates whose bodies had been left in the original trenches were disinterred in the 1870s and their remains sent to Southern cemeteries.

There are many commercial attractions established to commemorate one or more aspects of the battle; they are briefly reviewed here. It is possible to see and recreate the history of the Battlefield and Cemetery without visiting any of the commercial enterprises, and possibly even without taking a guided tour, if you've done some reading and study beforehand. However, while very touristy, each of these attractions adds a certain insight to your visit. The most practical approach is to decide in what ways you would like to supplement your knowledge and experience of visiting Gettysburg, and then go to the attraction(s) that fit your desires. Most are located on the south side of town, within walking distance of the Visitors Center and many motels. If at all possible, leave your car at your motel or parked at one location and walk to the attractions. Traffic congestion during the high season and on most weekends is horrendous.

The following attractions participate in **package plan** admission prices. If you plan to visit several of them, you can purchase one of two packages at the Gettysburg Tour Center, 778 Baltimore St. The Tour Center is open daily year round from 7:30 AM approximately until dark. Battlefield bus tours are given all year, but most other attractions close after the Thanksgiving weekend and reopen about Easter. If you're visiting out of the main season, it's best to call first (334-6296) to verify the hours of the place(s) you want to see.

★★ **Jennie Wade House** and **Olde Town** (⑤)(30-45 min.), 500-block of Baltimore St., 334-4100. Open daily—summer 9 AM-10 PM, spring and fall 9 -5. Regular admission: adults, $3.85; children 6-12, $2.20; under 6, free. Jennie Wade, 21 years old, was the only civilian casualty of the Battle of Gettysburg. She lived in one side of this double house and was killed when a stray bullet pierced the kitchen wall. A number of bullet holes in the interior walls and furniture have been "preserved", and the house restored to what it probably would have looked like in 1863. The tour provides a taped narration and pamphlet describing each room and its history. Behind the house is Olde Town, a series of shops as they might have appeared at the time of the war: there is a blacksmith, carpenter, printer, barber, and a general store.

★★ **Soldier's National Museum** (⑥)(30-45 min.), 777 Baltimore St., 334-4890. Open daily—summer 8 AM-9 PM, spring and fall 9-5. Regular admission: adults, $3.85; children 6-12, $2.20; under 6, free. The museum tour starts with an exhibit of Battlefield relics and dioramas. You then move into the "Southern Encampment", a life-sized display of a Confederate camp, followed by narrated dioramas depicting the major events of the War.

★★ **Hall of Presidents** and **Hall of First Ladies** (⑦)(about 1 hour), 789 Baltimore St., 334-5717. Open daily—summer 9 AM-10 PM, spring and fall 9-5. Closed December thru February. Regular admission: adults, $3.85; seniors, $3.50; children 6-12, $2.20; under 6, free. Full-sized wax figures of each President through

Ronald Reagan and brief summaries of the major events and accomplishments of their administrations as they might have spoken them. Famous quotes of Presidents from the 1920s to the present are heard in their actual voices. The Hall of First Ladies, a more recent addition to the Hall of Presidents, presents wax statues of each of these women in reproductions of the Smithsonian Institution's collection of First Ladies' gowns. A separate section is devoted to "The Eisenhowers at Gettysburg", including photographs of important events that took place at the Eisenhower farm while Ike was in office.

★★ **National Tower** (⑧)(30-40 min.), 999 Baltimore Pike, 334-6754. Open daily March thru November, hours as follows: March and November 10-4, April and October 9-5, May and September 9-6, June, July, August 9-7:30. Regular admission: adults, $3.50; seniors $3.00; children 6-12, $1.75; under 6, free. The Tower rises 307 feet above the Battlefield, affording a panoramic view of the entire Gettysburg area. There are two levels inside with exhbits and sound dramatizations of the battle, and two outside observation decks with high-powered telescopes and maps.

★★ **National Civil War Wax Museum** (⑨)(45-60 min.), 297 Steinwehr Ave., 334-6245. Open daily 9-7. Regular admission: adults, $3.95; children 13-17, $2.50; 6-12, $1.75; under 6, free. Over 30 displays of wax figures depicting events of the war and those leading up to it. A re-enactment of the Battle and Lincoln's Gettysburg Address is given in the auditorium (every 45 min.; show takes approx. 30 min.).

★ **Lincoln Train Museum** (⑩)(45 min.), 425 Steinwehr Ave., 334-5678. Open daily March thru November—summer 9 AM-10 PM, spring and fall 10-8. Regular admission: adults $3.85; children 5-12, $2.20; under 5, free. Package tickets also sold here. A collection of over 1,000 trains, and operating layouts of various gauges from all over the world, as well as dioramas portraying the role of railroads in the Civil War. Features a "ride with Lincoln" as he came to deliver his Address in 1863.

★★ **Gettysburg Battle Theater** (⑪)(30-45 min.), 571 Steinwehr Ave., 334-6100. Open daily—summer 7 AM-9 PM, spring and fall 8-5. Closed 1st weekend after Thanksgiving thru President's Day weekend, open weekends only President's weekend to Easter. Regular admission: adults $3.85; children 6-11, $2.20; under 6, free. Package tickets also sold here. Orientation program using electronic map and multi-media presentation to set the scene for the Battle.

Old Gettysburg Village of Quaint Shops (⑫), west side of Baltimore St. opposite the Gettysburg Tour Center. Admission free. A place to get a snack, cold water, use the restrooms, or simply sit a while and relax.

★★★ **Lincoln Room Museum** (⑬)(30 min.), 2nd floor of Wills House, SE corner of Lincoln Square, downtown, 334-8188. Open in season—Sun.-Thurs. 9-7, Fri.-Sat. 9-9; reduced hours out of season. Regular admission: adults $2.50; children $1.50. This is the room in which Lincoln stayed the night before delivering his famous Address. There is a 10-minute taped narration of what a conversation between Lincoln and his host David Wills might have included. Some furnishings are known to have been in the room during Lincoln's stay, others come from other rooms in the house, and the rest are copies. There is an exhibit of five copies of drafts of the Address, photos from the war, and cancelled first-day covers from anniversary observances of the Battle. This is probably the least "touristy" of any of the commercial attractions in town.

The following attractions are not affiliated with the Gettysburg Tour Center package plans.

★★"**The Conflict**" (⑭)(1 hour), 213 Steinwehr Ave., 334-8003. Open all year except Christmas and New Year's Day; mid-June thru Labor Day 10-9, remainder of year 10-8. Four separate 50-min. audio-visual programs, each telling a sequence of the Civil War story. Programs are: #1: "The Road to War" (Ft. Sumter to New Orleans); #2: "On to Richmond!" (Peninsula Campaign to Chancellorsville); #3: "Reaching the High Water Mark" (Vicksburg and Gettysburg); #4: "The Violent Road to Appomattox" (Murfreesboro to Appomattox). Two additional 50-min. programs, "The War Within" and "Three Days at Gettysburg", deal, respectively, with the entire war and the Battle of Gettysburg. Admission: any single program $4.00, any two $7.50, any four $14.50. Beginning in 1989, James Getty, well-known locally for his portrayals of Lincoln, will present one performance each evening from mid-June through Labor Day of "Mr. Lincoln Returns to Gettysburg". Admission: adults $5.00; children 6-12, $4.00.

★★ **Colt Heritage Museum of Fine Firearms** (⑮)(30 min.), 241 Steinwehr Ave., 334-6852. Open daily March thru Thanksgiving—daily 8 AM-9 or 10 PM, other times by appointment. Admission: adults $3.30; children 6-18, $2.20, under 6, free. No admission charge to souvenir shop in front part of museum. The museum is the only one authorized by the Colt Firearms Company (now Colt Industries) to use its name. It contains an extensive and attractively displayed collection of guns manufactured by the Hartford, Conn., company since its founding by Samuel Colt in 1836, including some prototypes, special issues, and low serial number specimens. The background of each piece is also described in the exhibits. The museum also contains some reproductions of Civil War guns and Pennsylvania long rifles. This museum would be of special interest to historians and firearms collectors.

★★★ **Cyclorama** (16)(45 min.), adjacent to Visitor Center, 334-1124. Open daily 9-5, shows every half hour. Admission: age 16 & over, $1.00; Golden Age, Golden Eagle, Golden Access Passport holders, free. No admission charge to view hall of paintings, murals, and photographs dealing with the Battle, or for the 15-20 min. movie in the auditorium preceding the Cyclorama show. The Cyclorama, measuring 356 by 26 feet, is one of only two in the U.S., and was painted between 1881 and 1884 by Paul Philippoteaux, a French artist who came to Gettysburg to study the Battlefield and specifically Pickett's Charge. A sound and light show recreates the Charge.

★★★ **Eisenhower National Historic Site** (17)(1-1/2-2 hrs.). Open daily April thru October, Wed.-Sun. November thru March, except closed for 31 days beginning the Sun. after New Year's Day. Admission: adults, $2.25; children 6-12, 70¢; Golden Age, Golden Eagle Pass holders, $1.25; Golden Access Passport holders, free. Purchase tickets and begin tours at the National Park Visitor Center. Buses depart approximately every 15 min. during the summer, every half hour beginning the last week in October, and every hour on weekdays November thru March. No

private vehicles allowed at the site. This is the farm that Dwight and Mamie Eisenhower bought in 1950 and retired to after his Presidency ended in 1961. It was the only home they ever owned, as they moved an average of once a year during Ike's military days. The tour includes the entire main house (except for one of the upstairs bedrooms), the barn, garage (formerly a chicken coop), reception center (once a storage building), guest house, guardhouse, barbecue, and putting green. A National Park Service brochure and floor plan of the main house tell the history of the farm and the Eisenhowers' ownership and residency.

Battlefield Military Museum ([18])(30-45 min.), 900 Baltimore Pike, 334-6568. Open Easter to December 1—daily 9-9 in summer, otherwise 12-5. Admission: adults $2.00, children $1.50. Reputedly the largest collection of authentic military items in Gettysburg, with over 10,000 guns, swords, medals, uniforms, and other effects representing most of the wars the country has been involved in. However, the museum is kept "low key" because the owner is usually busy with an on-premises store and mail order business dealing in war relics.

★★ **Lee's Headquarters** ([19])(30-40 min.), US 30, 1 mi. west of Lincoln Sq. Open daily mid-March thru November, 9-9. Admission free. Located in a house built in the 1700s and owned during Lee's occupancy by Thaddeus Stevens, noted Abolitionist and Congressman from Pennsylvania. Contains collection of military equipment from Union and Confederate sides, including uniforms, rifles, bullets, saddles, buttons, powder flasks, and other items, as well as photographs and documents.

★★ **Downtown Walking Tour** (45-60 min.). Pick up descriptive folder and start tour at the Gettysburg Travel Council Information Center. The tour covers 14 blocks and 1.5 miles, and presents a good view of the historic and well preserved central portion of the town. A worthwhile addition (about 20-30 min.) to the tour is the attractive campus of **Gettysburg College** ([20]), two blocks north of the information center on the west side of Carlisle St. Gen. Eisenhower maintained an office on the campus after he retired to Gettysburg.

There is an easy way to tell if you're getting closer to Lincoln Square or moving away from it: the even house numbers are always on your right as you approach the square or any of the streets that pass through it.

Outside Gettysburg

Adams County Winery, 251 Peach Tree Rd., Orrtanna, 334-4631. Open Thu.-Mon. 12:30-6. Tours by appointment only. Directions: From Lincoln Sq., go west on US 30 for 8.1 mi., turn left on High St. (SR 3011) for 0.8 mi. to Cashtown. Turn left, then immediately right in Cashtown to stay on SR 3011, go another 0.9 mi. to a "T" intersection, turn right and immediately left for 0.4 mi., turn right on Peach Tree Rd. to winery.

Land of Little Horses (☒21☒)(1-2 hrs.), Knoxlyn Rd., 3 mi. west of Gettysburg, 334-7259. Open daily April 1 to November—Memorial Day thru Labor Day 10-6, other times 10-5. Admission: adults, $4.95; seniors, $3.85; children 3-12, $3.30. Directions: From Lincoln Sq., go west on US 30 3.0 mi. to Knoxlyn Rd. (SR 3013), turn left about 1 mi. to farm. A variety of miniature breeds performing, exercising, being trained, and fed. Shows in arena daily at 11, 1, and 3, with additional 5 PM show Memorial Day to Labor Day.

★★ **Scenic Valley Tour** (1-1/4-1-1/2 hrs. by car, at least half a day by bicycle). This 36-mile ride through the countryside to the west and north of Gettysburg incorporates a small portion of the Battlefield, several historic churches, one of the county's covered bridges (see page 87), South Mountain, part of the county's apple orchard region, and small villages. A brochure describing the 29 points of interest is available at the Gettysburg Travel Council office. The route is signed and could be followed without the brochure, but you wouldn't have the background information about the stops, and it's always possible that some of the direction signs are missing.

Community Resources

Gettysburg Travel Council Information Center: 35 Carlisle St., 334-6274. Information desk: Taneytown Rd., 334-9410
Gettysburg-Adams Co. Area Chamber of Commerce: 33 York St., 334-8151
PO: 115 Buford Ave., 337-3781
Public Library: 59 E. High St., 334-5716
Gettysburg Hospital: 147 Gettys St., 334-2121
Court House: 111 Baltimore St., 334-6781
Borough Offices: 34 E. Middle St., 334-1160
Borough Police: 334-1168 or 334-8101
State Police: Fairfield & Old Mill Rds., 334-8111
Bus: 45 N. Stratton St., 334-7064

McSherrystown, pop. 2,900.

★ **Conewago Chapel** (☒22☒), the oldest Jesuit chapel west of the Susquehanna, is located about 1 mile north of town in the village of Edgegrove. The present building, on the NRHP, was completed in 1787, replacing a mass house that had been built about 1740. Open daily, admission free, 637-2721. Directions: from center of town, turn north off PA 116 on 2nd St. (SR 2011) for 1.2 mi., then left on Edgegrove Rd. (SR 2008) for 0.2 mi. Chapel is on left. (Also listed under Hanover, York Co.)

Mt. Pleasant, unincorporated, pop. about 100.

★ **Hanover Shoe Farms** (23), north side of PA 194, about one mile west, 637-8931. Open daily 7 AM-5 PM. Admission free. Self-guided walk-through tours—get brochure at the office just inside the entrance. Noted for its famous trotters and pacers. (See also Hanover, York Co.)

New Oxford, pop. 2,000. Noted as an antiques center. Lincolnway (US 30) for several blocks east and west of the town square is especially pretty, with many Victorian homes.

York Springs, pop. 600.

York Springs Vineyard and Winery, 420 Latimore Rd., 528-8490. Open daily 10-6 for tours. Directions: north on PA 94 for 2 mi., turn right on Latimore Rd.

COVERED BRIDGES

Jack's Mountain, Jacks Mountain Rd. (SR 3021) (Toms Creek), 1-3/4 mi. west of Fairfield, Burr truss design, built 1890.
Sauck's (Sachs) Mill Just south of Pumping Station Rd. (SR 3005) (Marsh Creek), about 1 mi. west of Eisenhower National Historic Site, Town truss design, built about 1854.

RECREATION FACILITIES

Ski Liberty, PA 116, 1 mi. south of Fairfield, 642-8282. 24-hr. snow report, 642-8297, out of state, (800) 423-0227.
Gettysburg Railroad, Reading RR Station, Constitution Ave., 1 block west of N. Washington St., 334-6932. Steam-powered excursions to Biglerville (16 mi. round trip, takes 1 1/4 hrs.) and Mt. Holly Springs (50 mi, round trip, takes 5 hrs.). Trains to Biglerville run June thru October. Mt. Holly Springs trains make only six runs from July thru October. For schedule and fares, write P.O. Box 1267, Gettysburg, PA 17325.

CALENDAR OF EVENTS

Note: Unless otherwise indicated, the contact for all events is the Gettysburg Travel Council, 35 Carlisle St., Gettysburg, PA 17325, 334-6274.

1st weekend in May, Fairfield. **Gettysburg Spring Bluegrass Festival**, Granite Hill Campground, PA 116, 6 mi. west of Gettysburg. c/o Granite Hill Campground, 3340 Fairfield Rd., Gettysburg, PA 17325, 642-8749.

1st weekend in May, Arendtsville. **Apple Blossom Festival**, South Mountain Fairgrounds, PA 234. c/o Gettysburg Area Chamber of Commerce, 33 York St., Gettysburg, PA 17325, 334-8151.

3rd Sat. in May, Gettysburg. **Gettysburg Spring Outdoor Antiques Show**, Lincoln Sq. and adjacent streets.

4th weekend in May, Gettysburg. **Gettysburg Square Dance Round-Up**, Gettysburg College.

May 30, Gettysburg. **Memorial Day Observance**. Parade and memorial service at National Cemetery.

3rd Sat. in June, New Oxford. **New Oxford Outdoor Antiques Show**, Lincolnway, New Oxford.

Last weekend in June and 1st week in July, Gettysburg. **Civil War Heritage Days**. Encampment, outdoor church services, band concerts, lectures by Civil War historians, Battle re-enactment.

1st weekend in July, Gettysburg. **Civil War Collectors Show**, Sheraton Inn, 2634 Emmitsburg Rd.

1st weekend in July, Gettysburg. **Civil War Book Fair**, Gettysburg Jr. High School. c/o GBPA, Box 1863, Gettysburg, PA 17325.

End of August or beginning of September, Arendtsville. **South Mountain Fair**, South Mountain Fairgrounds, PA 234.

2nd Sat. in September, East Berlin. **Colonial Days**.

2nd weekend after Labor Day, Fairfield. **Gettysburg Fall Bluegrass Festival**. See Spring Bluegrass Festival for contact.

4th Sat. in September, Gettysburg. **Gettysburg Fall Outdoor Antiques Show**, Lincoln Sq. and adjacent streets.

1st two weekends in October, Arendtsville. **Apple Harvest Festival**, South Mountain Fairgrounds, PA 234.

Sat. closest to November 19, Gettysburg. **Remembrance Day**, National Cemetery.

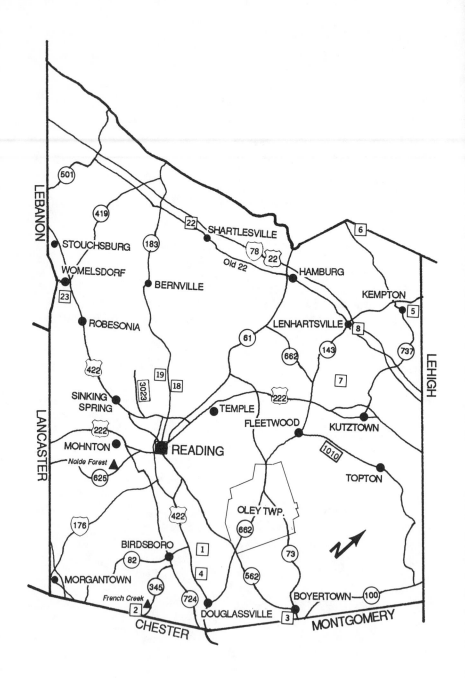

BERKS

Created: March 11, 1752, as the 7th county, from parts of Philadelphia, Lancaster, and Chester Counties
County Seat: Reading
Land Area: 862 square miles
Population (1989 est.): 328,000
Area code: 215, except for Bethel area (933 exchange), which is 717

Most of the northern half of Berks County lies within a gently rolling valley whose northern limit is Blue Mountain. The southern half of the county is generally hilly, particularly the portion south of US 422. The Schuylkill River, which drains virtually the entire county, flows south through a gap in Blue Mountain to Reading, where it turns in a more easterly direction to its mouth at the Delaware in Philadelphia. Despite a large amount of wooded and hilly terrain, nearly half the county's land area is devoted to farming. Berks County ranks fourth in the PDC in average farm sales per acre and third in total value of farm products sold and number of farms.

Reading (pronounced RED-ing) is the county's dominant community in employment and retail trade, and is the state's sixth largest city. No other Berks County town outside the greater Reading area has as many as 5,000 residents.

Among Berks County's largest industries are VF Corporation (Vanity Fair) and Carpenter Technology, both "Fortune 500" firms; AT&T Technologies, Glen Gery Brick Company, and General Battery, all located in Reading; and Caloric Company, a well-known appliance manufacturer, in Topton.

Berks County is known for its "Gay Dutch" population, a group not to be confused with the Old Order Amish concentrated primarily in Lancaster County. The Gay Dutch are neither Amish or Mennonites, but primarily Lutherans, Reformed, and other German-based religious groups. Their customs include decorating their barns with brightly colored "hex signs" (see Shartlesville).

Historical Highlights

Berks County, and Reading, its seat, were named for Berkshire County in England by William Penn's sons Richard and Thomas, who organized the county.

91

The county's earliest settlers, however, preceded the Penns and represented a variety of European origins, including Swedes, Welsh, Scottish, Irish, and French Huguenots as well as the more common English and Germans. The Swedes are believed to be the first white inhabitants of the county, near present-day Birdsboro and Monocacy. The earliest Amish settlement in America was at Northkill, near Shartlesville, about 1738. German immigration predominated in Berks County until the heavy industry of the late 19th century began to develop. At that time, eastern Europeans started to arrive in large numbers. Today Berks County has the highest percentage of Poles of any PDC county, although their number relative to the still-dominant Germans is not high.

The county's most famous early settler was German-born Conrad Weiser, who arrived here about 1729 from Schoharie County in eastern New York. His time spent as a young man among the Iroquois nations had educated him as to their language and customs. He was able to establish peace between Indians and white settlers, and thus served as an ambassador, both official and unofficial, to the Iroquois tribes inhabiting Pennsylvania.

Two even more famous Americans have their roots in Berks County. Daniel Boone, 19th century pioneer, was born in the county, and direct ancestors of Abraham Lincoln first settled here.

Berks County's history is very much tied to industrial and transportation development. The first iron ore furnace in Pennsylvania, established about 1720, was located at Colebrookdale, near Boyertown. A number of other furnaces were built later at various locations in the county, among them Hopewell Forge, Joanna Furnace, Charming Forge, and Robesonia. Revolutionary War munitions were made in these furnaces, as was the case at nearly all furnaces in operation at that time.

The county was near the center of Pennsylvania's network of canals, with the Schuylkill and Union Canals joining at Reading. The Philadelphia and Reading Railroad (shortened to just "the Reading" today) is the state's oldest chartered line still in operation, dating from 1833.

Textile, iron, and steel manufacturing began in the last quarter of the 19th century. The VF Corporation, for example, began as a manufacturer of braiding and knitting machines, the first such enterprise in the country. The Reading Iron Works started operations in 1878, and Carpenter Steel, now Carpenter Technologies, in 1889.

Berks was a pioneer in the auto industry before it became centered in Detroit. Some fifteen different makes were made in Reading, and there were also factories in Boyertown and Fleetwood. The factories are gone now, but local names like Duryea and Fleetwood are familiar even to casual observers of the auto world.

PLACES OF INTEREST

Bernville, pop. 800.

Calvaresi Winery, Bernville-Shartlesville Rd., 488-7966. Open Thu.-Fri. 1-6, Sat.-Sun. 12-5. Free tours and tastings. Directions: Turn right (north) off PA 183 on Bernville-Shartlesville Rd. (SR 4011) just north of Bernville. Winery is 1/4 mi. on right.

Birdsboro, pop. 3,600. A small manufacturing town along the Schuylkill about 8 miles southeast of Reading.

★★★ **Daniel Boone Homestead** ([1])(1 hour), 2 mi. north on Daniel Boone Rd., 582-4900. Open Tue.-Sat. 9-5, Sun. 12-5, closed Mon. and holidays except Memorial Day, Independence Day, and Labor Day. Admission to guided tour of house: adults, $1.50; seniors, $1.00; children age 6-17, 50¢; under 6, free. No charge to visit other buildings on the property. The fabled pioneer was born here in 1734 in a log house that was replaced by a two-story stone house built on the same site. However, an addition to the original log house, built about 1750, may have been built by the Boones prior to their leaving Pennsylvania that year for North Carolina. Other buildings include a Pennsylvania bank barn, smokehouse, blacksmith shop (not the one that Daniel's father, who was a blacksmith, would have used), an 1810 sawmill relocated to the property, the Bertolet log house (1737) from the Oley Valley, and visitor center. Property is administered by the State Historical and Museum Commission and is on the NRHP. Directions: From center of town, go north on PA 82 for 1 mi. to US 422 eastbound. Turn right, go 0.4 mi. to Daniel Boone Rd. (SR 2041), turn left for 3/4 mile to entrance on left.

★★★★ **Hopewell Furnace National Historic Site** ([2])(1 hour), 5 mi. south on PA 345, 582-8773. Open daily 9-5 except Christmas and New Year's Day. Admission: $1.00. An attractive and interesting re-creation of this charcoal-fueled iron furnace and surrounding "village" that operated from 1771 to 1883. A brochure describes the iron-making process and the self-guided walking tour of the grounds. The 10-minute instructive slide show should be seen before starting the tour. Recorded narrations can be heard at several stops on the tour. During the summer costumed guides demonstrate some of the jobs performed at the village. The furnace made numerous products, but its most profitable were coal- and wood-burning stoves. Directions: From center of town, go east on E. Main St. (PA 724) for 0.6 mi. to PA 345, turn right for 5.0 mi. Entrance is on right at intersection of SR 4020.

Boyertown, pop. 4,300. The community has long been associated with vehicle manufacturing, and remains so today as the home of Boyertown Auto Body Works, a truck body maker, and the home of a manufacturer of motorized trolleys now being used in a number of cities.

★★★ **Boyertown Museum of Historic Vehicles** (③)(45-60 min.), 28 Warwick St., 367-2090. Open Tue.-Fri. 8-4, Sat.-Sun. 10-2, and most holidays. Admission: $2.00; under age 7, free. An interesting and unusual museum of different types of transportation, many manufactured in Berks County. Vehicles include bicycles, sleds, farm wagons, motorcycles, and steam, electric, and gasoline powered cars and trucks. Plaques identify the vehicles and their history. Photos, advertising posters, and other memorabilia line the walls. The only shortcoming of the museum is that it has outgrown its space, so the vehicles have to be crowded together in rows instead of being arranged in a more attractive manner. Directions: In the center of town, just off S. Reading Ave. (PA 562), one block south of Philadelphia Ave. (PA 73).

Douglassville, unincorporated, pop. about 1,300. Settled in 1693.

★ **Merritt's Museum of Childhood** and **Mary Merritt Doll Museum** (④) (20-30 min. each), US 422, 2.9 mi. west of PA 662 at Limekiln Rd. (SR 2025), 385-3408. Open Mon.-Sat. 10-5, Sun. and hol. 1-5. Closed New Year's Day, Easter, Independence Day, Labor Day, Thanksgiving, and Christmas. Admission to both: adults, $2.00; children 5-12, $1.00. Two museums devoted to dolls and antiques, most of the latter related to children. The Museum of Childhood contains a wide variety of American and European toys, baby carriages, pottery, mechanical banks, trains, ships, costumed wax figures, and Indian relics, as well as two rooms furnished circa 1785-1820. The Doll Museum houses 1,500 dolls from 1725 to 1900 and over forty miniature furnished and "inhabited" period rooms. Most pieces are identified as to date and origin. The museums are rather cluttered, but anyone especially interested in the subject would overlook that and could easily spend much more than half an hour in each.

Fleetwood, pop. 3,400. A manufacturing and food processing center. The town was famous in the 1910s and 20s as the home of the Fleetwood Metal Body Company. The firm built bodies for many different top-of-the-line automakers such as Packard, Lincoln, Duesenberg, and Rolls-Royce. General Motors bought the plant in 1928 and produced bodies for Cadillacs and LaSalles. The Fleetwood name was retained for many years by Cadillac limousines. The plant, a brick building alongside the Reading Railroad, is at 29 W. Locust St., one block south of Main St. (SR 1010) and one-half block east of S. Richmond St. (PA 662); the name of the company is still faintly visible on the north wall near the roofline.

Kempton, unincorporated, pop. about 400.

★★ **Pennsylvania Dutch Farm Museum** (5)(45-60 min.), 683-7130 (Kutztown). Open May thru October—Sat.-Sun. 11-6, other times by appointment. Admission: age 12 and up, $2.00. A collection of the usual implements found on farms and in farm homes—butchering, butter-making, and hand tools, hand-operated washing machines, kitchen utensils, tractors, and the like. Demonstrations of some equipment and domestic trades are given by Howard Geisinger, creator and owner of the museum and a noted authority on Pennsylvania Dutch folklore. He realized a long-time dream in 1964 when he purchased the barn and built the museum. The contents are part of his personal collection and his guided tours reflect a lifetime of interest in this field. Directions: Just north of the center of town. Turn off PA 737 onto SR 1019 for 0.1 mi. at the point where 737 makes a 90-degree turn (southbound turn left, northbound continue straight), then left across small bridge onto SR 1017.

Hawk Mountain Sanctuary (6)(1/2 hour, longer if you hike to the lookouts), 8 mi. west atop Blue Mountain, 756-6961. Open daily except Thanksgiving, Christmas, and New Year's Day, 8-5. Admission: adults, $2.50; children 6-12, $1.00. One of the first private wildlife refuges in the country, established in 1934. A refuge for birds of prey—hawks, eagles, falcons, and ospreys—that migrated over the mountain. Orientation displays in the visitor center, special nature programs at various times throughout the year. Trails to the North and South Lookouts may be walked—wear suitable shoes. The best season to visit is the fall, when birds migrate. Directions: From PA 143, 1/2 mile south of Kempton turnoff, go west on Hawk Mountain Rd. for 7 mi., through Albany and Eckville, to the top of Blue Mountain. Entrance on right.

W.K.&S. Railroad (See Recreation Facilities).

Kutztown, pop. 3,900. Home of Kutztown University, one of the fourteen State-run colleges formerly oriented to teacher training, now offering a liberal arts program. The famous Kutztown Folk Festival is held here annually around Independence Day.

★★ **Crystal Cave** (7)(45-60 min.), Crystal Cave Rd. (SR 1012), 4 mi. northwest, 683-6765. Open March 1 thru Thanksgiving weekend. March 1 until Memorial Day weekend—daily 9-5, except 6PM closing on weekends in May. Memorial Day weekend thru Labor Day—Mon.-Fri. 9-6, Sat., Sun., hol. 9-7. After Labor Day thru October 31—Mon.-Fri. 9-5, Sat., Sun., hol. 9-6. November—Fri.-Sun. only 9-5. Admission: adults, $5.00; children 4-12, $2.50; under 4, free. The cave was discovered in 1871 and is the oldest operating cavern in the state. Cave formations are highlighted by indirect lighting. A 10-min. slide show precedes the guided tour. On the grounds are a playground and picnic area. Directions: From US 222 westbound, take Virginville exit, turn right on Crystal Cave Rd. (SR 1006) for 1.4 mi., turn right on SR 1012 (still Crystal Cave Rd.) for 1.7 mi. to entrance on left. From center of Kutztown, follow W. Main St. (old US 222, now SR 1014, for 2 mi. to Crystal Cave Rd. (SR 1006), turn right, cross US 222, and proceed as above.

Lenhartsville, pop. 200.

★★**Folklife Museum** ([8])(30-45 min.), center of town on PA 143 between Old US 22 and I-78/US 22, 562-4803. Open April thru October—weekends only April, May, September, and October; daily June thru August. Weekday and Sat. hours 10-5, Sun. 1-5. Admission: adults, $3.00; chilren $1.50. Guided tour (about 30 min.) of the several buildings comprising the museum: log house, fashions barn, one-room school, farm equipment building, and folk culture center. Museum is operated by the Pennsylvania Dutch Folk Culture Society, whose headquarters and research library are on the premises. While it does not contain any unique artifacts or relics, it represents a worthy effort by the Society to preserve various aspects of Pennsylvania German farm life.

Morgantown, unincorporated, pop. about 500. Located at the interchange of the Pennsylvania Turnpike and I-176 in the southernmost part of Berks County. Originally a highway junction, it is now famous as an outlet shopping center. The **Manufacturers Outlet Mall** is on PA 10 immediately south of the Turnpike interchange (access also from PA 23 via Walnut St.), 286-2000. Open Mon.-Sat. 10-9, Sun. 12-5. The mall is built in the same manner as any other large enclosed shopping center; the difference here is that all of the 60-plus stores are outlets. There is also a food court and, perhaps unique to this mall, a 200-room hotel attached directly to the building.

Oley Township, pop. 3,300. The entire township was designated a **Historic District** in 1983 as a rural preservation area, so it differs from the usual NRHP sites in that, in effect, a way of life rather than a structure is being protected. The township includes the small unincorporated villages of Oley and Pleasantville and two of Berks County's five covered bridges. PA 73 and 662 are the main highways through the district.

Reading, pop. 78,000, with suburbs 175,000. The greater Reading area includes the surrounding incorporated communities of Kenhorst, Laureldale, Mohnton, Mount Penn, St. Lawrence, Shillington, Sinking Spring, Temple, West Lawn, West Reading, Wyomissing, and Wyomissing Hills. These twelve boroughs have a combined population of about 40,000.

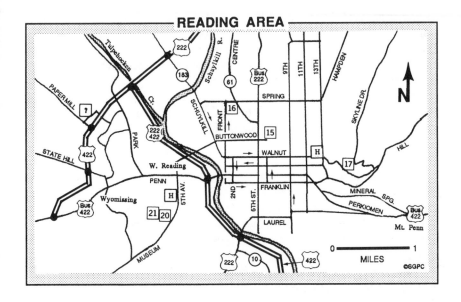

Reading was founded in 1748 by William Penn's sons Thomas and Richard. The city has been a manufacturing center for most of its history, but its greatest industrial development occurred after the Civil War. Charles Duryea, the inventor of the first successful hill-climbing gasoline powered automobile, built and tested his cars in Reading beginning in 1900. He was one of several auto manufacturers in the city in the early 20th century, including Acme Motor Company, Dile and Daniels Motor Car Companies, and Schwartz Motor Truck Corporation. The Acme bicycle plant employed 1,200 and produced 60,000 bicycles before production was shifted to chain-drive automobiles.

Despite the high proportion of people of conservative German background, labor unions became quite strong in the early 1900s, which led to the strength of the Socialist party in the city. One local Socialist labor leader, James H. Maurer, served three terms in the Pennsylvania General Assembly, and was a candidate for Governor in 1906, for Vice President of the United States in 1928 and 1932, and for U.S. Senate in 1934.

A number of well-known consumer products are made in Reading: Luden's cough drops, Bachman's pretzels and snack foods, Godiva chocolates, Exide automotive batteries, Vanity Fair hosiery and lingerie, and Glidden paints. The city's largest industrial employers are VF Corporation, Carpenter Technologies, General Battery, and AT&T Technologies research labs.

The concept of outlet shopping developed in Reading, when textile manufacturers began to sell overruns and seconds to employees. The VF Factory Outlet in the suburb of Wyomissing was among the first to open to the public. It now encompasses over 400,000 square feet of space in what had been the world's largest hosiery mill.

The city experienced a significant decline in its manufacturing base when some of the heavy industry closed, but in recent years has rebounded with growth in the high tech area.

Reading has four colleges: Albright College, a coeducational liberal arts college founded in 1856, located at 13th and Exeter Sts.; Alvernia College, a small Catholic institution on St. Bernadine St.; a branch of Penn State University on Tulpehocken Rd. just northwest of the city; and Reading Area Community College at 10 S. 2nd St.

★★ **Downtown** (about 1 hour). The city's traditional main shopping district is centered around **Penn Square** (9), the intersection of 5th and Penn Streets. The Square actually extends from 4th to 6th Streets along Penn. The major public buildings, with the exception of the library, are all within a few blocks north and east of the Square.

There are three **Historic Districts** in the city, two of them in or near downtown. **Callowhill** extends along N. and S. 5th St. (originally called Callowhill St.) from Buttonwood to Laurel, a distance of nine blocks, and includes both blocks of Penn Square. **Prince** encompasses about six blocks of S. 6th St. from Cherry to Canal, and parts of 5th, 7th, and the east-west cross streets. A **walking tour** brochure covering about a 10-block walk in parts of both Districts is available from the Berks Co. Pennsylvania Dutch Travel Association. The highlights of the area, not all of which are listed in the brochure, are:

Widow Finney's Restaurant, John Hiester House, and West Reading Market House (10), all located on the south side of Cherry St. from 4th to Carpenter, the north-south alley mid-block between 3rd and 4th Sts. All three properties are on the NRHP. The restaurant occupies a log building estimated to have been built in the late 1750s, making it one of the oldest in the city. The Hiester House is of 1810-vintage Federal style and is named for one of its prominent early owners. The market house, no longer in use, was built in 1895.

Numerous Victorian era homes in a variety of architectural styles (Federal, Italianate, Reading German, and Queen Anne) dating from the second half of the

19th century line the 100- to 300-blocks of S. 5th and S. 6th Sts. in the Prince Historic District. The **South Reading Market House** (no longer used as such), at the SW corner of 6th and Bingaman, was the social and business center of the neighborhood. The **South 7th St. Railroad Shops,** on the west side of the street between Chestnut and Spruce, were built starting in 1845 and eventually completed in 1884. The first anthracite burning locomotive was designed and built here in 1847.

Berks County Court House (⟦co⟧), 33 N. 6th St. (NE corner of Court), built in 1931 in the then popular Art Deco style.

Trinity Lutheran Church (⟦11⟧), NW corner of 6th and Washington Sts. Built in 1792 of Georgian style, on the NRHP.

Rajah Theater (⬚12), 136 N. 6th St., 375-0185. A well-known 2,000-seat theater used for concerts, plays, the Shrine Circus, and other community events. It was built as a market house in 1874 and was occupied by the Academy of Music until purchased in 1917 by the Rajah Temple Masonic Lodge, which converted it to a theater.

Christ Episcopal Church (⬚13), NW corner of 5th and Court Sts. A Gothic-Revival building with a 200-foot tower.

431-33 Penn St. (⬚14). One of the few Beaux-Arts façades in the city. The building behind it has no historical or architectural significance, but it happened to be within a few inches of the same width of the Reading News Building at 22 N. 5th St., where the façade was originally built in 1912. Considered worth preserving because of its intricate detail work, it was moved here in 1982 during a reconstruction project.

Outside Downtown

Skew Bridge (⬚15), 400-block of N. 6th St., at Reading RR. Considered the best example of this type of bridge design in the U.S., built in 1857. Each stone in each arch is properly curved, so no keystone is needed.

The city's third Historic District, **Centre Park,** is located generally from Greenwich to Robeson Sts. between and including N. 5th St. and Centre Ave. This is primarily a residential zone, with most homes dating from 1895 to 1915. The dominant architectural styles are Queen Anne and Reading German; the latter is typically a 2-1/2 story structure with gabled or mansard roofs and a flush dormer. The focal point of the District is Centre Park, at the southeast corner of Centre and Douglass St. The largest mansions are located on Centre Ave., but there are also some large townhouses in the 600- and 700-blocks of N. 5th St. (between Greenwich and Douglass).

Berks County Historical Society (⬚16)(1 hour), 940 Centre Ave. (SW corner of Spring St.), 375-4375. Open Tue.-Sat. 9-4. Admission: adults $2.50, seniors $2.00, children age 5-12 $1.00, under 5 free. Contains products manufactured and household items used in Berks County. Museum reopened early in 1989, after extensive renovations.

★**Pagoda** (⬚17), Skyline Dr. On NRHP, the only Japanese Pagoda east of California. Open summer 11-9, other seasons 12-9. Admission: 25¢. Standing at an elevation of 900 feet, it affords a commanding view of the city and many miles beyond. The 7-story Pagoda was built in 1908 as a resort at a cost of $50,000. However, the difficulty of access made it a commercial failure and it was donated to the City. It has been restored and now serves as a snack bar, gift shop, and exhibit of native birds and animals. Directions: From the intersection of 13th and Walnut Sts., follow Duryea Dr. uphill through City Park to Skyline Dr., turn left, continuing uphill.

★★ **Skyline Drive**, a 2-1/2-mile-long scenic drive atop Mt. Penn (elevation 1,100) extending from the Pagoda northeast to McKnight Gap.

★★ **Mid-Atlantic Air Museum** ([18])(30 min.), MacArthur Rd., 372-7333. Open daily except major holidays 9:30-4. Admission free. A collection of vintage civilian and military aircraft, housed in a hangar on the north side of Reading Municipal Airport. The museum relocated to Reading from Harrisburg International Airport early in 1988, and plans to occupy a new building at the extreme north end of the airport in the summer of 1989. Consequently, only a few of the museum's 32 aircraft are on display at any one time. All are kept in flying condition by museum member volunteers. There is also an exhibit of military and commercial aviation effects inside the hangar. An interesting and different museum. Directions: From Warren St. Bypass (US 222), go north on Bernville Rd. (PA 183) for 2.0 mi. to MacArthur Rd., turn right for 0.1 mi., then right on dead end street to museum.

★★★ **Berks County Heritage Center** ([19])(1 hour), Red Bridge Rd. along Tulpehocken Creek, 374-8839. Open May thru October—Tue.-Sat. 10-4, Sun. 12-5. Admission: adults, $2.50; seniors age 60 and over, $2.00; children age 7-18, $1.50; under 7, free. There are two excellent museums here. The **C. Howard Hiester Canal Center** (30 min.) is the result of one man's goal of commemorating Berks County's place in the development of canals. Mr. Hiester was a prominent authority on canals in the county, and wanted to preserve as many artifacts related to them as possible. Many were already in his possession. The result is a very attractively presented display of a canal boat, pilot house, locktender's house, tools, and other memorabilia from the short-lived canal era in Pennsylvania. The **Gruber Wagon Works** (30 min.) is a reconstructed wagon-manufacturing and repair facility that operated from 1882 to 1972 near Obold, about 5 miles northwest of the present site. In 1976 the building was disassembled and moved to the Heritage Center to make way for construction of Blue Marsh Lake, a flood control and recreation area upstream on Tulpehocken Creek. The building was intact at the time of relocation, permitting reassembly exactly as it had been left when production ceased. The tools and techniques used by the wagon makers are demonstrated on the guided tour of the factory, and are an education in themselves. The building is now on the NRHP. Directions: Turn south off Bernville Rd. (PA 183) 2.4 mi. NW of

Warren St. Bypass (US 222) or 0.3 mi. SE of SR 3055, the expressway known locally as the "Road to Nowhere".

Union Canal Towpath Tour (1 hour), a 4.2-mile walking or bicycling tour along the canal towpath, following Tulpehocken Creek from near its mouth to Reber's Bridge Rd. There are 12 stops on the tour, including Stonecliffe Recreation Area, six locks, Wertz's (Red) Covered Bridge, one of five in the county and the longest single-span covered bridge in the state (the bridge can also be seen at the Heritage Center), and the sites of a grist mill and mule bridge. The towpath is on Berks County parkland, and no motor vehicles are allowed. The Heritage Center (see above) can be visited as part of this tour; allow an extra hour if you include it.

Blue Mountain & Reading Railroad (See Recreation Facilities).

★★★ **Reading Public Museum and Art Gallery** ([20])(1 hour), 500 Museum Rd., 371-5850. Open Mon.-Fri. 9-4, Sat. 1-4, Sun. 1-5. Admission: adults, $1.50; students, $1.00. A good museum in an attractive building. Permanent exhibits include ancient civilizations (Chinese, Egyptian, Greek, Babylonian, American Indian, and South American), birds of Eastern Pennsylvania, art by Chinese, and by French Impressionists. Also a portrait gallery. One gallery is used for changing exhibits. Owned by Reading School District.

Reading Planetarium ([21])(45 min.), 1211 Parkside Dr. S., 371-5854. Open for shows during school year—Thu. 7:30 PM, Sun. 2 and 3 PM; June and July—Mon.-Fri. 1 PM, closed Independence Day. Owned by Reading School District. Directions: Turn west off Museum Rd. at Reading Public Museum; planetarium is adjacent to the museum.

Outlets

There are three outlet complexes in the Reading area, and one each in Morgantown and Robesonia. The three Reading areas are: N. 9th St., Hiesters Lane, and VF in Wyomissing. If you're driving to Reading, you'll see color-coded signs on all major roads approaching the city directing you to each complex and parking areas.

N. 9th St. Area:

Reading Outlet Center, 800-block of N. 9th, between Douglass and Windsor, 373-5495. Open Mon.-Wed. 9-6, Thu.-Sat. 9-8, Sun. 11-5. 60 stores.
9th St. Outlet Mart, 916 N. 9th, between Windsor and Spring (Down East, 372-1144. Open Mon.-Sat. 9:30-5:30, Sun. 12-5).

Big Mill Factory Outlet, NW corner of 8th & Oley, 378-9100. Open Mon.-Sat. 9:30-5:30, Sun. 11-4. 20 stores

Hiesters Lane Area:

Hiesters Lane, Hiesters Lane and Kutztown Rd. (Burlington Coat Factory, 929-4777. Open Mon.-Sat. 9:30-0, Sun. 10-5); and 13th and Rosemont Ave. (David Crystal, 921-0201. Open Mon.-Fri. 9-9, Sat. 9-6, Sun. 12-5).

Hiesters Lane Outlet Center, 800 Hiesters Lane, 921-9394. Open Mon.-Sat. 9:30-5:30, Fri. to 9 PM, Sun. 12-5. 4 stores.

Four Square Outlet Center, 755 Hiesters Lane, 921-9394. Open Mon.-Sat. 9:30-5:30, Sun. 12-5. 4 stores.

Wyomissing:

VF Factory Outlet Complex, Hill Ave. and Park Rd., 378-0408. Open Mon.-Fri. 9-9, Sat. 9-6, Sun. 12-5, extended hours in fall. There are 9 separate buildings, each color-coded, as are the parking lots. A shuttle bus serves the parking lots.

Community Resources
Berks Co. Pennsylvania Dutch Travel Association, Sheraton Berkshire Inn, US 422 & Paper Mill Rd., 375-4085
Berks Co. Chamber of Commerce, 645 Penn St., 376-6766
PO: 2100 N. 13th St., 921-7000
    59 N. 5th St., 378-5065
Public Library: 5th & Franklin Sts., 374-4540
Community General Hospital: 145 N. 6th St., 376-4881
Reading Hospital: 6th Ave. & Spruce St. (W. Reading), 378-6000
St. Joseph Hospital: 12th & Walnut Sts., 378-2000
Court House: 33 N. 6th St., 378-8000
City Police: emergency 320-6111, all other business 320-6116
City Hall: 8th & Washington Sts., 320-6234
State Police: Kenhorst & Pershing Blvds., 378-4011; (800) 332-6036
Bus: 3rd & Court Sts., 374-3182

Robesonia, pop. 1,900.

Robesonia Outlet Center, US 422 at east end of town, 693-3144. Open Mon.-Fri. 9:30-8:30, Sat. 9-6, Sun. 11-5. 15 stores.

Shartlesville, unincorporated, pop. about 400. Small farming community along old US 22.

★ **Roadside America** (22)(about 1/2 hr.), 1/2 mi. west on old US 22, 488-6241. Open July thru Labor Day—Mon.-Fri. 9-6:30, Sat.-Sun. 9-7; Labor Day thru June—Mon.-Fri. 10-5, Sat.-Sun. 10-6. Admission: adults, $3.25; children 6-11, $1.00; under 6, free. A series of miniature villages and rural scenes (scale 3/8 inch to the foot) supplemented with operating model trains. The culmination of the hobby of founder Laurence Gieringer. The kids would enjoy it.

Hex Sign Area. Some barns in this region are adorned with "hex signs", a form of Pennsylvania German folk art. The signs are more correctly called barn signs, although they originated with baptismal certificates, chests, chairs, and pottery. Their common design feature is a round shape with a hexagonal star, a turning sunwheel in the center, and bright colors. A few barns along old US 22 between Shartlesville and Strausstown have hex signs, but the number of signs appears to be diminishing.

Stouchsburg, unincorporated, pop. about 300. The entire village is a NRHP **Historic District,** set up to preserve this Union Canal era community. All 100-or-so houses were built in the 1830s-80s, when the Canal was at its peak. The village has been able to retain its appearance in part because US 422 was built to bypass it, so there are no highway-oriented businesses intruding.

Womelsdorf, pop. 1,900. **Historic District** includes the center of this attractive farming community, although no individual buildings are listed on the NRHP. Settlement dates from the 1720s, and Stouch's Tavern, built around 1780, is still operating.

★★ **Conrad Weiser Park** (23)(30-40 min.), just east of town on the south side of US 422, 589-2934. Open Wed.-Sat. 9-5, Sun. 12-5, open Memorial Day, Labor Day, and Independence Day if it falls on a Monday or Tuesday. Admission: adults $1.50; seniors, $1.00; children 6-17, 50¢. No charge to use the park grounds. On the NRHP, the home if the famous treaty maker with the Indians who helped maintain peace on the frontier from about 1737 until the French and Indian War began in 1756. The house was built in 1729 and had only one large room. An addition was built in 1751. A larger stone house was built in 1824 and is now occupied by the caretaker. Little of the original is left, other than the outer shell of the building, following a tornado in 1904 and a fire in 1907; the period furnishings are from elsewhere in the area. This detracts from the historical value of the property, but not from the history of Weiser himself. The property is scheduled to be "re-restored" in 1989.

COVERED BRIDGES

All five of Berks County's remaining covered bridges are in good or excellent condition, and are of the Burr truss type, the method of construction most frequently used in Pennsylvania.

Dreibelbis Station, PA 143 (Maiden Creek), 1-1/2 mi. S of Lenhartsville, built 1869.

Griesemer's Mill, Church Rd. (Manatawny Creek), 0.4 mi. E of Covered Bridge Rd. (SR 1030), 1.7 mi. S of PA 73 at Pleasantville, built c. 1832.

Kutz's, Kutz Mill Rd. (Sacony Creek), 0.6 mi. W of PA 737, 3 mi. N of Kutztown, built 1854. Portal design is the only one of its type in Pa.

Pleasantville, Covered Bridge Rd. (SR 1030) (Little Manatawny Creek), 1/2 mi. S of PA 73 at Pleasantville, built 1850.

Wertz's (Red), (Tulpehocken Creek) Berks Co. Heritage Center, Red Bridge Rd., W of PA 183, 4 mi. NW of Reading, built 1867. Pedestrian and bicycle traffic only—in county park.

RECREATION FACILITIES

French Creek State Park, PA 345, 4 mi. S of Birdsboro, 582-1514 (also listed in Chester Co.).

Nolde Forest State Park (Environmental Education Center), New Holland Rd. (PA 625), 2 mi. S of PA 724, 775-1411.

Blue Marsh Lake Recreation Area, County Welfare Rd., west of PA 183, 7 mi. NW of downtown Reading, 693-6000.

Blue Mountain & Reading Railroad, P.O. Box 425, Hamburg, PA 19526, 562-4083. Stations at Temple (Tuckerton Rd. between US 222 and PA 61) and S. Hamburg (Station Rd., just west of PA 61 at S. 4th St.). 26-mile, 1-1/2 hour steam-powered roundtrip between the two stations. Operates weekends from last Saturday in March to Sunday before Christmas, daily from 3rd Sunday in June until Labor Day, also several other special excursions.

Doe Mountain Ski Area, SR 1010, about 1 mi. SE of Maple Grove and 4 mi. NW of the intersection of PA 29 & 100 in Hereford, 682-7109; mailing address: Macungie, PA 18062.

W.K.&S. (Wanamaker, Kempton & Southern) Railroad, Box 24, Kempton, PA 19529, 756-6469. 6-mile, 40-minute steam-powered train rides and 9-mile, 35-minute trolley rides from Kempton station, 1/4 mi. north of PA 737 on SR 1019. Steam train operates Sun. only in May, September, and October, Sat. and Sun. June thru August, and Memorial Day, Independence Day, and Labor Day. Trolley operates Sun. in April, Sat. only in May, September, and October, and the first two

Sun. in November. Station located 1/4 mi. N of PA 737 in Kempton via SR 1019 to SR 1017.

Maple Grove Raceway (Auto Racing), Bowmansville Rd. (SR 3026), 3.5 mi. west of PA 10 at Plowville, 856-7812.

Reading Phillies (Baseball, Class AA Eastern League), Municipal Stadium, Centre Ave. & Berks St., 375-8469.

CALENDAR OF EVENTS

Late April, Boyertown. **Quilt Show.** c/o Boyertown Area Historical Society, 43 S. Chestnut St., Boyertown, PA 19512, 367-9843.

Early June, Reading. **Fiddle Festival**, Berks Co. Heritage Center. c/o Berks Co. Parks & Recreation Dept., RD 5, Box 272, Sinking Spring, PA 19608, 372-8939 or 374-8839.

Mid-June, Sinking Spring. **Pennsylvania German Day**, Gring's Mill Recreation Area. c/o Berks Co. Parks & Recreation Dept., RD 5, Box 272, Sinking Spring, PA 19608, 372-8939.

Late July-Early July, Kutztown. **Kutztown Folk Festival.** c/o Kutztown Folk Festival, 461 Vine La., Kutztown, PA 19530, 683-8707.

Late July, Sinking Spring. **Fine Arts Festival**, Gring's Mill Recreation Area. c/o Berks Co. Parks & Recreation Dept., RD 5, Box 272, Sinking Spring, PA 19608, 372-8939.

Late July, Reading. **Scenic River Days**, Riverfront Park. c/o Robert Kerper, P.O. Box 1442, Reading, PA 19603, 375-6508.

Early August, Kutztown. **Kutztown Fair**, Kutztown Fairgrounds. c/o Marvin I. Beltzner, P.O. Box 177, Kutztown, PA 19530, 683-3324.

Mid-August, Reading. **Air Show**, Reading Airport. c/o Kent G. George, RD 9, Box 9416, Reading, PA 19605, 372-4666.

Early September, Boyertown. **Duryea Day**, Community Park. c/o Boyertown Museum of Historic Vehicles, 28 Warwick St., Boyertown, PA 19512, 367-2090.

Early September, Lenhartsville. **Harvest Home Jubilee,** Pennsylvania Dutch Folklife Museum. 682-7432 (Topton).

Early September, Shartlesville. **Mountain Springs Bluegrass Festival.** c/o Mountain Springs Camping Resort. Shartlesville, PA 19554, 488-6859.

Mid-September, Mohnton. **Keystone Nationals**, Maple Grove Park. c/o Maple Grove Raceway, RD 3, Box 3420, Mohnton, PA 19540, 856-7612.

Mid-September, Lyons. **Fall Fiddle Festival**, Community Park. 682-6103.

Mid-September, Reading. **Reading Fair**, Fairgrounds Square Mall, 5th St. Hwy. (US 222 north). 921-9223 or 370-3473.

Mid-September, Oley. **Oley Valley Community Fair**, Oley. 929-0488 or 375-4085 (Reading).

Late September, Wernersville. **Fall Festival,** Old Dry Run Farm. 693-6000.
Early October, Reading. **Heritage Celebration,** Gruber Wagon Works, Berks Co. Heritage Center. c/o Berks Co. Parks & Recreation Dept., RD 5, Box 272, Sinking Spring, PA 19608, 372-8939 or 374-8839.
Early November, Reading. **Juried Holiday Craft Show,** Penn State University, Berks Co. Campus. 779-4488.

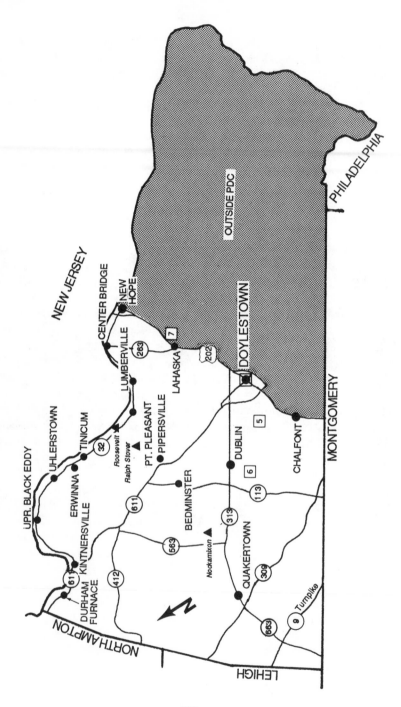

BUCKS

Created: November, 1682, as one of the three original counties
County Seat: Doylestown
Land Area: 635 square miles, of which approximately 350 in PDC
Population (1989 est.): 545,000, of which approximately 130,000 in PDC
Area code: 215

Bucks County is geographically oriented from northwest to southeast, and most of its roads run in the same pattern, with what are considered east-west roads actually running in a northeast-to-southwest direction. The major roads that deviate from this pattern are, probably not coincidentally, the county's first turnpikes, established well before the present highway network was laid out. Bucks County's highway pattern is continued in adjacent Montgomery County to the southwest.

Bucks is a county in transition, from primarily rural a generation ago to predominantly suburban today. The southern portion (outside the PDC) borders Philadelphia, and is very heavily developed. The central portion—the area near the US 202 corridor—has been feeling the push of suburbanization for about twenty years, and now the northern part is also seeing construction of housing tracts, shopping centers, and industrial parks. Some of the suburban growth in the north comes from the Allentown-Bethlehem area and from New Jersey, not all from Philadelphia. According to the latest population trends of individual townships, it is clear that growth in the PDC portion is faster than for the county as a whole, and Bucks County has been the fastest growing county in the state numerically (but not proportionately) since the 1980 Census.

Despite rapid growth, much of the area of the county within the PDC is still rural. The Pennsylvania Dutch influence, while not as strong in Bucks as in most other counties in the region, is still evident, especially in the northern sections. Actually, Bucks County's population mix reflects several different influences: the waves of European immigration that initially populated America, the middle-class move from city to suburbs, and a smaller influx of wealthy Philadelphians and New Yorkers who maintained summer and weekend homes in the county's lush country-side. These influences have given Bucks County a cosmopolitan aspect that is not present in most of the rest of the PDC. The county's economy is prosperous, even though there is a net export of labor, primarily to jobs closer to Philadelphia.

BUCKS CO.

One of Bucks County's greatest assets is its nearly sixty miles of Delaware River frontage. This waterway was the catalyst in the county's growth for almost the first 200 years of its history. Today the river is both a work and a play area; the portion south of Morrisville (opposite Trenton, New Jersey) is heavily industrialized, but from there north the river's primary use is recreational, with a 60-mile long state park along its west bank and quaint little towns loaded with antique shops and bed and breakfast inns hugging the narrow band of flat land in the river valley.

Historical Highlights

Bucks County's earliest white settlers were English who followed William Penn to America. The English gave the names to most of the townships in the county and to many of the incorporated boroughs as well, although the Indians had already named the creeks and rivers, and their choices stuck. Most of the county was included in Penn's initial land purchase from the Indians. A later, more famous, acquisition, which caused ill will among the peaceful Delaware Indians because of the manner in which it was made, was the "Walking Purchase" of 1737. This gave the Penns much of present-day Lehigh and Northampton Counties, although the area north of Blue Mountain was ceded back to the Indians after they protested their mistreatment.

The influx of Germans during the waves of immigration from that country was strongest in the northern portion of the county, and many descendants of those early settlers remain. German is still the dominant single nationality, but accounts for less than 13 percent of the total county population (the ratio is undoubtedly somewhat higher in the PDC portion, however). The other major nationalities represented are Irish, English, and Italian.

Early Bucks County farmers benefited from their proximity to Philadelphia markets and many built substantial stone farmhouses, some of which are still standing.

Iron ore mining was the dominant early industry, starting in 1727 at Durham Furnace. The furnace operated until 1789, then was dormant until the coming of the canals in the 1820s. The furnace was reactivated and remained in operation until 1908.

The canal industry played a major role in the county's development in the first half of the 19th century. The Delaware Canal, running along the entire length of the county, was probably the most important waterway in Pennsylvania. Several other canals in Pennsylvania and New Jersey intersected it. Remains of numerous locks are still visible.

PLACES OF INTEREST

Chalfont, pop. 3,000.

> **Peace Valley Winery,** 300 Old Limekiln Rd., 249-9058. Open Wed.-Sat. 12-6, Sun. 12-5. Directions: Go NW for 2.5 mi. from N. Main St./Easton Rd. in Doylestown on Swamp Rd. (PA 313) to New Galena Rd., turn left for 2 mi. to north entrance of Peace Valley Park, turn right on Old Limekiln Rd. for 1 mi. to winery.

Delaware River Towns. Each of the small communities along the river were stops on the Delaware Canal. In the sixty miles between Easton and Bristol, the inland-most reach of ocean tides, there were 24 locks, 9 aqueducts, and 106 bridges. The level of the river drops 165 feet in that distance. **New Hope** is about at mile 24, northward from Bristol, and is the southernmost town in the PDC portion of the Canal. Other than Easton, it is also the largest town on the Pennsylvania side of the river within the PDC (see the detailed write-up on New Hope later in this chapter). River Road, true to its name, is a delightfully scenic road following the river valley. It is numbered PA 32 from New Hope to Kintnersville, and then PA 611 the rest of the way to Easton. This road is meant to be traveled in leisurely fashion; it is quite narrow, with a maximum speed limit of 45, and there are many opportunities to stop, whether at one of the locks or bridges, picnic areas, or historical markers, or at an antique shop, restaurant, or bed and breakfast inn. The Canal is on the east side of the highway (between the road and the river) for most of the 35 miles between New Hope and Easton. It is on the west side in New Hope itself and from just north of Tinicum to Upper Black Eddy.

The River Road drive takes you through the small villages of Center **Bridge** (3-1/2 miles from New Hope), **Lumberville** (7 miles), **Point Pleasant** (8-1/2), **Tinicum** (12), **Erwinna** (13-1/2), **Uhlerstown** (15), **Upper Black Eddy** (18-1/2), and **Kintnersville** (23 miles upstream from New Hope). PA 611 passes through Durham Furnace, Riegelsville, and Raubsville before reaching Easton; this section of River Road does not lend itself as well to sightseeing—it carries heavier traffic and some trucks, is somewhat industrialized, and in addition, is quite narrow. Weekends are the busiest times along Route 32, so if you can plan your tour on a weekday you'll have less traffic, and the business establishments will be less crowded. This advice especially applies if you're bicycling; the River Road is a great ride, but weekend motor traffic can be bothersome even though it moves at a relatively slow speed. The towpath is open to bicyclists, although it's unpaved.

Center Bridge and Lumberville are NRHP Historic Districts, and a few of the inns are also listed on the NRHP. One of Bucks County's eleven remaining covered bridges in the PDC region crosses the Canal at Uhlerstown, and another is just west of it at Erwinna. Several others are within a mile or two of River Road.

Doylestown, pop. 9,100. This beautiful and quaint town was settled in 1735 and has been the Bucks County seat since 1812. About at the geographic center of the county, it was originally just a rural crossroads, but after the court house was moved here it began to grow rapidly. Doylestown is the home of Delaware Valley College, a small agriculture-oriented school located just west of town.

Doylestown is a feast for the architecturally minded. Designs run the gamut from colonial to federal to Victorian to modern. Brick, fieldstone, and frame construction have all been used extensively, which makes for an eclectic mix of styles. There are **three walking tours** of different parts of town (brochure available from Chamber of Commerce or Tourist Association), each highlighting the historic landmarks and noteworthy architectural features of the districts. The Central and West Side walks are about a mile each, while the East Sider is approximately a mile and a half long. There are no excessively steep hills on any of the walks, but neither are they completely level.

Doylestown is one of the few sizeable towns in Pennsylvania that does not have regular street address numbering (100 numbers to the block). Finding particular locations can thus be a little confusing, but the town isn't so large that you'll get hopelessly lost.

The highlights of the community and surrounding area are:

★★★ **Mercer Museum** (1)(1-1 1/2 hours), SE corner of Ashland and Green Sts., 345-0210. Open March thru December—Mon.-Sat. 10-4:30, Sun. 1-4:30, except Thanksgiving and Christmas. Admission: adults, $3.00; seniors, $2.50; students, $1.50. A collection of tools and artifacts from colonial America that had belonged to Dr. Henry Mercer forms the theme of the museum. Mercer was a historian, archæologist, and ceramist, and this NRHP building is one of three monuments he left in town. The unique six-story poured concrete building is perhaps as much of an attraction as its contents. This is a large (40,000 pieces) and varied collection, but the indiscreet placement of identification numbers on the outside faces of objects is a minor but noticeable detraction.

★★★ **James A. Michener Museum** (2)(30-40 min.), 138 S. Pine St. (former Bucks County Prison), 340-9800. Open Mon.-Fri. 10-4, Sat.-Sun. 11:30-4:30. Admission by donation; suggested amounts: adults, $3.00; seniors, $2.50; students, $1.50. A new museum, opened in the fall of 1988 to display 20th-century American art, including Michener's personal collection. As yet small, but attractive.

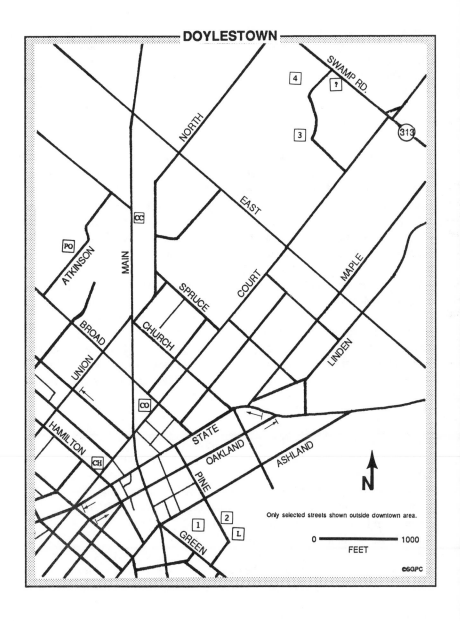

DOYLESTOWN

Only selected streets shown outside downtown area.

0 ———— 1000
FEET

©SGPC

★★★ **Fonthill** (③)(1 hour), E. Court St. and Swamp Rd., 348-9461. Open Mon.-Sat. 10-5, Sun. 12-5 (last tour at 4), closed Thanksgiving, Christmas, and New Year's Day. Admission: adults, $4.00; seniors, $3.50; students, $1.50. Guided tours only of this NRHP castle that was Henry Mercer's residence. This building, like the Mercer Museum, is of poured concrete construction, predating the latter by several years. The home is filled with the fruits of Mercer's collecting around the world. The design and method of construction alone make it a unique attraction. It's advisable to call before visiting to make sure your preferred tour time is available. There is a limit of 10 persons per tour.

★★★ **Moravian Tile Works** (④)(45-60 min.), Swamp Rd. (PA 313) just north of E. Court St., 345-6722. Open March thru December—Wed.-Sun. 10-4, except Easter, Thanksgiving, and Christmas. Admission: adults, $1.75; seniors and students, $1.00; families $3.50. The tile factory has nothing at all to do with Moravians or the Moravian Church—it's just that Henry Mercer was impressed by Moravian stoveplate designs, so he called his factory the Moravian Tile Works. The NRHP structure was built in 1911-12 and operated until the mid-1950s (Mercer died in 1930). A 10-minute orientation slide program begins on the hour and describes how tiles were made and decorated, and the history of the factory. The tour is self-guided. A unique sight well worth seeing.

★★ **National Shrine of Our Lady of Czestochowa** (⑤), Ferry Rd., 345-0600. Open for tours Mon.-Sat. by appointment. Admission free. Polish religious shrine. Directions: Go NW on Swamp Rd. (PA 313) for 1.4 mi. from N. Main St./Easton Rd. (SR 1001-old PA 611) to Ferry Rd. (SR 1006), turn left for 2 mi. to shrine on right.

Community Resources
Bucks County Tourist Commission, 152 Swamp Rd., 345-4552
Central Bucks Chamber of Commerce, 379 N. Main St., 2nd fl., 348-3913 or 345-7051
PO: 8 Atkinson Dr., 348-8114
Public Library: Pine St. & Scout Way, 348-9081
Doylestown Hospital: 595 W. State St., 345-2200
Court House: Main & Court Sts., 348-6000
Borough Police: emergency 348-4680, all other business 345-4143
Borough Offices: 57 W. Court St., 345-4140
State Police: PA 313, Dublin, 343-1234 (Doylestown)

Dublin, pop. 2,000.

★★ **Pearl S. Buck Home** (⑥)(1 hour), Maple Ave., 249-0100. Open March thru mid-January; tours 10:30 AM and 2 PM daily, 1:30 and 2:30 on Sun. May thru September. Admission: adults, $4.00; seniors and students, $3.00; children under 6, $2.00. Green Hills Farm was Pearl Buck's home from the late 1930s until her death in 1973. The rambling stone farmhouse was built in 1835 but largely rebuilt by Pearl Buck. Its contents reflect the life of the author, the only woman to have won the Pulitzer and Nobel Prizes for literature. Pearl Buck was born in China of American missionary parents. Her Oriental upbringing is depicted in the art objects found throughout the house. The guided tour begins with a 15-minute video describing the work of the Pearl S. Buck Foundation, which seeks sponsors of needy Amerasian children, and whose headquarters are on the property. The author's life, writings, and personal effects are fully covered in the guided tour. Directions: In center of town, turn SW (coming from Doylestown, it's a left turn) off PA 313 on Maple Ave. (SR 4003), go 1.2 mi. to entrance on right.

Lahaska, unincorporated, pop. about 200. Well-known antiques center between Doylestown and New Hope.

Peddlers Village, a "village" of shops, restaurants, crafts barn, dinner theater, and country inn that draws shoppers and browsers from all over the East Coast. Located in the triangular-shaped area bordered by US 202, PA 263, and Street Rd., the Village is the creation of Earl Jamison, whose intention was to create a tastefully built shopping center, but not in the usual shopping center style. The stores are designed to be unusual and unique, and no two are exactly alike in their merchandise. While touristy, the Village is beautifully designed and landscaped, with Mr. Jamison's personal involvement. Open daily at 10 AM; normal closing is 5:30, but 9 PM on Friday and 6 on Saturday. Sunday hours 12-5:30. Closed Thanksgiving, Christmas, and New Year's Day. Individual shop, and the restaurants', hours may vary.

Quarry Valley Farm (⑦), 2302 Street Rd., 794-5882 or -8185. Open April thru December—daily 10-5. Admission: adults, $3.50, children under 12, $3.00. An educational farm with gardens, animals, and a museum of implements. Numerous "please touch" displays and a petting zoo. Designed primarily for children. Directions: 0.2 mi. south of US 202.

New Hope, pop. 1,800. Founded about 1722 when John Wells received authorization to operate a ferry here. The town was originally named Coryell's Ferry for the owner about the time of the Revolution. Two mills were soon built, but after they burned down in 1790 and were rebuilt, the town's name became New Hope Mills, and later, just New Hope. Today it's a trendy antiques and arts center, drawing an upscale clientele to this genteel but genuinely attractive town. There are a number of NRHP sites and a **Historic District**. In addition to bed and breakfast inns, fashionable restaurants, and antique and craft shops, there is also summer stock theater at the **Bucks County Playhouse** (S. Main St., 862-2041) as well as at least one dinner theater. A walk through the center of town, along Main, Bridge, Mechanic, and Ferry Sts., is a delightful way to spend an hour or two, even if you don't go into any of the shops. While you're roaming about, take in the **Delaware Canal Gardens** at the Mule Barge Landing up the hill from S. Main St. This is a community effort to beautify and help draw attention to the historical significance of the Canal. Open daily, admission free. **Ghost Tours** (1 hour) are given on Saturday evenings from June thru early November (additional Friday night tours in October and November); these are lantern-led walks to the historic places in town. Admission: $4.00. For information, contact Ghost Tours, 135 Grasshopper Dr., Ivyland, PA 18974, (215) 357-4558.

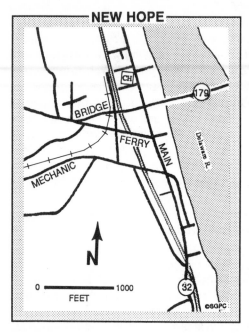

Bucks Country Vineyards, US 202, 2.5 mi. south of PA 179, 794-7449. Open Mon.-Fri. 10-5, Sat. and hol. 10-6, Sun. 12-6. Admission to tours: adults, $1.00 on weekends and holidays only; children free. Tours, tastings, and sales.

Quakertown, pop. 9,900. The major commercial center for northern Bucks County. The 1200-block of W. Broad St (PA 313) and the first two blocks of S. Main have a number of historic homes, two of which, Liberty Hall (1237 W. Broad) and the Enoch Roberts House (1226 W. Broad) are on the NRHP. This was the original part of the town. After the arrival of the North Pennsylvania (now Reading) Railroad in 1855 another village developed around the station about 3/4 of a mile farther east. Within a few years the two were consolidated within essentially the present limits of the borough.

Little Vineyard and Winery, 951 E. Cherry Rd., 536-8709. Open Wed.-Sat. 10-6, Sun. 12-5. Directions: From center of town, go north on California Rd. (N. Main St). (SR 4051) for 3 mi. to Cherry Rd., turn right for 1/2 mi.

COVERED BRIDGES

There are 11 covered bridges in the PDC portion of Bucks County. The Tourist Commission has prepared a brochure outlining a tour of the 13 in the county; therefore, the bridges are not listed individually. One bridge, in Perkasie (PERK-uh-cee), does not cross water; it was relocated to a park after being condemned by the county.

RECREATION FACILITIES

Nockamixon State Park, PA 563, 3 1/2 mi. NE of PA 313 and 4 mi. SW of PA 412, 538-2151.
Ralph Stover State Park, 4.2 mi. NE of PA 611 at Plumsteadville on Stump Rd. (SR 1010), 982-5560 (Upper Black Eddy).
Roosevelt State Park, PA 32 and 611 along the Delaware from Easton, Northampton Co., to Bristol, 982-5560 (Upper Black Eddy).
Coryell's Ferry Boat Rides, 22 S. Main St., New Hope, 862-2050.
Mule Barge Company, S. Main St., New Hope, 862-2842. Mule-drawn barge rides on the Delaware Canal.
New Hope Steam Railway, Bridge St., New Hope, 862-2707. Steam-powered 14-mi. round trip to Buckingham Valley. Operates Sat., Sun. in May, June, and September thru 1st weekend in November, Wed.-Sun. in July and August. For fares and schedules, write: New Hope Steam Railway, Bridge St., New Hope, PA 18938.
Point Pleasant Canoeing and Bucks County River Rafting, PA 32 along Delaware River at Point Pleasant and Upper Black Eddy, 297-TUBE (8823), 297-8181, or 982-9282 (See also **Lehigh Valley**).
Wells Ferry Boat Rides, Ferry St., New Hope, 862-5965.

CALENDAR OF EVENTS

Note: All Lahaska events are held at Peddlers Village and are c/o Peddlers Village, Box 218, Lahaska, PA 18931, 794-7055.

Late April, Doylestown. **A-Day Fair**, Delaware Valley College. c/o Delaware Valley College, US 202, Doylestown, PA 18901, 345-1500.

Late April-Early May, Lahaska. **Strawberry Festival.**

Mid-May, Doylestown. **Folk Fest**, Mercer Museum. c/o Bucks County Historical Society, Pine & Ashland Sts., Doylestown, PA 18901, 345-0210.

Late May, Dublin. **Fantasy of Flowers**, Green Hill Farm. c/o Pearl S. Buck Foundation, Dublin Rd., Perkasie, PA 18944, 249-0100.

Early June, Tinicum. **Tinicum Antique Show**, Tinicum Park. c/o Bruce Davidson, P.O. Box 234, Erwinna, PA 18920, 294-9601.

Mid-June, Doylestown. **Village Fair**, War Memorial Field. c/o Mary Ann Garton, P.O. Box 182, Doylestown, PA 18901, 345-0597.

Mid-June, Lahaska. **Arts Festival.**

Mid-June, Buckingham. **Buckingham Antiques Show**, Tyro Grange Hall. 275-4148 (Norristown).

Late June, Bedminster. **Deep Run Festival of the Arts**, Deep Run Presbyterian Church. c/o Mrs. Schmidt, RD 2, Box 370, Perkasie, PA 18944, 249-3689.

Early July, Tinicum. **Tinicum Art Festival**, Tinicum Park. c/o Civic Association, Erwinna, PA 18920, 294-9309.

Early August, Doylestown. **Art Day at Fonthill**, Fonthill Museum. 343-6760.

Mid-August, Quakertown. **Market Day and Festival**, Burgess-Foulke House. c/o William Amey, 26 N. Main St., Quakertown, PA 18951, 536-3298.

Mid-August, New Hope. **Auto Show**, New Hope-Solebury High School. c/o New Hope Borough Information Center, 1 W. Mechanic St., New Hope, PA 18938, 862-5880.

Early September, Doylestown. **Polish Festival**, Shrine of Czestochowa. c/o Our Lady of Czestochowa, Ferry Rd., Doylestown, PA 18901, 345-0600.

Early September, New Hope. **Arts Festival.** c/o New Hope Borough Information Center, 1 W. Mechanic St., New Hope, PA 18938, 862-5880.

Mid-September, Doylestown. **Children's Art Festival**, Fonthill and Moravian Tile Works. 348-6114.

Mid-September, Pipersville. **Scottish Festival.** c/o Bucks County Tourist Commission, 152 Swamp Rd., Doylestown, PA 18901, 345-4552.

Late September, Lahaska. **Scarecrow Weekend Festival.**

Early November, Lahaska. **Apple Festival.**

Mid-November, Lahaska. **Christmas Open House.**

Late November, New Hope. **Historical Society Antiques Show & Sale**, Eagle Fire Co. c/o New Hope Historical Society, S. Main St., New Hope, PA 18938, 862-5652.

Late November-Early December, Dublin. **Christmas House Tour**, Green Hills Farm. c/o Pearl S. Buck Foundation, Dublin Rd., Perkasie, PA 18944, 249-0100.
Early December, Lahaska. **Christmas Festival.**
December, Doylestown. **Doylestown Christmas House Tour,** James-Lorah House. c/o Junior Women's Club of Doylestown, 132 N. Main St., Doylestown, PA 18901, 348-2187.

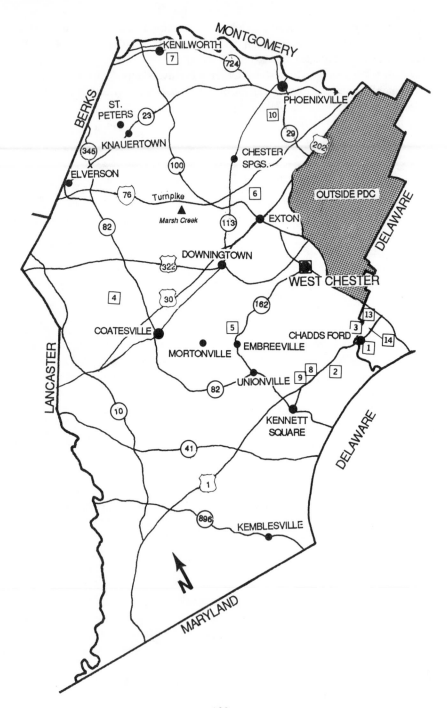

CHESTER

Created: November, 1682, as one of the three original counties
County Seat: West Chester
Land Area: 765 square miles, of which approximately 635 in PDC
Population (1989 est.): 350,000, of which approximately 250,000 in PDC
Area code: 215

Included with the portion of Chester County in the PDC is the westernmost part of Delaware County, an area that is more allied geographically and economically with Chester than with Delaware. Most of central Chester and the adjacent western part of Delaware County are referred to as the Brandywine Valley by the local chambers of commerce and tourism promotion agencies, who recognize the common socio-economic and historical characteristics that transcend the county boundary.

Chester County is probably the most culturally and developmentally diverse county in the PDC. Its population mix is notably different from others in the region. Undoubtedly because of its proximity to Philadelphia, the county has substantial variations in its land usage. It has flashy new corporate office parks and grimy old steel mills. It has suburban townhouse subdivisions and large estates. It has large corporate farms and small Amish family farms. It has quaint upscale historic villages and plain working-class towns.

Much of exurban Chester County is characterized by narrow, twisting country roads meandering over hills and valleys, passing stone farmhouses and barns and fields dotted with thoroughbred horses grazing, with pretty little villages here and there and occasionally a covered bridge. The tourist bureau uses the term "elegant countryside" to describe the county, a tag that befits the area quite well.

Topographically, Chester County is rolling to hilly. Most of the northern portion is heavily wooded, with limited land used for farming. The southern half is the major agricultural area. The narrow Chester Valley runs generally west to east through the center of the county and is the transition zone between the northern and southern areas. This valley has long been an important transportation corridor, with Indian trails, the nation's first toll turnpike, the Pennsylvania Railroad, and the Lincoln Highway in succession over the course of the county's history.

Historical Highlights

Chester County, as one of the three established by William Penn in 1682, originally extended from the Delaware River to the Susquehanna. Its name is derived from Cheshire (Chester-shire) in England, where many of its early settlers came from. By 1789 the last of the adjacent counties had been carved from it and it assumed its present boundaries. The border with Maryland was surveyed by Mason and Dixon in 1765, and that with the state of Delaware, known as the New Castle Arc, in 1701. The latter boundary, in fact, was defined in Penn's charter, as a "circle drawne at twelve miles distance from New Castle northward and westward".

The Dutch were the first Europeans to settle the county, in 1616, followed by the English about 1734, the Swedes in 1638, and Finns in 1640. However, these groups settled in the portion that was later established as Delaware County. The English predominated among the county's early settlers, perhaps explaining why they are today the largest single nationality represented in the county. Germans from the Palatinate arrived in the northern part of Chester County about 1730, and some Amish came about 1760 after first settling in Berks County.

Farming was the major occupation from the earliest days until the late 1800s. Industry developed in the northern part of the county, perhaps because the terrain there was not as readily conducive to farming. There were several iron ore furnaces in this region, and the first steel manufactured in the U.S. was made at Coventry in 1732. Agriculture is still an important segment of the economy, as the county ranks second only to Lancaster in value of farm production on an overall and per acre basis. The major crops are tobacco, corn, dairy products, and mushrooms. Southern Chester County is one of the largest mushroom growing areas of the United States, producing about 15% of the nation's total output. Most of the mushroom farms are in the Kennett Square, Toughkenamon, Avondale, and West Grove areas.

The Battle of Brandywine, which occurred in 1777 at Chadds Ford, Delaware County, represented the beginning of the low point for the American cause in the Revolution. General George Washington, trying to stop a British advance from the west on Philadelphia, was routed in the battle. The British advanced to Philadelphia, again defeating Washington's army at Germantown as it attacked from the northwest. The Continental Congress fled to Lancaster and York, and Washington spent the winter at Valley Forge while the English troops partied in Philadelphia.

The National Register of Historic Places lists 228 sites and 22 Historic Districts in the PDC portion of Chester County, which is far more places than any other county in this region and second only to Philadelphia County statewide. The fact that there are such a large number of locations is due to a very active effort made by local people to preserve relics from the past by nominating them for inclusion in the Register. Chester County has a fulltime Historic Preservation Office and Officer, something few other counties have. Considering the growth rate of urbanization in parts of the county, it would seem that the historic preservation effort has been well advised. The NRHP sites of greatest importance are described in the following section.

PLACES OF INTEREST

Chadds Ford, unincorporated, pop. about 1,200. Originally a stage stop on the Philadelphia-Baltimore road at the Brandywine Creek crossing, now an antiques and art center.

★★★★ **Brandywine Battlefield State Park** (⊞14)(1-1/2-2 hours), US 1, 1 mi. east of PA 100, 459-3342. Open Tue.-Sun. 9-8. Admission: adults, $1.00; seniors, 75¢; children 6-17, 50¢; under 6, free; no charge to tour the grounds. A 50-acre NRHP park on the site of the second largest and one of the Revolution's bloodiest battles. Exhibit hall in visitor center with slide show (10 min.) portraying the events of the battle. Guided tours of Washington's and Lafayette's headquarters (about 45 min. each) help give an understanding of the event and of life in the area in 1777; you should take one, or preferably, both, tours. Lafayette's headquarters occupied a farmhouse built in 1698 and is original, although additions to the house were made before and after the battle. Washington's headquarters is a reconstruction of a farm-house that stood on the property.

★★★★ **Brandywine River Museum** (⊞1)(1-1-1/2 hours), US 1, 200 feet west of PA 100, 459-1900. Open daily 9:30-4:30 except Christmas. Admission: adults, $3.00; seniors age 65 and over and full-time students, $1.50; under age 6, free. A premier museum in a beautiful setting. Opened in 1971, the museum houses the largest collection of works by three generations of the Wyeth family and other 19th and 20th century American art. Galleries include still-lifes and illustrations, and landscape paintings, plus changing exhibits. The converted Civil War-era grist mill contains three gallery floors and a lecture room, restaurant, and museum shop. Two glass towers added to the building afford views of the adjacent creek and landscaped gardens.

★★★ **Barns-Brinton House** (☑)(30 min.), US 1, 1-1/2 mi. west of PA 100, 388-7376. Open June thru August—Sat.-Sun. 10-5, remainder of year by appointment. Admission: adults, $1.00; seniors and children, 50¢. Owned by the Chadds Ford Historical Society and on the NRHP, this is a restored tavern built in 1714. It's valued for its interior woodwork and exterior brickwork. Tours conducted by costumed guides, and colonial crafts demonstrations given.

★★ **John Chad House** (③)(30 min.), PA 100, 0.2 mi. north of US 1, 388-1132 or -7376. Open June thru August—Sat.-Sun. 10-5, remainder of year by appointment. Admission: adults, $1.00; seniors and children, 50¢. This was the home of the namesake of Chadds Ford, who was a farmer and ferryman. The house was built about 1725 and is on the NRHP as an example of early Pennsylvania architecture. Like the Barns-Brinton House, it is owned by the Chadds Ford Historical Society, and tours are conducted by costumed guides who also demonstrate baking in the beehive oven.

Chadds Ford Winery, US 1, 1.9 mi. west of PA 100, 388-6221. Open Tue.-Sat. 10-5:30, Sun. 12-5 for tastings and sales. Tours offered on weekends or by appointment.

Chester Springs (30-40 min.), unincorporated, pop. 200. Formerly called Yellow Springs, the small community was a health resort from as early as 1722 until 1860 and had been the site of a hospital during the Revolutionary and Civil Wars. Now an art center maintained by Historic Yellow Springs, Inc. The resort buildings, on the NRHP, can be seen; for information on self-guided tours (Mon.-Fri. 9-4, weekends by reservation; free, donation requested), call 827-7911 or -7414. Directions: Turn left off PA 113 at the crossroads of Chester Springs on Yellow Springs Rd. (SR 1024) for 0.5 mi. to Art School Rd.

Fox Meadow Farm Winery, Clover Mill Rd., 827-7898. Open Sat.-Sun. 1-5 for tours and tastings. Admission free. Directions: Turn south off PA 113 on Clover Mill Rd. (SR 1026), 1.0 mi. north of Chester Springs crossroads and 2.5 mi. north of intersection of PA 113 and 401.

Coatesville, pop. 11,000. Industrial town in the Chester Valley, dominated by Lukens Steel Company headquartered here. The firm's Corporate Office Building at 50 S. 1st Ave. is on the NRHP. There is also a large Veterans Administration Hospital just east of town along US 30. The downtown business district, extending along E. Lincoln Hwy. and a block on either side from 1st to 6th Aves., is a NRHP **Historic District**.

★★ **Hibernia Ironmaster's Mansion** (④)(1 hour), home of a wealthy iron forge owner, probably built about 1763 and on the NRHP. Another wing, now the center section, was added in the 1830s, and the ballroom in the east wing was built in 1904. The furnishings belonged to the last owner, who deeded the home to the county in 1963 after it had been unused and vandalized for several years. Thus, the house represents a combination of architectural styles, but there is no particular historic significance to the furnishings. Open for tours Sun. 1-4. Admission: $1.00. Located in an 800-acre county park. Other historic structures in the park are Hibernia Church and five cottages occupied by workers in the iron furnace. Directions: From PA 82, 2.1 mi. north of US 30, turn left on Cedar Knoll Rd. (SR 4005) for 1.5 mi. to entrance to Hibernia Park.

Downingtown, pop. 9,300. An attractive manufacturing community in the Chester Valley, settled 1739 as Milltown. The section of Lancaster Ave. (US 30 Business) east of the East Branch of Brandywine Creek is a **Historic District**. Within this zone are two NRHP sites: the **Downingtown Log House** at 15 E. Lancaster Ave., and **General Washington Inn**, at Lancaster and Uwchlan Aves.

Elverson, pop. 600. **Hopewell Furnace National Historic Site** and **French Creek State Park** are 6 mi. northeast on PA 345, just north of the Berks Co. line. See complete listings under Birdsboro, Berks Co.

Embreeville, unincorporated. A mile north is the **Star Gazer Stone** (⑤), the marker set up in 1764 by surveyors Mason and Dixon to determine the placement of the boundary line bearing their names. From this point they measured 15 miles south, the place where, through an agreement with successors of William Penn and Lord Baltimore, they began their westward survey that took four years to complete. Directions: go north on Star Gazers Rd. (SR 3051) for 0.1 mi. from PA 162 to field on right. Star Gazers Rd. is 7-1/2 mi. west of downtown West Chester and 3.5 mi. north of the intersection of PA 82/842 in Unionville. Stone is surrounded by low cement block wall.

Exton, unincorporated, pop. about 2,000. Formerly a country crossroads, at the intersection of the Lincoln Highway. (US 30) and Pottstown Pike (PA 100), it has grown into one of the largest shopping areas in Chester County and a center for research and light industry.

★★★ **Thomas Newcomen Library and Museum** (⑥)(1 hour), 412 Newcomen Rd., 363-6600. Open Mon.-Fri. 9-5, admission free. Englishman Thomas Newcomen (1663-1729) was the inventor of the steam engine, considered the harbinger of the Industrial Revolution. This museum, which is the North American headquarters of the Newcomen Society, displays full-size steam engines and working scale models of equipment powered by them, such as locomotives, marine equipment, and automobiles. While oriented to enthusiasts of machinery, even the non-mechanically inclined will find the displays interesting and educational. The library contains 2,700 volumes dealing with steam power and its history. Directions: Go north on PA 100 for 1.5 mi. from US 30 to the Ship Rd. exit. Turn right at the end of the exit ramp on Ship Rd. (SR 1001) for 0.3 mi., then left on Newcomen Rd. (SR 1025) for 0.4 mi. to museum on right.

Kemblesville, unincorporated.

Brandywine Vineyards and Winery, PA 896, 0.8 mi. N of PA 841, 4.6 mi. N of Maryland line, 255-4171. Open Tue.-Sat. 11-6, Sun. 12-5. Tours given anytime during winery hours.

Kenilworth, unincorporated, pop. about 2,100. Located in North Coventry Township, just across the Schuylkill from Pottstown, Montgomery County. In fact, the Pottstown postal delivery area and telephone exchanges include most of North Coventry.

★★★ **Trumpet Museum** (⑦)(30-45 min.), Fairway Farm, Vaughan Rd., 327-1351. Open regular hours, but call first to arrange visit. Admission by donation, $2.50 suggested. A highly unusual museum, the only one in the world devoted to brass instruments. There are 600 in all, dating from as early as the 17th century. A sampling includes, in addition to trumpets, post horns, French horns, trombones, and cornets. The museum, owned and operated by the Streitwieser Foundation, is the work and collection of Franz Streitwieser, the German-born curator who has converted a large barn into an imaginative display of instruments, sheet music, band uniforms, and figurines. Brass concerts are held several times a year in the barn. Directions: From US 422 (Pottstown bypass), take PA 724 exit, turn left off ramp for 0.2 mi., then right on Vaughan Rd. for 0.2 mi. to entrance on left. From PA 100, take exit for US 422 east to PA 724 exit, proceed as above.

Kennett Square, pop. 5,500. The town, called simply "Kennett" by the locals, is in the center of the mushroom growing area of Chester County. The downtown area, along State and Broad Sts., is quite picturesque. A 13-stop **walking tour** of the central part of town is described in a brochure from the Kennett Square Main Street Association, 148 W. State St., Suite 202A, Kennett Square, PA 19348, 444-5737. There are 22 NRHP Historic Districts in Chester County yet, curiously, this is not one of them. The tour includes some of the oldest buildings remaining in town and several well preserved specimens of Federal, Queen Anne, and Victorian architecture.

★★★★ **Longwood Gardens** ([8])(3-4 hours), 3 mi. east, at US 1 and PA 52, 388-6741. Open daily—outdoor gardens, 9-6 April thru October, 9-5 November thru March; conservatories 10-5 year-round. From mid-June thru August, when illuminated fountain shows are presented, outdoor gardens and conservatories close at 10:30 PM. Admission: adults, $6.00; children 6-14, $1.50; under 6, free. Admission prices do not include some special events. One of the finest garden displays anywhere, covering 350 acres outdoors and 20 indoor conservatories. There are 11,000 different varieties of plants. Seasonal gardens and displays supplement the permanent ones. Longwood was developed by Pierre S. DuPont, chairman of the DuPont Company and of General Motors. He purchased the land in 1906 and the first gardens opened the following year. Longwood is on the NRHP. Concerts and special programs are given throughout the year; most are included in the regular admission. A 4-min. slide show describing the Gardens is presented in the visitor center. The **Peirce-du Pont House**, a 1730 mansion on the property, is open for tours daily April thru December, 11-3 (till 4 PM on weekends from April thru August); additional admission: $1.50.

The **Brandywine Valley Tourist Information Center** (388-2900), (800) 228-9933, relocated in 1988 from Longwood Gardens to the NRHP Longwood Meeting of Progressive Friends, a Quaker church built in 1855 and located just outside the Gardens and behind the Longwood Fire Department on US 1 at Cemetery Rd. The meetinghouse was used by an activist segment of the local Quaker society that was disowned by the established church in Kennett Square because of its radical stand on slavery and participation in the Underground Railroad. This meetinghouse was in use until 1940. The Information Center shows a beautifully photographed 18-min. video titled **"Chester County, Quiet Surprise"** an introduction to the county's attractions. Two additional videos cover the Underground Railroad, and the Brandywine River Museum and Conservancy and fairs and festivals in the Brandywine Valley.

★ **Phillips Mushroom Place** ([9]) (20-30 min.), 2-1/2 mi. east, at US 1 and Orchard Ave., 1/2 mi. west of Longwood Gardens, 388-6082. Open daily 10-6. Admission: adults, $1.25; seniors, 75¢; children 7-12, 50¢; under 7, free. A small museum explaining the cultivation of mushrooms via photos, motion pictures, dioramas, and slide shows. Unique, but not an especially noteworthy museum.

Phoenixville, pop. 14,000. Former center of iron and steel making. Phoenix Bridge Company was headquartered here. Some of the homes and businesses in the downtown area are adorned with locally made wrought iron railings.

★★ **Swiss Pines** ([10]) (45-60 min.), Charlestown Rd., 933-6916. Open mid-March to mid-December—Mon.-Fri. 10-4, closed holidays. Admission free. Not a

Swiss, but a Japanese garden developed by a Swiss industrialist and located on a steep hillside in a still rural part of Chester County. The 15-acre garden is centered around a pond and teahouse. Directions: from Phoenixville, go south from PA 23/113 for 3.1 mi. on Charlestown Rd. (SR 1019). Entrance is on left 1/4 mi. south of Church Rd., parking lot on right. From US 202, take Great Valley exit (PA 29), go north on 29 for 1.9 mi to Devault. PA 29 turns right here, but continue straight on Charlestown Rd. (SR 1019) for another 1.6 mi. to entrance on right, parking lot on left.

St. Peters (15-20 min.), unincorporated, pop. about 100. A quaint, restored Victorian village of perhaps a dozen antique shops, restaurants, and boutiques, in the woods of northern Chester County at the falls of French Creek. The natural setting is more of a reason to come here than the manmade restoration.

Unionville, unincorporated, pop. about 600. The small community comprises a **Historic District** extending along PA 82 and 162.

Valley Forge National Historical Park (See Montgomery County).

West Chester, pop. 19,000. The county seat and largest incorporated town in the county. An exceptionally pretty town that has been called the "Athens of Pennsylvania" because of its Greek Revival architecture and genteel appearance. The town was named for Chester, the original seat of Chester County, but which became part of Delaware County when it was formed in 1789. Actually, West Chester became the county seat a year earlier, which perhaps fomented a secession movement that resulted in Delaware being formed. The most notable buildings within and outside the downtown **Historic District** are the **Chester County Court House** (⊠), 10 N. High St. (NW corner of Market), the **First National Bank Building** (⑪) at 17 N. High (now Fidelity Bank), and the **Chester County Historical Society** (⑫), 225 N. High (see description of this building on the next page). All are on the NRHP and were designed by Thomas U. Walter, architect of the 1851 wings added to the U.S. Capitol.

In each of the borough's four quadrants there are numerous architecturally, if not historically, interesting structures. A West Chester **walking tour** map, published by Blue Cross and Blue Shield and designed as a fitness aid, can be used to explore the town's well-kept but narrow streets. The map is available at the Chester County Tourist Bureau. Each of the four walking tours is approximately 1-1/2 miles long, excluding a minor amount of overlap where they converge downtown. If six miles is a bit much walking for you, the tours can be covered comfortably by bicycle, or even more comfortably by car. But you should at least stroll around the downtown area. West Chester University, one of fourteen in the state

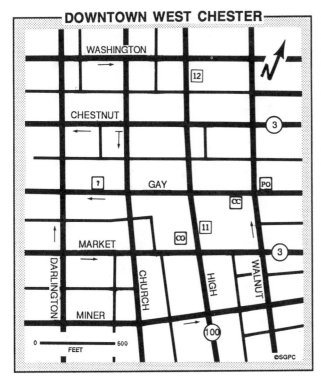

DOWNTOWN WEST CHESTER

WASHINGTON

12

CHESTNUT

3

7   GAY   PO

CC

11

CO

MARKET

3

DARLINGTON

CHURCH

HIGH

WALNUT

MINER

100

0   FEET   600

©SGPC

system, is at the south end of the borough; its Quadrangle is on the NRHP.

★★★**Chester County Historical Society** (1 hour), 225 N. High St., 692-4800. Open Tue., Thu.-Sat. 10-4, Wed. 1-8, Sun. 12-4. Admission: adults, $2.00; seniors, $1.00; students, 50¢. Of the four galleries in the museum, three have rotating exhibits, so there is almost always something new to see. This is unusual in any museum, particularly so in a smaller one such as this. The main theme of the exhibits is aspects of Chester County life, and there is a permanent display of American furniture, decorative arts, and family and home artifacts used in or formerly in the possession of Chester County residents. Chester County was a clock making center, and there are approximately a dozen examples made locally in the early 1800s. A very good museum.

★★★ **Brinton 1704 House** (13)(30-45 min.), Oakland Rd., 692-4800. Open May thru October—Tue., Thu., Sat., except holidays, 1-4. Admission: adults, $1.00; seniors and children, 50¢. Owned by the Chester County Historical Society, although the house is just over the line in Delaware County. Built by Quaker William Brinton and restored by his descendants using an inventory compiled at Brinton's death in 1751. This made for a very complete and accurate restoration, and the house is regarded as one of the finest of its type. Directions: south on US 202/322 for 5 mi. from downtown West Chester to Brintons Bridge Rd. (SR 2002). Turn right for 0.1 mi. to the Dilworthtown intersection. Turn left on Oakland Rd. (also known as Old Wilmington Rd.) for 0.5 mi. to house on left.

Community Resources

Chester County Tourist Bureau, 117 W. Gay St., 344-6365
Visitors Information Center, US 1 at Longwood Gardens, 388-2900, (800) 228-9933
Chamber of Commerce of Greater West Chester, 40 E. Gay St., 696-4046
PO: Walnut & Gay Sts., 696-5831
Public Library: 415 N. Church St., 696-1721
Chester County Hospital: 701 E. Marshall St., 431-5000
Court House: 10 N. High St., 431-6000
West Chester Police: emergency 431-1212, all other business 696-2700
Borough Offices: 400 E. Gay St., 696-0249
State Police: PA 162, Embreeville, 486-0300

Yellow Springs (See **Chester Springs**).

COVERED BRIDGES

There are eleven covered bridges on public land in Chester County, including two spanning Octoraro Creek that are shared with Lancaster County. All are of the Burr truss design, the most widely used construction method in Pennsylvania. Nine bridges in good condition are listed below.

Gibson's, Harmony Hill Rd. (East Branch, Brandywine Creek), at US 322 intersection, about halfway between West Chester and Downingtown, built 1872.
Glen Hope, Providence Rd. (Little Elk Creek), about 1/2 mi. north of Maryland border, built 1889.
Hall's, Sheeder, Sheeder Rd. (SR 1033) (French Creek), about 1-3/4 mi. south of PA 23, built 1850.
Knox, Yellow Springs Rd. (SR 1016) (Valley Creek), at intersection of PA 252 in Valley Forge National Historical Park, built 1865.
Linton Stevens, Kings Row Rd. (Big Elk Creek), about 3/4 mi. north of PA 472 just east of Hickory Hill, built 1886.
Mercer's Mill, Baileys Crossroads Rd. (Octoraro Creek), on the Lancaster Co. line about 1 mi. southwest of Atglen, built 1800.
Rapp's, Rapps Dam Rd. (SR 1049) (French Creek), 0.3 mi. south of PA 23 and 0.7 mi. north of PA 113, just west of Phoenixville.
Rudolph and Arthur, Rudolph's Camp Bonsul Rd. (Big Elk Creek), about 3/4 mi. east of PA 472, about 2 mi. north of Maryland border, built 1880.
Speakman No. 1, Hepzibah Rd. (SR 3047) (Buck Run), about 1-1/2 mi. south of Strasburg Pike (SR 3062), built 1881.

RECREATION FACILITIES

French Creek State Park, PA 345, 3 mi. N of Warwick, 582-1514 (also listed in Berks Co.)
Marsh Creek State Park, off PA 100, 5 mi. N of Exton, 458-8515

CALENDAR OF EVENTS

Mid-February, Valley Forge and Chadds Ford. **Washington's Birthday Celebration.** c/o Valley Forge National Military Park, Valley Forge, PA 19460, 783-7700, or Brandywine Battlefield Park, Chadds Ford, PA 19317, 459-3342.

Mid-March, Coatesville. **Maple Sugar Festival,** Hibernia Park. c/o Chester Co. Parks & Recreation Dept., 235 W. Market St., West Chester, PA 19382, 431-6415.

Mid-April, Mortonville. **Northbrook Canoe Challenge,** Brandywine River. c/o Northbrook Canoe Co., 1810 Beagle Rd., West Chester, PA 19382, 793-2279.

Late April, Chester Springs. **Historic Yellow Springs Art Show and Sale,** Village of Yellow Springs. c/o Sandy Momyer, P.O. Box 627, Art School Rd., Chester Springs, PA 19425, 827-7414.

Late April, Chadds Ford. **Pennsylvania Crafts Day.** c/o Brandywine River Museum, P.O. Box 141, Chadds Ford, PA 19317, 459-1900. Also Early September.

Late May, West Chester. **Chester Co. Historical Society Antiques Show,** Hollinger Field House, West Chester Univ. c/o Chester Co. Historical Society, 225 N. High St., West Chester, PA 19380, 692-4800.

Memorial Day weekend, Chadds Ford. **Memorial Day Encampment.** c/o Brandywine Battlefield Park, Chadds Ford, PA 19317, 459-3342.

Late May, Chadds Ford. **Antique Show.** c/o Brandywine River Museum, P.O. Box 141, Chadds Ford, PA 19317, 459-1900.

Late May, Exton. **Car Show and Flea Market.** c/o Chester County Antique Car Club, 580 Pine Dr., Phoenixville, PA 19460, 933-0381.

Mid-June, Chester Springs. **Yellow Springs State Craft Festival.** c/o Sandra Momyer, P.O. Box 627, Chester Springs, PA 19425, 827-7414.

Late June, Knauertown. **Warwick Summer Festival,** Warwick Park. c/o Chester Co. Parks & Recreation Dept., 235 W. Market St., West Chester, PA 19382, 431-6415.

Late July, Kimberton. **Kimberton Fair.** 933-9715.

Mid-August, Coatesville. **Old Fiddlers' Picnic,** Hibernia Park. c/o Chester Co. Parks & Recreation Dept., 235 W. Market St., West Chester, PA 19382, 431-6415.

Early September, Chadds Ford. **Pennsylvania Crafts Day.** See Late April listing for details.

Mid-September, Chadds Ford. **Chadds Ford Days and Country Fair.** c/o Chadds Ford Historical Society, 388-7376.

Mid-September, Chadds Ford. **Brandywine Battlefield Muster.** c/o Brandywine Battlefield Park, Chadds Ford, PA 19317, 459-3342.

Mid-September, Coatesville. **Buffalo Bill Days,** Main St. 383-0584.

Late September, Kennett Square. **Mushroom Festival.** c/o Southeastern Chester County Chamber of Commerce, P.O. Box 395, Kennett Square, PA 19348, 444-0774 or 388-7806.

Early October, countywide. **Chester County Day.** c/o Chester Co. Tourist Promotion Bureau, 117 W. Gay St., West Chester, PA 19380, 344-6365.

Early October, Unionville. **Unionville Community Fair,** Unionville High School. 347-2087.

Late October, Unionville. **Chesterland International Three-Day Event,** PA 82. 347-2333 or 933-2712 (Phoenixville).

Late November thru New Year's weekend, Chadds Ford. **Brandywine Christmas.** c/o Brandywine River Museum, Chadds Ford, PA 19317, 459-1900.

Early December, Coatesville. **Candlelight Tours,** Hibernia Mansion. c/o Chester Co. Parks & Recreation Dept., 235 W. Market St., West Chester, PA 19382, 431-6415.

Early December, Chadds Ford. **Christmas Celebration.** c/o Brandywine Battlefield Park, Chadds Ford, PA 19317, 459-3342.

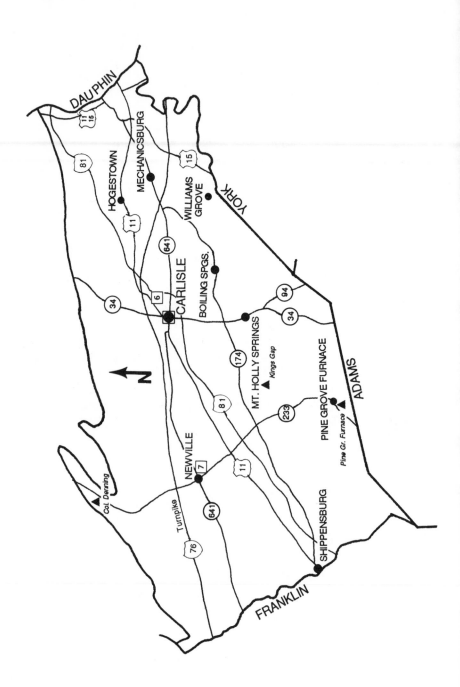

CUMBERLAND

Created: January 27, 1750, as the 6th county, from part of Lancaster County
County Seat: Carlisle
Land Area: 555 square miles
Population (1989 est.): 194,000
Area code: 717

Cumberland County was named for the county in England and is located at the northern end of the Cumberland valley. The county is bordered on the north by Blue Mountain and partially on the south by South Mountain. Although the Cumberland valley is underlain by limestone, its soil depth is shallow in some places. Numerous rock outcroppings can be seen as you drive through the farm areas. North of Conodoguinet Creek, which meanders from west to east across the northern part of the valley, there is shale and slate.

The eastern quarter of the county is part of the Harrisburg metropolitan area (see **West Shore**, page 139), and is considerably different in character from the remainder, which is much less heavily populated. The major industries in the portion outside the suburban Harrisburg area are a carpet manufacturer, C.H. Masland & Sons; tire maker, Carlisle Tire & Rubber; and Kinney Shoe Corporation, all in Carlisle; and PPG Industries with a float glass manufacturing facility at Mount Holly Springs.

Historical Highlights

The area was first populated by Europeans about 1720, and because the valley provided a natural travel route toward the south and west, settlement was relatively rapid after that time. Shippensburg, the oldest town in the county and the first county seat, was founded in 1730, and Carlisle, the present seat and largest town, was laid out in 1751 but had been settled earlier. When first established, Cumberland County included all the land west of the Susquehanna River that the Penns had purchased from the Indians, except for York County, which had been created a year earlier (and also included present-day Adams County until 1800). The earliest settlers were primarily Scotch and Irish, although the first European settler at Carlisle, James LeTort, was French. The Penns in their original land policy felt that Scotch-Irish and Germans might not co-exist amicably, so they decided to reserve separate lands for each. The Cumberland Valley was to be Scotch-Irish, but these people soon began to treat land as a profit-making commodity and sold it off, primarily to Germans who viewed it as a valuable possession to be nurtured and preserved. Thus, Germans began arriving in large numbers after about 1770. As it turned out, the mixing of Germans and Scotch-Irish brought no significant conflicts. Each had their own way of life so there was no rivalry.

Being located on the route to the West, a series of forts was established in the county in the early and mid-1750s. Carlisle Barracks, built in 1757, was the largest and best fortified stockade, and was the dispatch point for provincial troops sent to the French and Indian War battles in western Pennsylvania. It served a similar purpose in 1794 during the Whiskey Rebellion, with President George Washington on hand to command the government's forces.

Although the Revolutionary War was not fought here, Cumberland County had an important role in it. Carlisle Barracks served as an arsenal, and the first American artillery school was established there in 1777. The town of Carlisle is famous as the home and burial place of Mary Hays McCauley, better known as Molly Pitcher, heroine of the Battle of Monmouth, New Jersey. Three signers of the Declaration of Independence lived in the county.

Confederate soldiers marched through the county in 1863 as part of their northern offensive. Carlisle was temporarily captured and shelled, and the Southern army reached its northernmost point a few miles west of Harrisburg in Cumberland County, from where they were commanded to return to Gettysburg.

PLACES OF INTEREST

Boiling Springs, unincorporated, pop. about 1,500. NRHP **Historic District**, bounded by High and 1st Sts., Boiling Springs Lake, and Yellow Breeches Creek, includes many homes from the 19th century. The lake (the eastern boundary of the district) is man-made and dates from the 1740s when it was created to power a grist mill that stood on the site of the present mill. Boiling Springs began as a mill town and iron making center, but in the late 19th century it became a summer resort. A self-guided **walking tour** (30-45 min.) of the Historic District (brochure available from the Boiling Springs Civic Association or from the Greater Carlisle Area Chamber of Commerce) includes 22 sites, but the district covers only a few square blocks, so it can easily be seen on foot. The major sites are around the lake, and include the Ege-Bucher Mansion (1795), restored blast furnace (1760), grist mill (the building as it now stands was renovated in 1897), and Ege's Bridge, a stone arched span built in 1854. The main part of the town is on the west side of the lake, and includes numerous old homes and churches. A limestone clock tower is on the southeast corner of Front and 1st Sts., at the northern end of the lake. The lake is fed by natural springs in caves estimated to be 1,800 feet below the surface. Across from the clock tower, on the northeast corner, is the Boiling Springs Tavern, which dates from about 1832; it was originally a hotel. About 3/4 of a mile east of town on PA 174 is **Allenberry Playhouse,** a summer stock theater.

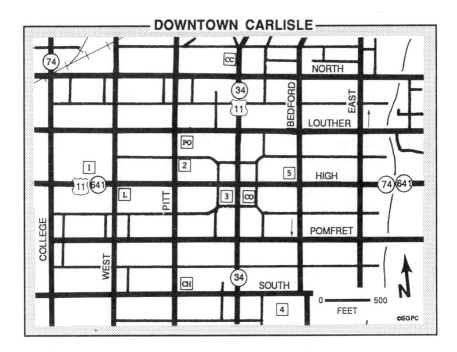

DOWNTOWN CARLISLE

Carlisle, pop. 20,000. Carlisle is a major transportation hub, with the Pennsylvania Turnpike (I-76) and I-81 crossing just east of town. A very pretty town, especially the downtown business district radiating from Public Square (intersection of High and Hanover Sts.). The NRHP **Historic District** is bounded by Penn, East, Walnut, and College Sts., and covers about 30 square blocks in the center of the community. A self-guided **walking tour** (1-1/2-2 hours, not including museum) (brochure available from Chamber of Commerce) covers 20 sites within the district, including:

Dickinson College (☐1), High and West Sts. Founded 1773, it is the oldest college west of the Susquehanna. **West College,** on the Rush Campus (west side of West St.), dates from 1803 and was designed by Henry Latrobe, the architect of the U.S. Capitol. **Denny Hall,** on the NE corner of High and West, was built in 1905. The Washington Redskins football team takes its pre-season training at Dickinson.

137

Bosler Free Library (⬜L⬜), 158 W. High St. (SE corner of West), is a beautiful 1899 Greek Revival building.

★★★ **Hamilton Library** (⬜2⬜)(30-45 min.) 21 N. Pitt St., 249-7610, houses the Cumberland County Historical Society offices, library, and museum. Museum open Mon. 7-9 PM, Tue.-Fri. 1-4. Admission free. The museum contains an attractive collection of Indian artifacts, crafts, Schimmel and Mountz woodcarvings, tools, paintings by local artists, and other items pertaining primarily to Cumberland County. There are also changing exhibits.

Old Court House (⬜3⬜), SW corner of Public Square, built 1845. The present Court House is on the SE corner.

Molly Pitcher Monument (⬜4⬜) in the Old Graveyard in the unit block of E. South St. The Revolutionary War heroine is buried in this cemetery.

Old Cumberland County Prison (⬜5⬜), NW corner of High & Bedford Sts. Built 1854 and used until 1984. A replica of jail in Carlisle, England.

Several noteworthy churches and numerous 18th and 19th century homes described in the brochure line the streets in the Historic Districts, principally High and Hanover. Some of the homes are open during special events in town.

Outside Downtown

★★★ **Carlisle Barracks** (⬜6⬜), 1 mi. NE of Public Sq. on Harrisburg Pike (US 11), 245-3131. In existence since 1757, the Barracks has served as a stockade, arsenal, military training station, Indian school, hospital, and since 1951, the home of the U.S. Army War College. Located on the campus are the **Hessian Museum**, built in 1777 as a powder magazine, and the **Omar N. Bradley Museum** (30 min.), a collection of the General's personal letters, uniforms, weapons, and other memorabilia. The Hessian Museum is open weekends and holidays from May 15-September 30, 1-4 PM. The Bradley Museum is open Mon. 8-12N, Wed. and Fri. 1-4 PM. Admission is free to both. The Bradley Museum is located in Upton Hall.

Community Resources
Greater Carlisle Area Chamber of Commerce: 212 N. Hanover St., 243-4515
PO: 66 W. Louther St., 243-3531
Public Library: 158 W. High St., 243-4642
Carlisle Hospital: South & Wilson Sts., 249-1212
Court House: SE corner of Public Sq., 249-1133
Police: emergency 911, all other business 243-5252

Borough Offices: 53 W. South St., 249-4422
State Police: 1501 Commerce Ave., 249-2121
Bus: MJ Mall, S. Hanover St. & I-81, 249-6955

Newville, pop. 1,500. Just east of town, on the south side of PA 641, is **Laughlin Mill** (7), originally built in 1763 and recently restored.

Ramp's Bridge, Cumberland County's only remaining authentic covered bridge in good condition, spans Conodoguinet Creek about 8 miles west of Newville. The bridge, built in 1870, is on Covered Bridge Rd. just north of SR 4003 and about 1 mile southwest of PA 641.

Shippensburg, pop. 5,300, of which 4,500 in Cumberland Co. The oldest town in the county and its first seat. Founded 1730 by Edward Shippen. Trading center for a prosperous farming region of Cumberland and Franklin Counties. The borough's NRHP **Historic District** is bounded by Lutz, Kenneth, Spring, and Fort Sts. The original court house was on the SW corner of King and Queen Sts., known as **Widow Piper's Tavern**, a NRHP property. Now owned by the Shippensburg Civic Club; interior tours by appointment. **Shippensburg University**, one of 14 colleges in the state system, was established in 1871 as the Cumberland Valley State Normal School. On the campus, at the north edge of town on N. Earl St. (PA 696), stands the **Little Red Schoolhouse**, a one-room school that operated from 1865 to 1954 in Hopewell Township, about 9 miles north of Shippensburg. SU alumni raised funds for its preservation and relocated it to the campus. Open to the public during spring and fall celebrations at the University; at other times, call the Alumni Affairs office (532-1218).

Community Resources
Shippensburg Area Chamber of Commerce: 75 W. King St., 532-5509
PO: 46 W. King St., 532-2314
Public Library: 73 W. King St., 532-4508
Police: emergency 911, all other business 532-8878
Borough Offices: 60 W. Burd St., 532-2147
Bus: 29 W. King St., 530-1329

The "West Shore" (see map on page 144). The portion of Cumberland County east of a north-south line drawn approximately through Mechanicsburg, is part of the greater Harrisburg area and is known locally as the "West Shore". This area has a population of nearly 100,000 and to some extent has an economic life of its own independent of Harrisburg. Most of Cumberland County's, and many of greater Harrisburg's, largest employers are located in this area, including the headquarters of Harsco, a Fortune 500 company, Quaker Oats, and The Book-of-the-Month Club.

Two large military facilities are on the West Shore: the Navy Ships Parts Control Center just east of Mechanicsburg, and the New Cumberland Army Depot. The latter, while associated with Cumberland County, is actually located in the northernmost portion of York County, and is the Army's largest distribution center in the world.

★ **Peace Church** ([8]), NW corner of Trindle Rd. (PA 641) and St. Johns Rd. (SR 2029) in Hampden Twp., is a NRHP site built in 1798 as a house for all Christian denominations. It has been maintained in its original form and is used on special occasions. Open for visitation from about April 1 to December; to visit, call 737-6492; if no answer, 787-3602.

Community Resources
West Shore Chamber of Commerce: 4211 Trindle Rd., Camp Hill, 761-0702
PO: Camp Hill, 2139 Market St., 737-1461
    Enola, 21 N. Enola Dr., 732-2221
    Lemoyne, 333 Market St., 737-4129
    Mechanicsburg, 702 E. Simpson St., 697-4641
    New Cumberland, 318 Bridge St., 774-7092
Public Libraries: Mechanicsburg, 51 W. Simpson St., 766-0171
                West Shore, 30 N. 31st St., Camp Hill, 761-3900
Holy Spirit Hospital: N. 21st St., Camp Hill, 763-2100
Seidle Memorial Hospital: Simpson & Filbert Sts., Mechanicsburg, 766-7691
Police: emergency 911
State Police: Harrisburg 787-7777
Bus: Capital City Airport, Old York Rd., New Cumberland, 774-5483

COVERED BRIDGE (see Newville)

RECREATION FACILITIES

Colonel Denning State Park, PA 233, 8 mi. north of Newville, 776-5272.
Kings Gap State Park (Environmental Education Center), 500 Kings Gap Rd., 10 mi. SW of Carlisle, 486-5031. Directions: From Carlisle, south on PA 34 3.8 mi. from I-81, turn right for 5.4 mi. on Pine Rd. (SR 3006).
Pine Grove Furnace State Park, PA 233, Pine Grove Furnace, 486-7174.
Williams Grove Amusement Park, Williams Grove, 697-8266. Directions: From US 15 at Pa. Turnpike interchange, go south on 15 for 3.1 mi. to Mosers Lane (SR 2026), turn right for 1.2 mi.
Willow Mill Park, 100 Willow Mill Park Rd., Mechanicsburg, 766-9639. Directions: just north of US 11 at Hogestown, 1/4 mi. west of jct. of PA 114.

CALENDAR OF EVENTS

Late April, Carlisle. Spring Collector Car Flea Market and Corral, Carlisle Fairgrounds, Carlisle Springs Rd. c/o Flea Marketeers, 1000 Bryn Mawr Rd., Carlisle, PA 17013, 243-7855.

Late May, Carlisle. Old House Fair and Antiques Show, Downtown. c/o Carlisle Economic Development Center, 114 N. Hanover St., Carlisle, PA 17013, 245-2648.

Early June, Boiling Springs. Foundry Day. c/o Boiling Springs Civic Assn., 619 Lerew Rd., Boiling Springs, PA 17007, 258-3256 or 766-8739 (Mechanicsburg).

Late June, Carlisle. Antiquarian Book Fair, Holland Union Bldg., Dickinson College. c/o Carlisle Economic Development Center, 114 N. Hanover St., Carlisle, PA 17013, 245-2648.

Late July, Shippensburg. Shippensburg Community Fair, Shippensburg Fairgrounds. c/o Shippensburg Area Chamber of Commerce, 75 W. King St., Shippensburg, PA 17257, 532-5509.

Mid-August, Carlisle. Carlisle Fair, Carlisle Fairgrounds

Late August, Shippensburg. Corn Festival, King St., Shippensburg. c/o Rose Dillner, Box F, Shippensburg, PA 17257, 532-5509 or 532-3940.

Late September, Carlisle. Fall Collector Car Flea Market and Corral, Carlisle Fairgrounds. (See Spring Collector Car Flea event above for contact.)

Early October, Carlisle. Arts Festival, Downtown. c/o Carlisle Economic Development Center, 114 N. Hanover St., Carlisle, PA 17013, 245-2648.

Early October, Carlisle. Grand Finale Collector Car Auction, Carlisle Fairgrounds. (See Spring Collector Car Flea event above for contact.).

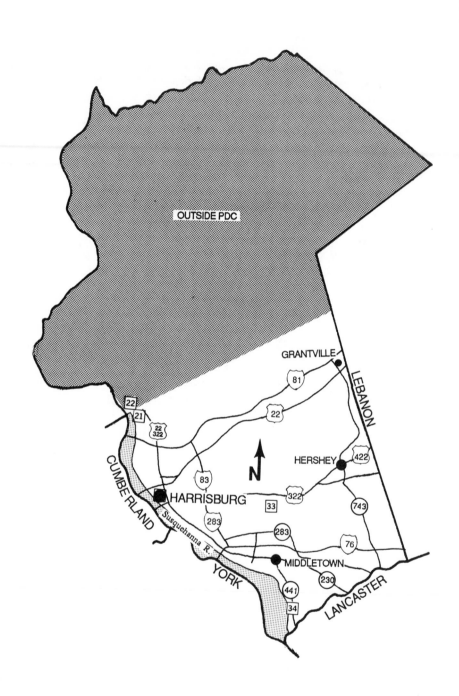

OUTSIDE PDC

GRANTVILLE

LEBANON

81

22

22

21

22
322

422

HERSHEY

N

83

322

HARRISBURG

33

743

CUMBERLAND

283

Susquehanna R.

283

76

441

MIDDLETOWN

230

YORK

34

LANCASTER

DAUPHIN

Created: March 4, 1785, as the 16th county, from part of Lancaster County
County Seat: Harrisburg
Land Area: 548 square miles, of which approximately 225 in PDC
Population (1989 est.:): 238,000, of which approximately 205,000 in PDC
Area code: 717

Dauphin County was named for the title of the French king's oldest son. While only about 40% of Dauphin County's land area is south of Blue Mountain and therefore within the PDC, some 86 percent of the county's population lives in this portion. This area is predominantly urban and forms the core of the Harrisburg metropolitan region.

The terrain in southern Dauphin County is rolling, with a band of flat land ranging up to a mile wide along the east bank of the Susquehanna. This region bridges the gap between the widely recognized and identified Cumberland and Lebanon Valleys; while it essentially is all the same valley, the portion in Dauphin County has no name of its own.

Historical Highlights

The first settlement in the county was at the present location of Hershey, where a church was established in 1724. Harris' Ferry, now Harrisburg, was established in 1733 by John Harris, but there was no real settlement here until 1785. Once Harrisburg became the state capitol in 1812, the history of most of southern Dauphin County, with the exception of Hershey, became virtually indistinguishable from that of the city.

Harrisburg was a target of the Confederate invasion of the North in 1863, but the troops were stopped a few miles west of the city when Gen. Robert E. Lee ordered them to Gettysburg.

The steel industry has been important in Dauphin County's history. Pennsylvania Steel Company's plant in Steelton was the first in the country (1866) built solely to make steel and steel rails. It was acquired by Bethlehem Steel in 1916, who operates it today. Harrisburg Steel Company, now Harsco, a diversified "Fortune 500" company, began as a railroad car manufacturer in 1853.

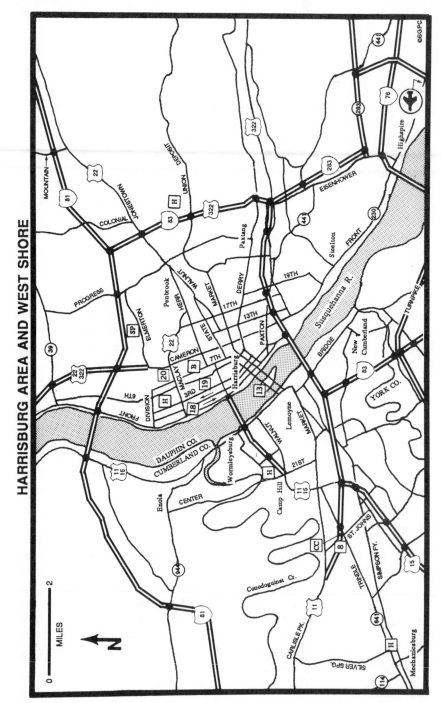

HARRISBURG AREA AND WEST SHORE

PLACES OF INTEREST

Harrisburg, pop. 52,000, with suburbs 280,000. Harrisburg has been the county seat since the county's creation, and from the time it was formally laid out (at the time of Dauphin County's establishment) it has been an important transportation hub for every major mode of travel used by the public. Circumstances of geography were largely responsible for the city's development. The gap in Blue Mountain created by the Susquehanna River was a natural transportation funnel for north- and west-bound traffic. A further boost to development was gained from its location at the juncture of the Cumberland and Lebanon Valleys.

Because of Harris's ferry, early Colonial roads converged on the town. Later, Harrisburg was in the center of Pennsylvania's extensive canal network—directly on the Susquehanna Canal and only a few miles north of the terminus of the Union. Then came railroads, and the city became and still remains an important freight and passenger rail center. Both the Pennsylvania and Reading Railroads had large yards just outside the city (the Pennsy had two); these are now operated by Conrail. The highway network of central Pennsylvania converged on Harrisburg, although by the time of its development the city was long established not only as the capital but also as an economic center in its own right. Most recently, Harrisburg's enlarged and modernized International Airport has become the state's third busiest.

In the past few years the Harrisburg area has been recognized by several national business magazines for its strong economy and high quality of life. The central business district is the scene of extensive building as the shopping core area undergoes a revitalization. A new city hall, hotel and convention center, bank headquarters, multi-level shopping mall, and office buildings have become part of the landscape. While the city admittedly has had its share of urban problems, among them the outmigration of 40% of its population in just 30 years, it has now entered a new phase of development, and is taking on a more cosmopolitan character.

The city has been divided into five districts (see map) to help you organize your sightseeing: Downtown, Shipoke, Capitol District, Uptown, and Allison Hill. Two self-guided tour brochures, "Center City Sights" and "City Wide Sights", are available free at the Chamber of Commerce and the Mayor's office at City Hall. Also ask at the Chamber for "A Walk Through History", which contains two walking tour itineraries for Downtown, Shipoke, Capitol District, and Uptown (these itineraries define the neighborhoods in a slightly different manner than this book). The major attractions in all three brochures are described below. Sightseeing is best done on foot Downtown and in the Capitol District, but a car or bicycle is the most effective way to get around in the other districts. However, you may wish to

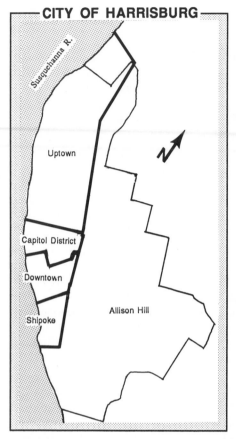

CITY OF HARRISBURG

(map labels: Susquehanna R., Uptown, Capitol District, Downtown, Shipoke, Allison Hill)

cover some parts of these districts on foot as well to get a more leisurely look that urban traffic conditions usually don't permit. Parking is plentiful, and usually free, outside Downtown and the Capitol Complex. On weekends and holidays, parking in reserved permit spaces on Capitol property is free to the public. Parking on City Island is free on weekends and holidays, and after 11 AM on weekdays; a shuttle trolley operates between the Island and downtown. Be sure to carry a good lock if you park your bike outdoors.

Do not miss a **view of Harrisburg's Riverfront**; if this is your first sight of the city, so much the better. The five-mile-long park with its concrete steps at the water's edge, the majestic bridges, and the skyline, all lying before you creates a memorable sight. There are several good vantage points: as you drive across the John Harris (I-83) and M. Harvey Taylor Bridges, from City Island (accessible from the Market St. and Walnut St. Bridges—by car only from Market St., by bicycle and on foot from both), or from the top of the hill on the west bank.

★★★★ **Downtown** (2-3 hours). This area accents the dramatic contrast between the old and new Harrisburg. Most of the historic buildings have been spared in the revitalization. A good place to begin your walking tour is **Market Square** (⬜1⬜), 2nd & Market Sts., the commercial hub of the city. There were once market houses here as there were in other Pennsylvania cities, but they were torn down a century ago. Harrisburg's new **City Hall** (⬜CH⬜), built in 1981, is on the NW corner of the Square, and features an indoor atrium and outdoor plaza and sculpture.

The unit block of N. Front St. has been called **Governor's Row**, so named for the fact that several of its town houses were occupied by the state's early chief executives. The Art Deco **Dauphin County Court House** (⬜CO⬜) is on the SE cor-

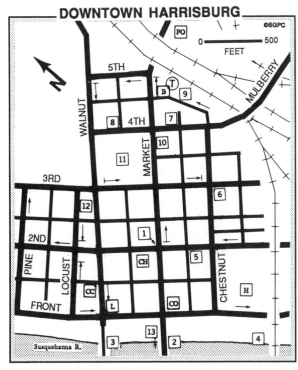

DOWNTOWN HARRISBURG

ner of Front and Market. The present **Market Street Bridge** (2) is the third structure to cross the river at this location. The first, called the "Camel Back", was a covered bridge built in 1813 that stood until 1902. The **Walnut Street Bridge ("Old Shaky")** (3), one block to the north, is a NRHP structure built in 1890. Since structural damage by Hurricane Agnes in 1972 made it unsafe for motor vehicle traffic, it has been open only to bicycles and pedestrians. A walk along the **Riverfront** can be done at street level on paths in Riverfront Park on the west side of Front St., or at water level on the concrete steps, reached by any of the stairways from the street level. The Park extends virtually the entire length of the city, although the steps go only as far north as Maclay St. (2100 N. Front). The **Pennsylvania Railroad Bridge** (4) marks the southern limit of Downtown, and is the northerly of the two railroad bridges.

Four 19th century churches of historical significance are Downtown. **Market Square Presbyterian Church** (5), at the south end of the Square on the west side of 2nd St., houses a congregation formed in 1794; the present building was built in 1860. **Salem United Church of Christ** (6), 231 Chestnut St. (SW corner of 3rd), is the city's oldest church building, dating from 1822, and is on the NRHP. **Zion Lutheran Church** (7), 15 S. 4th St., was the site of the 1840 Whig Party convention, when it nominated William Henry Harrison for President and John Tyler for Vice President. Harrisburg is the smallest American city to host a national political convention. **First Church of God** (8), 15 N. 4th St., is considered the "mother church" of this denomination, which was founded in the city in 1827.

147

A completely "function-oriented" landmark, now beautifully restored, is the NRHP **Pennsylvania Railroad Station** (⑨) on the south side of Market St. between 4th and 5th. The building was built in 1884. Amtrak and SEPTA (Southeastern Pennsylvania Transportation Authority) commuter trains to and from Philadelphia use the station, which retains its cavernous sheds. Capitol Trailways' bus depot is on the lower level of the station, facing Market St.

Among the newer landmarks are **333 Market St.** (⑩), the tallest building in the city (341 feet), housing the Pennsylvania Departments of Banking and Education; the **Federal Building** (⑫), 3rd and Walnut Sts.; and **Strawberry Square** (⑪), a multi-level enclosed mall of shops, offices, and food court, on the south side of Walnut St. extending from 3rd to 4th. Expansion of the mall is under way, and when finished, it will occupy the entire block bounded by Walnut, Market, 3rd, and 4th Sts., and part of the block between 2nd and 3rd. On the third level of Strawberry Square is the★★★**Museum of Scientific Discovery** (30-45 min.), 233-7969, a small but very good "hands-on" showcase of applications of principles of science. Geared primarily to kids, but adults would enjoy it too. Open Tue.-Sat., 10-6, Sun. 12-5. Admission: adults, $2.75; seniors age 60 and over, $2.00; children 3-17, $2.00; under 3, free. Free parking in any of three city-owned garages with validated ticket—2 hours weekdays, 5 hours Saturdays.

City Island (⑬), Harrisburg's playground in the middle of the Susquehanna, houses RiverSide Stadium, home of the city's Eastern League professional baseball team, the Senators, and its Continental Interstate Football League team, the Patriots. Concerts, Independence Day fireworks, and carnivals are held there throughout the summer. The Island also has a large parking lot used by downtown workers; a shuttle bus operates to and from the "mainland". Parking is free here on weekends and holidays and after 11 AM on weekdays. The **"Pride of the Susquehanna"**, a 65-foot paddle-wheeler cruising the river during the summer, docks here. The boat, operated by the not-for-profit Harrisburg Area Riverboat Society, offers 45-50 minute cruises daily at 2, and hourly from 4 to sunset. The trips include City Island, Shipoke, and the West Shore. There are dinner cruises with jazz concerts in the fall, and 30-minute lunch cruises (from the Pine St. dock in Riverfront Park) at 12:15 and 1 PM. Regularly scheduled trips are $4.00 for adults, $3.50 for persons over age 65, and $1.00-2.50 for children under 17, depending on age. Lunch cruises are $3.00 for adults of all ages, and $1.00-2.00 for children. The season usually runs from Memorial Day to the end of October, but depends on river conditions. Call HARS at 234-6500 to verify schedules and operating status.

Shipoke (SHY-poke) is a late 19th century NRHP residential area just south of Downtown, extending along the river from the Pennsylvania Railroad

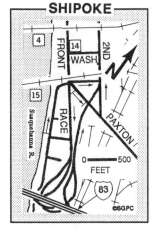

Bridge to I-83, and bounded on the east by the Pennsy main line. Part of Shipoke's original area was torn down about 1960 to make way for the I-83 interchange. This was one of the first city neighborhoods to undergo "gentrification", spurred largely by heavy damage from Hurricane Agnes. The ★★ **John Harris Mansion** (14̄)(1 hour), 219 S. Front St. (NE corner of Washington St.), 233-3462, a NRHP property, was owned by the founder of Harrisburg and later by Simon Cameron, a U.S. Senator, the first Secretary of War under Lincoln, and an important Republican boss in Pennsylvania after the Civil War. The front part of the house was built in 1766, and the rear addition about 1850. The first floor has been restored to the Simon Cameron period by the Dauphin County Historical Society, and the second floor serves as a museum, with three galleries, two of which have changing exhibits. Open Mon.-Fri. 11-4, tours on the hour. Admission: adults, $2.50; seniors, $2.00; children $1.00. DCHS's offices are in the brick stable behind the mansion. Across Front St. from the mansion is the grave of John Harris, which is near the site of his ferry, and thus, the site of the founding of Harrisburg. Just south of the park is the **Reading Railroad Bridge** (15̄), the southernmost of the city's four historic bridges.

The **Capitol District** includes the Capitol grounds and the area directly to the west from 3rd St. to the river. The present ★★★ **Capitol Building** (16̄) was completed in 1906 and dedicated by President Theodore Roosevelt. Its architecture is Italian Renaissance; the dome is modeled after St. Peter's Basilica in Rome, and the stairs leading up from 3rd St. after the Grand Opera in Paris. The Capitol is on the NRHP. Free tours (30 min.) given on the hour Tue.-Sat. 9-4; no tour at noon.

A block north of the Capitol, on the NE corner of 3rd and North Sts., is the ★★★★ **State Museum of Pennsylvania** (17̄)(about 2 hours), 787-4978. Open Tue.-Sat., 9-5, Sun., 12-5. Closed Mon. except Memorial Day, Labor Day, and Independence Day if it falls on Monday. Admission free. Children under 12 must be accompanied by adult. An outstanding museum, with exhibits covering a wide range of subjects related to Pennsylvania—its natural resources, manufacturing, the arts, and history. There is a planetarium with shows Sat. and Sun., 1:30 and 3. Admission to show: adults, $1.00; seniors and children, 50¢. There is a snack bar and museum store on the ground floor; the store sells a wide variety of state-related books, pamphlets, and handicrafts.

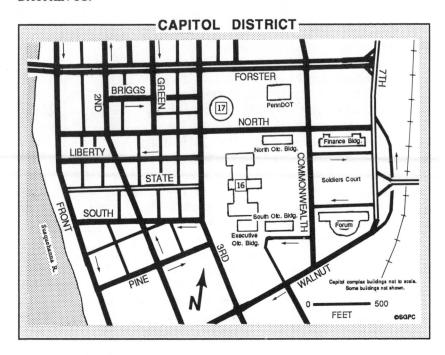

The portion of the Capitol District outside the Capitol grounds is a mixed residential and professional office area. Many trade associations, unions, and lobbying groups have offices in this zone because of its proximity to the government. The two blocks of State St. between Front and 3rd are especially attractive, as is Front between Locust and North. State St. is known as Harrisburg's "street of churches". The 100-block of South St. was the first in the city to be restored and is similar in appearance to Boston or Georgetown in Washington, D.C. Three notable homes on N. Front St. in the district are the **William Maclay Mansion** at 401 (NE corner of South), the **J. Donald Cameron Mansion** at 407, and the **Civic Club** at 612, just south of North St. The Maclay home was originally built in 1792 by U.S. Senator Maclay, but the Georgian remodeling occurred in 1901 long after the family had left. The Italianate Victorian Cameron home, which belonged to Simon Cameron's son and successor in the U.S. Senate, was built in 1863. The Civic Club, of Tudor design, is the only residential building on the west side of Front St. in the city, and dates from about 1862. The second floor ballroom was added by the Civic Club in 1916.

The **Uptown** district begins at Forster St. and extends north to I-81 and east to the Pennsylvania Railroad. The portion between Forster and Verbeke Sts. from Front to 3rd comprises the NRHP **Old Midtown Historic District**. Forster St., a broad boulevard in a neighborhood of mostly narrow streets, was widened when the

M. Harvey Taylor Bridge was built in the early 1950s as a bypass of the central business district.

The highlight of this district are the many beautiful mansions lining Front St. from about Reily St. (1500-block) northward, a distance of over 3 miles. Originally private homes, nearly all are now professional or trade association offices. Some homes have been razed to make way for apartment and office buildings and religious institutions. The transformation from private residence to office building has, on the whole, been a positive change. It is doubtful that many of these large homes could have remained intact as single-family residences, given today's high energy and labor costs and smaller family size. While the change to professional occupancy has brought the paving of front yards to provide parking lots and the installation of large signs to provide identity, many of the exteriors have remained largely unblemished, and some have even been enhanced, because these associations are able to apply the necessary resources to maintain the properties.

The Georgian style ★★★ **Governor's Mansion** ([18]) is at 2035 N. Front St. (SE corner of Maclay). Completed in 1968, it suffered severe damage in the 1972 flood. Open for tours (30 min.) April thru October, Tue. and Thu. on the half hour from 10-2, last tour 1:30. Admission free. Phone 787-1192.

The blocks immediately north of Forster St. on 2nd, Penn and Green Sts., where many homes date from the mid-19th century, have been renovated.

North 3rd St. is the commercial zone of the Uptown neighborhood, and at its center is the ★★★ **Broad Street Market** ([19]), 236-7923, at the corner of Verbeke. Open Thu., Fri., Sat. 7-3:30. This is the oldest continuously operating markethouse in the United States; the original (easterly) building was built in 1860, and the second in three sections beginning in 1874. Despite a downgrading of the neighborhood, the market remains a viable entity.

Farther uptown, at 3rd and Division Sts. (2900-block) are **Italian Lake** and the **Obelisk**. The lake was created in the 1930s from a swamp and is in a baroque park setting. The obelisk, erected originally in 1867 at 2nd and State Sts., is a memorial to Civil War soldiers from Dauphin County.

Just outside the Uptown district, at the NW corner of Cameron and Maclay Sts., is the **Pennsylvania Farm Show Complex** ([20]), a 13-acre exposition hall that hosts many of Harrisburg's largest public events.

Allison Hill is the local name given to the eastern portion of the city that rises above the Susquehanna valley. It contains the **Mount Pleasant Historic District**, the area bounded generally by Martin L. King Blvd. (Market St.), Berryhill, Crescent, and 19th Sts. The city's oldest building, the **John Elder House**, is at 2426 Ellerslie St. Built about 1740, it is a private residence. **Bellevue Park**, an early planned residential community, was laid out in 1910 and lies south of Martin L. King Blvd. from 21st St. to Hale Ave. **McFarland House**, 2101 Bellevue Rd., was built in 1876 and was the home of the famous horticulturalist J. Horace McFarland.

Outside Harrisburg

Six miles north of downtown Harrisburg is the world-famous **Rockville Bridge** (⧄), a massive stone arch viaduct carrying the Pennsylvania Railroad main line over the Susquehanna at the base of Blue Mountain. The present bridge was built in 1902 and is the third span at this location. On the NRHP.

One-quarter mile north of the Rockville Bridge, at 5300 N. Front St., is ★★ **Fort Hunter Mansion and Park** (⧅)(1-1-1/2 hours), 599-5751, owned by the Dauphin County Parks and Recreation Department. The Federal style mansion, enlarged to its present size in 1814 and incorporating an older and smaller house, was the home of several prominent Harrisburg families. The house and park are on the NRHP. Open May thru December—Mon.-Sat. 10-4:30, Sun. 12-4:30. Guided tours of the mansion include a 10-minute slide presentation on the history of the house and fort. Tour admission: adults, $2.00; seniors, $1.50; students, $1.00; children under 6, free. No admission charge to the park, which includes picnic facilities, riverside walking path, and play area. The property also contains an ice house, barn, stable, corncrib, spring house, blacksmith shop, stable, and herb garden. There was originally a fort at this location, built in 1754 as one of a series along the Susquehanna from Harrisburg to Sunbury (Fort Augusta). The fort got its name from Samuel Hunter, who had built a mill here in 1725. Hunter was the son-in-law of one of Benjamin Chambers' brothers; Chambers was the founder of Chambersburg (see Franklin County).

Community Resources
Capital Region Chamber of Commerce, 114 Walnut St., 232-4121
PO: 813 Martin L. King Blvd. (Market St.), 257-2100
    Federal Sq. branch: 228 Walnut St., 257-2290
Public Library: 101 Walnut St., 234-4963
Harrisburg Hospital: Front & Chestnut Sts., 782-3131
Polyclinic Hospital: 2601 N. 3rd St., 782-4141

Community General Osteopathic Hospital: 4300 Londonderry Rd., 652-3000
Court House: Front & Market Sts., 255-2711
City Police: emergency 911, all other business 255-3131
City Hall: 10 N. 2nd St., 255-3011
State Police: Elmerton Ave. & Kohn Rd., 787-7777
Amtrak: Pennsylvania RR Station, 5th & Market Sts., 232-3916; (800) USA-RAIL
(872-7245)
Bus (Capitol Trailways): Pennsylvania RR Station, 5th & Market Sts., 232-4251
Bus (Greyhound): 1303 N. 7th St., 232-8601

State Resources

State Archives, 3rd & Forster Sts., 787-3023. Collects and preserves records of State
government, and some private papers relating to Pennsylvania history. Open Mon.-
Fri., 8:30-4:45.
State Library, Forum Bldg., 787-4440. Serves the reference needs of state government and acts as a regional library resource center for public, college, and special
libraries. Open for public use. Some materials may be borrowed by Pennsylvania
residents and by out-of-state residents attending Pennsylvania colleges. Main
reading room open Mon., and Wed.-Fri., 8:30-5, Tue., 8:30-8:30.

Hershey, unincorporated, pop. about 13,000. Arguably the most famous, and
probably the most beautiful, "company" town in America, the headquarters of
Hershey Foods Corporation, a Fortune 500 company and the largest non-govern-
mental employer in Dauphin County. The community has no legal status since it is
an unincorporated part of Derry Township, but there has been a settlement here
since 1724, when Derry Church was organized by Scotch-Irish immigrants.

Hershey as it is known today was developed beginning in 1903 by Milton
S. Hershey, founder of Hershey Foods. In that year he began construction on his
chocolate factory, moving the operation from Lancaster where it was already a
successful business. Mr. Hershey envisioned a storybook-like town for his employees that became a reality. Homes are well maintained, with tidy lawns along tree-
lined streets. Recreational and cultural facilities were provided and, as if to complete
the fairy tale, the streets were given names such as Chocolate and Cocoa, and the
street lights were in the shape of Hershey's chocolate kisses. Many of the landmarks
date from the Depression, which was part of Mr. Hershey's campaign to provide
jobs. The influence of the Hershey organization over the government of Derry Twp.
has resulted in carefully controlled development. Thus, the town has very little of
the unsightly strip type of development that lines main roads leading into most
American towns of this size and larger.

The Life and Work of Milton S. Hershey

Mr. Hershey was born in 1857 at "The Homestead", a large stone and frame home that is now the corporate headquarters of Hershey Foods Corporation. His great-grandfather had purchased this land and several other tracts in 1796. Milton Hershey lived at The Homestead only until 1866, when his parents moved to Lancaster. He began his business career at the age of 19 manufacturing caramels in Philadelphia. After working at his trade in Denver, Chicago, and New York, he returned to Lancaster in 1886 to start his own caramel making plant. His first ventures, for which his aunt had provided some capital, were not particularly successful. However, this business was profitable and was sold to the American Caramel Company in 1900 for $1 million. Hershey retained the right to manufacture chocolate and the machinery with which to do it, and broke ground in Hershey in 1903 for his new chocolate factory. By 1905, when the factory was completed, the community, still named Derry Church but changed to Hershey the next year, began to take on its present form. A bank was chartered, volunteer fire company organized, a ballroom and theater were built, and Hershey Park (now with the modernized name of Hersheypark) opened, all within the next two years.

Milton Hershey married rather late, at age 41. His wife Catherine, 15 years his junior, died after a long illness before her 43rd birthday, in 1915. The Hersheys had no children of their own, but as the business began to earn more money than they had the opportunity or desire to spend, they decided to establish a school for indigent boys. Milton, remembering his own unhappy childhood and early business failures, wanted to ensure that the boys learned a trade as well as the biblical values he had grown up with. This led them to establish the Hershey Industrial School (renamed the Milton Hershey School in 1951), which opened in 1909 with four students on 486 acres of farmland a short distance south of the chocolate factory. The school became coeducational in 1976. Its current enrollment is about 1,200.

The Hersheys' philanthropic work brought the town a library, zoo, consolidated elementary school, department store, streetcar line, and convention hall, all before 1925. The Depression years brought the Hershey Hotel, Rose Garden, hospital, sports arena, 16,000-seat stadium, and community center. All the while the Hershey Chocolate Corporation continued to prosper; the five-cent Hershey bar sold well during the Depression because it provided quick energy at a low price.

Milton Hershey died in 1945 at the age of 88, but he had provided for his philanthropy to continue after his death. The Hershey School Trust and M.S. Hershey Foundation are the charitable arms of the Hershey Foods and Hershey Entertainment & Resort Company operations.

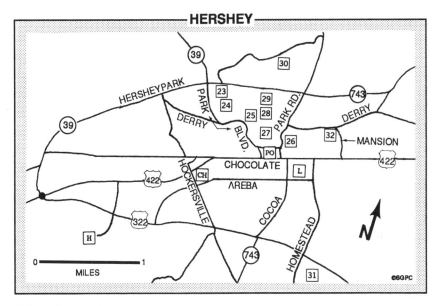

Points of Interest

Most attractions in Hershey are located within walking distance of each other. There are large parking lots accessible from Hersheypark Drive, adjacent to the **Information Center** (23) 534-3005, or (800) 533-3131, where you can leave your car and proceed on foot to any or all of the following places:

★★★★ **Chocolate World** (24)(15-20 min.), 534-4903. Open daily 9-4:45, except as follows: closes at 6:45 from first weekend in June thru Labor Day; opens at noon on Sun. only, January thru March; closed Thanksgiving, Christmas, New Year's Day, and Easter. Admission free. A beautiful building housing an outstanding attraction showing a simulated factory tour, using a tram ride with the audio-video show viewed on monitors on each car. The show is timed to coincide with displays along the walls, some animated. The stories of Milton Hershey's life and Hershey Foods are told in photos and overhead videos as you enter the museum. The displays are designed in a way that allows many people to be in the building at once without it seeming crowded. The trams end at the "Village of Shops", a tastefully (no pun intended) done area of souvenir stores and snack bars. Chocolate World was built in 1973 to replace tours of the factory which had to be abandoned due to excess demand.

★★★ **Museum of American Life** (25)(30-45 min.), 534-3439. Open daily except Thanksgiving, Christmas, and New Year's Day—Memorial Day thru Labor Day, 10-6, remainder of year 10-5. Admission: adults, $3.00; seniors age 62 and up

$2.50; children 4-18, $1.25; under 4, free. A very good museum depicting various eras and aspects of American life, including crafts, Conestoga wagons, musical instruments, clocks, firefighting equipment, and Indian and Eskimo artifacts. Displays are attractively presented, some are hands-on. A furnished house and three 12-minute videos tell the story of early Pennsylvania German life, covering their crafts, beliefs and practices, and language and cultural survival (viewing time for the videos is not included in the total museum visiting time above). There is also a theater and special exhibits gallery.

★★★ **Zoo America** (26)(45-60 min.), 534-3860. Open daily—June thru August 10-8, remainder of year 10-5, closed Thanksgiving, Christmas, and New Year's Day. Admission: adults, $3.00; seniors age 62 and up; $2.50, children 4-18, $1.75; under 4, free. Admission free if also going to Hersheypark (see fees below). Over 200 animals representing 75 species found in five regions of North America. Plant species also on display, all in natural settings.

Hersheypark (27) 534-3900. Open mid-May thru mid-September—weekends only before Memorial Day and after Labor Day, otherwise daily. Open 10:30 AM every day, closing hours vary, from 6 PM weekdays thru the first week in June, 8 PM second week in June, the week before Labor Day, and weekend days after Labor Day, and 10 PM all other times. Admission: Age 62 and over, $9.75; age 9-61, $16.75; age 4-8, $13.75; under 4, free. Admission includes all rides (except where height restrictions apply), all live entertainment, and Zoo America, excludes paddleboats and miniature golf. Other special rates available if staying all or part of two days—check at ticket office, or call information office (534-3900) between 8 AM and 5 PM. One of America's oldest amusement parks, open since 1907, remodeled in 1972. In addition to 45 rides, the park includes theaters, an amphitheater, six full-service restaurants as well as many snack stands, and theme areas such as Tudor Square, Der Deitschplatz, Rhine Land, and Carousel Circle.

The **Hersheypark Arena** (28) and **Hersheypark Stadium** (29) are open only when events are scheduled. The Arena seats about 10,000 and is home to the Hershey Bears American Hockey League team, the Hershey Impact of the American Indoor Soccer League, and regular shows such as Ice Capades and the Harlem Globetrotters. The Stadium has a seating capacity of 17,000 and is the site of football, drum and bugle corps competitions, and concerts. General information: 534-3900; box office: 534-3911.

★★★ **Hershey Gardens** (30)(1 hour), 534-3492, a 23-acre park near the Hershey Hotel, overlooking the town, containing nearly 14,000 roses of 800 varieties. There is an excellent collection of specimen trees—towering bald cypress, chestnut oak, China fir, and others—and four theme gardens: English, Colonial,

Japanese, and Rock. Open daily April thru October, 9-5, except 9-7 Memorial Day thru Labor Day. Admission: adults, $3.00; seniors age 62 and up, $2.50; children 4-18, $1.00; under 4, free.

A **package plan** offers admission to any two of the following: Museum of American Life, Zoo America, Hershey Gardens, and Hershey Lodge Cinema. Prices: adults, $5.00; children 4-18, $2.00; under 4, free. Package tickets are available at all of the above, plus the Information Center, Hotel Hershey, and Hershey Highmeadow Camp.

★★★ **Founders Hall** (31) 534-3557, headquarters of the Milton Hershey School, is located just off Homestead Rd. south of Governor Rd. (US 322). Built of native limestone, its most striking feature is the magnificent domed Rotunda, whose interior is made of Vermont marble. The Rotunda is a memorial to Milton Hershey. In the center of the floor is the Founders Medallion, a mosaic of Italian marble portraying twelve significant experiences in Hershey's life. Another highlight is the bronze statue of Mr. Hershey with his arm around the shoulder of one of his students. It was presented by the alumni on the school's 50th anniversary in 1959. The Visitors' Lounge features maps, slides, models, and dioramas intepreting the School's programs. The Chapel and Auditorium are behind the Rotunda. A carillon announces the Sunday morning chapel services. Open Mon.-Fri. 9-4, Sat.-Sun. 10-4, closed Thanksgiving, Christmas, and New Year's Day. Admission free. See also information on Milton Hershey School in this chapter.

Derry Church (32), Derry and Mansion Rds., is the oldest church in the community, founded in 1724. The original log building (1732), now encased in glass, had been used as a church, school, and post office of the village of Derry Church.

★★ **Indian Echo Caverns** (33)(45-60 min.), 566-8131, 3 mi. west of Hershey, 1 mi. south of Hummelstown. Open daily—Memorial Day to Labor Day, 9-6; April, May, September, and October, 10-4; March and November, weekends only 10-4. Admission: adults, $5.00; seniors 62 and up, $4.50;.children 4-11, $2.50. Guided tour takes 45 min. Some steep steps to reach cave entrance from ticket office. This cave was discovered about 1783, and has been open commercially since 1928. Directions: 500 feet south of Hummelstown-Middletown exit of US 322 on SR 2003, on the banks of Swatara Creek.

<u>Community Resources</u>
Information Center: 400 W. Hersheypark Dr., 534-3005
PO: 50 N. Linden Rd., 533-3356
Public Library: 30 E. Granada Ave., 533-6555

Hershey Medical Center: 500 University Dr., 531-8521
Derry Twp. Police: emergency 911, all other business 534-2202
Township Offices: 229 Hockersville Rd., 533-2057

Middletown, pop. 10,000. Originally named Portsmouth, Middletown is the oldest incorporated settlement in the county, founded in 1761. The present name stems rom its location halfway between Lancaster and Carlisle, the two major communities in the area at the time. Located at the mouth of Swatara Creek, it had been a transportation focus in Indian times. The town was the western terminus of the Union Canal, which joined the Susquehanna with the Schuylkill at Reading.

★★★**Three Mile Island** (34), 948-8395. 3 mi. south on PA 441. **Visitors Center** (30 min.) open daily 10-5 except Thanksgiving, Christmas, and New Year's Day. Admission free. Exhibits with photos, scaled-down models, and explanations of how nuclear reactors work. Outdoor observation deck overlooks plant. **Drive-around plant tours** (60 min.) by bus available, but may require advance notice due to plant activities. Use of cameras in the plant is restricted, but not at the Visitors Center. Very instructive exhibits and tour.

RECREATION FACILITIES

Harrisburg Senators (Baseball, Class AA Eastern League), RiverSide Stadium, City Island, Harrisburg, 255-3117.
Harrisburg Patriots (Football, Continental Interstate League), RiverSide Stadium, City Island, Harrisburg, 652-5006.
Hershey Bears (Hockey, American Hockey League), Hershey Arena, Hershey, 534-3911.
Hershey Impact (Soccer, American Indoor Soccer League), Hershey Arena, Hershey, 533-5170.
Penn National Race Course (Horse Racing), PA 743, 1 mi. north of I-81, exit 28, Grantville, 469-2211.
Middletown & Hummelstown Railroad, M&H RR Station, 136 Brown St., Middletown, 944-4435. Steam powered 11-mile round trip to Hummelstown. Operates June to October—Sat. and Sun. 1, 2:30, and 4 PM.

CALENDAR OF EVENTS

Note: Farm Show Complex is at 2300 N. Cameron St., Harrisburg, PA 17110. Events at this location list only the phone contact.
Mid-January, Harrisburg. **Pennsylvania Farm Show**, Farm Show Complex, 787-5373.

Late January, Harrisburg. **Pennsylvania International Auto Show**, Farm Show Complex, 657-1310.

Mid-February, Hershey. **Great American Chocolate Festival**, Hotel Hershey, 533-2171.

Late March, Harrisburg. **Pennsylvania National Arts and Crafts Show**, Farm Show Complex, 763-1254.

Early April, Harrisburg. **Pennsylvania Relief Show and Sale of Mennonite Crafts**, Farm Show Complex. 944-0293 (Middletown).

Early April, Harrisburg. **Shrine Circus**, Farm Show Complex. 236-4591.

Mid-April, Hershey. **Tulip Display**, Hershey Gardens, 621 Park Ave., Hershey, PA 17033, 534-3492.

Late April, Harrisburg. **Eastern National Antique Show and Sale**, Farm Show Complex. (215) 437-5534 (Allentown).

May 1, Fort Hunter. **May Day**, Fort Hunter Mansion. c/o Dauphin Co. Parks & Recreation Dept., 5300 N. Front St., 599-5751.

Late May, Harrisburg. **Arts Festival**, State Museum of Pa., 3rd & North Sts. c/o Nick Feher, P.O. Box 770, Harrisburg, PA 17108, 238-5180.

Mid-June, Middletown. **Historical Society Colonial Arts and Crafts Fair**, Hoffer Park. c/o Leon Daily, P.O. Box 248, Middletown, PA 17057, 944-3420.

Mid-June, Hershey. **Lady Keystone Open Golf Tournament**, Hershey Country Club. c/o LKO Office, 2101 N. Front St., Harrisburg, PA 17110, 238-9344.

Mid-June, Hershey. **Rose Display**, Hershey Gardens, Hotel Rd. 534-3492.

Mid-June, Harrisburg. **Central Pennsylvania Jazz Festival**, Sheraton East Hotel, I-83 & Union Deposit Rd. (exit 29). c/o Joe Intreri, P.O. Box 10738, Harrisburg, PA 17105, 257-5441.

Late June, Hershey. **Hershey Arts Festival**, Hershey Botanical Gardens. c/o Hershey Gardens, 534-3492.

Late June, Grantville. **Sherwood Hall Country Festival**, Harrison School Rd. c/o Sherwood Hall Country Festival, P.O. Box 288, Grantville, PA 17028, 865-3911 (Annville) or 469-7486.

Mid-July, Harrisburg. **Antique Fire Apparatus Show and Muster**, Riverfront Park. c/o Dave Buskey, 7210 Chambers Hill Rd., Harrisburg, PA 17111, 564-6935.

Mid-July, Harrisburg. **Harrisburg Historic Canoe Tour**, Susquehanna River, Fort Hunter to City Island. c/o Dauphin Co. Parks & Recreation Dept., 255-1369.

Labor Day weekend, Harrisburg. **Kipona Celebration**, Riverfront Park. c/o Harrisburg Parks & Recreation Dept., 255-3020.

Mid-September, Harrisburg. **RV Expo**, Farm Show Complex, 774-3470.

Mid-September, Fort Hunter. **Fort Hunter Day**, Fort Hunter Mansion, 5300 N. Front St., 599-5751.

Late September, Harrisburg. **All-American Dairy Show**, Farm Show Complex, 787-2905.

DAUPHIN CO.

Early October, Hershey. **Fall Meet of the Antique Auto Club of America,** Hersheypark Stadium, 534-3829.

Mid-October, Harrisburg. **Pennsylvania National Horse Show,** Farm Show Complex, 236-1600.

Late October, Middletown. **Pennsylvania International Air Show,** Harrisburg International Airport, 948-5760.

Late October, Harrisburg. **Pennsylvania 4-H Horse Show,** Farm Show Complex, (814) 863-3657 (State College, PA).

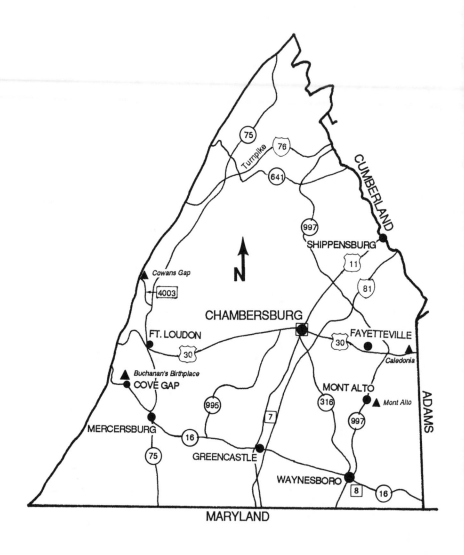

FRANKLIN

Created: September 9, 1784, as the 14th county, from part of Cumberland County
County Seat: Chambersburg
Land Area: 754 square miles
Population (1989 est.): 121,000
Area code: 717

Franklin, the westernmost county in the PDC, is bordered on the east and west by mountains, and has both the highest point (2,450 feet) and the highest average elevation of any PDC county. The central portion of the county lies in the Cumberland Valley and contains most of the population. This is a productive farming area; the county ranks fourth among the thirteen in the PDC in value of farm products sold. Dairying, general farming, and fruit growing are the major agricultural pursuits. There is a small Amish community in Path Valley in the northernmost part of the county and another near Shippensburg.

Franklin County's economy today reflects a mix of manufacturing, agriculture and food processing, and government employment. The county's largest employer is the Letterkenny Army Depot, headquarters for the U.S. Army Depot System Command, or DESCOM, which coordinates 12 depots around the world and more than 39,000 employees.

Several food companies in the county produce snack and frozen foods and process locally grown fruit. The major manufactured products are clothing, industrial power transmission equipment, and refrigeration equipment. The county's industrial centers are Chambersburg, Waynesboro, and Greencastle.

Historical Highlights

Despite being on the "frontier" of Pennsylvania in the 1700s, the county was settled relatively early because the Cumberland Valley provided a natural travel corridor for people moving west along already established paths from the eastern part of the colony. Chambersburg dates from 1735, and Shippensburg, straddling the Cumberland County border, was founded in 1730. Benjamin Chambers arrived with his three brothers from Ireland in 1726 and settled along Conococheague Creek at the present site of the town which bears his name. He received from William Penn's heirs a license to sell lots in a 400-acre tract. A majority of early inhabitants

163

were Scotch-Irish; the Germans, the largest single nationality now, did not arrive in great numbers until about 1810. Early relations with Indians were peaceful, but as a result of troop movements through the county to reach the fighting in western Pennsylvania during the French and Indian War, forts were built beginning in 1756, among them Chambers Fort (at Chambersburg), Fort Loudon (two miles southeast of the small present-day community bearing its name), Fort McCord (about 10 miles northwest of Chambersburg), and Steele's Fort (3 miles east of Mercersburg at Church Hill).

The county was the birthplace of Pennsylvania's only President, James Buchanan, born a few miles west of Mercersburg in 1791.

Franklin County was visited three times by Confederate soldiers during the Civil War. In October, 1862, a raiding party of Gen. J.E.B. Stuart visited the Chambersburg area in an attempt to cut off Union supplies funneling through the town via the Cumberland Valley Railroad. Several buildings were burned but on the whole the mission was a failure. About nine months later, in late June, 1863, part of Lee's army spent several days at Chambersburg as it passed through the county on its drive into Northern territory. While restocking his 80,000 troops with supplies, Lee made the decision to move east toward Philadelphia rather than north toward Harrisburg. It is thought that this decision doomed the Confederate cause, as the Union forces took advantage of Lee's delay in Chambersburg to move south. They met several days later at Gettysburg. The most lasting effect of Confederate incursions into the county occurred in July, 1864, when 3,000 troops led by Gen. Jubal Early burned Chambersburg, then a town of 5,000, when it failed to deliver a high ransom. The town was unable to defend itself and was virtually leveled, but with a minimal loss of life. Chambersburg was the only northern city destroyed or intentionally attacked during the war.

PLACES OF INTEREST

Chambersburg, pop. 16,000. Has been the seat since Franklin County was created in 1784. Established as a town in 1764 by Benjamin Chambers, who had settled there in 1726. Originally Falling Spring, Chambers Fort, and then Chambers Town, the present name was adopted in 1784. Due to the burning by Confederate troops in 1864, few buildings predate the Civil War. Despite the lack of Colonial period structures, Chambersburg is a very attractive town, particularly the downtown area and the neighborhood around Wilson College on Philadelphia Avenue (US 11). Main St. and Lincolnway in the downtown business district comprise the NRHP **Historic District**. The entire community is tidy and well-kept.

A brochure describing a **downtown walking tour** (45 min., not including museum stops) is available from Greater Chambersburg Chamber of Commerce. The tour includes, among others, these sites:

★★ Old Franklin County Jail and Heritage Center (1)(30-40 min.), 175 E. King St. (NW corner of 2nd), 264-6364. Open January to mid-April—Tue. 5-8 PM, Wed.-Thu. 12-4; mid-April thru November—the preceding hours plus Fri.-Sat., 9:30-4, closed December. The Georgian building, on the NRHP, was the county prison from 1818 to 1970, the longest continuous period of operation of any prison in Pennsylvania. Saved from destruction by local residents, the original front portion of the building now houses the Heritage Center, displaying home implements, coins, women's and children's clothing, guns, and other items from Franklin County. There is a kitchen and apothecary shop set up as they might have appeared in colonial times. Unfortunately, due to inadequate space and the interior design of the jail, the museum materials can't be properly displayed. The 1880 cellblock to the rear of the original jail can also be toured; some original furnishings and hardware from that period remain.

Presbyterian Church of Falling Spring (②), 221 N. Main St., on the north side of Falling Spring. The main part of the church was built in 1803, but the congregation dates from 1734. Benjamin Chambers is buried in the cemetery behind the church. Church is open during regular services.

Site of Fort Chambers (③), on the south side of W. King St., 1/2 block west of Main. Benjamin Chambers lived on this site, and later built the fort here. The fort was torn down prior to the Civil War.

Memorial Square (④), intersection of Main St. and Lincolnway, on NRHP. The square was established by Benjamin Chambers as the main focal point for the community, and it has remained so ever since. The centerpiece (literally!) is **Memorial Fountain**, erected in 1878 to honor Franklin County casualties from all wars the country had been involved in up to that time. On the southwest corner of

the square, in front of Unitas National Bank, is the **Burning of Chambersburg Stone Marker**, indicating the number of buildings destroyed and the value of property lost during the burning. The northeast corner houses the **Franklin County Courthouse** (⌂), built in the 1840s and on the NRHP. The interior was gutted during the burning and then rebuilt.

Borough Building (□), 100 S. 2nd St. (SE corner of Queen), was built in 1830 and survived the burning. It was a market house at the time of the Civil War.

Masonic Temple (⑤), 74 S. 2nd St. (NE corner of Queen), the oldest such building in Pennsylvania, built 1823-24, and still used for masonic purposes. On NRHP.

John Brown House (⑥), 225 E. King St. The abolitionist John Brown and some of his assistants boarded at this house while he secretly transported weapons south in preparation for the raid in 1859 at Harpers Ferry. The owners of the home were supporters of the Underground Railroad.

Outside Downtown

★★★**Museum of Natural History**, 1015 Philadelphia Ave. (US 11 north), in the Paul Havens Science Center on the campus of Wilson College, 264-4141, ext. 241. Open Mon. 7-9 PM, Tue.-Thu. 10-2, Sat. 9-11 AM. Admission free. A new and still evolving museum containing a 3,000-specimen egg collection, all dating from before 1890; a herbarium with 8,200 specimens, insects, rocks, fossils, bird collection, and Pennsylvania waterfowl collection. Among the prized specimens are a passenger pigeon egg and an extinct Carolina parakeet. The native American passenger pigeon became extinct about 1914. Special programs and workshops for school children are offered. Wilson is one of the oldest four-year women's liberal arts colleges in the country, founded 1869.

★★ **Frontier Trail Auto Tour** (2-1/2-3 hours, not including stops), a 95-mile tour of southern Franklin County featuring historic churches, sites of forts, James Buchanan's birthplace, Mercersburg, both of Franklin County's covered bridges, a one-room school, the Renfrew Museum, two state parks, and several other features. There are 19 points of interest in all, not including two in Chambersburg described above. Route is signed, but brochure, available from Chamber of Commerce, is essential for descriptions. Tour includes all of the sites described under Fayetteville, Fort Loudon, Greencastle, Mercersburg, and Waynesboro.

Community Resources

Greater Chambersburg Chamber of Commerce: 75 S. 2nd St., 264-7101
Visitors Information Center: 1235 Lincolnway E., 261-1200
PO: 308 Lincolnway E., 263-8581
Public Library: 102 N. Main St., 263-1054
Franklin Co. Library: 35 Ragged Edge Rd., 264-9663

Chambersburg Hospital: 112 N. 7th St., 264-5171
Court House: NE corner Memorial Sq., 264-4125
Police: 264-4131
Borough Offices: 100 S. 2nd St., 264-5151
State Police: 440 Walker Rd., 264-5161
Bus: 56 S. 3rd St., 263-1914

Fayetteville, unincorporated, pop. about 3,200. **Totem Pole Playhouse**, 9555 Golf Course Rd. (SR 2028), four miles east, just south of intersection of US 30 & PA 233), 352-2164. Well-known summer theater. **Thaddeus Stevens Blacksmith Shop**, US 30 just west of jct. of PA 233 in Caledonia State Park. Site of iron furnace and blacksmith shop built in 1837 by Thaddeus Stevens, noted abolitionist and Congressman from Pennsylvania. Furnace was destroyed by Confederates on June 26, 1863.

Fort Loudon, unincorporated, pop. about 700. Site of **Fort Loudon**, 1.5 mi. east, turn south off US 30. Display board shows site plan; original buildings no longer standing.

Greencastle, pop. 3,900. Founded 1782. Pretty town with center square. The 300-600 blocks of E. Baltimore St. (PA 16), and the square itself, are particularly attractive.

Old Brown's Mill School (7), 3-1/2 mi. north at Kauffman, a memorial to the one-room school, maintained by the Pennsylvania Historical and Museum Commission. On the NRHP, built in 1836 and used until 1921. Directions: From US 11, 3.3 mi. north of PA 16, turn right (east) on Kauffman Rd. (SR 2016), go 0.5 mi., bear right after railroad underpass on Browns Mill Rd. (SR 2001). School is 0.3 mi. on left at Angle Rd.

Site of **Enoch Brown School Massacre** of July 26, 1764, is commemorated by monument and small park, located 3 miles NW of Greencastle. Enoch Brown, the teacher, and all but one of his pupils in attendance that day were scalped and killed by Indians. Directions: Turn left off US 11 0.2 mi. north of PA 16 on Williamson Ave. (SR 3002), go 1.9 mi., turn right on Stone Bridge Rd. (SR 3013) for 0.7 mi., then left for 0.2 mi. on Enoch Brown Rd. to park.

Mercersburg (1-1-1/2 hours), pop. 1,800. Founded 1750 and originally called Black's Town. A beautiful small community, worth seeing for its unspoiled charm alone. The NRHP **Historic District** encompasses Main and Seminary Streets. Mercersburg is the home of **Mercersburg Academy**, which had its origins as

Marshall College, founded in 1787 and merged in 1853 with Franklin College, at which time it was relocated to Lancaster. The Academy is two blocks east of Main St. (PA 16/75/416) on Seminary St.—turn at the square in the center of town. A noted 43-bell English Carillon is housed in the Gothic stone chapel. The log cabin in which President James Buchanan was born stands on the campus, having been relocated from its original site at Cove Gap. Buchanan was the only President born in Pennsylvania and the only bachelor. First Lady duties at the White House were assumed by his niece, Harriet Lane, who was born in the house at 16 N. Main St. Buchanan as a boy lived across the street at no. 17; historical markers commemorate both houses. Jane Irwin, wife of President William Henry Harrison, and Elizabeth Irwin, mother of President Benjamin Harrison, were born in a stone home adjacent to Anderson's Mill along the West Branch of Conococheague Creek about 4 miles southeast of town.

Buchanan's Birthplace State Park, 3.3 mi. NW, bear right off PA 16 at Cove Gap onto SR 3011, go 0.7 mi.. Monument marking the site of the log cabin, picnic facilities.

Mont Alto, pop. 1,600. Site of Mont Alto State Park and branch of Penn State University.

Shippensburg, pop. 5,300, of which 800 in Franklin Co. See Cumberland Co.

Waynesboro, pop. 10,000. Established 1749 by John Wallace. A prominent early inhabitant was John Bourns, a nephew of the poet Robert Burns; he ran a blacksmith shop here. Today a manufacturing and farming center and the second largest town in the county. The borough hall and library are on the NRHP. The largest industries are the Frick Co., makers of refrigeration equipment, and Landis Tool Co. There is an outlet shopping center with 25 stores at 3rd & Walnut Sts. (turn south off Main St. (PA 16) one block east of the square).

★★ **Renfrew Museum and Park** (⑧), 1010 E. Main St. (SW corner of Welty Rd., 762-4723. Museum open last weekend in April thru mid-November—Thu., Sat., Sun. 1-4. Admission: age 12 & over, $1.00. Park open daylight hours, free. Museum contains decorative arts and furniture from 1790-1830 and is located in the 1815 Royer-Nicodemus stone farmhouse, on the NRHP.

Community Resources
Greater Waynesboro Chamber of Commerce: 323 E. Main St., 762-7123
PO: 118 E. Main St., 762-1513
Public Library: 45 E. Main St., 762-3335
Waynesboro Hospital: 501 E. Main St., 765-4000
Borough Police: 762-2131
Borough Offices: 55 E. Main St., 762-2101

COVERED BRIDGES

Martin's Mill, Weaver Rd. (Conococheague Creek), 4 mi. SW of Greencastle, Town truss design, built 1839, rebuilt after 1972 flood.
Witherspoon, Welty Rd. (Licking Creek), 4 mi. SE of Mercersburg, Burr truss design, built 1883.

RECREATION FACILITIES

Buchanan's Birthplace State Park, Cove Gap, 485-3948 (see **Mercersburg**).
Caledonia State Park, US 30, 4 mi. east of Fayetteville, 352-2161.
Cowans Gap State Park, summit of Tuscarora Mtn., 7 mi. NW of Fort Loudon, 485-3948. Directions: From US 30 at Ft. Loudon, go north on PA 75 for 3.8 mi., turn left on Richmond Rd. (SR 4003) for 3.0 mi.
Mont Alto State Park, PA 233, 1-1/2 mi. east of Mont Alto, 352-2161.

CALENDAR OF EVENTS

Mid-July, Mont Alto. **Visiting Artists Festival**, 210 Main St. c/o A Little Gallery, P.O. Box 397, Mont Alto, PA 17237, 749-3831.
Late July, Chambersburg. **Chambersfest**, Downtown. c/o Chamber of Commerce, 75 S. 2nd St., Chambersburg, PA 17201, 264-7101. (In 1989 the 125th anniversary of the burning of the town will be commemorated.)
Late August, Chambersburg. **Franklin County Fair**, Chambersburg Rod & Gun Club, 3725 Warm Spring Rd. (PA 995), 8 mi. SW of Chambersburg. c/o Franklin Co. Fair, P.O. Box 49, Chambersburg, PA 17201, 264-6359.
Mid-September, Chambersburg. **International Food Festival**, Memorial Sq. c/o Chamber of Commerce, 75 S. 2nd St., Chambersburg, PA 17201, 264-7101.
Late September, Mercersburg. **Apple Fest and Town Fair**, E. Seminary St. c/o Tuscarora Tourist Council, 328-5701.

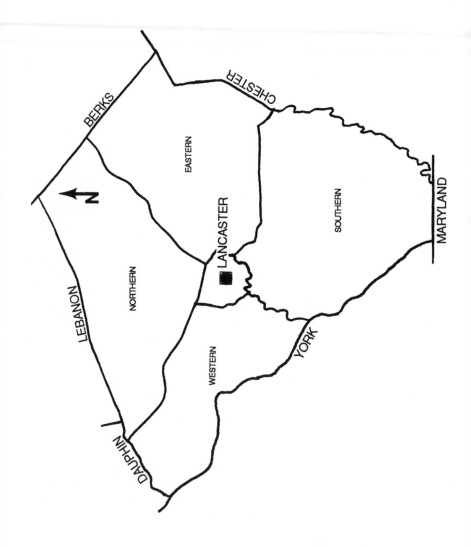

LANCASTER

Created: May 10, 1729, as the 4th county, from part of Chester County
County Seat: Lancaster
Land Area: 946 square miles
Population (1989 est.): 410,000
Area code: 717, except for Adamstown (484 exchange), Christiana (593), Denver (267), and Terre Hill (445) areas, which are 215

Lancaster (pronounced LANK-uh-stir, not LANG-kas-ter as are most of the Lancasters in America) is the largest county in the PDC and is considered by most people to be the heart of the Pennsylvania Dutch region. It is home to the largest concentration of Amish and Mennonite people in the state.

The dominant ancestry group, as expected, is German, yet this group represents a smaller percentage of the total population than it does in Adams, Berks, or York Counties. The next largest groups are English and Irish. In recent years there has been a large influx of Hispanic residents, with most settling in Lancaster city.

The county has an extensive amount of level to gently rolling terrain, which, combined with extremely fertile soil, contributes to the high proportion of land being farmed. The southern portion of the county, particularly near the Susquehanna River, is the hilliest region. There are only two small isolated mountainous areas: the Furnace Hills, lying along the Lebanon County border in the extreme north, and Welsh Mountains, in the eastern section southeast of New Holland. Most of the county is underlain by limestone.

Lancaster is Pennsylvania's leading agricultural county by any standard, and is justly deserving of its title "The Garden Spot". Lancaster County farm production per acre is about double the average for the PDC, and four times that of the state.

Lancaster is also one of Pennsylvania's fastest growing counties, and for the past 20 years has been adding an average of over 4,000 new residents a year. While this is a sign of a strong economy, it is putting pressure on the agricultural sector through the conversion of farmland into housing developments, shopping centers, industrial parks, and roads. This in turn escalates land values of the remaining farms well above what they could command as working farms. The bountiful farmland is the county's greatest natural resource, and its gradual diminution is of concern, not only to farmers, but to other local residents. In 1984 the Lancaster Farmland Trust was established to work to protect county farmland from succumbing to urban sprawl, and to encourage the designation of Agricultural Preserve Areas. The Trust is a not-for-profit organization with about 300 members, most of whom are Lancaster Countians. It attempts to influence planning and zoning decisions made by the county's 61 separate and autonomous municipalities in ways that preserve what it views as an irreplaceable asset.

Historical Highlights

Lancaster was the first county to be established after the three original counties (Philadelphia, Bucks, and Chester) were set up by William Penn in 1682.

The earliest permanent European settlement was that of Hans Herr and a group of Swiss Mennonites who established a community a few miles south of Lancaster. The house named for him, but built by his son Christian, dates from 1719, and stood along what had been an Indian path from the Delaware to the Susquehanna.

The first wave of German immigration arrived in the county beginning about 1732, when the Ephrata Cloister was established by Conrad Beissel. This was one of the first religious communal societies in America. The Moravians followed in 1746, setting up a school at Lititz. The first of the Amish and Mennonites probably arrived about 1760 from Berks County, although there may have been a community in the northernmost part of the county, in what are now East and West Cocalico Townships, as early as 1742.

Prior to the time of the Revolution, the town of Lancaster had become the largest and most important inland town in the colonies. The Germans were by then building large wagons in the Conestoga Creek valley to take their crops to market, hence, the derivation of the name "Conestoga wagon". They were also making what became known as the Pennsylvania long rifle, but the basic design originated in Germany. Thus, Lancaster became the first center of rifle manufacturing. Several iron ore furnaces dotted the countryside in the county. Glass making started at Manheim in 1764.

Lancaster served as the colonies' capital, but only for one day, September 27, 1777, as the Continental Congress fled Philadelphia during the British occupation. The city was not considered safe enough from possible British advances, so the capital was relocated to York, on the west side of the Susquehanna, where it remained for nine months before being returned to Philadelphia. Lancaster had a longer tenure as the seat of Pennsylvania's government, serving as the capital from 1799 to 1812.

The county is noteworthy for its place in transportation development. The country's first toll turnpike, linking Lancaster and Philadelphia, a distance of 65 miles, was built between 1792 and 1794. One of Pennsylvania's first railroads, the Harrisburg, Portsmouth, Mt. Joy, and Lancaster, was chartered in 1833. The Strasburg Railroad, the oldest short line in America, still takes sightseers over the "road to Paradise". Robert Fulton, inventor of the first successful steamboat, the *Clermont*, was born in southern Lancaster County.

Lancaster County had numerous stations on the "Underground Railroad" in the 1840s and 1850s, among the most important of which was Columbia. What some consider the first skirmish of the Civil War occurred in 1851 at Christiana, on the Chester County border. There, a man named Edward Gorsuch, attempting to retrieve his runaway slaves, was killed by local sympathizers. The courts refused to prosecute the killer or any of the townspeople who stood by and watched the killing, thus infuriating Southerners.

A few years later, James Buchanan, an attorney, Secretary of State under James Polk, Minister to Russia, and the only Pennsylvanian to occupy the White House, was elected President while living at Wheatland, the estate just west of Lancaster that he had purchased in 1848. After his term he retired to Wheatland and lived there until his death in 1868.

Lancaster County is noted today as the home of several well-known industries: Armstrong World Industries (formerly Armstrong Cork), maker of floor and ceiling coverings; Hamilton Watch; Victor F. Weaver (Weaver's frozen chicken); Playskool, Inc. (toys); and Ford Motor Company New Holland division (farm equipment).

PLACES OF INTEREST

Because of the large number of attractions, the county has been divided into five regions, as shown on the map heading this chapter: Lancaster and Environs, and Northern, Eastern, Southern, and Western. A good place to begin your visit to Lancaster County is at the **Pennsylvania Dutch Convention & Visitor's Bureau** (1), 501 Greenfield Rd., 299-8901. Located at the Greenfield Rd. exit of US 30 on the east side of Lancaster. Open daily except Thanksgiving, Christmas, and New Year's Day. Hours vary month to month—the minimum hours are 9-5. The earliest opening in peak season is 8 AM and the latest closing is 8 PM Fri. & Sat., 7 PM Mon.-

Thu., and 6 PM Sun. Free information on tourist attractions, accommodations, restaurants, shopping, and services, and personnel on hand to answer questions. You should be aware, however, that the Center does not have brochures for establishments that are not members of the PDCVB, and this includes some non-profit museums. The 36-minute movie shown in the auditorium, "**The Lancaster Experience**", is an introduction to the area, mainly to the Amish and their way of life, but it shows little about the county's major places of interest. Admission: adults, $2.00. Shows April to November—daily on the hour from 9-4, Sun. 10-4; additional 5 PM show Mon.-Sat. in June, July, and August; no 4 PM show in November. Shows Sat. and Sun. 10-3 in March, Sat. only 10-3 in December. By appointment only January and February.

The attractions with an Amish or "Dutch" theme are overwhelmingly oriented toward tourists. Most are true to life in their representations, a few are less authentic. Some knowledge of the area, its history, and its people can be gained at each attraction. Using the descriptions and ratings, you can decide for yourself which sights are most worth visiting.

LANCASTER AND ENVIRONS

Lancaster, pop. 57,000, with suburbs 160,000. County seat, and major industrial and trading center for the county. First settlement dates from 1721, known as Hickorytown. Town laid out 1730 by John Wright, who named it for his home in England, Lancashire. The boundaries were set in 1742 at one mile from the central square (now Penn Square) in all the cardinal directions. They remained unchanged for 200 years until a series of annexations of parts of adjoining townships began. The city boundary now looks like a masterpiece of gerrymandering, although its original square shape is still recognizable.

Lancaster is the home of the oldest tobacco shop in the U.S. under the same family ownership, one of Pennsylvania's first Jewish synagogues, Woolworth's first successful five-and-ten, and the largest stockyards east of Chicago which operated until just a few years ago. The central business district mixes attractively its many historic sites with new office buildings, parking garages, and shops.

Lancaster is the home of Franklin and Marshall College, founded as Franklin College in 1787, the nation's 14th oldest, located along College Ave. on the west side of the city. Three of its buildings—Old Main, Goethean Hall, and Diagnothian Hall—are on the NRHP.

★★★★ **Downtown** (about 4 hours). Plan to explore this area on foot, the only way to really see the many worthwhile and unheralded sights. Begin at the **Information**

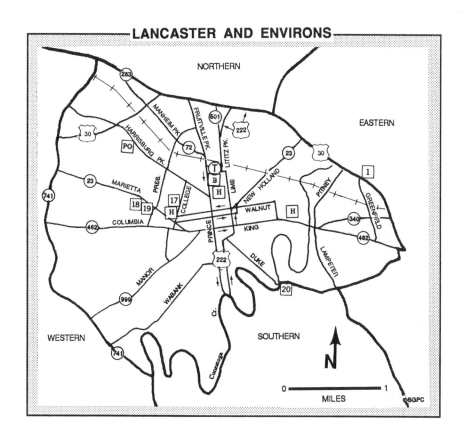

LANCASTER AND ENVIRONS

Center (2)(10-15 min.) in the former NRHP Southern Market house at 100 S. Queen St. (SW corner of Vine), 392-1776. This is the origination point of the ★★★ **Historic Lancaster Walking Tour** (1-1/2-2 hours), an enjoyable guided walk to and through some of the city's finest historic sites. Information Center open daily April thru October—Mon.-Sat. 9-4, Sun. and hol. 12-3. Walking Tours daily Mon.-Sat. 10 and 1:30, Sun. and hol. 1:30 only, twilight tours Mon. at 6:30, June thru August. Tours by reservation only November thru March. Admission $3.00. The guides are knowledgeable and reveal many unknown facts about the places and the city, and there is an excellent 10-minute narrated slide show before the walk gets underway. However, the tour misses some of the important attractions, so take time to see them afterwards.

The Walking Tour includes some, but not all, of the places described below, and some not listed:

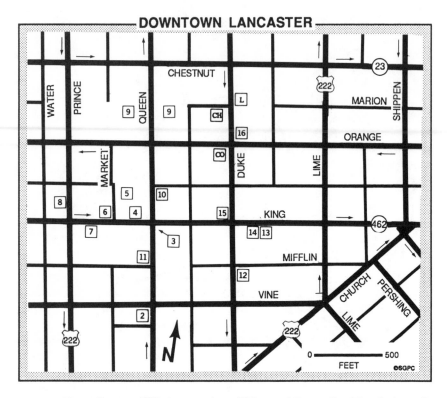

DOWNTOWN LANCASTER

Penn Square (③), intersection of King and Queen Sts. The city's traditional central focal point. The **Soldiers and Sailors Monument** in the center of the Square was erected in 1874 to honor Civil War dead. In the early 1970s the Square was remodeled—the quadrants were converted from parking areas to sidewalks, and for the first time, the Monument was no longer isolated in a sea of moving traffic. The original county court house, and meeting place of Continental Congress on September 27, 1777, the one day that Lancaster was the nation's capitol, stood on the southwest corner.

On the King Street side of the northwest quadrant is the old city hall building, built 1795 and on the NRHP, now the ★★ **Heritage Center of Lancaster County** (④)(20-30 min.), 299-6440. Open May thru mid-November—Tue.-Sat., 10-4. Admission free. It houses works by Lancaster County craftsmen, including long rifles, clocks, quilts, frakturs, woodenware, and other items. There are also changing exhibits, a lecture series, and gallery talks.

A walkway in the northwest quadrant of the Square leads to ★★★ **Central Market** (⑤), on the NRHP and the only remaining true farmers' market in the city, built 1889. Open Tue., Fri., Sat. 6 AM-2 PM. These markets, and the buildings housing them, are unique to the PDC (there are similar ones in Harrisburg, York, Columbia, and Hanover).

Steinman Park, a small pedestrian arcade on the south side of W. King St., was built in the mid-1970s, and connects with the Central Parking Garage, one of four city-owned garages serving the downtown area. The park was donated by the Steinman family, who owns the three local newspapers and a number of other businesses in town.

The **Hager Arcade** (⑥), 25 W. King St. (NW corner of Market, the alley running north past Central Market), houses boutiques in a NRHP building that had been Hager's Department Store. The building's unique architecture has largely been retained.

Steinman Hardware Company stood at 26-28 W. King St. from its founding in 1744 until it closed in 1965. At the time it was the oldest continuously operating hardware store in the country.

Major General John Reynolds (⑦), killed on the first day of the Battle of Gettysburg, was born and lived in the house at 42 W. King St. A historic marker commemorates the site.

★★★ The **Fulton Opera House** (⑧), 12 N. Prince St., 394-7133, is one of the oldest theaters in the country, built in 1852 and on the NRHP. The interior has been magnificently restored, and tours are available Mon.-Fri. 9-5; call in advance for an appointment. Admission: adults, $1.50; seniors and students, $1.00; children under 12, 75¢. The theater is now used for concerts, dance, and special events.

Lancaster Square (⑨), an office-retail-hotel complex, straddles the 100-block of N. Queen St. Some corporate offices of Armstrong World Industries occupy the building on the west side of the street, and the Brunswick Hotel is at the SE corner of Chestnut St. The large building on the NE corner of Queen and Orange is occupied by offices and manufacturing facilities of Hamilton Technologies, the well-known watch and clock manufacturer headquartered in Lancaster.

F.W. Woolworth Variety Store (⑩), 21 N. Queen St., was the first successful store in the chain. It was opened, at a different site, by Frank W. Woolworth in 1879, following the failure of his initial store in Utica, N.Y.

★★ **Newseum** (⑪)(5-10 min.), 28 S. Queen St., 291-8600, is a window exhibit of the evolution of newspaper production in Lancaster. It is located in the production building of Lancaster Newspapers, Inc.

Trinity Church (⑫), 31 S. Duke St. (SE corner of Mifflin), houses Lancaster's oldest congregation. The present building was dedicated in 1766. The interior of the church houses a 1774 Tannenberg organ. The steeple is 195 feet high, is modeled after, and was second only in height to Christ Church in Philadelphia at the time of its completion in 1794. Free guided tours of the church are given Sunday at 10 AM and 12:15 PM; the church is also on the Walking Tour. Thomas Wharton, President of Pennsylvania in 1777-78, and Governor (1790-99) Thomas Mifflin, are buried in the churchyard.

★★ **Charles Demuth House and Garden** (⑬)(30 min.), 120 E. King St., 299-9940, the home of the noted early 20th century artist (1883-1935). Open Mon.-Sat. 10-4, Sun. 12-3. Admission free. A small gallery of art and educational exhibits occupy the second floor parlor. The home was built in the late 18th century and is typical of its day. The garden in the rear was Demuth's inspiration for many of his paintings.

Demuth Tobacco Shop (⑭), 114 E. King St., 397-6613, is the oldest tobacco shop (founded 1770) in America still in business, now owned by the Demuth Foundation. There is a collection of antique firemen's memorabilia in the shop.

Old Lancaster County Court House (⑮), 43 E. King St. (NW corner of Duke). This Roman Revival structure was built in 1852; the two additions on either side of the steps were built in the 1920s. The present court house was built in the 1970s and is directly behind this building at 50 N. Duke St. (SW corner of Orange).

St. James Episcopal Church (⑯), NE corner of Duke and Orange Sts. One of Lancaster's oldest churches, founded 1744. Open to visitors Mon-Sat. 8:30-5, and on Sun. during services, also on the walking tour. George Ross, a signer of the Declaration of Independence, and General Edward Hand, Revolutionary War adjutant to George Washington (see **Rock Ford Plantation**, below), are buried in the church cemetery.

Several blocks north and east of Penn Square are especially attractive for their elegant row houses; these include the 100-block of E. King St., the 100- and 200-blocks of E. Orange St., and the unit and 100-blocks of N. Lime St. Especially attractive is a Georgian colonial mansion on the NW corner of Orange and Shippen

Sts. It was built in the 1750s and had been occupied by John Passmore, Lancaster's first mayor.

Outside Downtown

★★★ **North Museum** ([17])(1 hour), NW corner College and Buchanan Aves., 291-3941. Open Wed.-Sat. 9-5, Sun. 1:30-5. Admission free, donation appreciated. An excellent natural history museum containing Egyptian artifacts, American Indian tools and implements, stuffed Pennsylvania mammals and birds, Lancaster County rocks and minerals, fossils, wildflowers, and more.

★★★ **Wheatland** ([18])(45-60 min.), 1120 Marietta Ave. (PA 23), 392-8721. Open daily except Thanksgiving, April 1 thru November 30—10-4:15. Admission: adults, $3.75; children 6-12, $1.50; under 6, free. The Federal style house was built in 1828, and was the home of President James Buchanan from 1848 until his death in 1868. Much of the furniture was Buchanan's. Other than a few improvements such as indoor plumbing, made by the person who owned the house from the time of Buchanan's niece Harriet Lane's death in 1903 until the Lancaster County Historical Society bought it in 1936, the house and furnishings are authentic. The property originally contained 22 acres, but now has only four.

Lancaster County Historical Society ([19])(45-60 min.), 230 N. President Ave. (SW corner of Marietta), 392-4633. Open Tue., Wed., Fri., Sat. 9:30-4:30, Thu. 9:30-9:30. Admission free. Scheduled to reopen April, 1989 following renovations. Contains changing exhibits of local artifacts, the largest private collection of Jacob Eichholtz portraits, and works of other local artists, as well as items related to Lancaster County history and culture.

Victorian Wine Cellars, 2225 Marietta Ave. (PA 23), 295-WINE (9463). Open Tue.-Sat. 12-6:30 and holiday Mondays. Production facility only, no vineyard on premises. Small group tours, tastings and sales. At press time no charge for tours, but format of tours may change, and a charge was being considered.

★★★ **Rock Ford Plantation** ([20])(45-60 min.), 881 Rock Ford Rd., 392-7223. Open April thru November—Tue.-Sat. 10-4, Sun. 12-4, closed Thanksgiving and day after. Admission: adults, $2.50; children 6-18, $1.00; under 6, free. Built about 1792, this was the home of General Edward Hand, an Irish-educated doctor who was adjutant general to George Washington in the Revolution, then later served in Congress, the Pennsylvania General Assembly, and was a burgess of Lancaster. All furnishings date from 1810 or earlier, and the house has been very well preserved, even down to the original color paint on the walls. Also on the property is the

Kauffman Museum, located on the second floor of the barn, containing 18th and 19th century pewter, kitchen utensils, furniture, stoneware, armoires, rifles, and frakturs. Directions: follow S. Duke St. from downtown to Conestoga Creek bridge, then immediately turn right on Rock Ford Rd.

Community Resources
Pennsylvania Dutch Convention & Visitors Bureau, 501 Greenfield Rd., 299-8901
Lancaster Chamber of Commerce & Industry, 100 S. Queen St., 397-3531
PO: 1400 Harrisburg Pike, 396-6916
    East branch: 1813 Olde Homestead La., 291-2900
Public Library: 125 N. Duke St., 394-2651
Lancaster General Hospital: 555 N. Duke St., 299-5511
Community Hospital of Lancaster: 1100 E. Orange St., 397-3711
St. Joseph's Hospital: 250 College Ave., 291-8211
Court House: 50 N. Duke St., 299-8000
City Police: emergency 911; all other business 291-4911
City Hall: 120 N. Duke St., 291-4711
State Police: 2099 Lincoln Hwy. E., 299-7650
Amtrak: N. Queen St. & McGovern Ave., 392-6717; (800) USA-RAIL (872-7245)
Bus: 22 W. Clay St., 397-4861

NORTHERN LANCASTER COUNTY

Neffsville, unincorporated, pop. about 2,500. Once a small crossroads village, now part of suburban Lancaster.

★★★★ **Pennsylvania Farm Museum** ([21])(2 hours), 2451 Kissel Hill Rd., 569-0401. Open Tue.-Sat. 9-5, Sun. 12-5. Closed Mon. and most legal holidays except Memorial Day, Labor Day, and Independence Day if it falls on a Monday. Admission: age 11-64, $2.00; age 65 and up, $1.40; under 11, free. An excellent and comprehensive museum depicting all aspects of farm life, with live demonstrations in some of the 22 buildings open to the public. Orientation slide program and exhibit gallery in Visitor Center. Directions: From US 30, go north 1.8 mi. on Oregon Pike (PA 272), turn left at traffic light on Landis Valley Rd. for 0.1 mi. From PA 501 in Neffsville, turn east at traffic light on Valley Rd. (SR 1014) for 1.4 mi. From US 222 southbound, take Oregon Pike exit, go south on PA 272 for 1.7 mi. to traffic light at Landis Valley Rd., turn right for 0.1 mi.

Ephrata, pop. 12,000. A busy farming community and the commercial center for northeastern Lancaster County.

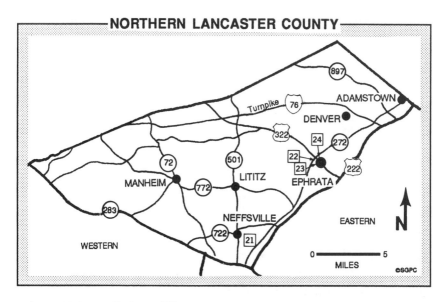

NORTHERN LANCASTER COUNTY

★★★★ **Ephrata Cloister** (22)(1-1/2 hours), 632 W. Main St. (US 322, at the SE corner of the interchange of PA 272), 733-6600. Open Mon.-Sat. 9-5, Sun. 12-5, closed holidays except Memorial Day, Independence Day, and Labor Day. Admission: adults, $3.00; seniors, $2.00; children 6-17, $1.50; under 6, free. Guided tours on the hour, but self-guided visits permitted—get brochure at visitor center. The Cloister was established by Conrad Beissel in 1732 as a religious commune. The 20 buildings on this NRHP property, most of which are original, trace the lifestyle of the residents. The society dwindled after Beissel's death in 1768, and finally disbanded in 1814. During the summer, Ephrata Cloister Associates presents **"Vorspiel"**, a musical pageant about life at the Cloister. Performances are held in the amphitheater, or in case of rain, in the Meetinghouse with a reduced seating capacity. Show is Sat. at 9 PM from early July thru Labor Day weekend. Admission: adults, $6.00; seniors, $5.00; children 6-17, $4.00; under 6, free. For information on Vorspiel, call 733-4811.

★ **Eicher Indian Museum and Shop** (23)(20-30 min.), Ephrata Community Park, Cocalico St., 738-3084. Open Thu.-Sat. 11-5, Sun. 12-5. A small museum, opened in 1987, of Pennsylvania, southwestern U.S., and Mayan Indian artifacts. Most of the collection belongs to the curator, Gordon McQuate. Directions: 0.2 mi. southeast of Ephrata Cloister on W. Main St., turn west at Cocalico Creek bridge on Cocalico St., go 0.2 mi. along creek to Community Park.

Ephrata Museum (24)(20-30 min.), 249 W. Main St., 733-1616. Open June 1 thru Labor Day—Mon.-Sat. 11-4, Sun. 1-4; open September thru May by appointment. Operated by the Historical Society of The Cocalico Valley in the Connell Mansion, a NRHP Victorian home built in the mid-1800s. Contains household items of the mid- and late 19th century.

Community Resources

Ephrata Area Chamber of Commerce, 501 S. State St., 733-4454
PO: 129 E. Main St., 733-2390
Public Library: 205 W. Fulton St., 733-4411
Ephrata Community Hospital: Martin Ave., 733-0311
Police: emergency 911, all other business 733-8611
Borough Offices: 114 E. Main St., 733-1277
State Police: PA 272, 733-8691

Lititz, pop. 9,000. A charming and tidy community, one of the most attractive in the county. The NRHP **Historic District** includes E. Main, N. and S. Broad, W. Orange, and Sturgis Sts. The square, at the intersection of Main and Broad, with its fountain and park, is especially pretty. The town was named by the Moravians for the community in Bohemia where Moravians had been protected in the 1400s. The Moravians established in a school here in 1746 and a church in 1749, but the town was not laid out until 1756. For the first 100 years, only Moravians were permitted to live in Lititz. The best way to see the downtown area is on foot; parking is available on the street, but spaces may be hard to find at times in the center of the area.

Start your **walking tour** at the **Johannes Mueller House** (30 min.), 137-39 E. Main St., the home of the Lititz Historical Foundation (626-7958). Open Sat. 10-4 (last tour 3:30) Memorial Day thru October 31. Admission: adults, $1.00; students and seniors, 50¢. Pick up a brochure there describing the other sights in the first two blocks of E. Main St. The Mueller house contains a museum of early Lititz artifacts.

There are 17 points of interest on the walking tour; the major sites are:

Moravian Church Square, south side of E. Main St. in the 200-block. The Square includes the Church (1787), Parsonage (1762), Brothers' House (1759), Sisters' House (1758), and Linden Hall Girls School (1767). Linden Hall is the oldest girls' boarding school in the U.S., founded in 1746. The Parsonage, originally the *Gemeinhaus*, or community house, was used for church services before the present church was built. The **Archives**, in a building on the west side of the square, houses old musical instruments; the Moravians were noted for their use of brass instruments in their earliest days in America. Open Sat. 12-4. Admission free, donation requested.

★★★ **Sturgis Pretzel Company** (20-30 min.), 215 E. Main St., 626-4354. Open for tours Mon.-Sat. 9-4:30 (Fri.-Sat. only in January and February). Admission: $1.00. The building originally housed the Moravian bakery. The tour goes into the 110-degree oven room to show the actual production process. An interesting tour.

Moravian Congregational Store, 120 E. Main St. Except for the addition of dormers, the house is unchanged from its original 1762 design. On NRHP.

John Augustus Sutter House, 19 E. Main St. On the NRHP, General Sutter of California gold rush fame had this home built in 1871 at a cost of $10,000. He lived in it until his death in 1880. He is buried in the cemetery behind Moravian Church Square.

General Sutter Inn, 14 E. Main St. Originally built in 1764 and named Zum Anker, the building still offers overnight lodging and meals.

Not on the walking tour, but a worthwhile attraction, is the ★★ **Candy Americana Museum** (20 min.) at the Wilbur Chocolate Company factory and outlet store, 46 N. Broad St., 626-1131. Open Mon.-Sat. 10-5. Admission free. Photos, antique molds, tools, packaging supplies, and European chocolate pots from the 19th century.

Community Resources
Lititz Area Chamber of Commerce, 7 S. Broad St., 626-2044
PO: 74 E. Main St., 626-2329
Public Library: 302 S. Broad St., 626-2255
Police: emergency 911, all other business 626-0231
Borough Offices: 7 S. Broad St., 626-2044

Manheim, pop. 5,000. Founded 1761. Known for the manufacture of Stiegel glass in pre-Revolutionary times. Baron Henry William Stiegel's factory was located at 102 W. Stiegel St. His home, at 1 N. Main St., was built in 1763, and was also the residence of Robert Morris, the Revolutionary War financier.

★★ **Mount Hope Estate and Winery** (30 min.), 5 mi. north on PA 72, just south of Pa. Turnpike crossing and interchange, 665-7021. The original part of the mansion was built in 1800 by Henry Grubb, whose family owned the Cornwall Iron Furnace, a few miles to the north (see Lebanon County). Between 1890 and 1905 another 22 rooms were added to the original ten. Little of the original furnishings remain, as the various owners took their shares. The house, on the NRHP, is somewhat gaudy, with an opulence that seems out of place in this conservative area. Open for tours Mon.-Sat. 10-6, Sun. 12-6. Admission: adults, $4.00; children 6-11, $1.50; under 6, free. Tours include wine tasting. The winery began operation on the property in 1980, and now produces 60,000 gallons a year. For 15 weekends beginning in early July, the Estate presents the **Pennsylvania Renaissance Faire**, a re-creation of an Elizabethan country fair, held in the gardens on the property. Hours: Sat., Sun., and Mon. 12-7 thru Labor Day; Sat. and Sun. 11-6 until season ends. Admission to Faire: adults, $10.50; children 6-11, $3.00.

EASTERN LANCASTER COUNTY

This area contains most of the Amish population and the Pennsylvania Dutch tourist attractions. There are four main travel corridors in this region, not including US 222, which forms the area's northern limit. These corridors are: US 30 (Lincoln Highway), PA 340 (Old Philadelphia Pike), PA 23 (New Holland Pike), and PA 741. All except the latter radiate out from Lancaster, and 741 loops to the west and south around the city and then heads due east to Strasburg and Gap, forming the southern boundary of this region. Nearly all points of interest and business establishments serving the tourist industry are located along or very near these roads. Therefore, the listings of places of interest are arranged by these corridors, from south to north, and within each corridor in a west to east direction.

Route 741 Corridor

Strasburg, pop. 2,400. A picturesque village, with well-kept homes along tree-lined streets. The town's NRHP **Historic District** includes E. and W. Main, S. Decatur, and W. Miller Sts.

★ **Gast Classic Motorcars** (25)(30 min.), PA 896, 1/2 mi. north, 687-9500. Open May thru October—daily 9-9, November thru April—Sun.-Thu. 9-5, Fri.-Sat. 9-9. Admission: adults, $4.00; children 7-12, $2.00; under 7, free. A varied collection cars dating from the 1920s to the 60s. Gift shop on premises with scale models, reference books, and memorabilia for sale.

Strasburg Railroad (See Recreation Facilities)

★★★ **Railroad Museum of Pennsylvania** (26)(1 hour), 3/4 mi. east on PA 741, 687-8628. Open Mon.-Sat. 9-5, Sun. 11-5, closed Mon. from October thru April and all holidays except Memorial Day, Independence Day, and Labor Day. Admission: adults, $3.00; seniors, $2.00; children 6-17, $1.50; under 6, free. Indoor and outdoor displays of various types of locomotives, passenger coaches, baggage cars, sleepers,

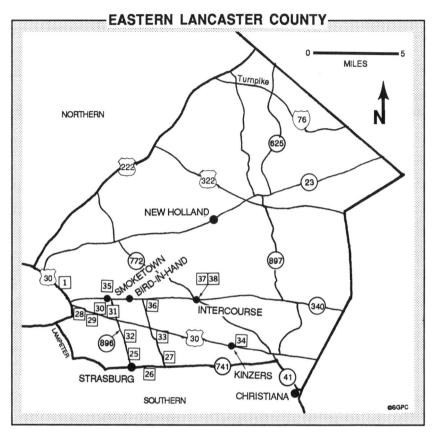

EASTERN LANCASTER COUNTY

diners, parlor cars, observation cars, and hoppers. Platform in indoor hall permits overhead viewing of rolling stock. Some cars may be entered. Additional exhibits include a waiting room, trackside signs and signals, timetables, and other memorabilia. Railroading film shown in the "station". An extensive collection of rolling stock that is added to as space allows.

★ **Toy Train Museum** (⟨27⟩)(30 min.), Paradise La., 1/4 mi. north of PA 741, 687-8976. Open daily May thru October, weekends in April and November, the first two weekends in December, Good Friday, Easter Monday, the day after Thanksgiving and Christmas, and December 31. Hours are 10-5 all open days. Headquarters of the Train Collectors Association. Three operating layouts and showcases of toy trains. A short comedy movie related to model railroading, probably made in the 1940s, is shown every 45 min. A railroading slide show fills in the remaining time. A good place to keep the kids entertained.

Christiana, pop. 1,100. Located on the Chester County line, the town was the site in 1851 of the Christiana Raid. The town was a stop on the Underground Railroad, and when a man named Edward Gorsuch, searching for his escaped slaves, found them here, the locals refused to release them. Gorsuch was killed and his son injured in the ensuing fight. The courts refused to prosecute the residents for the murder or for failing to try to stop it. Some historians consider this to be the opening skirmish in the Civil War.

Route 30 Corridor

★★ **Amish Homestead** ([28])(1 hour), 2034 Lincoln Hwy. E. (between Strasburg Pike and the eastern end of the US 30 bypass), 392-0832. Open daily: Memorial Day thru Labor Day, 9-7 (last tour 6 PM), remainder of year, 9-5 (last tour 4 PM), closed Thanksgiving, Christmas, New Year's Day. Admission: adults, $3.75; seniors, $3.25; children 6-11 $1.75; under 6, free. 50-min. guided tour of a farmhouse and barn. The house is furnished as an Old Order Amish home might be. A Dunkard family operates the farm and lives in a part of the house not on the tour. During busy times the tours may seem like an assembly line, with two groups in different parts of the farmhouse at the same time. Visitors are free to explore the other farm buildings after the guided tour.

★★★★ **Mennonite Information Center** ([29]), 2209 Millstream Rd., (SW corner of Lincoln Hwy. E.), 299-0954. Open Mon.-Sat. 8-5, closed Thanksgiving, Christmas, New Year's Day. The Center has information on Mennonite religious practices, lifestyles, outreach services, and culture, as well as on general tourist attractions in Lancaster County. Their 22-min. movie **"Morning Song"**, shown every half hour, is an excellent introduction to the religion and people. Admission free, donation requested. The Center sells literature on the Mennonites and Amish. **Farm Country Tours,** with a Mennonite guide in your vehicle, are available with advance reservations. Costs: $7.00 per hour plus $2.50 set-up service fee, for vehicles with 1-9 persons; $9.00 per hour plus $5.00 set-up fee for vehicles with 10-16 persons, both with 2-hour minimum. **Hebrew Tabernacle Reproduction** (1 hour), located in a building next to the Information Center, is a 50-min. tour and lecture explaining the history, function, and spiritual meaning of the tabernacle. Tours are given April thru October—every hour from 8-4, November thru March—11, 1, and 3. Admission: adults, $2.50; seniors age 65 and up; $2.00, children 7-12, $1.50; under 6, free.

★ **National Wax Museum** ([30])(30-40 min.), 2249 Lincoln Hwy. E., 393-3679. Open daily: Memorial Day thru Labor Day, 9-9, until Thanksgiving, 9-8, after Thanksgiving until April, 9-6. Admission: adults, $3.90; seniors, $3.50; children,

$2.60. A series of three-dimensional narrated exhibits portraying significant events in Lancaster County's history. The displays are attractively done, but very touristy.

★★ **Amish Farm and House** (31)(45-60 min.), 2395 Lincoln Hwy. E., 394-6185. Open daily except Christmas—8:30-6 summer, 8:30-4 remainder of year; last tour 1/2 hour before closing. Admission: adults $3.90; seniors $3.50; children 5-11 $2.25; under 5, free. Guided tours of the house, which is furnished as an Amish home, and self-guided tours of the buildings on the working farm, which include a barn, chicken house, spring house, corn crib, operating waterwheel, former blacksmith shop, tobacco shed, and smokehouse. The blacksmith shop contains Indian relics, dolls, china, and other local crafts.

★★ **The Amish Village** (32)(45-60 min.), PA 896, 1.0 mi. south of US 30, 687-8511. Open daily: summer, 9-6, spring and fall, 9-5. Closed from weekend after Thanksgiving until approximately mid-March. Admission: adults, $3.85; children 6-12, $1.10. Guided tour of the 1840 furnished farmhouse, preceded by an explanation of Amish customs. Self-guided visit to the spring house, operating smokehouse, blacksmith shop, windmill, operating waterwheel, barnyard, and simulated village store and schoolhouse.

★ **Mill Bridge Village** (33)(30-45 min.), S. Ronks Rd., 0.5 mi. south of US 30, 687-8181. Open April thru November—daily 9-5:30. Admission: adults $7.00; seniors $3.50; children 6-12 $2.50; under 6, free. Operating mill, built 1738, craft shops, quilt making, and 1890s nickelodeon. Admission includes Amish buggy ride.

Rough and Tumble Museum (34)(30 min.), Lincoln Hwy., 0.3 mi. east of Kinzer Rd. in Kinzers, 442-4249. Open Sat. 10-5. A semi-open air museum of antique farm equipment and implements. Demonstrations given during festivals (see Calendar of Events).

Route 340 Corridor

Anderson Bakery (30-45 min.), 2060 Old Philadelphia Pike (1 block east of US 30 bypass), 299-2321. World's largest pretzel bakery. Tours Mon.-Fri. 8:30-3. Factory store on premises.

★★ **Folk Craft Museum** (35)(30-40 min.), 441 Mt. Sidney Rd. (1/2 mi. north of PA 340), 397-3609. Open April 1 thru November 1—Mon.-Sat., 9-5, Sun., 12-4. Admission: adults, $4.00; seniors, $3.00; children 6-16, $2.00; family rate (parents and all children under 16), $10.00. Contains farm implements, dishes, lithographs, furniture, quilts, and photographs. Some displays are arranged by subject, e.g., butchering, barn decorations, etc. Operating woodworker's shop and 100-year-old weaving loom. A 15-min. slide show, **"The Land We Love"**, presenting Pennsylvania German folk art, the Amish lifestyle, and changing seasons, shown on demand.

Bird-in-Hand Farmers Market, PA 340 at Maple Ave., 393-9674. Open 8:30-5:30 as follows: Fri. and Sat., year-round; Wed., April thru November; Thu., July thru October. Stands are more oriented to selling handcrafts and souvenirs than farm products. If it's farm products you want, go to Central Market in Lancaster.

★ **Weavertown One-Room Schoolhouse** (36)(15-20 min.), PA 340, 0.3 mi. east of N. Ronks Rd., 768-3976. Open Easter weekend thru Thanksgiving weekend—daily 9-6. Admission: adults, $1.75; seniors, $1.50; children 5-11, $1.25. A re-created one-room school with animated "students". The school building was in use until 1969.

Intercourse, unincorporated, pop. about 500. A quiet farming village until the tourist trade began to grow, now a bustling attraction, probably largely due to its curious name.

Kitchen Kettle Village (37), PA 340, center of town, 768-8261. Open daily except Sun. and Christmas—usually 9-5, but 5:30 or 6 PM closing in summer and on Saturdays from late March thru December. A community of 30 shops, restaurant, and snack shops. The stores sell gifts, pewter, leathercrafts, smoked meats and cheeses, sportswear, furniture, brass items, flowers, etc. The Village is pleasantly laid out and unabashedly designed for tourists.

★★ **The People's Place** (38), PA 340, center of town, adjacent to Kitchen Kettle Village, 768-7171. Open daily except Sun. 9:30-9:30, November thru March 9:30-4:30. A combination arts and crafts exhibit, bookstore, interpretive center, and theater presenting works by and about the Amish and Mennonites. A good place to learn about these people from the works of Merle and Phyllis Good, authors of several books dealing with Amish and Mennonite life. Two films are presented: **"Who Are the Amish?"** (25 min.), shown continuously from 9:30-5 daily except Sunday; and **"Hazel's People"** (105-minutes), a fictionalized documentary about Mennonite culture in Lancaster County, shown daily except Sunday from April thru October at 6 and 8 PM. Admissions to either Amish World and "Who Are the Amish?": adults $2.50; children $1.25; combination admission: adults $4.25; children $2.10. Admission to "Hazel's People": adults $4.00; children $2.00. No admission charge for bookstore or gallery, both located on the first floor.

Route 23 Corridor

New Holland, pop. 4,300. Best known as the home of New Holland farm equipment, now a division of Ford Motor Company. The town's other large employer is Victor F. Weaver, Inc., a producer of frozen poultry.

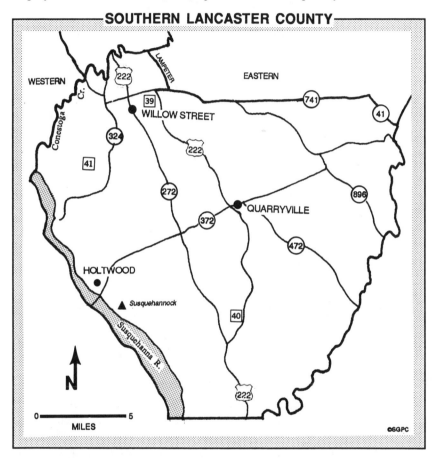

SOUTHERN LANCASTER COUNTY

SOUTHERN LANCASTER COUNTY

★★★ **Hans Herr House** (39)(45 min.), 1849 Hans Herr Dr., 0.7 mi. south of US 222, 464-4438. Open April thru December—Mon.-Sat. 9-4, closed Thanksgiving and Christmas. The house, built in 1719, is the oldest building in Lancaster County and the site of the first permanent white settlement. On the NRHP. The two-story home is of medieval German architecture and was in the Herr family until 1969, when it was bought by the State. Other buildings on the site include the blacksmith's shop, barn and sheds. The house has been restored to depict 18th century life. A museum in another house (circa 1890) has displays dealing with Mennonite beliefs. Admission: adults, $2.50; children 7-12, $1.00; under 7, free. Worthwhile as one of the few examples of its type of architecture found anywhere in America.

★ **Robert Fulton's Birthplace** (40)(30 min.), US 222 and Swift Rd., 6.5 mi. south of Quarryville. Open Memorial Day to Labor Day—Sat. 11-4, Sun. 1-5. Admission: adults, $1.00; children under 12, free. The house where the inventor of the first successful steamboat was born in 1765 was nearly destroyed by fire in 1822 and then rebuilt. Fulton had lived here less than two years when his family moved to Lancaster. House is administered by the Southern Lancaster County Historical Society, Box 33, Quarryville, PA 17566, 548-2679.

★★ **Sickman's Mill** (41)(20-30 min.), Sickman's Mill Rd. at Pequea Creek, 872-5951. Open daily 10-5 from first weekend in May thru Labor Day, weekends only 10-5 after Labor Day until Christmas, rest of year by appointment. A 4-1/2 story mill with 30-inch thick stone walls originally built in 1793 and rebuilt in 1862. Farm machinery over 100 years old is on display. Directions: From intersection of PA 324 and 741 at New Danville, go south on 324 for 4.7 mi. to Marticville. Turn right on Frogtown Rd. (SR 3023) for 1.3 mi.

Lancaster County Winery, Rawlinsville Rd. (SR 3009) south of Willow Street, 464-3555. Open February thru December—Mon.-Sat. 10-4, Sun. 1-4. Tours anytime during hours. Directions: From intersection of US 222, PA 272 southbound, and PA 741, go south on 272 for 1.9 mi., turn right on Baumgardner Rd. for 0.7 mi. Turn left on Rawlinsville Rd. (SR 3009) for 1.9 mi. to winery, on left opposite Creek Rd.

Tucquan Vineyard, Drytown Rd. (SR 3012) just east of Holtwood, 284-2221. Open April 1 to December 31—Mon.-Sat. 11-5. Salesroom open Sat. only January thru March. Tours by appointment. Directions: From intersection of PA 272 and 372 at Buck, go west on 372 for 4.5 mi., turn right on Hilldale Rd. for 0.4 mi. to Drytown Rd. Left on Drytown for 0.1 mi. to winery on left.

WESTERN LANCASTER COUNTY

Columbia, pop. 11,000. Founded 1726 by John Wright as Wright's Ferry on the site of the Indian village Shawannah. Because of its location on the Susquehanna, it has always been a locally important transportation focus, with the ferry, canal, railroad, and highway. The first bridge spanning the river, over a mile wide at this spot, was

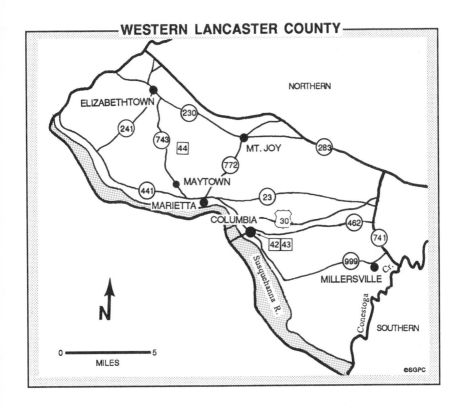

WESTERN LANCASTER COUNTY

built in 1812. The Lincoln Highway bridge (PA 462) is the longest multiple arch span in the world and was built in 1930 with contributions of Lancaster and York County residents. The town came close to being selected as the location of the U.S. capital in 1789. Arguments that followed a favorable vote in the House of Representatives determined that the capital would be built on the Potomac rather than on the Susquehanna. Columbia was an important station on the Underground Railroad partly because of its strategic location. The borough's **Historic District** includes the 200- and 300-blocks of Locust St. (the downtown business district), the 200-block of Cherry, and the unit blocks of N. and S. 2nd and 3rd Sts. The **Market House** at 17 S. 3rd, built in 1869, is the oldest continuously operating market in Lancaster County.

★★★ **Wright's Ferry Mansion** (42)(45 min.), 2nd & Cherry Sts., 684-4325. Open May thru October—Tue., Wed., Fri., Sat. 10-3. Admission: adults, $3.00; children 6-18, $1.50; under 6, free. A beautifully preserved, not restored, 1738 Pennsylvania Quaker mansion that was the home of Susanna Wright, the sister of John (Jr.) and JamesWright, who operated the ferry, and the daughter of John

Wright, a founder of Columbia and for many years the chief burgess of Lancaster County. The house, on the NRHP, remained in the Wright family until 1922. In addition to being the oldest house in Columbia, it is the only one of this type architecture furnished from the period. Several pieces of furniture are the only known ones in existence. The home reflects at the same time elegance and simplicity of the Quaker lifestyle. Directions: from US 30, take 3rd St. (PA 441) exit south for 6 blocks to Cherry St., turn right for 1 block.

★★★ **The Watch and Clock Museum** (43)(30-45 min.), 514 Poplar St. (NE corner of 5th), 684-8261. Open Tue.-Sat. 9-4, closed holidays. Admission: adults, $1.50; seniors, $1.20; children 6-17, 50¢; under 6, free. The headquarters of the National Association of Watch and Clock Collectors, the museum was established in 1977. More than 6,000 timepieces of all varieties of American and European manufacture are displayed in three galleries. Clocks made by Association members are also on view. Fortunately, not all clocks are kept wound, or there would be quite a din at the top of each hour! An out-of-the-ordinary and enjoyable museum. Directions: from US 30, take 3rd St. (PA 441) exit south for 2 blocks, turn left on Poplar St. for 2 blocks.

Community Resources
Columbia Area Chamber of Commerce, 40 N. 3rd St., 684-5249
Visitors Information Center: Linden St. at US 30 eastbound off-ramp to 3rd St. (PA 441), 684-2199
PO: 4th & Walnut Sts., 684-2733
Public Library: 24 S. 6th St., 684-2255
Columbia Hospital: 7th & Poplar Sts., 684-2841
Police: emergency 911, all other business 684-2120
Borough Hall: 308 Locust St., 684-2468

Elizabethtown, pop. 9,000. Farming and manufacturing community in northwestern Lancaster County. Home of Elizabethtown College, founded 1899, a small liberal arts college.

Marietta, pop. 3,000. An old factory town along the Susquehanna, but with an unexpectedly attractive **Historic District** encompassing four blocks of Market Street and several side streets. The downtown is quiet since River Road (PA 441) was rebuilt to bypass the borough, but this enhances the beauty of the many Victorian and older homes lining Market Street.

Maytown, unincorporated, pop. about 1,000. A delightful little community, appearing almost as if someone forgot to tell the residents about neon signs and shopping centers. The area within a block in all directions of the central square is the most picturesque.

Nissley Vineyards, Maytown-Bainbridge Rd. (SR 4004), 426-3514. Open Mon.-Sat. 12-5, Sun. 1-4. Free self-guided tours Sun.-Fri., guided tours Sat. only, admission $2.00 age 12 and up. Closed New Year's Day, Easter, Thanksgiving, and Christmas. Directions: From Maytown, 3.9 mi. NW of Maytown square on SR 4004. From PA 441 at Marietta, go north on 441 for 4.4 mi. from the intersection of PA 743, turn right on Wickersham Rd. for 0.9 mi. to end at Maytown-Bainbridge Rd., turn left for 0.6 mi. to entrance.

Millersville, pop. 7,400. Home of Millersville University, the oldest (1859) of the fourteen colleges established as "normal schools" for the training of teachers, founded as a private academy in 1854.

Mount Joy, pop. 6,300. Southwest of town is ★ **Donegal Church and Witness Tree** (44), a NRHP church and cemetery established around 1721 (the present building was erected in 1740). The large white oak in the churchyard, estimated to be at least 300 years old, was the scene of a pledge of patriotism by the parishoners in 1777 when told of the British advance. Located on Donegal Springs Rd. (SR 4002). Directions from Mt. Joy: Southwest from PA 230 (Main St.) on Marietta St. (PA 772) for 2 blocks, bear right on Donegal St. which becomes Donegal Springs Rd. Go 3.0 mi. to Colebrook Rd., turn left, then immediately right for 0.2 mi. to church on right.

Donegal Mills Plantation is a 1736 mansion, bake house, garden, and grounds now operated as a bed and breakfast inn and restaurant. Guided tours are available—phone 653-2168. Located on Trout Run Rd. between Mt. Joy and Maytown. Directions from Mt. Joy: West on PA 772 from PA 230 for 2.6 mi., turn right on Musser Rd. (SR 4017) for 0.4 mi., then left on Trout Run Rd. for 0.3 mi. to Plantation.

COVERED BRIDGES

There are 22 publicly owned covered bridges in Lancaster County, plus two spanning Octoraro Creek that are shared with Chester County. Only those in good condition are listed; the locations are coded to correspond with the regions of the county as outlined earlier in this chapter. All Lancaster County covered bridges are of the Burr truss design, the most widely used type in the state, probably because the inventor, Theodore Burr of Connecticut, built some of the earliest of this type himself in Pennsylvania.

Baumgardner's Mill (S), Covered Bridge Rd. (Pequea Creek), about 1 mi. west of Rawlinsville Rd. (SR 3009), built 1860.

Bitzer's Mill (E), Covered Bridge Rd. (SR 1013) (Conestoga Creek), 1 mi. north of Fairmount, built 1846.

Bucher's Mill (N), Creek Rd. (Cocalico Creek), just south of PA 272 at Reamstown, built 1881.

Colemanville (S), Fox Hollow Rd. (Pequea Creek), just south of PA 324 at Colemanville, built 1856, rebuilt after 1972 flood.

Erb's (N), Erb's Bridge Rd. (Hammer Creek), about 1-1/2 mi. northeast of Rothsville, Burr truss type, built 1887.

Guy Bard's (Keller's) (N), Rettew Mill Rd. (Cocalico Creek), just north of Akron, built 1891.

Hunsecker's Mill (E), Hunsecker Rd. (SR 1029) (Conestoga Creek), about 1 mi. northwest of PA 23 and 1-1/2 mi. east of PA 272, built 1843, rebuilt after 1972 flood.

Jackson's Mill (S), Mt. Pleasant Rd. (West Branch, Octoraro Creek), about 1-1/2 mi. south of PA 372 between Green Tree and Quarryville, built 1878, rebuilt 1984 after flood damage.

Herr's Mill (E), S. Ronks Rd. (Pequea Creek), 1/2 mi. south of US 30, built 1885.

Kauffman's Distillery (N), Sun Hill Rd. (Chickies Creek), 1-1/2 mi. southwest of Manheim, built 1874.

Kurtz's Mill (L), S. Duke St. in Williamson Park, Lancaster, built 1876, moved to present location after 1972 flood.

Leaman Place (Eshelman's Mill) (E), Belmont Rd. (Pequea Creek), 1/2 mi. north of US 30, built 1893.

Lime Valley (S), Breneman Rd. (Pequea Creek), at Lime Valley, about 1 mi. east of US 222, built 1871.

Mercer's Mill (S), Creek Rd. (Octoraro Creek), on the Chester Co. line about 1 mi. south of Christiana, built 1800.

Neff's Mill (S), Penn Grant Rd. (Pequea Creek), about 1-1/2 mi. west of Strasburg, built 1875.

Pinetown (E), Pinetown Rd. (Conestoga Creek), adjacent to Oregon exit of US 222, built 1867 (replaced and rebuilt after 1972 flood).

Schenck's Mill (N), Schenck Rd. (Chickies Creek), about 1-1/2 mi. northwest of Landisville, built 1855.

Siegrist's Mill (W), Siegrist Rd. (Chickies Creek), about 1/2 mi. west of Prospect Rd. (SR 4001) and 1 mi. north of PA 23, built 1885.

White Rock (S), White Rock Rd. (West Branch, Octoraro Creek), about 2 mi. south of PA 472 near Kirkwood, built 1847.

Zook's Mill (N), Log Cabin Rd. (Cocalico Creek), about 1 mi. northwest of Brownstown, built 1849.

RECREATION FACILITIES

Susquehannock State Park, State Park Rd., overlooking Susquehanna River 3 mi. south of Holtwood, 548-3361.

Muddy Run Recreation Park, PA 372, 3/4 mi. east of the Norman Wood Bridge just south of Holtwood, 284-4325. Owned by Philadelphia Electric Company, featuring fishing, boating (no gas powered boats), camping, picnicking, ballfields, playground equipment, and an environmental information center (open 9-4: April thru November, Wed.-Sun.; December thru March, Tue.-Sat. Closed Christmas and New Year's Day).

Strasburg Railroad, PA 741, 3/4 mi. east of Strasburg, 687-7522. Steam train rides on the "road to Paradise", the oldest operating short-line in the country. Open daily from 1st week in May thru October, weekends only mid-March to 1st week in May and November thru 2nd weekend in December.

Dutch Wonderland, 2249 Lincoln Hwy. E., Lancaster, 291-1888. Open daily Memorial Day weekend thru Labor Day—Mon.-Sat. 10-7, Sun. 11-7. Out-of-season: open, weather permitting, weekends only from Easter to Memorial Day weekend and from the day after Labor Day thru October—Sat. 10-6, Sun. 11-6. Admission: adults, $1.75; seniors, $1.50; children 5-11, $1.25; under 5, free. Admission to any 5 rides, $9.00; unlimited rides, $12.75.

Ed's Buggy Rides, PA 896, 2 mi. south of US 30, Strasburg, 687-0360. 3-mile backroads tour of farmlands.

Aerial Tours, Smoketown Airport, Mabel Ave., north off PA 340 and just east of Mt. Sidney Rd., Smoketown, 394-6476. Hours: June 1 thru October 1—daily 9-6, other hours by appointment. Admission: adults, $12.50, children age 8 and under, $6.25. Minimum charge 2 adults.

"Dutch Country Digest" videotape tour. Action Video Productions, 1828 State St., E. Petersburg, PA 17520, 560-0605. Price: $19.95 plus $3.00 shipping. VHS and Beta available.

CALENDAR OF EVENTS

Early April, Lancaster. **Quilters Heritage Celebration**, Host Farm Resort, 2300 Lincoln Hwy. E. c/o Rita Barber, Rt. 3, Box 119, Lancaster, PA 17601, 854-9323 (York).

Early May, Willow Street. **Lancaster County Spring Pilgrimage**, Hans Herr House, 1849 Hans Herr Dr. c/o Steve Friesen, 464-4438.

Mid-May, Kinzers. **Spring Steam-Up**, Rough and Tumble Museum, US 30, 442-4249.

Late May, Intercourse. **Rhubarb Festival**, Kitchen Kettle Village, 768-8261.

Late May, Lancaster. **Spring Craft Show**, Central Park. c/o Pennsylvania Dutch Convention & Visitors Bureau, 501 Greenfield Rd., Lancaster, PA 17601, 295-1500.

Early June, Intercourse. **Outdoor Woodcarving Show**, Kitchen Kettle Village, 768-8261.

Early June, Landis Valley. **Landis Valley Fair**, Pennsylvania Farm Museum, 2451 Kissel Hill Rd., Lancaster, PA 17601, 569-0401.

Mid-June, Manheim. **Red Rose Payment**, Zion Lutheran Church. c/o Zion Lutheran Church, 2 S. Main St., Manheim, PA 17545, 665-5880.

Late June, Columbia. **Antique & Craft Fair.** c/o Columbia Area Chamber of Commerce, 40 N. 3rd St., Columbia, PA 17512, 684-5249.

Late June thru Labor Day, every weekend, Adamstown. **Bavarian Beer Fest**, Stoudt's Black Angus Brewery Hall, PA 272, (215) 484-4385.

Early July, Lititz. **Antique Show & Sales**, Warwick Middle School. c/o Lititz Historical Foundation, 431 W. Orange St., Lititz, PA 17543, 626-8427.

Early July thru early October, every weekend, Manheim. **Pennsylvania Renaissance Faire**, Mt. Hope Estate and Winery. c/o Mt. Hope Estate & Winery, P.O. Box 685, Cornwall, PA 17016, 665-7021.

Early July, Strasburg. **All American Ragtime Festival and Contest**, Mill Bridge Village. c/o Karen Reynolds, P.O. Box 86, Strasburg, PA 17579, 687-6521.

Late July, Lancaster. **Pennsylvania State Craft Fair**, Franklin & Marshall College. c/o Pennsylvania Designer Craftsmen, P.O. Box 718, Richboro, PA 18954, (215) 860-0731.

Mid-August, Kinzers. **Annual Threshermen's Reunion**, Rough and Tumble Museum, US 30, 442-4249.

Late August, Elizabethtown. **Elizabethtown Fair**, Fairgrounds, E. High St. c/o Sally K. Nolt, 25 Iris Cir., Elizabethtown, PA 17022, 367-7256.

Late August, Strasburg. **Lost Dutchman Gemboree**, Historic Strasburg Inn. c/o Richard Hasner, 217 Nevin St., Lancaster, PA 17603, 392-6825.

Mid-September, Bird-in-Hand. **Plain and Fancy Craft Fair**, Plain and Fancy Farm. c/o Plain and Fancy Farm, PA 340, Bird-in-Hand, PA 17505, 768-8281.

Mid-September, Denver. **Denver Community Fair**, Denver Memorial Park, (215) 267-2831.

Mid-September, Intercourse. **Harvest Festival**, Kitchen Kettle Village, 768-8261.

Mid-September thru mid-October, weekends only, Strasburg. **Family Oktoberfest**, Mill Bridge Village, 687-6521.

Late September, Ephrata. **Ephrata Fair**, 733-8132.

Late September, Lancaster. **Collector Auto Auction**, Dutch Wonderland, 2249 Lincoln Hwy. E., 291-1888.

Late September, New Holland. **New Holland Farmers Fair**, 354-0423.

Late September, Quarryville. **Southern Lancaster County Fair**, 786-1054.

Early October, Landis Valley. **Harvest Days**, Pennsylvania Farm Museum, 2451 Kissel Hill Rd., Lancaster, PA 17601, 569-0401.

Early October, Manheim. **Manheim Community Fair**, Memorial Park, 665-7480.

Early October, Kinzers. **Time of Harvest**, Rough and Tumble Museum, US 30, 442-4249.

Late October, Strasburg. **Halloween Lantern Tours**, Railroad Museum of Pennsylvania, PA 741 east, 687-8628.

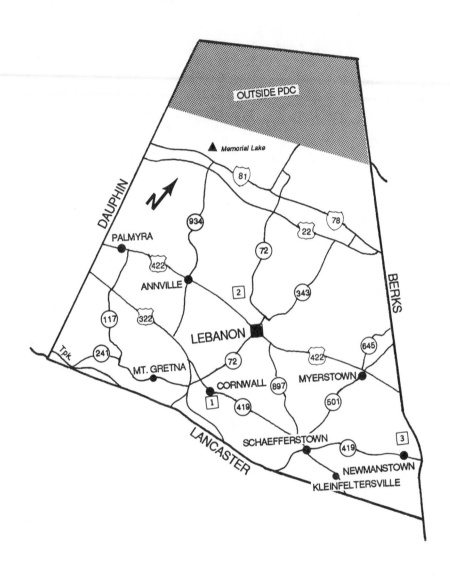

LEBANON

Created: February 16, 1813, as the 43rd county, from parts of Dauphin and Lancaster Counties
County Seat: Lebanon
Land Area: 363 square miles, of which approximately 300 in PDC
Population (1989 est.): 114,000
Area code: 717, except for Newmanstown area (589 exchange), which is 215

Most of Lebanon County's land area, and virtually the entire population, is in the broad Lebanon Valley between Blue Mountain and the Furnace Hills. The portion north of Blue Mountain that is technically outside the PDC has, at most, only a few hundred residents. The valley is relatively level along and to the south of US 422, the county's main east-west highway, and rolling to hilly to the north. This road roughly bisects the valley, and connects all the heavily populated communities. Lebanon is one of the state's smallest counties in land area, and is barely ahead of Lehigh as the smallest in the PDC.

Lebanon has the highest proportion of Germans in its population of any PDC county—42%, counting only residents who claim a single nationality. The second largest group, the English, comprise only 4.5% of the population. Except for a few Scotch-Irish in the early 1700s, Germans have, until modern times, been the dominant immigrant group.

Historical Highlights

Early county history is intertwined with industry and transportation. Iron ore was mined starting in the 1730s at Cornwall Furnace, where there was a ready supply of timber and limestone in addition to the ore. The furnace made cannons as well as ammunition for the Revolutionary Army.

The county's earliest settlements were at Myerstown, Newmanstown, and Schaefferstown. Newmanstown was the site of Fort Zeller, originally built in 1723. Schaefferstown, believed to have been settled by Jews about the time of the founding of Pennsylvania, had the first public water works in the United States, in 1744.

The Union Canal, completed in 1827 and extending from the Schuylkill River at Reading to the Susquehanna at Middletown, crossed the midsection of

201

Lebanon County. One of the first tunnels built in America (for any purpose) was constructed through a ridge just northwest of Lebanon; it still exists and may be visited.

Railroads reached the county in 1850, but the first line ran between two mountains in the extreme northern area and did not serve any populated places. The second, the Cornwall and Lebanon, was built in 1853 to carry coal from the Union Canal to Cornwall Furnace, a distance of seven miles. It was later extended to Lancaster and offered passenger service. This railroad operated until 1915, when it merged into the Pennsylvania, and there was never an accident during its tenure.

Farming has always been an important component of the county's economy. Favorable land and soil conditions help make Lebanon County the PDC's third most productive in terms of value of products sold per acre. There is an Amish community in the eastern part of the county, in the Newmanstown-Schaefferstown area.

Lebanon County is the birthplace of Lebanon bologna, a sweet and spicy sausage that originated with German settlers in the early 1800s. The county still produces nearly all the Lebanon bologna made in America.

PLACES OF INTEREST

Annville, pop. 4,400. Home of Lebanon Valley College, a coed liberal arts college founded in 1866. **Historic District** on E. Main St. (US 422) features some attractive Victorian-era homes.

Cornwall, pop. 2,700.

★★★ **Cornwall Iron Furnace** (☐1☐)(45-60 min.), Rexmont Rd. and Boyd St., 272-9711. On the NRHP, the property is maintained by the State Historical and Museum Commission. Open Tue.-Sat. 9-5, Sun. 12-5, closed Mon. except Memorial Day, Labor Day, and Independence Day if it falls on a Monday. Admission: adults, $1.50; seniors 65 and over, $1.00; children 6-17, 50¢; under 6, free. The furnace operated from 1742 until 1883, but the nearby mines were worked until 1974. The guided tour (30 min., last tour 4 PM) includes the furnace building and connecting shed. The Visitor Center, roasting ovens, coal bins, and several other outbuildings can be toured on your own. Exhibits in the visitor center show how iron ore was made and depict life in the company town (actually, "towns"—there were several within the borough of Cornwall). The mines contain the largest ore deposits east of Lake Superior. This furnace, and the community around it, are very well preserved and are a good representation of the importance of this industry in early America.

Lebanon, pop. 26,000. Trading and industrial center for the county, founded 1750. Originally named Steitztown for its founder George Steitz, a Palatinate immigrant who had arrived in 1737. It has been the county seat for Lebanon County's entire history.

The steel industry came to Lebanon around 1911, when Lebanon Steel Company, later acquired by Bethlehem Steel, opened a mill. The Upton automobile was manufactured in Lebanon from 1904 to 1907; it featured a double chain drive and headlights that turned with the steering wheel.

★★**Stoy Museum (Lebanon Co. Historical Society)** (about 1 hour), 924 Cumberland St. (US 422 westbound), 272-1473. Museum open Sun., Mon, Wed., and Fri. 1-4:30, and Mon. 7-9 PM. Closed Sun. and Mon. of holiday weekends and other non-Monday holidays. Admission: adults, $2.00. Museum occupies a home built in 1773 by a prominent local doctor and minister. The second floor was used as Lebanon County's first court house. Contains a series of rooms, each set up to depict a different aspect of Lebanon County or Pennsylvania life: drug store, doctor's office, dress shop, industries such as blacksmithing, milling, weaving, and shoemaking, railroad transporation, World War I memorabilia, and Pennsylvania German arts and crafts. Hauck Memorial Library is the Historical Society's reference department. Generally good presentation of exhibits.

★**Union Canal Tunnel** (2̲), Tunnel Hill Rd. (SR 4002), 2 mi. NW of downtown. Built 1823 and operated from 1827-84 as part of the 78-mile Union Canal. On NRHP, but worthwhile mostly for its uniqueness. Picnic tables at site. Directions: North on PA 72 for 1.9 mi. from Cumberland St. (US 422), then bear left on Tunnel Hill Rd. for about 1/3 mi. Parking area on left.

Cornwall & Lebanon, and Reading Railroad Stations, 161 and 250 N. 8th St., respectively. Both on NRHP. The Reading station, whose architecture is typical of the line, has been restored and now houses a bank and the Lebanon Chamber of Commerce. The striking C&L station, a large red brick structure with an ornate tower, houses an insurance company office.

Weaver's Bologna (about 30 min.), 15th Ave. & Weavertown Rd., 274-6100. Factory tours and retail outlet. Open Mon.-Sat. 9-4. Admission free, free samples. Oldest producer in U.S. (1885). New museum and displays in the sales outlet. Directions: From US 422 at east end of city, turn north at traffic light on N. 15th Ave., go 0.6 mi. to Weavertown Rd.

Community Resources

Lebanon Valley Tourist and Visitors Bureau, 625 Quentin Rd. (lower level of Quality Inn), 272-8555
Lebanon Valley Chamber of Commerce: 252 N. 8th St., 273-3727
PO: 101 S. 8th St., 274-2594
Public Library: 7th & Willow Sts., 273-7624
Lebanon Valley General Hospital: 4th & Willow Sts., 273-8521
Good Samaritan Hospital: 4th & Walnut Sts., 272-7611
Court House: 400 S. 8th St., 274-2801
City Police: emergency 911, all other business 272-6611
City Hall: 400 S. 8th St., 273-6711
State Police: PA 72, Jonestown, 865-2194
Bus: 603 Cumberland St., 272-0161

Mount Gretna, pop. 300. Located on PA 117, 2 mi. west of the interchange of US 322/PA 72. Former summer resort, now the home of summer theater, concerts, arts and crafts classes and shows, and religious programs at **Mt. Gretna Playhouse**, a century-old Chautauqua-style open auditorium. For program information, call Mt. Gretna Arts Council, 964-2028.

Myerstown, pop. 3,200. Tidy farming community in the eastern part of the county, home of Evangelical School of Theology.

Tulpehocken Manor, 650 W. Lincoln Ave., 1-1/2 mi. west on US 422, a NRHP plantation dating from 1732. The Michael Ley Mansion, the main house on the property, was built in 1769. Guided tours are available daily 10-5 with advance reservations. The mansion also serves as a bed & breakfast. Phone 866-4926 or 392-2311 (Lancaster).

Kutztown Bologna Company, 689 Kutztown Rd., 933-5626, (800) 822-2063 in PA, offers free tours of its factory Mon.-Fri. 9-3. Plant is about 1-1/2 mi. north of US 422 on PA 465.

Newmanstown, unincorporated, pop. about 1,400.

★ **Fort Zeller Museum** ([3]), 1/4 mi. north of PA 419 on N. Fort Zeller Rd., (215) 589-4301. Open by appointment, donation requested. This is the oldest existing fort in the state, built in 1723. The building as it now stands was rebuilt in 1745. Established by followers of Conrad Weiser (see Berks Co.) who migrated south from Schoharie County, New York, its architecture reflects the Germanic background of its builders, the Zeller family from the Palatinate.

Palmyra, pop. 8,000. Second largest community in Lebanon County and a small manufacturing center.

Palmyra Bologna Co., 230 N. College St., 838-6336, maker of Seltzer's brand Lebanon bologna, offers free tours (about 15 min.) and samples at its plant. Open Mon.-Fri. 8-11:45 AM, 12:30-3:15 PM. Sales outlet open Mon.-Fri. 7 AM-8 PM, Sat. 7-4:30. Directions: turn north off US 422 on College St. one block west of center of town.

Schaefferstown, unincorporated, pop. about 1,000. The area is believed to have first been settled by Jews, as a Jewish trading post existed here shortly after William Penn established Pennsylvania. The oldest public waterworks in North America was established here in 1744 by the town's acknowledged founder Alexander Schaeffer. He needed a constant supply of water for the hotel he built on the NW corner of the square (the intersection of Main and Market Sts., now the Franklin House, a restaurant and tavern). The only visible remnants of the waterworks are fountains in the square and at Fountain Park maintained by the water company's trustees located one block south on Market St. Curiously, the water flowed by gravity uphill from the spring in the park to the hotel. There has never been a charge for water taken from the spring.

★ **Brendle Museum** (20-30 min.), N. Market St. (PA 419), just north of the square, 949-3795 for information. Open mid-June to 2nd weekend in September—Sat.-Sun. 12-5. Admission: adults $1.00, children 25¢. Located in a former lodge hall, this museum contains relics related to the local community, including home implements, the original telephone switchboard, cigar making equipment, quilts, Indian artifacts, and an ice refrigerator.

★ **Alexander Schaeffer Farm Museum,** on PA 501, 1 block south of the traffic light at its intersection with PA 419/897, operated by Historic Schaefferstown, Inc., the local historical society. Open by appointment and for special events. The farm buildings contain 18th and 19th century implements, and the house is a typical 18th century Swiss farmhouse. Call 949-2244 or 949-3705 for appointment and schedule of events.

★★ **Michter's Distillery,** Michter's and Distillery Rds., 949-6521. Tours (about 30 min.) Mon.-Sat. 10:15-4:15, Sun. 12:15-4:15. Admission: over age 14, $1.00; seniors, 50¢. "Jug House" (sales outlet) open Mon.-Sat. 10-5, Sun. 12-5. The oldest operating distillery in America, established in 1753, and the only place in Pennsylvania legally able to sell liquor by the bottle on Sunday. On the NRHP. Because of the plant's small size, visitors are able to see up close the whiskey making process. Directions: south on PA 501 from PA 419/897 for 1.1 mi., turn right on Michter's Rd. for 0.5 mi., turn right on Distillery Rd.

Middle Creek Wildlife Management Area, SR 2013, 1 mi. south of Kleinfeltersville, 949-3582 or 733-1512 (Ephrata). 5,000 acres of waterfowl, forest and farmland wildlife habitat, operated by the Pennsylvania Game Commission. Visitor center has environmental displays. Picnic areas, hiking and nature trails, fishing. Visitor center open March 1 to November 30—Tue.-Sat. 9-5, Sun. 12-5, picnic areas open daily 8 AM-10 PM. Admission free. Directions from Schaefferstown: east from the square on PA 897 south for 2.3 mi. to Kleinfeltersville, turn right on SR 2013 for approximately 1 mile to visitor center on right.

RECREATION FACILITIES

Memorial Lake State Park, Fort Indiantown Gap, 865-5444, ext. 2806. Directions from I-81 exit 29: north on SR 4020 for 0.6 mi., turn left on Asher Miner Rd. (SR 4019) for 0.3 mi., then left on Boundary Rd. (SR 4018) for 0.6 mi. to park.

CALENDAR OF EVENTS

Note: All Schaefferstown events are held at the Alexander Schaeffer Farm Museum and are c/o Historic Schaefferstown, Inc., P.O. Box 307, Schaefferstown, PA 17088, 949-3795.

Early January, Lebanon. **Train Display**, Stoy Museum, 924 Cumberland St. c/o Lebanon Valley Tourist & Visitors Bureau, P.O. Box 626, Lebanon, PA 17042, 272-8555.

Late June, Schaefferstown. **Cherry Fair.**

Mid-July, Schaefferstown. **Schaefferstown Folk Festival.**

Mid-July, Cornwall. **Cornwall Country Fair**, Cornwall Iron Furnace. c/o Manager, Cornwall Iron Furnace, P. O. Box 251, Cornwall, PA 17016, 272-9711.

Late July-Early August, Lebanon. **Lebanon Area Fair**, Lebanon Area Fairgrounds, Rocherty Rd. c/o Ben Bow, RD 1, Box 829, Annville, PA 17003, 867-1305.

Late August, Mt. Gretna. **Outdoor Art Show**, Chautauqua Grounds. c/o Mt. Gretna Art Show, P.O. Box 419, Mt. Gretna, PA 17064, 964-2028.

Late August, Lebanon. **Lebanon Bologna Fest**, Lebanon Area Fairgrounds. c/o Lebanon Valley Tourist & Visitors Bureau, P.O. Box 626, Lebanon, PA 17042, 272-8555.

Mid-September, Schaefferstown. **Harvest Festival and Horse Plowing Contest.**

Mid-December, Schaefferstown. **Candlelight Tour of Historic Schaefferstown.**

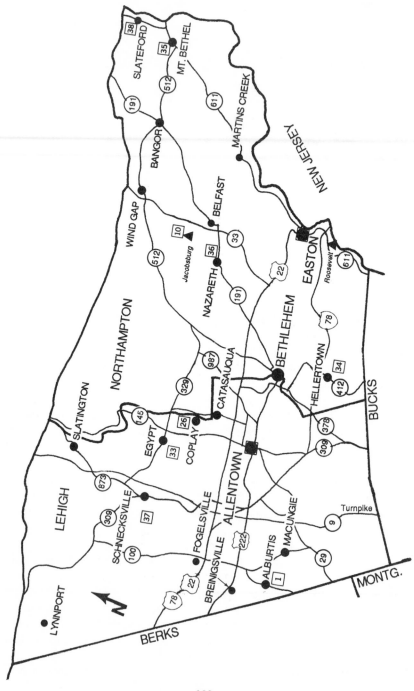

LEHIGH VALLEY

LEHIGH VALLEY (LEHIGH and NORTHAMPTON)

LEHIGH

Created: March 6, 1812, as the 42nd county, from part of Northampton County
County Seat: Allentown
Land Area: 348 square miles
Population (1989 est.): 287,000
Area code: 215

NORTHAMPTON

Created: March 11, 1752, as the 8th county, from part of Bucks County
County Seat: Easton
Land Area: 376 square miles
Population (1989 est.): 240,000
Area code: 215, except for Portland area (897 exchange), which is 717

Following local practice, Lehigh and Northampton Counties are considered as one unit. The boundary between the two is diminished in importance due to the overriding influence of the Allentown-Bethlehem metropolitan area. The city of Bethlehem is located in both counties, one of the few such municipalities in the state. Even when combined, the two counties are smaller in land area than five other PDC counties. The Allentown-Bethlehem urbanized area in effect comprises one large city, and would thereby be the state's third largest, after Philadelphia and Pittsburgh.

Sociologically, the two counties are similar in the makeup of their populations, although Germans comprise a notably larger proportion in Lehigh, and Italians in Northampton. However, German is by far the dominant single nationality in both.

The term "Lehigh Valley" refers to the broad relatively level valley lying between Blue Mountain on the north and South Mountain, a steep ridge bordering Allentown and Bethlehem on the south. The Lehigh River, which flows south from the anthracite coal region through a gap in Blue Mountain, makes an abrupt turn to the east when it reaches the base of South Mountain and empties into the Delaware River at Easton. The terrain west of the Lehigh and south of South Mountain is quite hilly and generally not heavily populated, although some increase in growth in this area may be anticipated with the completion of the last unfinished link in I-78.

The Lehigh Valley has long been noted as for its heavy manufacturing, but that is changing now as cleaner industries and high tech research and development become more important. Steelmaking, truck building, cement production, and slate mining, while still present to some degree, have given way to the manufacture of electronics parts, textiles, and pollution control equipment. Among the Valley's largest employers are AT&T Technologies, Fuller Company, Greif Company, and Kraft, Inc. Farming is not as large a part of the economy here as in most other parts of the PDC.

Historical Highlights

Few European settlers came to the Lehigh Valley before the "Walking Purchase" of 1737, which bought from the Delaware Indians all of what is now Northampton County and most of Lehigh. The Moravians were probably the first to arrive, in 1741, when they founded settlements at Bethlehem and Nazareth. Other Germans soon arrived, as did a smaller number of Scotch-Irish and Huguenots.

Several forts to protect against expected Indian attacks dotted the Valley in the mid-1700s, including those at Egypt, Lynnport, Slatington, and Wind Gap. The Delawares, the main tribe in this area, were peace-loving, but after the Walking Purchase cheated them out of a large portion of their lands, they were more easily incited. Internal squabbles with the Iroquois further weakened them, and they eventually moved west.

The area played an important support role during the Revolutionary War. While the Continental Congress fled Philadelphia to Lancaster and York during the British occupation in the winter of 1777-78, the Liberty Bell was taken from Independence Hall to Zion's Reformed Church in Allentown (then called Northampton). Government records were stored at Easton. While the war was going on, Iroquois in the northern part of the state who were loyal to the British began attacking largely unprotected white settlements in the upper Susquehanna valley. General John Sullivan set out from Easton in 1779 with a contingent of about 2,000 men to stop the pillaging. With the help of an equally large force from New York State, he routed the Indians and destroyed virtually every village in the "Five Nations."

Industrial development began with iron furnaces in the 1720s, followed by iron mining in 1812 in the hills south of Easton, slate mining about 1845 in the foothills of Blue Mountain, commercial cement making at Coplay in 1889, and steel manufacturing around 1900. It was during the first two decades of this century that the Valley experienced its greatest population growth, spurred by development of Bethlehem Steel and the arrival of Mack Trucks, which relocated to Allentown from

Brooklyn. However, other industries died out, such as iron mining in the early 1920s and silk manufacturing about the time of World War II. The area had been home to a number of small breweries, and they also closed or were absorbed by larger brewers. Modern-day industrial development has brought new industries to the Valley—Day-Timers, Inc., and Rodale Press among them, and the return of breweries with Stroh's modern facility at Fogelsville.

PLACES OF INTEREST

Alburtis, pop. 1,600. A small community along the Reading Railroad at the base of Lock Ridge.

Lock Ridge Furnace Museum (☐1)(45 min.), Franklin St., 435-4664 (Allentown). Open May thru September—Sat.-Sun. 1-4. Owned by the Lehigh County Historical Society, this NRHP site depicts anthracite iron production as it existed in the 19th century. Directions: In center of town, bear left at fork off Main St. onto Franklin St. for 0.3 mi. to Lock Ridge Park entrance on left.

Allentown, pop. 104,000, with Bethlehem and suburbs 304,000. The fourth largest city in Pennsylvania, founded in 1762 by William Allen. Originally called Northamptontowne or just Northampton, the present name was not adopted until 1834.

The iron industry, whose success was guaranteed by the arrival of the Lehigh Canal and later by the Lehigh Valley Railroad, began to develop about this time. The city became an important silk making center in the 1880s. This industry developed because of steps taken by German residents after the depression of 1873 to diversify manufacturing.

The city's greatest growth occurred between 1910 and 1930, when industrial development reached its peak. The population rose from 52,000 to 92,000 during this period. Pennsylvania Power and Light Company, which resulted from the consolidation of several smaller utilities, located its headquarters here and in 1927-28 built the city's tallest building. After World War II Western Electric built a large plant (the transistor was invented there), and Air Products and Chemicals Corporation was founded.

Allentown is the home of Muhlenberg and Cedar Crest Colleges, both located in the western section of the city. Muhlenberg was founded in 1848 as an affiliate of the Lutheran Church of America, and Cedar Crest, a women's college, opened in 1867. Penn State University's Allentown branch campus is about 8 miles west of the city, just north of Fogelsville.

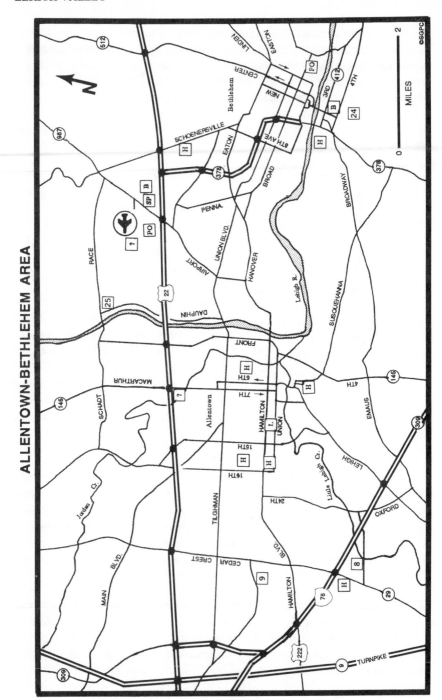

ALLENTOWN-BETHLEHEM AREA

The city is split geographically into four separate areas by the Lehigh River and Jordan and Little Lehigh Creeks. Connections between these areas are limited to relatively few bridges and viaducts, and in fact, there is no direct link between the eastern and southern sections of the city. The bulk of the city's factories and warehouses are in these two zones.

Although Allentown is one of the few PDC cities without an NRHP Historic District, the city is not lacking in historic sites.

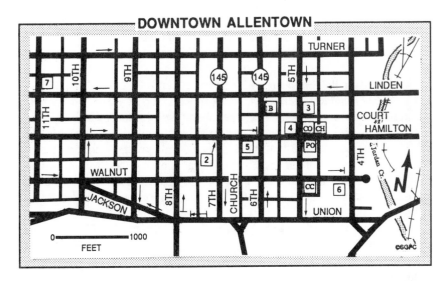

★★★ Downtown. The central business district is focused around **Center Square** (2) at 7th and Hamilton Sts. Hamilton St. from 6th to 10th has been renamed Hamilton Mall and has been converted into a pedestrian arcade with canopies over the widened sidewalks, poster displays, trees, and restricted vehicle traffic in an effort to compete with suburban shopping centers. A free trolley circles the downtown area on Hamilton and Linden Sts. between 5th and 12th. Pennsylvania Power & Light, Lehigh Portland Cement Company, and city and county government offices are downtown. PP&L's headquarters occupies the city's tallest building on the NW corner of 9th and Hamilton. The flagship of Hess's department store chain, one of Pennsylvania's largest, is on the NE corner.

★★★ Allentown Art Museum (3)(45 min.), 31 N. 5th St. (NE corner of Court), 432-4333. Open Tue.-Sat. 10-5, Sun. 1-5, extended evening hours during winter holiday season. Admission free, donation requested. An excellent museum originally housed in a church but since expanded into adjacent quarters. In addition to the paintings, which are very attractively displayed, there are old prints, a textile collection, drawings and photographs, a children's gallery with hands-on activities, and one room from the Francis Little House designed by Frank Lloyd Wright (the rest of the house is at the Metropolitan Museum in New York). Gallery talks and other special programs take place frequently throughout the year.

★★★ **Old Court House County Museum** (⓸)(30-45 min.), NW corner of 5th and Hamilton Sts., 435-4664. Open Mon.-Fri. 9-4, Sat.-Sun. 1-4. Admission free. This NRHP building was built around 1815 and now houses the Lehigh County Historical Museum, a well arranged collection of Indian relics, minerals, and educational displays relating to the county's history and industrial development. An expansion of the museum was underway at press time.

★★★ **Liberty Bell Shrine** (⓹)(20-30 min.), Zion's Reformed United Church of Christ, 622 Hamilton Mall, 435-4232. Open Mon.-Sat. 12-4, Sun. 2-4 from April 15 thru October 15. Admission free. The Liberty Bell was hidden in the basement of this church for nine months during the British occupation of Philadelphia in 1777-78. The shrine includes a 46-foot mural, accompanied by a taped narration, portraying the important events in eastern Pennsylvania during the Revolution. Other paintings, artifacts, colonial flags, and a full-size replica of the bell round out the interesting and well assembled display. The church is on the NRHP.

★★ **Trout Hall** (⓺)(30 min.), 414 Walnut St. (SW corner of 4th), 820-4043 or 435-4664. Open Tue.-Sat. 12-3, Sun. 1-4, closed January thru March. Admission free. The city's oldest home, built in 1770 and on the NRHP. James Allen, the son of the city's founder lived here. After the Civil War, it was the home of Muhlenberg College. Nicely furnished (nearly all items come from individuals and organizations in the area, since most of the Allens' possessions have been lost), reflecting the wealth of its builders.

Frank Buchman House (⓻)(20 min.), 117 N. 11th St., 435-7398 or -4664. Open Sat.-Sun. 1-4. Admission free. This Victorian home was built in 1895 and had been the residence of Dr. Frank Buchman, founder of the Oxford Group and Moral Re-armament. It is owned by the Lehigh County Historical Society.

Outside Downtown

★★ **Bieber Farmhouse (Lenni Lenape Historical Society)** (⓼)(30-45 min.), Fish Hatchery Rd. (SR 2010) in Little Lehigh Parkway, 797-2121 or 434-6819. Open Tue.-Sun. 10-3 or by appointment—organized groups with reservations have priority, so it's best to call to make sure there are no groups scheduled for the time you want to visit. Admission: adults, $1.50; children under 6, $1.00.

Primarily a privately funded learning center devoted to telling the story of the Lenni Lenape Indians who inhabited this area before the Europeans came. Some artifacts date from 12,000 BC. Exhibits change seasonally. Directions: 0.3 mi. east of Cedar Crest Blvd. (PA 29), 0.8 mi. west of S. 24th/Oxford St.

★★ **Haines Mill Museum** (⑨)(30-45 min.), 3600 Dorney Park Rd., 435-4664. Open Sat.-Sun. 1-4. Admission free. This NRHP mill was originally built in 1759 and rebuilt in 1909 after a fire. Lehigh County now owns the mill and has set it up as a milling museum. All the equipment is powered by the flow from Cedar Creek. A very good reconstruction. Directions: 1/2 mi. west of Cedar Crest Blvd. on Linden St. (SR 2008), at the corner of Main Blvd.

Community Resources

Lehigh Valley Convention and Visitors Bureau, A-B-E Airport Terminal Bldg., 3rd fl., 266-0560 (mailing address P.O. Box 2605, Lehigh Valley, PA 18001)
Visitors Information Center (open 9-6 daily Memorial Day thru Labor Day and weekends in Sept.), George Washington Lodge, MacArthur Rd. & US 22, 432-0181
Allentown-Lehigh Co. Chamber of Commerce, 462 Walnut St., 437-9661 or -9685
PO: 5th & Hamilton Sts., 821-8451
    1000 Postal Rd. (adjacent to A-B-E Airport), 266-3256
Public Library: 12th & Hamilton Sts., 820-2400
Allentown Hospital: 17th & Chew Sts., 778-2300
Allentown Osteopathic Medical Center: 1736 Hamilton St., 770-8300
Sacred Heart Hospital: 421 Chew St., 776-4500
Lehigh Valley Hospital Center: 1200 S. Cedar Crest Blvd., 776-8000
Good Shepherd Hospital: 6th & St. John Sts., 776-3120
Court House: 455 Hamilton St., 820-3000
City Police: emergency 911, all other business 437-7751
City Hall: 435 Hamilton St., 437-7511
State Police: Peach Lane & Mohr Rd., Fogelsville, 285-4444
            2930 Airport Rd., Bethlehem, 861-2026
Bus (Greyhound): 27 N. 6th St., 434-6188
Bus (Trans-Bridge): 2012 Industrial Dr., Bethlehem, 868-6001; 434-4110

Bangor, pop. 5,300. Once the center of the soft slate mining area of northern Northampton County, now primarily a textile manufacturing town, as are its neighbors Pen Argyl and Wind Gap.

Franklin Hill Vineyards, Franklin Hill Rd., 588-8708. Open Sat.-Sun. 12-6. Tours and other hours by appointment. Directions: From the (only) traffic light in Martins Creek, go west on Front St. (SR 1002) for 0.9 mi., turn right on Franklin Hill Rd. (SR 1013) for 1.6 mi. to dirt lane on right leading to winery.

Belfast, unincorporated, pop. about 700.

Andrew Benade House (⑩), Belfast Rd. (SR 1012) at Jacobsburg Environmental Education Center, 759-7616 (Nazareth). Built in the mid-1700s and named for a Moravian bishop who lived here at that time. Currently closed for renovation, anticipated opening Fall, 1989.

Bethlehem, pop. 70,000, with Allentown and suburbs 304,000. About 50,000 of the city's population is in Northampton County, the remainder in Lehigh. Founded in 1741 by Moravians, who named the settlement for the Biblical town. This was the first permanent Moravian community in America, and the Bethlehem church is considered the "mother" church of the denomination in the United States.

A prosperous industrial center developed along Monocacy Creek just north of the Lehigh River soon after the Moravian settlement. A total of 32 industries were located here before 1750, including a tannery, forge, oil mill, springhouse, and one of the first municipal waterworks in America (1754). Most of the industries remained in operation for about 100 years. The coming of the canals and railroads helped keep Bethlehem prosperous because of its location along the Lehigh River.

Bethlehem Steel Company's predecessor Saucona Iron built its first mill in the city in 1857 to make railroad rails. The firm became Bethlehem Steel in 1899, by which time it had expanded production to forgings for electric generators, metal cutting tools, and armor plate for Navy ships. Despite having a steel mill as its major employer, Bethlehem never acquired the grimy and shabby appearance that characterizes many steelmaking towns. Even the area around the plant has been kept relatively well maintained. The city's downtown area and **Historic District** are among the most attractive in the PDC.

The city is famous for its Christmas tours and activities. Many of the special events are held downtown. There are also evening bus tours to view the thousands of traditional white Christmas lights and the star at the summit of South Mountain overlooking the entire Lehigh Valley.

The city is home to Lehigh University, which occupies three campuses on South Mountain, and Moravian College, whose main campus is at Main and Locust Sts. about half a mile north of downtown. Northampton County Community College occupies a modern campus about 5 miles northeast of downtown.

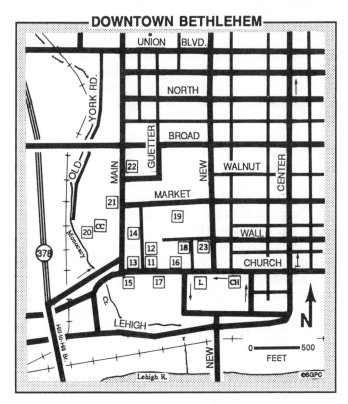

Downtown. The area bounded by Monocacy Creek and New, Church, and Broad Streets contains nearly all of the city's historic and cultural attractions. This area approximately four blocks square should be covered on foot.

★★★★**Moravian Community** (1-1/2-2 hours), 867-0173. The Community Walking Tour starts at the **Gemeinhaus** (⑪), 66 W. Church St. Open for tours Tue.-Sat. 1-4, closed January, Good Friday, Easter Saturday, Independence Day, Thanksgiving, and Christmas Eve and Day. Admission to Moravian Museum only: adults, $2.00; students, $1.00. The complete Moravian Community tour, including the Museum, is for groups of 10 or more, and is available Mon.-Sat. 10-4. Admission: adults, $4.00; students, $1.50.

The Gemeinhaus is the oldest surviving building in the city, built in 1741. This is a five-story log structure that houses the **Moravian Museum**. Each room depicts a different aspect of Moravian life: school, kitchen, bedroom, musical instruments, and others. The building is on the NRHP and may be the largest log structure in continuous use in America; the clapboard exterior was added about

1860. The second floor was used for church services until 1751, when the **Old Chapel** (⏨) was built. It is immediately adjacent to the Gemeinhaus and can be viewed from the inside, as can the 1803 **Central Church** (⏩). This massive Federal-style building has six-foot thick walls, enabling the roof to be supported over the sanctuary without pillars. The church has a seating capacity of 1,500 and was built at a time when Bethlehem's population was less than half that. The **Apothecary Museum** (⏨), rear of 424 Main St., is open by appointment only; call or apply at the Gemeinhaus (867-0173). Admission: adults, $1.00; students, 50¢. The drug store was founded in 1752 and operated continuously until 1951. The small quarters contain pharmacists' tools and artifacts and the original fireplace where prescriptions were prepared.

Other buildings in the Moravian Community that can be viewed from the outside are the **Brethren's House** (⏨)(1748), which now houses Moravian College's music department; **Sisters' House** (⏨) (1744, added to in 1752 and 1773), a dormitory originally built for single men but turned over to women's use after the Brethren's House was completed; **Widow's House** (⏨)(1768, with additions in 1794 and 1889); **Schnitz House** (⏨)(1801), a small stone house built for the the preparation of cut and dried apples, or *schnitz*; and the **Bell House** (1746, additions in 1748 and 1749), originally a residence for married couples. The latter buildings, except for the Schnitz House, are used as private apartments for Moravian widows and single women and are not open to the public. The entire row of buildings on the south side of W. Church St. between the City Center and Main St. belong to the Moravian Community. Before leaving the Community, take a walk through God's Acre (⏨), the graveyard fronting on Market St. behind the Gemeinhaus. All the gravestones are flat, indicating the Moravian belief in the equality of man. There is an Indian buried there who became a character in James Fenimore Cooper's The Last of the Mohicans. The Moravian Community is truly an outstanding combination of preservation and restoration.

★★★ **18th Century Industrial Area** (⏩)(1 hour), along Monocacy Creek behind and downhill from the west side of the 400-block of Main St. This NRHP area is accessible by vehicle from Old York Rd. via W. Union Blvd., and on foot via a walkway leading downhill from the Main St. end of the Hill-to-Hill Bridge. Begin at the **Visitor Center** (691-5300 or -0603) located in **Luckenbach Mill**, an 1869 flour mill restored in 1982. In addition to tourist information, the mill contains a contemporary crafts gallery, interpretive exhibit, and the offices of the Bethlehem Area Chamber of Commerce. A 30-min. orientation film on Bethlehem is shown daily at 11 and 2; admission: adults, $1.50; students, 50¢. Tours are available as follows: July and August—Tue.-Sat. 10-4, Sun. 12-4; April thru June and September thru December—Sat. 10-4, Sun. 12-4, and Tue.-Fri. by appointment. Closed January thru March. Admission to tours: adults, $3.00; seniors and students, $2.00;

children under 6, free; families, $10.00. The buildings can be viewed at other times from the outside; these include the 1762 **Waterworks, Tannery** (1761), and **Spring House** (1764). The Waterworks housed the first pumped municipal water supply in America.

★ **Goundie House** (㉑)(30-40 min.), 501 Main St., opposite Market, 691-5300. Open Mon.-Sat. 12-4. Admission free, donation requested. This 1810 Federal-style home belonged to John Goundie, a local brewer and mayor of Bethlehem, and is thought to have been the first brick townhouse in the city. It has had various uses in addition to being a residence, and a complete restoration of the interior is underway. Furnishings, donated by local residents, are from the period 1741 to 1885; possessions of the Goundie family have long since been lost.

★★ **Sun Inn** (㉒)(20-30 min.), 564 Main St., 866-1758. Open Tue.-Fri. 12:30-4, Sat. 10-4, or by appointment. This inn was built by the Moravians in 1758 and was widely known as one of the finest in the colonies. The inn was remodeled inside a number of times, so only the exterior walls are original. However, the Sun Inn Preservation Association, which acquired the building in 1975, located the original plans, so the reconstruction is precise. A restaurant now operates in several of the upstairs rooms, and the four first floor rooms have been made into a museum showing what the guest rooms of the Revolutionary period would have looked like. An interesting restoration of a building that was probably unique for its times.

★★★ **Annie S. Kemerer Museum** (㉓)(45 min.), 427 N. New St., 868-6868. Open Tue.-Fri., Sun. 1-4, Sat. 10-4, closed Mon., January, and major holidays. Admission by donation. Annie S. Kemerer was a well-to-do collector in Bethlehem; she collected Currier and Ives prints, locally made grandfather clocks, Bohemian glass, Oriental rugs, and other items. She never lived in the house, but left the money for the museum to be set up. The house was built in 1846 with 1-1/2 stories, but a second full story was added later by raising the roof; evidence of this can be seen on the outside. The second floor is devoted to changing exhibits. An eclectic collection, but well presented, and in a beautiful setting.

Also worth seeing downtown are beautiful Victorian and Colonial style homes in the 400-block of N. New St. and the unit blocks of E. and W. Market, Wall, and E. Church Sts. The 400- and 500-blocks of Main St., the center of the downtown retail area, are also very attractively refurbished. The **City Center**, located on the south side of Church St. at the foot of New, is a beautiful complex of public buildings built in 1967. The City Administration (CH), Public Safety, Town Hall, and Public Library (L) are in this complex, which overlooks the Lehigh River and the south side of the city.

Outside Downtown

★★ **Lehigh University Art Galleries** (☒)(30-45 min.), 758-3615. There are three galleries: Ralph Wilson and Hall, at the Alumni Memorial Building, and DuBois at Maginnes Hall. Wilson and Hall are open daily 9-5, Sat. 9-12, and Sun. 2-5; DuBois is open daily 9 AM-10 PM and Sat. 9-noon. Admission free to all galleries. Exhibits include porcelains, photography, paintings, sculpture, prints, and gold weights from America, Europe, Africa, China, and Japan; exhibits change periodically. The Alumni Memorial Building is a two-story Gothic stone structure with a central tower on the east side of Brodhead Ave. just south of Packer Ave.; there is a visitors' parking lot in front of the building. Maginnes Hall is a modern two-story yellow brick building on the NE corner of Packer Ave. and Vine St. The two buildings are about one block apart but one cannot be seen from the other.

<u>Community Resources</u>
Lehigh Valley Convention and Visitors Bureau, A-B-E Airport Terminal Bldg., 3rd fl., 266-0560 (mailing address P.O. Box 2605, Lehigh Valley, PA 18001)
Bethlehem Area Chamber of Commerce, 459 Old York Rd., 868-1513
PO: Broad & Wood Sts., 866-0911
    1000 Postal Rd. (adjacent to A-B-E Airport), 266-3256
Public Library: 11 W. Church St., 867-3761
Muhlenberg Hospital Center: Schoenersville Rd., 861-2200
St. Luke's Hospital: 801 Ostrum St., 691-4229
City Police: emergency 865-7171, all other business 865-7187
City Hall: 10 E. Church St., 865-7100
State Police: 2930 Airport Rd., 861-2026
Bus (Greyhound): Adams & Mechanic Sts., 867-3988
Bus (Trans-Bridge): 2012 Industrial Dr., 868-6001

Breinigsville, unincorporated, pop. about 400.

Clover Hill Vineyards & Winery, Old US 222, 398-2468. Open Wed.-Sat. 11-5, Sun. 12-5. Tours by appointment. Directions: From US 222 southbound, bear right on old 222 for 1.5 mi. to entrance on left. From US 222 northbound, bear left on Schantz Rd. (SR 3012) 1/2 mile east of Berks Co. line, go 1/4 mi., turn right on old 222 (first right after PA 863), go 0.1 mi. to entrance on right.

Catasauqua, pop. 6,700. An industrial town along the Lehigh River that has an NRHP **Historic District** bounded by Race, 2nd, and Mulberry Sts., and the Lehigh Canal. It includes the small business district of the borough and some industrial buildings.

George Taylor House (☒)(30 min.), Lehigh & Poplar Sts., 264-4367 or 435-4664. Open June thru October—Sat.-Sun. 1-4. Admission free. This NRHP house was built in 1768 by George Taylor, local ironmaster and signer of the Declaration of Independence, who used it as a summer residence. Now owned by the Lehigh County Historical Society which has restored it. Directions: From US 22, take Fullerton exit and go north on 3rd St. (SR 1015) for 1.1 mi., turn right on Bridge St., cross Lehigh River, then make first right onto Lehigh St. 1/2 block to house on left. From Union Blvd. in Allentown, go north on Dauphin St. (SR 1007) for 2.3 mi. to house on right.

Coplay, pop. 3,000. Industrial town along the Lehigh River, birthplace of the Portland cement industry in America.

★★ **David O. Saylor Cement Industry Museum** (☒)(30 min.), N. 2nd St. at Saylor Park, 435-4664 (Allentown). Open May thru September—Sat.-Sun. 1-4. Owned by the Lehigh County Historical Society and on the NRHP, the museum traces the history of cement making.

Easton, pop. 26,000. Established in 1752, the same year that Northampton County was created, although a settlement had already existed here for at least thirty years. Easton, at the juncture of the Lehigh and Delaware Rivers, was a strategically located industrial center, served by the canal system and later by railroads. Easton had the nation's first industrial park, along the Lehigh Canal.

The town was an important political and military center in its early history. In 1779 General John Sullivan amassed an army of 2,000 here and set out for the Iroquois settlements of northern Pennsylvania and the Southern Tier of New York. During this campaign he and an army from New York State virtually annihilated the Iroquois, who had sided with the British in the Revolution and had attacked white settlements in the region.

Just as Allentown is fragmented by creeks, so is Easton. The Lehigh River and Bushkill Creek converge on the Delaware a few blocks apart and divide the city into three separate areas. Easton is a hilly city, with the downtown area occupying the only flood plain land. Lafayette College, a highly regarded small liberal arts institution founded in 1826, is atop the hill overlooking Bushkill Creek on the north side.

Downtown. A brochure describing a **walking tour** of the central district is available from the Chamber of Commerce. The district extends about two blocks in all directions from Centre Square. It has significant historic and architectural value, and is a NRHP **Historic District**. The highlights of this area are:

221

Centre Square (⟨27⟩), the intersection of 3rd and Northampton Sts. The monument in the center honors local Civil War veterans. An open-air farmers' market is held here year-round on Tuesday, Thursday, and Saturday, a tradition dating from 1791.

Parsons-Taylor House (⟨28⟩), NE corner of 4th & Ferry Sts. Open by appointment. This NRHP home was built in 1757 by William Parsons, a surveyor and founder of Easton. George Taylor, a signer of the Declaration of Independence, lived here (he also had a summer home at Catasauqua (see listing)). The house is owned by the George Taylor chapter of the Daughters of the American Revolution and is open on special occasions for visitation; phone 253-1222 for information.

Mixsell House (⟨29⟩)(20-30 min.), SW corner of 4th & Ferry Sts., 253-1222. Open Apr.-Dec.—Thu.-Sun. 9-4. Admission free. This 1833 Federal-style brick home, on the NRHP, is the headquarters of the Northampton County Historical Society. The museum features changing exhibits relating to local history.

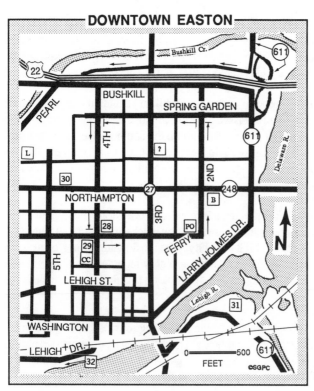

State Theater (⟨30⟩), 453 Northampton St., is a beautifully restored NRHP theater now used as a performing arts center. The 1,500-seat auditorium was built in 1878 and served as a bank until 1925. Tours are given for groups of 20 or more; phone 258-7766 for reservations.

The YWCA Building at 41 N. 3rd St. houses a **Visitors Information Center** (⟨?⟩) operated by the Two Rivers Area Chamber of Commerce. Open Tue.-Sat. 10-4, Sun. 1-4.

Brochures describing local attractions are available, and there are graphic displays of the community's highlights. The four-story building is of French chateau design, but there are also German and Italian influences in its architecture.

Numerous Victorian mansions line the 200-block of Spring Garden St., and there are other architectural styles evident in churches, stores, banks, and residences.

★★★ **Canal Museum** (31)(30-40 min.), 200 S. Delaware Dr. (PA 611), 250-6700. Open Mon.-Sat. 10-4, Sun. 1-5. Admission: adults, $1.00; children 5-12, 50¢; under 5, free. A very well developed and important museum depicting the development of the canal industry in Pennsylvania (where it was strongest) and the nation, and the only one in the country dealing with towpath canals. The museum treats the following subjects: what is a canal?, canals and economic growth, canals and technology, life on the canals, and canals today. Exhibits, lighted maps, a model canal boat cabin, and video tell the story in considerable detail. Canal boat rides are available from Memorial Day to Labor Day, and rentals of bicycles, pedal boats, and canoes are available. Free lectures on transportation and industrial history are presented during the fall and winter.

Outside Downtown

★★ **Locktender's House** (32)(20-30 min.), Hugh Moore Park, Glendon Ave., 250-6700. Open Memorial Day weekend thru Labor Day—Wed.-Sun. 12-4:30, weekends only rest of September. Admission, which includes the canal boat ride: adults, $3.00; children 5-12, $1,50. Located at Lock 8 on the Lehigh Canal, the house shows how the locktenders and their families lived. Four rooms of the house are open to visitors. The **Chain Bridge**, spanning the river and canal at the house, was used to hoist boats at the point where the canal shifted from the south side to a channel on the north side of the river.

<u>Community Resources</u>
Lehigh Valley Convention and Visitors Bureau, A-B-E Airport Terminal Bldg., 3rd fl., 266-0560 (mailing address P.O. Box 2605, Lehigh Valley, PA 18001)
Visitors Information Center (open 9-6 daily Memorial Day thru Labor Day and weekends in Sept.), 25th St. Shopping Center at Northampton St. & Nazareth Rd. (25th St. exit of US 22), 258-8525
Two Rivers Area Chamber of Commerce, 157 S. 4th St., 253-4211
Visitors Information Center: 41 N. 3rd St.
PO: 2nd & Ferry Sts.
Public Library: 6th & Church Sts., 258-2917
Easton Hospital: 21st & Lehigh Sts. (Wilson), 250-4000

Court House: 7th & Washington Sts., 253-4111
City Police: emergency 250-6666, all other business 250-6665
City Hall: 650 Ferry St., 250-6600
State Police: 207 E. Center St., Stockertown, 258-0816
Bus: 154 Northampton St., 253-4126

Egypt, unincorporated, pop. about 2,000. A small community in the northern part of Whitehall Township, originally a farming village, but now engulfed in suburbia.

★★ **Troxell-Stockel House and Farm Museum** (33)(30-45 min.), 4229 Reliance St., 435-4664. Open June thru October—Sat.-Sun. 1-4. Admission free. An NRHP property owned by the Lehigh County Historical Society. The house was built in 1756 and is an example of medieval German style. It is furnished to the period, and the barn, of later vintage, contains farm implements, carriages, and sleighs. Directions: Go west from PA 145 on PA 329 for 1.1 mi.to Reliance St., turn left for 0.3 mi. to house on right.

Fogelsville, unincorporated, pop. about 800. Originally a small crossroads community, now, because of good highway access, an important industrial area, with several industrial parks just east and south of the village. The Allentown branch of Penn State University is about a mile north of town.

Stroh Brewery (40-45 min.), PA 100 just south of I-78/US 22, 395-6811. Free tours weekdays 12-3—on the half hour in summer, on the hour remainder of year, closed holidays. This modern brewery was built in 1971.

Hellertown, pop. 5,900.

★★ **Lost River Caverns** (34)(30-40 min.), Durham St., 838-8767. Open daily except Christmas and New Year's Day 9-6. Admission: adults, $5.00; children under 12, $2.50. The cave was discovered in 1883 and has been open commercially since 1930. In the early years after its discovery the cave housed a dance hall. A small stream flows through part of the caverns, but its source and mouth are unknown, hence the name "Lost River". Directions: Just south of the center of town, turn east off PA 412 at traffic light on Penn St., go 1-1/2 blocks, follow left curve onto Durham St. for 1/2 mi.

Mount Bethel, unincorporated, pop. about 1,000.

★ **Slate Belt Museum** (35)(30 min.), PA 611, 0.1 mi. north of PA 512 intersection, (717) 897-6412. Open Memorial Day thru September—Sat.-Sun. 1-5. Admission by donation. A small museum, housed in a former church, commemorating the slate industry in the area as well as other facets of local history. Displays pertaining to the soft slate industry occupy only a small part of the museum; the remainder houses Lenni-Lenape Indian relics, old clothing and Army uniforms of local residents, and a nearly complete collection of Homefront magazine, published in nearby Pen Argyl during World War II and sent free to GIs. The magazine is believed to have been the only one of its type, and was financed by contributions from churches and residentsof the area. A worthy effort by the Slate Belt Historical Society to preserve its past, but the museum is too cluttered and the tiered church floor makes it a little tricky to move about.

Nazareth, pop. 5,700. A very pretty town in the center of the cement producing area. Especially attractive is Moravian Hall Square, Main and Center Sts., one block west of PA 191. Pennsylvania International Raceway (autos) is just south of town on PA 191.

★★ **Whitefield House** (⊠)(20 min.), 214 E. Center St. (PA 191) (SW corner of New), 759-5070. Open Wed.-Fri. 1-4. Admission free, donation requested. The first Moravians arrived here in 1740 and began construction of this building to be a school for Negroes, although it was never used for that purpose. It is now the Museum of the Moravian Historical Society, containing musical instruments, household items, maps and prints, Indian artifacts, and clothing from Moravian settlements around the world, documented as much as possible as to date and place of origin. Several instruments made in the mid-1700s are the only known ones in existence. The collections on display are limited, but the Society has many more items in storage. A varied exhibit that can appeal not just to Moravians.

Schnecksville, unincorporated, pop. about 1,500. Home of Lehigh County Community College.

★★ **Trexler-Lehigh County Game Preserve** (⊠)(1 hour), Game Preserve Rd. (SR 4007), 2.0 mi. west of PA 309, 799-4171. Open Memorial Day weekend thru Labor Day—daily 10-5; April, May, and Labor Day thru October—Sun. 10-dusk. Admission: adults, $2.00; children thru age 12 and seniors, $1.00. A 1,700-acre wildlife sanctuary housing a wide variety of unusual animals (sika deer, muntjas, aoudad, pigmy donkeys, reptiles, birds, and others). A nature study building features wildlife displays and films (weekends only). A good place for kids, but adults would also find the animals enjoyable.

Slateford, unincorporated, pop. about 100.

Slateford Farm (⎡38⎤)(45 min.), PA 611, 2.0 mi. north of Delaware River bridge at Portland, 1.6 mi. south of Monroe Co. line, (717) 588-6637 (Bushkill). Open late June thru Labor Day—Wed.-Sun. 12-5. Admission free. Owned by the National Park Service as part of the Delaware Water Gap National Recreation Area, this is an interpretive farm depicting agrarian life in the 19th century and the development of the slate industry in this area. The farmhouse and several outbuildings are furnished.

COVERED BRIDGES

There are six covered bridges in Lehigh County, for which a tour brochure is available from the Allentown-Lehigh Co. Chamber of Commerce. The tour is also marked by signs on the roads. Five bridges are on Jordan Creek within a few miles of each other northwest of Allentown; the sixth is in Little Lehigh Parkway in the city of Allentown. Since directional signs are posted, and a brochure is available, the bridges are not listed individually. Northampton County has one covered bridge, **Kreidersville**, located 3 miles north of Northampton just east of Kreidersville Rd. (SR 4003) at Hokendauqua Creek.

RECREATION FACILITIES

Jacobsburg State Park (Environmental Education Center), 435 Belfast Rd. (SR 1010), 1-1/4 mi. W of Belfast exit of PA 33, Belfast, 759-7616 (Nazareth).
Roosevelt State Park, PA 611 and 32 along the Delaware from Easton to Bristol, Bucks Co., 982-5560 (Upper Black Eddy).
Apple Valley X-C Ski Area, PA 29/100, 1/4 mi. north of Berks Co. line, Zionsville, 966-5525.
Doe Mountain Ski Area, Macungie (See **Berks County**).
Dorney Park & Wildwater Kingdom, 3830 Dorney Park Rd., Allentown, 395-3724. Open weekends from late April thru Memorial Day, daily except for certain Mondays until Labor Day. Admission to either Dorney Park or Wildwater Kingdom: age 7-61, $12.95; age 3-6, over 61, or handicapped, $7.50. After 5 PM, all ages $7.50. Combination admission: age 7-61, $16.95; others, $10.00. Additional $1.50 parking charge.
Lehigh County Velodrome, US 222, Trexlertown, 965-6930. Races Fridays 7:30 PM, mid-May thru August. Admission: $2.50-$7.00, depending on location and event.
Point Pleasant Canoeing, PA 611 along Delaware River, 5.8 mi. north of Easton, 1.5 mi. south of traffic light in Martins Creek, 252-TUBE (8823) or 258-2606 (See also **Bucks County**).

CALENDAR OF EVENTS

Early April, Easton. **Newport Jazz Festival All-Stars**, State Theater. c/o State Theater, 453 Northampton St., Easton, PA 18042, 252-3132.

Late April, Bethlehem. **Pulaski Festival.** 838-6858 (Hellertown)

Early May, Allentown. **Corn Planting Ceremony**, Lenni Lenape Historical Society. c/o Carla Messinger, Lenni Lenape Historical Society, Fish Hatchery Rd., Allentown RD 2, PA 18103, 797-2121 or 434-6819.

Mid-May, Bethlehem. **Shad Festival**, 18th Century Industrial Area. c/o Historic Bethlehem, Inc., 459 Old York Rd., Bethlehem, PA 18018, 868-6311.

Mid-May, Bethlehem. **Bach Music Festival**, Lehigh University. c/o Bonnie Salventi, Bach Choir of Bethlehem, 423 Heckewelder Pl., Bethlehem, PA 18018, 866-4382.

Late May, Easton. **Historic Easton House Tour.** c/o Toni Mitman, P.O. Box 994, Easton, PA 18042, 258-1612.

Late May, Allentown. **Mayfair**, Allentown Parks System. c/o Marie Conway, 2020 Hamilton St., Allentown, PA 18104, 437-6900.

Early June, Bethlehem. **Moravian College Antique Show.** c/o Patricia Helfrich, Alumni House, Moravian College, Bethlehem, PA 18018, 861-1366.

Mid-June, Bethlehem. **Martha Washington Strawberry Festival**, Sun Inn. c/o Jeannette MacDonald, Sun Inn Preservation Assn., 564 Main St., Bethlehem, PA 18018, 866-1758.

Early July, Easton. **Canal Festival**, Hugh Moore Park. c/o Hugh Moore Park, P.O. Box 877, Easton, PA 18044, 250-6700.

Early July, Easton. **Easton Area Heritage Day**, Downtown. c/o Two Rivers Area Chamber of Commerce, 157 S. 4th St., Easton, PA 18042, 253-4211.

Mid-July, Bethlehem. **Christmas City Fair**, Christmas City Fairgrounds. c/o Richard Szulborski, 669 Atlantic St., Bethlehem, PA 18015, 865-3751.

Late July, Allentown. **Lehigh Valley Balloon Festival**, Queen City Airport. c/o Lehigh County Convention & Visitors Bureau, P.O. Box 2605, Lehigh Valley, PA 18001, 266-0560.

Early August, Macungie. **Das Awkscht Fescht (August Festival).** 820-3393 (Allentown).

Late August, Bangor. **Blue Valley Farm Show.** 588-3693.

Late August, Bethlehem. **Musikfest**, Downtown. c/o Margaret Barshine, 556 Main St., Bethlehem, PA 18018, 861-0678.

Late August-Early September, Allentown. **The Great Allentown Fair**, Fairgrounds, 17th & Chew Sts. 433-7541.

Late September, Mt. Bethel. **Autumn Arts Festival**, Slate Belt Museum. (717) 897-6181.

October, Bethlehem. **Juried Exhibition of Contemporary Crafts**, Luckenbach Mill Gallery. c/o Bethlehem Visitor Center, 459 Old York Rd., Bethlehem, PA 18018, 691-0603.

Early October, Allentown. **A Time of Thanksgiving**, Lenni Lenape Historical Society. c/o Carla Messinger, Lenni Lenape Historical Society, Fish Hatchery Rd., Allentown RD 2, PA 18103, 797-2121 or 434-6819.

Mid-October, Bethlehem. **Living History Days**, 18th Century Industrial Area. 868-6311.

Mid-November, Allentown. **World of Wheels Custom Car Show.** 394-8365.

Late November, Easton. **Peace Candle Lighting Ceremony**, Centre Square. 250-6612.

Late November, Bethlehem. **Christmas City Lighting Ceremony**, City Center Plaza, 10 E. Church St. 868-1513.

Late November-January 1, Bethlehem. **Moravian Christmas Putz**, Christian Education Bldg. c/o Moravian Museum, 66 W. Church St., Bethlehem, PA 18018, 866-5661 or 867-0173.

Late November-Late December, Bethlehem. **Christmas City Night Light Tours**, Lehigh Valley Bank, 52 W. Broad St., 868-1513.

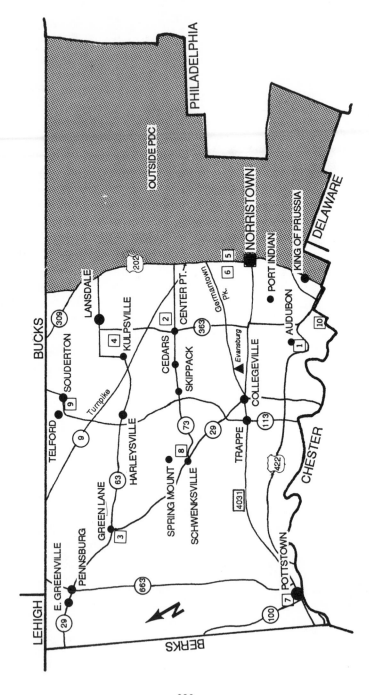

MONTGOMERY

Created: September 10, 1784, as the 15th county, from part of Philadelphia County
County Seat: Norristown
Land Area: 498 square miles, of which approximately 300 in PDC
Population (1989 est.): 685,000, of which approximately 252,000 in PDC
Area code: 215

The portion of Montgomery County northwest of US 202, the PDC's southeastern border, contains the county's rural area and a small part of its densely populated suburbs of Philadelphia. The PDC part of the county has about 60% of the land area but only 37% of the population. References to Montgomery County in this chapter, unless otherwise specified or where the meaning is obvious, are to the section in the PDC.

The county lies on a northwest-to-southeast axis with all but a very small section lying north of the Schuylkill River. Many of the main highways generally follow this axis, with other roads running at right angles to them. This highway pattern is also found in adjacent sections of neighboring Bucks County. Terrain in the southeastern half of the county is mostly level, but rolling in the northwestern half. The highest elevations are only about 600 feet near the Bucks County border, and are generally in the 200-300 foot range in the lowlands of the southeast. Montgomery County has the least hilly terrain among all PDC counties.

Despite the favorable topography and soil conditions for farming, agriculture is no longer a significant part of the county's economy. This is a heavily populated county and the land commands greater value for other uses. The county is an important industrial area, however. The largest industries in the PDC region are Merck & Company, the drug concern, whose headquarters are at West Point; Leeds & Northrup, a manufacturer of environmental equipment in North Wales; Ford Electronics Division in Lansdale; and Knoll International, an office furniture maker in East Greenville. Except for the King of Prussia area, the PDC portion of Montgomery County has yet to experience the development of high tech and research firms that neighboring Chester County has seen.

German is still the largest single nationality, and is stronger in the PDC area than in the county as a whole. However, no single group has an overwhelming presence.

Montgomery County has a relatively large Mennonite population, centered mainly around Souderton, Harleysville, and Kulpsville. The Schwenkfelders, a very small denomination, live primarily in the county; four of their five churches are in the central area (see description of Schwenkfelders on page 33).

Historical Highlights

The first European settlers in the county were English and Welsh, who began arriving at the same time as William Penn (1681). The English and Welsh left their names on nearly all the townships in the county, yet many of the local communities, whether incorporated as boroughs or unincorporated, have Germanic names.

The most famous site in America's war of independence is located in Montgomery County (and a small corner of Chester)—Valley Forge. However, no major military action of the Revolution occurred in the county, which, during the war, was still part of Philadelphia County.

The limestone soil that underlies most of the county led to early industrial development of lime kilns. Marble quarrying and lead, copper, and iron mining also developed during the county's early history.

Montgomery County has been the birthplace or home of a number of historically notable people, among them Henry Melchior Muhlenberg, pioneer of the Lutheran church in America; several of Muhlenberg's sons—Peter, a Revolutionary War general, and Frederick, the first speaker of the U.S. House of Representatives; David Rittenhouse, surveyor, astronomer, and builder of America's first telescope; naturalist and painter John J. Audubon; Winfield Scott Hancock, well-known Civil War general; and several Pennsylvania governors.

PLACES OF INTEREST

Audubon, unincorporated, pop. about 1,500. The community is named for John James Audubon, whose first home in America was located here.

★★★ **Mill Grove** (1)(1 hour), Audubon and Pawling Rds., 666-5593. Open Tue.-Sat. 10-4, Sun. 1-4, closed Thanksgiving, Christmas, and New Year's Day. Admission free. Now owned by Montgomery County, the NRHP home was built in 1762. Audubon moved here with his family in 1789 at the age of four and remained here until 1806. Audubon was noted not only for his paintings of birds and wildlife, but also for taxidermy. The home has been attractively restored, and there are gardens and nature trails on the 175-acre property. Directions: From PA 363 at US 422 interchange, go north for 0.2 mi. on 363, then left on Audubon Rd. for 1.2 mi. to Pawling Rd.

Center Point (Worcester), unincorporated, pop. about 500.

★★★ **Peter Wentz Farmstead** (②)(45-60 min.), Schultz Rd., 584-5104. Open Tue.-Sat. 10-4, Sun. 1-4 (last tour 3:30), closed the second week in September, Thanksgiving, Christmas, and New Year's Day. Admission free. The house dates to 1758, the barn to 1744. This was a wealthy man's farm, as evident in the style of construction and size of the house. Both have been restored by Montgomery County, the owner, to appear as they would have in 1777. At that time George Washington was headquartered here and planned his strategy for the Battle of Germantown. The property was in the Schultz family from 1794 to 1969, and they were the last of only three families that occupied it, including the Wentzes. Other buildings on the grounds include a log house and reception center as well as a garden and orchard. The house has been exceptionally well restored. Directions: From intersection of PA 73 and 363, go east on 73 for 0.4 mi., bear left on Schultz Rd. There are two roads going left at this point—Schultz is the lesser turn, and is marked as a dead end.

Collegeville, pop. 3,200. Home of Ursinus College, a liberal arts school founded in 1869. The **Perkiomen Bridge** on Ridge Pike (SR 4031) spanning Perkiomen Creek was built in 1799 and is one of the oldest in the state still in use. It's a beautiful stone arch structure—the best viewpoint is from the parking lot of the Collegeville Inn on the east side of the creek. Ridge Pike was the main road from Philadelphia to Norristown, Pottstown, and Reading before the advent of expressways, and formerly carried US 422.

Green Lane, pop. 500.

Goschenhoppen Folklife Library and Museum (③)(20-30 min.), PA 29, 0.1 mi. south of PA 63, 234-8953. Open April thru November—Sun. 1:30-4 and by appointment. Admission free, donations accepted. Located in Red Men's Hall, adjoining the post office, the ground floor recreates a late 19th-century store, both inside and out. The small museum upstairs is devoted to furnishings, folk art, music, and items of historical and genealogical interest of the 18th- and 19th-century Pennsylvania Germans who lived in the two communities called "Goschenhoppen". The communities were in the area of the villages of Zieglersville, Salford, Perkiomenville, Bergey, and Harleysville in Montgomery County, and Hereford, Bally, and Bechtelsville in Berks County. The Goschenhoppen Historians, who operate the museum, sponsor the Goschenhoppen Folk Festival on the second Friday and Saturday in August (see Calendar of Events).

King of Prussia, unincorporated, pop. about 9,000. Home of the massive shopping development that includes The Plaza, The Court, and several smaller shopping centers. This is the largest shopping complex in Pennsylvania and one of the largest on the East Coast. The roughly one-mile-square triangular shaped area bounded by US 202, the Turnpike, and the Schuylkill Expressway, also contains a number of large office buildings and hotels.

Lansdale, pop. 18,000. A manufacturing community and former shopping hub for the surrounding townships located on one of the Reading Railroad's commuter lines. The **Mennonite Historical Library and Archives** of Eastern Pennsylvania are located at Grebel Hall, Christopher Dock Mennonite High School, 1000 Forty Foot Rd. (PA 63), about three miles west of town.

★★★ **Morgan House** (④)(45-60 min.), Weikel Rd., 368-2480. Open April thru November—Sat.-Sun. 1-5, weekdays by appointment. Admission: $2.50; children under 10, free. This NRHP property built in 1695 went undiscovered until 1967 when it was to have been razed as an "eyesore". The house is the only example of medieval Welsh architectural style in America, and is over 90 percent original. Nicely furnished with 18th century antiques, but most of the attention on the guided tour is, as it should be, on the architectural aspects. The builder, Edward Morgan, and his wife were Welsh natives. Not much is known about their family or occupation, but one of their daughters was the mother of Daniel Boone, and another married a man named Thomas, an ancestor of the late broadcaster Lowell Thomas. Directions: From center of Lansdale, go west on W. Main St. (PA 63) for 0.7 mi., turn left on Valley Forge Rd. (PA 363) for 0.6 mi. to Allentown Rd. (SR 1001), right for 0.6 mi. to Weikel Rd., left 1/4 mi. to house on right.

Norristown, pop. 35,000. Montgomery County's seat since its establishment in 1784; in fact, the town was founded the same year to serve just that function. There are two **Historic Districts** in the borough, one covering the downtown area and the other encompassing the western part of town, west of Stony Creek from the Schuylkill to Elm St. The façade of the **Montgomery County Court House**, at Airy and Swede Sts., dates from 1854, but the rest of the building was torn down and a larger structure rebuilt around 1900. Norristown is primarily an industrial city today.

★ **Historical Society of Montgomery County** (⑤)(30 min.), 1654 DeKalb St., 272-0297. Open Mon., Wed.-Fri. 10-4, Tue. 1-9, Sat. during school year 9-12. Admission free. A small museum containing items from local homes, or donated by county residents. Society library (admission: adults, $2.00; students, $1.00) and reading room also in the building. Directions: SW corner of DeKalb (US 202 northbound) and Roberts Sts.

★ **Elmwood Park Zoo** ([6])(30-45 min.), Harding Blvd. and Fornance St., 277-3825. Open daily except Mon. 10-4:30. Admission free, donation requested. A small zoo, featuring a children's section, aviary, and pony rides. Directions: 2 blocks west of Markley St. (US 202 southbound); turn right at Fornance St.

Community Resources
Valley Forge Convention & Visitors Bureau, PO Box 311, Norristown, PA 19404, 278-3558, (800) 441-3549 (Visitors Center located at Valley Forge National Historical Park)
Greater Valley Forge Chamber of Commerce, 73 E. Main St., 277-9500
PO: 28 E. Airy St., 275-9780
Public Library: Swede & Powell Sts., 278-5100
Montgomery Hospital: Powell & Fornance Sts., 270-2000
Sacred Heart Hospital: DeKalb & Fornance Sts., 278-8200
Suburban General Hospital: 2701 DeKalb Pike, 278-2000
Valley Forge Medical Center: 1033 W. Germantown Pike, 539-8500
Court House: Airy & Swede Sts., 278-3000
Police: emergency 272-1111, all other business, 272-8080
Borough Hall: 235 E. Airy St., 272-8080
State Police: US 422 & Lewis Rd., Limerick, 631-5933
Bus: Valley Forge Shopping Center, King of Prussia, 265-2900

Pottstown, pop. 25,000. Located in the southwestern corner of the county, along the Schuylkill River. Founded 1752 by John Potts, son of Thomas Potts, who had set up the first iron forge in 1714 on a site along Manatawny Creek that is now within the borough limits. Iron and steel making had been the town's dominant industry, but today the town's largest employers are Mrs. Smith's Frozen Foods, Doehler-Jarvis, a castings manufacturer, and Dana Corporation, maker of motor vehicle parts. There is a **Historic District** covering the downtown area.

Pottsgrove Manor ([7]), W. King St., 326-4014. Open Tue.-Sat. 10-4, Sun. 1-4. Admission free. John Potts' home, built in 1754 and on the NRHP. Scheduled to reopen about June 1, 1989, after extensive renovations, and will be furnished using a 1768 inventory of John Potts. Directions: on PA 663, 1/2 block east of PA 100.

Trumpet Museum (See Kenilworth, Chester County).

Community Resources
Tri-County Chamber of Commerce, 1200 High St., 326-2900
PO: High & Madison Sts. 323-2100
Public Library: High & Washington Sts., 326-2532
Pottstown Memorial Medical Center: 1600 E. High St., 327-7000
Police: emergency 323-1212, all other business 326-3100
Borough Offices: King & Penn Sts., 326-3100
State Police: US 422 & Lewis Rd., Limerick, 495-7055
Bus: 10 N. Hanover St., 326-6121

Schwenksville, pop. 800. Located on Perkiomen Creek, five miles north of Collegeville.

★★★**Pennypacker Mills** (⁸)(30-45 min.), PA 73 and Haldeman Rd., 287-9349. Open Tue.-Sat. 10-4, Sun. 1-4. Admission free. Owned by Montgomery County, this NRHP home was built about 1730 and remained in the Pennypacker family's hands from 1747 until 1981 when it was sold to the county for preservation. The house as it now exists was remodeled extensively in 1901-02 by noted architect Arthur Brockie. Samuel Pennypacker, governor of Pennsylvania from 1903-07, bought the house in 1900 and lived in it until his death in 1916. The home reflects the family's wealth but at the same time a simple, unpretentious lifestyle. Directions: Entrance to property is at the intersection of Haldeman Rd. (SR 1022) and PA 73, just over the Perkiomen Creek bridge from PA 29.

Skippack, unincorporated, pop. about 600. **Historic Skippack Village** is a commercial venture that has brought a number of crafts shops, boutiques, restaurants, antique shops, and service businesses together in a half-mile strip along Skippack Pike (PA 73) between PA 113 and Store Rd. (SR 1006). The village itself was settled by Germans in 1702, and was on one of the routes linking upper Montgomery County with the markets and mills in the Philadelphia area. The merchants association sponsors special events several times a year.

Souderton, pop. 6,300. Small town in the heart of Montgomery County's Mennonite community, near the Bucks County line.

★★**Mennonite Heritage Center** (⁹)(20-30 min.), 24 Main St. (PA 113), 723-1700. Open Wed.-Sat. 10-4, Sun. 2-4. Admission free, donations accepted. Artifacts and handcrafts of Mennonite life from the time of their arrival in Pennsylvania to the present, including clothing, quilts, church photos, and frakturs. There is a scale model of the Franconia Mennonite Church, one of the largest in the area.

Telford, pop. 3,400, of which 800 in Bucks Co.

Country Creek Vineyard & Winery, 133 Cressman Rd., 723-6516. Open Mon.-Sat. 9-6, Sun. 10-6. Tours by appointment. Directions: about 5 mi. W of Telford. From intersection of PA 63 & 113 at Harleysville, go NW on 63 for 2.6 mi. to Long Mill Rd., turn right for 0.4 mi. to Moyer Rd., turn left for 0.2 mi. to Cressman Rd., and right to winery.

Trappe, pop. 1,700. The borough adjoins Collegeville to the east along Ridge Pike and houses three buildings of significance to the Lutheran church. **Augustus Lutheran Church,** 7th Ave. and Main St. (Ridge Pike, SR 4031), is on the NRHP and is the oldest Lutheran church in the country. It was built in 1743 by Henry Melchior Muhlenberg, who started the denomination upon his arrival from Germany the year before. He is buried in the church cemetery. The other two important buildings are houses where he and his large family had lived; one is at 201 Main St. and the other on E. 7th Ave., several blocks east of Main St.

Valley Forge, unincorporated.

★★★★**Valley Forge National Historical Park** ([10]). One of America's most important historical shrines, covering 2,800 acres between the Schuylkill River, Valley Creek, the Pennsylvania Turnpike, and US 422 (County Line Expressway). The Park overlaps the Chester County line, but most of it is in Montgomery. Despite the fact that no fighting actually took place here, Washington's encampment in the winter of 1777-78 represented the turning point for American forces in the Revolution. Begin your tour at the modern **Visitor Center** (30-45 min.), 783-7700, located just inside the main entrance to the Park on PA 23 at the US 422 interchange. Open daily 8:30-6. A 15-minute orientation film and exhibits describe Washington's encampment. A brochure is available (25¢) for a **self-guided tour** (at least 2 hours); signs along the route mark stops described in the folder. **Bus tours** featuring a taped narration of the encampment are offered daily from 9-4:30 from mid-April thru October (admission: adults, $5.00; children, $4.00). Bicycle rentals are available at the Visitor Center daily from 9-4:30 (last rental 3:30), or you may use your own. A marked bicycle trail covers part of the Park. Hikers are also permitted to use the bicycle trail and other dedicated hiking trails. Highlights of the Park include the **National Memorial Arch, Washington's Headquarters** (20-30 min.), and **Varnum's Quarters** (10-15 min.). The latter two sites, the Steuben Memorial Information Center, and Huntington's Quarters are fee areas; $1.00 admission covers all. Guided tours are given at Washington's headquarters, which were located in one of several houses owned by the Potts family, the region's leading iron manufacturers and founders of Pottstown (as well as Pottsville, a city in the anthracite coal mining area of Schuylkill County). The Steuben Center, located at the west entrance to the Park on PA 23, has furnished room displays; open Sat.-Sun. 1-5. Huntington's Quarters are located on the south side of PA 23 about 1 mile east of Washington's Quarters.

★★ **Washington Memorial Chapel** (15 min.), located on private land within the Park on the north side of PA 23 about 1 mile west of the Visitor Center. Open daily 9:30-5. The Bell Tower houses the Washington National Carillon, where recitals are given Sundays at 2 PM.

★★★ **Valley Forge National Historical Society Museum** (45-60 min.), adjacent to the Chapel, also on private land. Open Mon.-Sat. 9:30-4:30, Sun. 1-4:30. Admission: $1.00; children under 10, free. An extensive and well presented collection of Washington memorabilia, both of George and Martha. Displays include some items directly related to the encampment, 17th century guns, the General's letters and personal effects, 19th century chinaware, and souvenirs of encampment reunions.

RECREATION FACILITIES

Evansburg State Park, 3660 Germantown Pike, Evansburg, 489-3967.
Spring Mountain Ski Area, Spring Mount Rd., Spring Mount, 287-7900.

CALENDAR OF EVENTS

Mid-February, Valley Forge. **Washington's Birthday Weekend.** c/o Valley Forge Convention & Visitors Bureau, P.O. Box 311, Norristown, PA 19404, 278-3558; (800) 441-3549.
Early March, Skippack. **Doll and Teddy Bear Celebration**, Skippack Village. 584-6397 or -1438.
Early May, Pottstown. **Antique Show and Sale**, Sunnybrook Ballroom, Sunnybrook Rd. c/o Edna Smith, Box 164, Huntingdon Valley, PA 19006, (215) 947-1254.
Early May, Valley Forge. **French Alliance Day Celebration.** c/o Valley Forge National Historical Park, P.O. Box 953, Valley Forge, PA 19481, 783-7700 or -1066.
Early May, Harleysville. **Herb Festival**, Heckler Plains Farmstead. c/o Joan DiMaria, Morris & Landis Rds., Harleysville, PA 19438, 256-8087 or 822-7422 (Chalfont).
Third Saturday in May, June, July, and August, Cedars. **Up-Country Flea Market.** c/o Cedars Village Shops, P.O. Box 173, Cedars, PA 19423, 584-1490.

Mid-June, Center Point. **Muster Day**, Peter Wentz Farmstead. c/o Elizabeth Gannon, P.O. Box 240, Worcester, PA 19490, 584-5104.

Mid-June, Valley Forge. **Departure of the Continental Army**. c/o Valley Forge National Historical Park, P.O. Box 953, Valley Forge, PA 19481, 783-7700 or -1066.

Late June, Skippack. **Victorian Tyme Arts & Crafts Show**, Skippack Village. 584-6397 or -1438.

Mid-July, Port Indian. **Port Indian Regatta**, Schuylkill River. c/o Port Indian Civic and Boating Assn., 66 W. Indian Lane, Norristown, PA 19403, 666-9428 or 688-1426 (Wayne).

Late July, Skippack. **Historic Days**, Skippack Village. 584-6397 or -1438.

Mid-August, East Greenville. **Goschenhoppen Folk Festival**, New Goschenhoppen Park. c/o Goschenhoppen Historians, Box 476, Green Lane, PA 18054, 754-6013 (Sassamansville).

Late August, Schwenksville. **Philadelphia Folk Festival**, Old Poole Farm. c/o Philadelphia Folk Song Society, 7113 Emlen St., Philadelphia, PA 19119, (215) 242-0150.

Late August, Skippack. **Antique Car & Truck Show**, Skippack Village. 584-6397 or -1438.

Early September, Lansdale. **Traditional Irish Music and Dance Festival**, Fischer's Pool, 2375 Kriebel Rd., (215) 849-8899 (Philadelphia).

Late September, Harleysville. **Hecklerfest**, Heckler Plains Farmstead. 256-8087.

Early October, Pottstown. **Antique Show and Sale**, Sunnybrook Ballroom. See same listing, Early May.

Early October, Harleysville. **Apple Butter Frolic**, Indian Creek Farm. c/o Mennonite Heritage Center, 24 Main St., Souderton, PA 18964, 723-1700.

Early October, Center Point. **Laerneswert (Worth Learning)**, Peter Wentz Farmstead. 584-5104.

Early October, Skippack. **Skippack Days**, Skippack Village. 584-6397 or -1438.

Late November, Skippack. **Holiday Open House**, Skippack Village. 584-6397 or -1438.

Early December, Center Point. **Candlelight Tour**, Peter Wentz Farmstead. 584-5104.

Mid-December, Valley Forge. **Re-enactment of Washington's March**. c/o Valley Forge National Historical Park, P.O. Box 953, Valley Forge, PA 19481, 783-7700 or -1066.

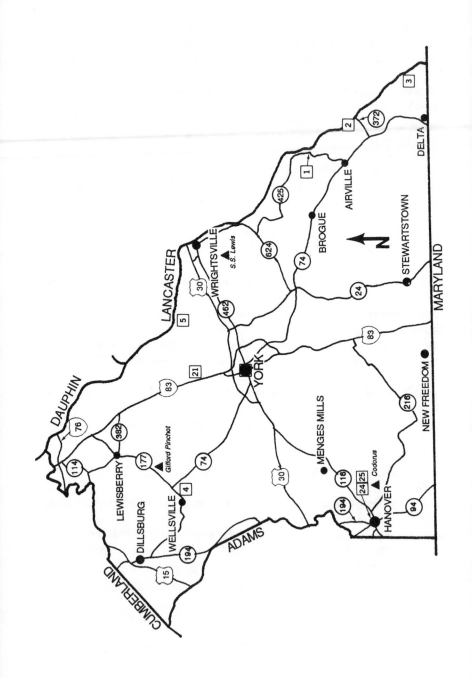

YORK

Created: August 19, 1749, as the 5th county, from part of Lancaster County
County Seat: York
Land Area: 909 square miles
Population (1989 est.): 335,000
Area code: 717

York County is composed almost entirely of rolling to hilly terrain, with the urban areas of York and Hanover occupying much of the limited amount of level ground. The county is bisected east-west by US 30, the Lincoln Highway, and north-south by I-83, the Susquehanna Expressway. The city of York, the largest town and county seat, is at the intersection of these two roads.

York County has always had a prosperous economy. It traditionally has ranked second only to Lancaster County in agricultural production, and its industries manufacture a wide variety of products. York city produces air conditioners, false teeth, turbines, and, over a period of about ten years, eight different makes of automobiles and trucks were made here. Hanover became famous for its shoe factory and canning company. Several smaller towns in the southern part of the county were furniture and cigar making centers. In recent years, York city has become a major East Coast distribution center because of its convenience to the heavily populated Northeast Corridor and its good highway access.

While land devoted to farming is declining due to relatively rapid population growth, the pressure on farm prices is not as severe as in neighboring Lancaster County, with the result that some Amish families are moving into the southeastern part of York County, where they can continue their agrarian life and still not be too far from their former community. The dominant crops in the county are corn, tobacco, apples, and peaches. The York Imperial apple was developed in 1820 on a farm a few miles south of York.

Historical Highlights

York is the oldest county in the state west of the Susquehanna River, and second largest in the PDC. It was named either for the Duke of York or for its namesake county in England. The first European settlers were English, arriving about 1728. Some English settlers also came from Maryland, seeking an escape

241

from taxes in that colony. The boundary between the two colonies that became the Mason-Dixon line was not surveyed in this area until 1765, so early settlers might have claimed exemption and protection from both colonies simultaneously.

Other early settlers, who came in larger numbers than the English, were Germans and Scotch-Irish. The Germans included Mennonites and Baptists, and they soon became the dominant group in York. The Scotch-Irish, and a small number of Welsh, settled in the southeastern part of the county, where the Welsh developed slate mines and limestone quarries. The northern part was settled by English Quakers.

The county played an important role in the Revolutionary War. Not only did the town of York serve as the headquarters of the Continental Congress for nine months in 1777 and 1778, but the county's iron ore furnaces helped supply ammunition to the colonial army. A plot to unseat George Washington as commander-in-chief of the Continental army, initiated by General Horatio Gates and his partisans, was thwarted by a toast to Washington by the Marquis de Lafayette during the Congress's tenure in York.

In the early 19th century the county began to develop as an industrial center. The first successful steam locomotive and first iron steamboat built in America were made here. The steamboat *Codorus*, named for one of the county's largest creeks, was launched on the Susquehanna just north of Wrightsville in 1825. The locomotive, the *York*, was built by Phineas Davis and won a competition sponsored by the Baltimore and Ohio Railroad in 1832. Several more engines were built for the B&O, but the city of York never became a locomotive manufacturing center. The area, however, did become an important location for another type of "railroad", the Underground Railroad, that ferried slaves from the south to freedom in the north in the years preceding the Civil War.

York County was touched only briefly by the Civil War, despite the fact that its most important battle was fought at nearby Gettysburg. Hanover and York were visited a few days prior to the battle by Confederate troops seeking supplies and money. York met the ransom demand and the town was spared. The first skirmish of the battle took place at Hanover on June 30, 1863, when J.E.B. Stuart's cavalry encountered Union soldiers eating lunch provided by the townspeople. Union troops in retreat burned the bridge over the Susquehanna at Wrightsville as a precaution against a further Confederate advance.

PLACES OF INTEREST

Airville, unincorporated, pop. about 100.

★★★ **Indian Steps Museum** (1)(30-45 min.). On the Susquehanna just south of PA 425, 4 miles northeast of PA 74, 862-3948 during museum hours; 741-1527 (York) at other times. Open April 15 thru October 15—Thurs.-Sun. Hours: Thu.-Fri., 10-4; Sat., Sun., hol., 11-6. Admission free, contributions welcome. Museum contains over 10,000 Indian artifacts found embedded in the walls of steps carved in rocks now submerged in the river. The artifacts tell the story of the Susquehannocks and other Indians who lived and traveled along the river. A self-guided walking tour (20-30 min., brochure available) covering plants, birds, and the Susquehanna & Tidewater Canal, starts at the museum.

★ **Lock 12** (2)(10-15 min.). On the banks of the Susquehanna at the west end of the Norman Wood Bridge, on the north side of PA 372. Remains of Susquehanna and Tidewater Canal lock, built 1836-39. 17 feet wide, 10 feet deep, 170 feet long. Picnic tables, rest rooms. Admission free. Approx. 300 yard walk to site from parking area.

Brogue, unincorporated, pop. about 100.

Allegro Vineyards, 927-9148. Open for tours Wed.-Fri. 2-7 PM, Sat.-Sun., 12-5. Directions: 2.2 mi. south of PA 74 on Muddy Creek Rd. (SR 2069), then turn left on Sechrist Rd. to entrance.

Stephen Bahn Winery, 927-9051. Open for tours Sat. 12-5, Sun. 1-5, other hours by appointment. Closed major holidays. Directions: 3.9 mi. south on PA 74, then turn left on Tomlinson Rd. (SR 2041) for 3 mi. to winery on right.

Delta, pop. 700. Located on the Mason-Dixon line, this community was the center of Welsh settlements and the slate industry in York County. The **Historic District** extends along Main Street for most of its one-mile length and features buildings with a variety of architectural styles, including the widespread use of locally mined slate.

Peach Bottom Atomic Power Station (3), 4 miles east, on the banks of the Susquehanna. Bus tours of the plant (45 min., plus 1 hour roundtrip bus ride from starting point), operated by Philadelphia Electric Company, are offered on Memorial Day, Labor Day, and Columbus Day weekends, starting at Muddy Run Recreation Park on Route 372 just east of the Susquehanna in Lancaster County (see Lancaster County for description of Muddy Run Recreation Park). Admission free.

Visitors normally may not leave the tour bus for safety and security reasons. Tour information: 284-2538 (Rawlinsville).

Hanover, pop. 15,000. A farming and manufacturing center and second largest town in York County. First settled in 1731, the town was laid out by Richard McAllister, a Scotch-Irish innkeeper, in 1763. The first skirmish of the Gettysburg campaign during the Civil War, and the first on Northern soil, occurred here June 30, 1863 (see Historical Highlights for details). Major industries include Hanover Shoe Co., Hanover Brands, Doubleday Book Club, and Hanover Horse Farms (owned by Hanover Shoe). Hanover House, a large mail-order concern, is located here. Center Square (intersection of York, Baltimore, Frederick, and Carlisle Sts.) is the hub of the downtown business district.

The Hanover Area Historical Society offers brochures describing a walking tour of downtown Hanover and a driving tour covering locally significant sites in the area. The walking tour highlights the town's varied architectural styles, while the driving tour visits several old churches and other features that were important in and around the community. The Society's offices are at the George Neas House (address and phone number follow).

★★**George Neas House** (24)(20-30 min.), 113 W. Chestnut St. (NE corner of High), 632-3207. Open Tue.-Fri. 10-2, closed January. Guided tours every half hour. Admission free, donation requested. Georgian mansion built about 1783 by the Neas (pronounced NACE) family, local tanners. House is on NRHP, now owned by Hanover Area Historical Society and contains a museum of local culture and 18th and 19th century crafts. Directions: 2 blocks west and 1 block north of Center Square. Chestnut St. is PA 194 southbound and High St. is PA 116.

★ **Conewago Chapel,** Edgegrove Rd. (SR 2009) & Basilica Rd. in the village of Edgegrove, just west of Hanover in Adams Co., 637-2721. Open daily. Oldest Jesuit chapel west of the Susquehanna. The present building, on the NRHP, was completed in 1787, replacing a mass house that had been built about 1740. Admission free. Directions: From Center Square, go west on PA 116 for 1.8 mi. to traffic light where 116 turns left. Continue straight on Oxford Ave. (SR 2008) 1.1 mi., then turn left on Edgegrove Rd. (SR 2008) for 0.4 mi. Chapel is on left (22 on Adams Co. map).

★ **Hanover Shoe Farms,** north side of PA 194, 3.2 mi. southwest of Center Square, about one mile west of Mt. Pleasant, Adams Co., 637-8931. Open daily 7 AM-5 PM. Admission free. Self-guided walk-through tours—get brochure at the office just inside the entrance. Noted for its famous trotters and pacers (23 on Adams Co. map).

Farmers Market (25), 210 E. Chestnut St. Open Sat. 6 AM-noon, 632-1353. Small market, but one of the few true markethouses remaining in towns of this size.

Community Resources
Hanover Area Chamber of Commerce: 146 Broadway, 637-6130
PO: 18 High St.
Public Library: 301 Carlisle St., 632-5183
Hanover General Hospital: 300 Highland Ave., 637-3711
Police: 44 Frederick St., emergency: 911
Borough Offices: 44 Frederick St., 637-3877
Bus: 1150 Carlisle St., 632-3717

Stewartstown, pop. 1,300. Small farming community near the Maryland border.

Stewartstown Railroad (See Recreation Facilities).

Naylor Wine Cellars, Inc., Ebaugh Rd., 993-2431. Open Mon.-Sat. 11-6, Sun. 12-5, closed Mon. and Tue. in January and February. Tours and sales during open hours. Directions: From Stewartstown, go north on PA 24 for 2 mi., turn left on Ebaugh Rd. for 0.3 mi.

Wellsville, pop. 400. **Historic District** on NRHP. Attractive stone homes line Main St. (PA 74).

Warrington Meeting House (4), SE corner of York Rd. (PA 74) & Quaker Meeting Rd., 0.5 mi. east of town and 1.0 mi. west of intersection of PA 74 & 177 in Rossville. Built in 1769, this house is still used by the Quakers, but no interior tours offered.

Wrightsville, pop. 2,600. Located on the west bank of the Susquehanna, founded 1732. Named for John Wright, who operated a ferry between here and Columbia. Thus, the town has always been a transportation center, first with the ferry and later with the Pennsylvania Canal and then with railroad and highway bridges. The original highway bridge, carrying the Lincoln Highway (now PA 462), is the longest multiple arch span in the world. It opened in 1930 and was paid for by contributions of York and Lancaster County residents. NRHP **Historic District** encompasses the blocks closest to the river; the oldest and most attractive homes and businesses are along Hellam (PA 462) and Locust Sts. (one block north of Hellam St.).

★ **Codorus Furnace** (⑤), Furnace Rd. (SR 1008), 8 mi. NW. Built in 1765 and once owned by James Smith, signer of Declaration of Independence from York, the furnace supplied iron and cannon balls for the Revolutionary Army. Outside viewing only. Directions: From Wrightsville interchange of US 30, go north following SR 1016, first on Cool Springs Rd., then Dark Hollow Rd., and finally Hauser School Rd. All turns are marked. It's 1.4 mi. from the interchange to Accomac Rd. (SR 1037). Then turn left and immediately right on Furnace Rd. (SR 1008), go 5.1 mi. to furnace, at the bottom of a steep hill, on right along Codorus Creek.

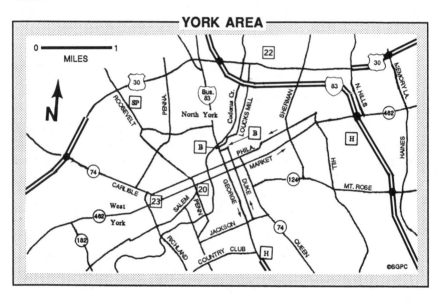

York, pop. 44,000, with suburbs 130,000. Established 1741 by Thomas Cookson, a surveyor authorized by the Penns. The town was laid out in a manner similar to Lancaster, with a gridiron street pattern, central square, and streets named for royalty. Most of the early inhabitants were German, the nationality that remains dominant today.

During the Revolution, the Continental Congress met in York from September 30, 1777, to June 27, 1778, a period that included Washington's encampment at Valley Forge and the British occupation of Philadelphia. York became the seat of government because the Congress felt that the Susquehanna River presented a reasonably safe barrier to a possible British advance. The government's printing press, which issued documents as well as money, was also brought to York and set up at a downtown site. It was during the Congress's tenure here that the Articles of Confederation were adopted, which included the first use of the name "United States of America". This gives York the basis for its claim as the first capital of the nation. The first National Thanksgiving Proclamation was also issued here. Two signers of the Declaration of Independence, Philip Livingston and James Smith (the latter a York resident), are buried in York.

The "Conway Cabal", a plot to unseat George Washington as commander-in-chief of the Continental Army following his defeat at the Battle of Brandywine and attributed to Generals Horatio Gates, Thomas Conway, and Thomas Mifflin, was cleverly exposed in York by Marquis de Lafayette, and Washington remained in command.

York was spared destruction during the Civil War. On June 28, 1863, a Confederate party led by General John B. Gordon entered the town, demanding supplies and money. A leading local industrialist, representing a committee of businesspeople, met the troops west of the city and concluded a deal in which the ransom would be met in exchange for sparing the town. Being close to the Mason-Dixon line, York had some Southern sympathizers, although its primary effort was clearly on the Union side.

The city became an industrial hub after the Civil War, and many of its present industries were founded during the late 1800s. Products made in York include air conditioners, hydraulic turbines, and farm equipment. York weighlifting apparatus, Pfaltzgraff pottery, and Harley-Davidson motorcycles are widely known products manufactured in York.

The city is the home of York College of Pennsylvania and a branch of Penn State University.

★★★ Downtown. The Historic District encompasses a large area in the central part of the city, extending north and south as far as the city line. A walking tour through the central part of the district will include the sights described below. A good place to start is at the corner of W. Market St. and Pershing Ave.

★★ York County Colonial Courthouse (6)(20-30 min.), 205 W. Market St. (NW corner of Pershing Ave.), 846-1977. Open Mon.-Sat., 10-4, Sun. 1-4. An exact replica of the courthouse occupied by the Continental Congress when it met in York. Features a multi-media presentation of the deliberations that took place in 1777-78.

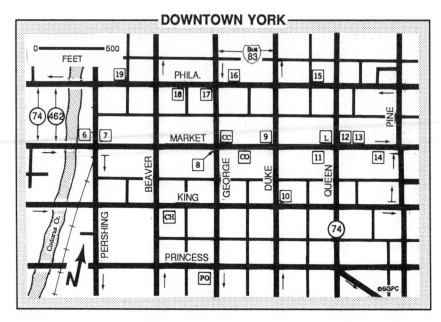

★★★ Gates House, Golden Plough Tavern, and **Barnett Bobb Log House** (⑦)(about 1 hr.), all located at the NE corner of Market St. & Pershing Ave., 845-2591. Open Mon.-Sat. 10-4, Sun. 1-4, last tour 3 PM. Admission: adults, $2.50; children 6-13, $1.25; under 6 with adult, free, or included with a combination admission ticket (adults, $4.50; children 6-13, $2.25; under 6, free) to all of the Historical Society of York County's properties on the walking tour. All are on NRHP. The Gates House, built in 1751, was the temporary home of Gen. Horatio Gates while the Continental Congress met in York. A substantial house for its time, furnished to reflect the period. The Golden Plough Tavern, built in 1741, is an example of Germanic half-timber construction, and includes the original wooden chimney. This is probably the oldest original building in York, dating from the year the city was founded. The Log House is typical of the early 19th century. The building originally stood three blocks south of the present site, and had been encased in clapboard. It was to have been demolished as part of expansion of William Penn High School, but was saved and later relocated.

Site of Hall and Sellers Press, SW corner of Market and Beaver Sts. Brought from Philadelphia while the Continental Congress met in York, the press produced documents and money.

Continental Square (⑧), the intersection of Market and George Streets. The original colonial courthouse stood on the SE corner. Market houses were located in the Square, as they were in other PDC cities, until 1887. The kiosk on the NE corner was used by the streetcar dispatcher until buses replaced the trolleys. The Square was remodeled in 1963; the quadrants, which had been used for parking, were converted to sidewalks and planters and expanded to create a normal right-angle intersection.

York County Court House (⊡), 28 E. Market St., built in 1898 using the granite columns and red tiled domes from the 1840 courthouse.

Lafayette Club (⑨), 59 E. Market St. (NW corner of Duke), an 1839 Greek revival townhouse. Houses a private men's club.

Laurel and Rex Fire Companies (⑩), NE corner of Duke and King Sts. The building, dating from 1877, is on the NRHP and is an outstanding example of Italianate Gothic architecture.

★★ **Bonham House** (⑪)(30-40 min.), 152 E. Market St., 845-2422. Open April thru December—Tue.-Sat. 10-4, Sun. 1-4 , Mon. by appt. only. Admission: adults, $1.00; children 6-13, 50¢; under 6 with adult, free. Owned by the Historical Society of York County (see combination ticket prices above). Home of Horace Bonham, local artist, and his family. Original period furnishings throughout the house, as it was occupied by the last surviving daughter until her death in 1965, and then willed to HSYC.

The 100, 200, and 300-blocks of E. Market St., and the unit blocks of N. Duke and N. Queen Sts. contain many attractive town houses dating from the 19th century. Some now house professional offices and civic clubs.

First Presbyterian Church (⑫), NE corner of Queen and Market Sts. James Smith, York signer of the Declaration of Independence, is buried in the churchyard (see historical marker).

Billmeyer House (⑬), 225 E. Market St., built in 1860 by Charles Billmeyer, a local railroad car manufacturer. The Italianate house, on the NRHP, is owned by First Presbyterian Church.

★★★ **Historical Society of York County** (⑭)(1 hour), 250 E. Market St., 848-1587. Open Mon.-Sat. 9-5, Sun. 1-4. Admission: adults, $1.50; children 6-13, 75¢; under 6 with adult, free. See also combination ticket prices above. An excellent collection and presentation of Colonial era furnishings, farm implements, exhibits depicting early life in York County, early vehicles, some made in York, and local artist Lewis Miller's watercolor sketches of 19th century York.

Home of William Goodridge ([15]), 123 E. Philadelphia St. Goodridge, a black Yorker influential in the Underground Railroad, had been a slave himself in Maryland. He operated several businesses in town, but was forced to flee when the Confederate Army approached York in 1863.

York Dispatch Building ([16]), 15-17 E. Philadelphia St. Distinctive cast iron façade on the offices and production facilities of York's evening and Sunday newspapers. The building was constructed in 1887 and is on the NRHP; it originally housed a wagon factory.

Strand-Capitol Performing Arts Center ([17]), SW corner of George and Philadelphia Sts., 846-1111. Two movie theaters were gutted and converted into a 1,200-seat hall for concerts and plays, and a 700-seat theater that features classic films. This is the home of the York Symphony Orchestra as well as other local cultural organizations.

★★★ **Central Market** ([18])(15-20 min.), 34 W. Philadelphia St. (additional entrances on N. Beaver St. and N. Cherry Alley), 848-2243. Open Tue., Thu., Sat. 6 AM-3 PM. On NRHP. York's largest farmers' market, built in 1888. While this and other markethouses are not as fully utilized or as well patronized as a generation ago, they remain outstanding and lasting traditions of life in the community.

Friends Meeting House ([19]), 135 W. Philadelphia St. Still in use, this NRHP structure is the oldest house of worship in the city, built in 1766. Tours by appointment only—call 854-8109.

Outside Downtown

★★★ **Farmers Market** ([20])(15-20 min.), 380 W. Market St. (SE corner of Penn St.), 848-1402. Open Tue., Fri., Sat. 6 AM-4 PM. The oldest surviving markethouse in the city, built 1866. On the NRHP. Smaller than Central Market, but otherwise on the same order.

★★ **Bob Hoffman Weightlifting and Softball Hall of Fame** ([21])(30-40 min.), 3300 Board Rd., 767-6481. Open Mon.-Sat. except holidays, 10-4. Admission free. A good museum of its type. Contains trophies, photos, and stories of US Olympic weightlifting records and other weightlifting, powerlifting, and body-building events. Amateur softball section highlights development of this sport by the late Bob Hoffman (not related to the author, although I knew him slightly), founder and owner of York Barbell Co., known world-wide for the manufacture of weightlifting equipment. York has become a major center of activity in both sports as a result of Hoffman's efforts. Directions: I-83 to exit 11. From York and south, cross PA 238 onto Board Rd., go about 1/4 mile to museum on left. From Harrisburg and north, turn left on PA 238 to first intersection, then left again on Board Rd. about 1/4 mile to museum on left.

★★ **Rodney C. Gott Harley-Davidson Motorcycle Museum** (22)(30 min. for museum alone, 80-90 min. for museum and plant tour), 1425 Eden Rd., 848-1177. Open for plant and museum tours Mon.-Fri. 10 and 2, museum only Mon.-Fri. 12:30, and Sat. 10, 11, 1, and 2. Admission free. Museum contains a sample of nearly every year's production of H-D motorcycles, plus advertisements, trophies, and other memorabilia. Small souvenir shop in lobby. This is the only motorcycle manufacturing plant in the United States. Directions: From US 30 (Arsenal Rd.) eastbound, turn left on Eden Rd. at third traffic light east of I-83 interchange. From US 30 westbound, turn right on Eden Rd. at third traffic light after limited-access expressway ends. Museum is 0.1 mi. on right.

★ **Fire Museum of York County** (23)(20-30 min.), 757 W. Market St. (NW corner of Carlisle Ave.), 843-0464. Open April 1 thru Nov. 1—Sat., and second Sun. of the month, noon-4. Admission free. Housed in the former Royal Fire House, built 1903, the museum contains old apparatus, equipment, uniforms, photos, and memorabilia from all 72 fire companies in York County and others outside the county. The building itself is interesting, with its ornate tile on the engine room walls, and heavy doors. Not the only such museum in existence, but this is a good presentation, done entirely with volunteer labor and private funds.

Community Resources
York Area Chamber of Commerce: 1 Marketway East (NE corner of Continental Sq.), 848-4000
Visitors Information Center: 2900 Whiteford Rd., 755-9638
PO: 200 S. George St., 848-2381
    East York branch: 3000 E. Market St., 755-0369
Public Library: 159 E. Market St., 846-5300
York Hospital: 1001 S. George St., 771-2345
Memorial Osteopathic Hospital: 325 S. Belmont St., 843-8623
Court House: 28 E. Market St., 771-9675
City Police: emergency 911, all other business 846-1234
City Hall: 50 W. King St.
State Police: 1195 Roosevelt Ave., 848-6355
Bus (Capitol Trailways): 53 E. North St., 845-6911
Bus (Greyhound): 315 N. George St., 843-0095

RECREATION FACILITIES

Codorus State Park, PA 216, 4 mi. SE of Hanover, 637-2816.
Gifford Pinchot State Park, 2200 Rosstown Rd. (PA 177), Lewisberry, 432-5011.
Samuel S. Lewis State Park, 2 mi. S of Wrightsville on Pisgah Rd. (SR 2009), 252-1134.
Otter Creek Recreation Area, PA 425 along Susquehanna River (RD 1, Airville, PA 17302), 862-3628. Camping (tents and travel trailers), boat ramp, dock, picnicking, hiking trails, natural area, trout fishing.
Ski Roundtop, 925 Roundtop Rd., Lewisberry, 432-9631. For snow conditions (800) 382-1390 in PA, and (800) 233-1134 in DE, DC, MD, NJ, NY, VA. Directions from I-83: Northbound, use exit 13, west on PA 382 3.7 mi. to PA 177 at Lewisberry. Southbound, use exit 15, west on PA 177 2.8 mi. to PA 382 at Lewisberry. Then both south on PA 177 for 0.9 mi., turn right on Pinetown Rd. (SR 4024) for 2.0 mi. to Moores Mtn. Rd. (SR 4031). Turn left and proceed 1.6 mi. to Roundtop Rd., turn right for 1.2 mi.
Stewartstown Railroad, W. Pennsylvania Ave., Stewartstown, 993-2936. Round-trip excursions Sundays and holidays, May thru October, to New Freedom and Hyde (south of York). Other special excursions (fall foliage, photo runs, breakfasts, twilight dinner trips, Santa Claus visits) also scheduled. Write to P.O. Box 155, Stewartstown, PA 17363, for schedules and fares.

CALENDAR OF EVENTS

Mid-April, York. **Country Crossroads Show and Sale**, Memorial Hall, York Fairgrounds. c/o Robert Goodrich, P.O. Box 236, Carlisle, PA 17013, (717) 243-7890.

Mid-April, York. **Art Competition**, Cora Miller Art Gallery, York College of PA. c/o York College, Country Club Rd., York, PA 17403, 846-7788, ext. 257.

May (Mother's Day), York. **Olde York Street Fair**, Market Street, downtown. Crafts, food, entertainment. c/o York Area Chamber of Commerce, 1 Marketway East, York, PA 17401, 848-4000.

Late May, York. **Greater York Antiques Show and Sale**, Memorial Hall, York Fairgrounds. c/o George Sheets, P.O. Box 1388, York, PA 17405, 741-0911 or 854-5907.

Early June, York. **Annual National Street Rod Association East Meet**, York Fairgrounds. c/o York Area Chamber of Commerce, 1 Marketway East, York, PA 17401, 848-4000.

Mid-June, York. **World's Greatest Yard Sale**, York Fairgrounds. c/o Sherry Ehrhart, 226 E. Market St., York, PA 17403, 848-1841.

Mid-June, York. **White Rose Square Dancing Festival**, York College of PA. c/o York College, Country Club Rd., York, PA 17403, 846-7788.

Early July, York. **Annual Antique Auto Show and Flea Market**, York Fairgrounds.

Mid-July, Menges Mills. **Historic Horse, Steam, and Gas Show**, Colonial Valley (1 mi. west of Spring Grove on PA 116, turn north on Colonial Valley Rd. (SR 3053) for 3/4 mi.). c/o Betty Staines, 621 E. Rocky Hill Rd., Sparks, MD 21152, (301) 472-2701 or (717) 225-4811.

Late July, Hanover. **Hanover Dutch Festival**, Wirt Park, 100-block of High St. c/o Hanover Area Chamber of Commerce, 146 Broadway, Hanover, PA 17331, 637-6130.

Late August, York. **Riverwalk Art Festival**, Codorus Creek Boat Basin, downtown. c/o York Area Chamber of Commerce, 1 Marketway East, York, PA 17401, 848-4000

Late August, Airville. **Annual Copperhead Snake Roundup**, Indian Steps Museum. c/o Conservation Society of York Co., 862-3948 or 741-1527 (York).

Early September, York. **York Interstate Fair**, York Fairgrounds. c/o York Co. Agricultural Society, 334 Carlisle Ave., York, PA 17404, 848-2596.

Late September, Lewisberry. **Pennsylvania Wild Horse and Burro Days.** c/o Wild Horse & Burro Adoption Center, Pleasant Hill Rd., Lewisberry, PA 17339, 938-2560.

Early October, York. **Country Crossroads Show and Sale**, Memorial Hall, York Fairgrounds. c/o Robert Goodrich, P.O. Box 236, Carlisle, PA 17013, (717) 243-7890.

Mid-October, Dillsburg. **Farmers Fair**, Baltimore St. 432-5228.

Mid-October, York. **"At the Sign of the Plough" Oyster Festival**, Golden Plough Tavern, 157 W. Market St. c/o Historical Society of York Co., 250 E. Market St., York, PA 17403, 848-1587.

Early November, York. **Christkindlesmarkt Fair**, downtown. c/o York Area Chamber of Commerce, 1 Marketway East, York, PA 17401, 848-4000.

Mid-Late December, Hanover. **Neas House Tour**, High & Chestnut Sts.. c/o Hanover Area Historical Society, 632-3207.

APPENDIX

The Appendix contains the following sections:

A	State Parks	pages 256-257
B	Bed & Breakfast Inns	258-269
C	Farm Vacation Homes	270-272
D	Hotels and Motels	274-289
E	Campgrounds	290-297
F	Restaurants	298-305

These businesses are described as to location, rates, facilities/specialties, and several other criteria but are deliberately not rated. The lists were compiled from responses to questionnaires sent to all lodging establishments and to a selected list of restaurants. Only those that returned a completed questionnaire are included, and no fee was charged for the listing. These lists are in alphabetical order by county, by town within each county, and by small geographic area within larger towns. Please note that restaurants in hotels and motels are not listed separately. While many of these restaurants are quite good, space considerations did not permit, in effect, two listings for the same establishment.

Information as to prices, hours and seasons of operation, and other services is listed as provided by these businesses. The information is subject to change, so you may want to call or write to confirm. Otherwise, it is best to use the prices in a comparative manner.

A. STATE PARKS

NAME (County) Mailing Address Phone	Location Description	Picnicking	Play area	Snack bar	Interpretive center	Swimming	Fishing	Boat rentals	Boat launch	Hiking	Hunting	Horseback riding	Ice sports	Camping	X-C skiing	Sledding	Handicapped-accessible sanitary facilities
BUCHANAN'S BIRTHPLACE (Fr'kln) HC 17266, Ft. Loudon 17224 (717) 485-3948	3 mi. NW of Mercersburg on PA 16 at Cove Gap	x					x										
CALEDONIA (Franklin) 40 Rocky Mt. Rd., Fayetteville 17222 (717) 352-2161	11 mi. E of Chambersburg at Intersection of US 30 & PA 233	x	x	x	x	x	x			x				x	x	x	x
CODORUS (York) RD 3, Box 118, Hanover 17331 (717) 637-2816	4 mi. SE of Hanover on PA 216	x	x	x	x	x	x	x	x	x	x	x	x	x	x	x	x
COL. DENNING (Cumberland) RD 3, Box 2250, Newville 17241 (717) 776-5272	8 mi. N of Newville on PA 233	x	x	x	x	x	x			x	x		x	x			
COWANS GAP (Franklin) HC 17266, Ft. Loudon 17224 (717) 485-3948	7 mi. NW of Ft. Loudon via PA 75 and Richmond Rd. (SR 4003)	x	x	x	x	x	x	x	x	x	x		x	x	x	x	x
EVANSBURG (Montgomery) Box 258, Collegeville 19426 (215) 489-3729	3660 Germantown Pike, 1 mi. E of Collegeville	x	x		x		x			x	x	x					x
FRENCH CREEK (Berks, Chester) RD 1, Box 448, Elverson 19520 (215) 582-1514	4 mi. S of Birdsboro on PA 345	x	x	x	x	x	x	x	x	x	x	x	x	x	x	x	x
GIFFORD PINCHOT (York) 2200 Rosstown Rd., Lewisberry 17339 (717) 432-5011	1 mi. E of Rossville on PA 177	x	x	x		x	x	x	x	x	x	x	x	x	x	x	x
JACOBSBURG (EE) (Northampton) 435 Belfast Rd., Nazareth 18064 (215) 759-7616	4 mi. NE of Nazareth via PA 33 to Belfast exit, 1 1/4 mi. W on Belfast Rd. (SR 1010)						x			x	x	x			x	x	x
KINGS GAP (EE) (Cumberland) 500 Kings Gap Rd., Carlisle 17013 (717) 486-5031	10 mi. SW of Carlisle via PA 34 and Pine Rd. (SR 3006)									x							x

EE: Environmental Education Center

NAME Mailing Address Phone	Location Description	Picnicking	Play area	Snack bar	Interpretive center	Swimming	Fishing	Boat rentals	Boat launch	Hiking	Hunting	Horseback riding	Ice sports	Camping	X-C skiing	Sledding	Handicapped-accessible sanitary facilities
MARSH CREEK (Chester) RD 2, Park Rd., Downingtown 19335 (215) 458-8515	5 mi. N of Exton, 1 mi. W of PA 100 via Lyndell Rd. (SR 4035)	x	x	x		x	x	x	x	x	x	x	x			x	x
MEMORIAL LAKE (Lebanon) RD 1, Box 7045, Grantville 17028 (717) 865-5444 ext. 2806	2 mi. NW of I-81, exit 29	x	x			x	x	x	x	x			x		x		x
MONT ALTO (Franklin) 40 Rocky Mt. Rd., Fayetteville 17222 (717) 352-2161	1 mi. E of Mont Alto on PA 233	x	x				x										
NOCKAMIXON (Bucks) RD 3, Box 125A, Quakertown 18951 (215) 538-2151	7 mi. SE of Quakertown via PA 313 and PA 563	x	x	x	x	x	x	x	x	x	x	x	x		x	x	x
NOLDE FOREST (EE) Berks RD 1, Box 392, Reading 19607 (215) 775-1411	4 mi. S of Reading on PA 625				x		x			x							
PINE GROVE FURNACE (Cumberland) RD 2, Box 399B, Gardners 17324 (717) 486-7174	on PA 233 at Pine Grove Furnace	x	x	x	x	x	x	x	x	x			x	x	x	x	x
RALPH STOVER (Bucks) 6011 State Park Rd., Pipersv. 18947 (215) 982-5560	11 mi. NE of Doylestown via PA 611 and Stump Rd. (SR 1010)	x	x							x							
ROOSEVELT (Bucks, Northampton) Box 615A, RR1, Upr. Blk. Eddy 18972 (215) 982-5560	along Delaware River from Easton to Bristol	x					x	x	x	x						x	
SAMUEL S. LEWIS (York) c/o Gifford Pinchot State Park (717) 432-5011	2 mi. SW of Wrightsville via Cool Creek Rd. (SR 2011) to Pisgah Rd. (SR 2009)		x							x							x
SUSQUEHANNOCK (Lancaster) c/p Gifford Pinchot State Park (717) 548-3361	along Susquehanna River 3 mi. S of Holtwood	x	x							x		x			x		x

EE: Environmental Education Center

257

B. BED AND BREAKFAST INNS

ADAMS CO.

Historic Cashtown Inn, 1415 Old Rt. 30, **Cashtown** 17310, (717) 334-9722. Owners: Charles & Carolyn Buckley. Open all year exc. Easter and Christmas. 4 rooms: dbl. w/ pvt. bath $70, w/ shared bath $60. Dep. req.: 50% per night per room, received within 7 days of making res. Accepts V, MC, personal checks for dep. only. 2 night stay req. summer wknds. and hol. Small tavern open daily, full dinner weekends. No children or pets. Smoking permitted exc. in bedrooms. First built in 1797, this Inn was a Confederate headquarters during the Battle of Gettysburg. Directions: 8 mi. W of Gettysburg off US 30 in center of Cashtown.

Goose Chase B&B, 200 Blueberry Rd., **Gardners** 17324, (717) 528-8877. Owners: Marsha & Rick Lucidi. Open all year. 3 rooms: dbl. w/ pvt. bath $65, sgl. or king w/ shared bath $55. Dep. req.: $25 per room. Accepts V, MC, personal checks. 10-day cancellation notice for refund, less $15 service charge. No children or pets. No smoking. A small (3-room) B&B in a 1760 home on 25 acres amid apple orchards. Complimentary fruit, afternoon tea or wine, terry robes, and bath supplies. Directions: From US 15 at PA 234 (Heidlersburg) exit, go west on 234 for 0.5 mi. to Old Harrisburg Rd.(SR 3001), turn right for 0.9 mi. to Oxford Rd. (SR 1016), left for about 2.5 mi. to Blueberry Rd., a gravel road. Turn left to house.

Abraham Spangler Inn, 264 Baltimore St., **Gettysburg** 17325, (717) 337-3997. Innkeeper: Joel C. Nimon. Open all year. 3 rooms: dbl. w/ shared bath $40, twin $35, sgls. $35 and $30. Lower rates Labor Day to Memorial Day. Dep. req.: 1 night. Accepts V, MC, personal checks. 2 night min. wknds. & hol. 48-hr. cancellation notice for refund, less $5 service charge. No children under 12, no pets. No smoking. House built 1907 on the foundation of a house that had been built in 1824. Directions: in town on US 15 Bus., 2-1/2 blocks south of Lincoln Sq.

The Brafferton Inn, 44 York St., **Gettysburg** 17325, (717) 337-3423. Owners: Mimi & Jim Agard. Open all year. 8 rooms: sgl. w/ pvt. bath $60, dbl. $80; sgl. w/ shared bath $55, dbl. $70. Dep. req. Accepts V, MC, personal checks for dep. only. Smoking permitted in atrium only. The house is the first built in town (1786) and is on the NRHP. During the Civil War it served as a church. Mural of Gettysburg buildings painted on dining room walls. Features atrium, living room, and garden area. Directions: in town on US 30, 1/2 block east of Lincoln Sq.

The Doubleday Inn, 104 Doubleday Ave., **Gettysburg** 17325, (717) 334-9119. Owners: Joan & Sal Chandon. Open all year. 11 rooms: sgl. w/ shared bath $60; king w/ pvt. bath $75-90, w/ shared bath $65; dbl. w/ shared bath $65. Dep. req.: 50% of stay. Accepts V, MC, and personal checks. Children over age 7 preferred, no pets. No smoking. The Colonial house stands atop Oak Ridge on the Battlefield at what was the center of the Union line on July 1, 1863 (the house was built in 1929, however). Collection of Civil War memorabilia, including 550 books written about the Battle of Gettysburg, are found throughout. Picnic basket lunches are available. Directions: from Lincoln Sq., go north on Carlisle St. (US 15 Bus.) to Lincoln Ave., turn left for 2 blocks, right on College Ave./Mummasburg Rd. for about 3/4 mi., left on Doubleday Ave. to house on left.

Keystone Inn, 231 Hanover St., **Gettysburg** 17325, (717) 337-3888. Owners: Wilmer & Doris Martin. Open all year. 4 rooms: twin or queen w/ pvt. bath $65, dbl. w/ shared bath $55. Dep. req.: 1 night. Accepts V, MC, and personal checks. No smoking. Dinner avail. Sat. only, Nov.-March. A large house built with lots of natural oak and chestnut, decorated with pastels, lace, and flowers. Access to tennis and basketball courts. Directions: in town on PA 116, SW corner of Hanover & 5th Sts.

BERKS CO.

Sunday's Mill Farm B&B, RD 2, Box 419, **Bernville** 19506, (215) 488-7821. Owners: Sally & Len Blumberg. Open all year. 2 rooms: queen w/ pvt. half bath, shared tub/shower $45 sgl., $55 dbl.; queen w/ shared bath $45 sgl., $35 dbl. Dep. req.: 1 night. Accepts personal checks, no credit cards. Children permitted but must be supervised at all times. No pets. Smoking permitted if there are no other non-smoking guests. Dinner avail. by res., $10. The 23-acre working farm is along Tulpehocken Creek and the Union Canal towpath in a NRHP Historic District. The stone mill dates from 1820 and most of its equipment is intact. The house was built about 1850 and is furnished with antiques and original paintings. Fishing and hiking on the premises. Directions: from PA 183 in Bernville, go SW on Heidelberg Rd. (SR 3033) for 0.2 mi., bear right on Christmas Village Rd. (SR 4010) for 2-1/2 mi. to Station Rd., turn left, cross steel bridge over Tulpehocken Creek to farm on right.

Twin Turrets Inn, 11 E. Philadelphia Ave., **Boyertown** 19512, (215) 367-4513. Owner: Gary Slade. Open all year. 9 rooms: queen w/ pvt. bath $70 sgl., $80 dbl.; King w/ pvt. bath $125 dbl. Dep. req.: 1 night. Accepts V, MC, AE, and personal checks. Smoking permitted in garden and on deck only. The house was built in the 1850s and renovated in 1987. Features old Victorian architecture and antique furnishings. Rooms have remote control cable TV and telephones. Continental breakfast served. Directions: on PA 73 in center of town, 3 doors east of intersection of PA 562.

The Loom Room, RD 1, Box 1420, **Leesport** 19533, (215) 926-3217. Owners: Gene & Mary Smith. Open all year. 3 rooms: dbl. w/ pvt. bath $45, king w/ shared bath $40. Extra person $15, children under 12 free. Dep. req.: $40. Accepts personal checks, no credit cards. Smoking permitted. 175-year-old farmhouse with herb and flower gardens and 18th-century log weaving studio on the property. Rooms furnished with antiques and handwoven accessories. Directions: 2-1/2 mi. N of Reading Airport, just off PA 183 at Old Bernville Rd. & White Oak La.

BUCKS CO.

Sevenoaks Farm B&B, 492 New Galena Rd., **Chalfont** 18914, (215) 822-2164. Owner: John T. Shafer. Open all year. 6 rooms: king w/ pvt. bath $75, w/ shared bath $55. Dep. req.: 1 night. Accepts V, MC, and personal checks. One week cancellation notice for refund, less than one week dep. refunded only if room is filled. Smoking permitted in downstairs common areas only. Traditional 18th-century farmhouse with beamed ceilings, sun porch. Features redwood hot tub, near Peace Valley County Park. Directions: from intersection of US 202 & PA 152 in Chalfont, go north on 152 for 1 mi. to Sellersville Rd., turn left for about 3/4 mi. to New Galena Rd., right to first driveway on left.

The Inn at Fordhook Farm, 105 New Britain Rd., **Doylestown** 18901, (215) 345-1766. Owners: Blanche Burpee Dohan and Jonathan Burpee. Open all year. 7 rooms: king or queen w/ pvt. bath $110, dbl. $82; king w/ shared bath $95, queen $87-95. Dep. req. within one week of making res.: 1 night. One week cancellation notice for refund. Accepts V, MC, AE, and personal checks. No children under 12, no pets. Smoking permitted only on terrace. A 60-acre estate on the NRHP owned by the Burpee Seed Co. family. Guest rooms are in the 18th-century stone house and 19th-century carriage house. Afternoon tea served in living room or on terrace. All rooms air-conditioned. Will pick up guests arriving by train with advance notice. Directions: Turn south off US 202, 1/4 mi. W of PA 611 interchange, go 1/4 mi. on New Britain Rd. to entrance on left.

Pine Tree Farm, 2155 Lower State Rd. (SR 3003), **Doylestown** 18901, (215) 348-0632. Owners: Ron & Joy Feigles. Open all year. 5 rooms: queen w/ pvt. bath $100; 2-bedroom suite w/ living room

& pvt. bath $150 for one couple, $190 for two. Dep. req.: 1 night. 10-day cancellation notice for refund, less $10 service charge. Accepts V, MC, AE, and personal checks. No children or pets. No smoking. A 1730 farmhouse furnished with antiques on 16 acres. Pool and tennis court on property. Directions: go SW from Doylestown on W. Court St., which becomes Lower State Rd. (SR 3003). Farm is just west of New Britain Rd.

Evermay-on-the-Delaware, River Rd. (PA 32), **Erwinna** 18920, (215) 294-9100. Owners: Ron Strouse & Fred Cresson. Open all year exc. Christmas Eve. 30 rooms: sgl. w/ pvt. bath $42-55, queen $95-100, dbl. $65-115, suites $155. Sgl. rate avail. weekdays only. Dep. req.: 1 night. Accepts V, MC, and personal checks. Dinner avail. Fri., Sat., Sun., and hol. by res. Smoking permitted, but no cigars or pipes in dining areas or parlor. Victorian country hotel on 25 acres situated between the river and canal. Lodging is in manor and carriage houses. Afternoon tea served. Directions: 13.5 mi. N of New Hope on PA 32.

Golden Pheasant Inn, River Rd. (PA 32), **Erwinna** 18920, (215) 294-9595. Owners: Michel & Barbara Faure. Open all year. 5 rooms: queen w/ pvt. bath $125, dbl. w/ shared bath $95. Dep. req.: 50% of stay. Accepts personal checks, no credit cards. Dinner avail. by res. Smoking permitted in dining area, porch, and private suite only. 1857 fieldstone inn located between the river and canal. Directions: 13 mi. N of New Hope on PA 32.

Barley Sheaf Farm, Box 10, Rt. 202, **Holicong** 18928, (215) 794-5104. Owners: Don & Ann Mills. Open Feb. 14 until week before Christmas, and weekends only from weekend after New Year's until Feb. 14. 10 rooms, all w/ pvt. bath: dbl. $100-110, queen $95-110, suite $135. High season rates (wknds. July 4-Oct.) $10-15 higher. Extra person $15. 15% disc. Sun.-Thurs. out of high season. 2 night min. wknds., 3 nights hols. Dep. req.within 10 days of making res.: 2 nights for hol. wknd., otherwise 1 night. 10-day cancellation notice for refund, less $10 service charge. Accepts AE and personal checks for dep. only. No children under age 9, no pets. Smoking permitted. This 30-acre farm in on the NRHP and was once the home of the playwright George S. Kaufman. The original part of the house dates from 1740, and the property includes a bank barn, swimming pool, and pond. Directions: on US 202/PA 263 between Buckingham and Lahaska.

The Bucksville House, RD 2, Box 146, **Kintnersville** 18930, (215) 847-8948. Owner: Joe Szollosi. Open all year, daily July, Aug., otherwise wknds. & hols. only. 4 rooms, all w/ pvt. bath: king $75, suite $120. Dep. req.: 1 night. 7-day cancellation notice for refund, less $15 service charge. Accepts V, MC, and personal checks. No children or pets. No smoking. A registered Bucks County landmark, formerly the Bucksville Hotel (1840-1930). Dining room has Mercer tile floor and walk-in fireplace. Rooms decorated with antiques and reproductions made by owner. Features cable TV. Directions: on PA 412, 2 mi. N of PA 611.

Lahaska Hotel, PO Box 500, Rt. 202, **Lahaska** 18931, (215) 794-0440. Owners: Susan & Ralph Kearney. Open all year. 6 rooms, all w/ pvt. bath: king $95, dbl. $80, queen $80, 85. Extra person $15. 10% mid-week & senior citizen discount. Dep. req.: full stay. 48-hr. cancellation notice for refund, less $10 service charge; no charge if res. is rebooked within 6 weeks. Accepts V, MC, and personal checks. No children under 12 or pets. Smoking permitted in common areas only. An 1885 Victorian home with country decor and antiques. Italian restaurant on the property. All rooms air-conditioned. Directions: on US 202 opposite Peddler's Village.

Black Bass Hotel, River Rd. (PA 32), **Lumberville** 18933, (215) 297-5770. Owner: Herbert Ward. Open all year exc. Christmas. 10 rooms: dbl. w/ shared bath $80, suites $150, $175. Dep. req.: 1 night. Accepts V, MC, AE, DC, CB, and personal checks. Dinner avail. by res. Smoking permitted in bar only. The inn has been operating since 1745 and houses the world's largest collection of British Royal commemorative memorabilia. Directions: on PA 32, 7 mi. N of New Hope.

The Inn at Phillips Mill, N. River Rd. (PA 32), New Hope 18938, (215) 862-2984. Owner: Joyce Kaufman. Open 1st wknd. in Feb. thru Dec. 6 rooms: dbl. w/ pvt. bath $78, w/ shared bath $68; cottage $125 (2 night min.). Dep. req.: full stay. Accepts personal checks, no credit cards. Rest. on premises open to public. Smoking permitted. On the NRHP. Lodging and country French cuisine in renovated 18th-century stone barn. Dining by the fireplace in winter and on the patio in summer. Directions: on PA 32, 1-1/2 mi. N of New Hope.

Pineapple Hill B&B, 1324 River Rd. (PA 32), New Hope 18938, (215) 862-9608. Owners: Suzie & Randy Leslie. Open all year. 5 rooms: dbl. w/ pvt. bath $75, w/ shared bath $65; 2-bdrm. suites w/ pvt. bath $85 & $95. Weeknights all rates $10 lower. Dep. req.: 1 night min. or 1/2 of stay. Accepts AE and personal checks. No pets. No smoking. Farmhouse dates from 1780s, with 18-inch thick walls and traditional woodwork. Country furnishings, folk art, and primitive antiques. Ruins of stone barn serve as foundation for swimming pool. Directions: On PA 32, 4.6 mi. S of PA 179 in New Hope.

The Wedgewood Inn, 111 W. Bridge St., New Hope 18939, (215) 862-2570. Owners: Nadine Silnutzer & Carl Glassman. Open all year. 12 rooms: dbl. w/ pvt. bath $75-100, w/ shared bath $65. Weeknights all rates $10-15 lower. Sgl. occupancy $5 less, extra person $15. Dep. req.: 1 night. 2-night min. on wknds., 3 nights on holiday wknds. 10-day cancellation notice for refund, less $15 service charge. Accepts personal checks, no credit cards. Inquire regarding accommodations for children and pets. Smoking permitted on veranda only. There are two houses: a Victorian built in 1870 on the foundation of a house that was built in 1720, and a Classic Revival stone manor house built about 1833. The inn was voted "Inn of the Year" in 1988 by readers of The Complete Guide to Bed & Breakfast Inns & Guesthouses in the US and Canada. Directions: on PA 179 in center of town.

The Whitehall Inn, 1370 Pineville Rd., New Hope 18938, (215) 598-7945. Owners: Mike & Suella Wass. Open all year. 6 rooms: dbl. w/ pvt. bath $90-100, w/ shared bath $95; Queen w/ pvt. bath $125, w/ shared bath $100. Dep. req.: 1 night. Accepts V, MC, AE, DC, CB, Discover, and personal checks. No smoking. An elegant 1794 manor house set on 12 acres of rolling hills with a working dressage farm. Rooms with high ceilings and wide pine floors furnished with antiques. Candlelight breakfast, rated "sumptuous" by Bon Appetit. Directions: Turn left off US 202, 2-1/2 mi. W of New Hope, on Lower Mountain Rd., go 1-3/4 mi. to 5-way intersection at Pineville & Street Rds., bear left on Pineville for about 1 mi. to inn on right.

Tattersall Inn, Cafferty & River Rds., Point Pleasant 18950, (215) 297-8233. Owners: Gerry & Herb Moss. Open all year. 6 rooms, all w/ pvt. bath: king $73-83, queen $73-95. Extra person $15, sgl. occ. $10 less. Senior citizen discount. Dep. req.within one week of making res.: 1 night. 2 night min. wknds. 10-day cancellation notice for refund, less $5 service charge. Accepts V, MC, AE, and personal checks. Smoking permitted. 18th-century plastered fieldstone house with wide porches was the home of the famous Stover family, prominent Bucks County mill owners. All rooms air-conditioned. Directions: center of village, turn left off River Rd. (PA 32) on Cafferty Rd. for 150 yards to inn on right.

Riegelsville Hotel & Inn, 10-12 Delaware Rd., Riegelsville 18077, (215) 749-2469. Owners: Harry E. Cregar, Jr. and Frances Cregar. Open all year. 12 rooms: sgl. w/ half bath $60, dbl. w/ pvt. bath $75, w/ shared bath $50, 2-room suite w/pvt. bath $85. Dep. req. Accepts V, MC, AE, and personal checks for dep. only. Dinner avail. by res. Smoking permitted on main and second floors only, not in rooms. Building dates from 1837 and has been a hotel and inn ever since. Dining areas and guest rooms furnished with antiques, fine china, and crystal chandeliers. Breakfast served on second floor enclosed balcony overlooking the river. Directions: center of town, by Delaware River bridge, between river and canal.

CHESTER CO.

Glen Run Valley Farm, RD 1, Box 69, **Atglen** 19310, (215) 593-5656. Owners: Harold & Hanna Stoltzfus. Open all year. 2 rooms w/ shared bath $40. Dep. req.: $10. Accepts personal checks, no credit cards. 50-acre farm operated by Mennonite family. Pick blackberries and wild strawberries in season. Dinner avail. by res. Homemade quilts for sale. Preferable for senior citizens. Directions: go east on PA 372 for 1 mi. from PA 41, turn right on Lenover Rd. for 1 mi. to farm on left.

B&B at Walnut Hill, 214 Chandler's Mill Rd., **Avondale** 19311, (215) 444-3703. Owner: Sandra F. Mills. Open all year. 2 rooms, both w/ pvt. bath: sgl. $50, dbl. $60. Dep. req.: 1 night. Accepts personal checks for dep. only, no credit cards. Smoking permitted downstairs area only. 1850 Chester County farmhouse with antique furnishings. VCR and ping pong available. Directions: Turn off PA 41, 3.5 mi. S of Avondale, 0.7 mi. N of Delaware state line, on Kaolin Rd. (SR 3013), go east 1 mi. to Chandler Mill Rd., turn left for 0.2 mi. (still SR 3013) to Bucktoe Rd.

Duck Hill Farm, 311 Little Washington Rd., **Downingtown** 19335, (215) 942-3029. Owner: Marie Reid. Open April to Nov. 2 dbl. rooms, both w/ pvt. bath, $65. Dep. req.: $15. Accepts personal checks for dep. only, no credit cards. Smoking permitted. Stone colonial house c. 1750 on 20 acres with swimming pool. Pick your own fruits and vegetables. Directions: 6 mi. NW of Downingtown, turn right of US 322 on Little Washington Rd. (SR 4006) for 1 mi. to farm.

The Conestoga Horse B&B, Box 256, Hollow Rd., **Glenmoore** 19343, (215) 458-8535. Owners: Richard & Patricia Moore. Open all year. 5 rooms: dbl. w/ pvt. bath $100, sgl., dbl., twin w/ shared bath $65. Dep. req.: $20 high season only. Accepts personal checks, no credit cards. Smoking permitted in living room only. A 1762 home and stone cottage with horse stable for boarding and riding lessons. Directions: from intersection of PA 100 and PA 401, go west on 401 for 2 mi. to Templin Rd., turn right for 1/4 mi. to Hollow Rd., right to first lane on right.

Campbell House, 160 E. Doe Run Rd., **Kennett Square** 19348, (215) 347-6756. Owners: Judy & Bill Campbell. Open all year. 3 rooms: dbl. w/ pvt. bath $60, sgl. & dbl. w/ shared bath $50. Dep. req.: 1 night. Accepts personal checks, no credit cards. No children or pets. Smoking permitted downstairs only. Farmhouse on 13 acres dates from 1745 with addition in 1794 and is decorated with 18th- and early 19th-century furniture. Pool available. Directions: go north on PA 82 from US 1 for 2.4 mi. to Doe Run Rd., turn right for 1 mi. to house on right.

Meadow Spring Farm, 201 E. Street Rd, **Kennett Square** 19348, (215) 444-3903. Owner: Anne I. Hicks. Open all year. 6 rooms: sgl. w/ pvt. bath $35, dbl. or queen $65. Dbl. or queen w/ shared bath $50. Dep. req.: $20. Accepts personal checks, no credit cards. Dinner avail. with res. An 1836 farmhouse furnished with antiques, Amish quilts, dolls, and animal collection. Live animals on farm. Pool, game room, hot tub, TV in rooms. Directions: NE of Kennett Square on PA 926 between PA 82 and PA 52.

Mrs. K's B&B, 404 Ridge Ave., **Kennett Square** 19348, (215) 444-5559. Owner: Charlotte Kanofsky. Open all year. 4 rooms, all w/ shared bath: sgl. $45, dbl. $50, king or twin $55. Dep. req.: 1 night. Personal checks accepted for deposit only, no credit cards. No pets. No smoking indoors. TV in rooms, wine and cheese served 5:30-6:30 PM. Directions: from center of town, go south on Union St. (PA 82) to high school on left, turn right on Ridge Ave. to house on left.

Cornerstone B&B Inn, Newark & Buttonwood Rds., **Landenberg** 19350, (215) 274-2143. Owner: Linda D. Chamberlin. Open all year. 4 rooms, all w/ pvt. bath: sgl. $65, dbl. $75, king $85. Dep. req.: 1 night. Accepts personal checks for dep. only, no credit cards. No smoking. Quaker fieldstone house originally built in early 1700s and expanded several times to reach its present size in 1820. Rooms have fireplaces, furnished with period pieces. Swimming pool. Directions: 2 mi. S of Avondale on PA 41, turn right on Newark Rd. (SR 3033) for 2-1/4 mi. to Buttonwood Rd.

Hershey's Vacationland B&B, Box 93, **Lincoln University** 19352, (215) 932-9257. Owners: Ephraim & Arlene Hershey. Open all year. 3 rooms, all w/pvt. bath: sgl. $25, dbl. $35. Dep. req.: none. Accepts personal checks, no credit cards. No smoking. Newly constructed house, picnic area in woods, basketball, ping pong, roller skating avail. Directions: 4 mi. N of Oxford on PA 10.

Fairway Farm, Vaughan Rd., **Pottstown** 19464, (215) 326-1315. Owners: Franz & Katherine Streitwieser. Open all year. 5 rooms, all w/pvt. bath: sgl. $45, queen $60, king $65. Children $10 addl. Dep. req.: none. Accepts personal checks, no credit cards. No pets. No smoking indoors. Oldest part of farmhouse dates from 1734, barn from 1860. Features hot tub, sauna, pool, tennis, TV, gazebo, Bavarian atmosphere. Directions: from US 422 (Pottstown bypass), take PA 724 exit, turn left off ramp for 0.2 mi., then right on Vaughan Rd. for 0.2 mi. to entrance on left.

Pheasant Hollow Farm, PO Box 356, **Thorndale** 19372, (215) 384-4694. Owners: Bob & Barbara Adams. Open all year. 2 queen rooms w/shared bath $65. Dep. req.: 1 night. Accepts personal checks, no credit cards. No smoking. A secluded wooded setting, fireplaces in rooms, gardens, hot tub. Directions: 1 mi. S of US 30 Bus. in Thorndale.

Whitethorne B&B, PO Box 92, **Unionville** 19375, (215) 793-1748. Owners: Jim & Marianne Hoy. Open all year. 10 rooms. Sgl. w/pvt. bath $55, w/shared bath $50; dbl., king, or queen $65 and $60. Dep. req.: 1 night. Accepts personal checks, credit cards if booked through B&B of Philadelphia or B&B of Chester County. No smoking in house. Stone farmhouse built early 1700s, has original locks and hardware, hand-pegged doors and woodwork. Horseback riding avail., nature trails surround house. Directions: 3 mi. E on PA 842.

The Barn B&B, 1131 Grove Rd., **West Chester** 19380, (215) 436-4544. Owner: Susan Hager. Open all year. 2 dbl. rooms w/shared bath, $55 1st night, $45 succeeding nights. Dep. req.: 1 night. Accepts personal checks, no credit cards. Smoking permitted but not encouraged. Restored 1800s stone barn furnished with antiques overlooking countryside with springhouse and pond. Directions: 1.7 mi. N of downtown West Chester, turn left on Grove Rd. (SR 3069) for 1/4 mi.

The Crooked Windsor, 409 S. Church St., **West Chester** 19382, (215) 692-4896. Owner: Mrs. Charles J. Rupp. Open all year. 4 rooms, all w/shared bath: sgl. $60, dbl. $65. Dep. req.: 20%. Accepts personal checks, no credit cards. No smoking. Historic Victorian home, furnished with antiques. House is on Chester County Day house tour. Pool, jacuzzi, basketball avail. Directions: in town, 1 block W of High St. (PA 100), between Dean & Price Sts.

Old Haines Mill, 680 Haines Mill Rd., **West Chester** 19382, (215) 793-1633. Owner: Sally E. Flynn. Open all year. 2 dbl. rooms w/pvt. bath $60. Dep. req.: none. Accepts personal checks, no credit cards. Smoking permitted on porch only. Restored grist mill, c. 1710, in the heart of fox hunting country. Trout stocked stream with swimming hole. Directions: from US 1 at Longwood Gardens, go north on PA 52 for 1-1/2 mi., bear left on Locust Grove Rd. for 0.3 mi., left on Haines Mill Rd.

CUMBERLAND CO.

Kellerhaus, 1634 Holly Pike, **Carlisle** 17013, (717) 249-7481. Owners: G.F. (Joe) & Mary Jane Keller. Open all year. 3 rooms: king w/pvt. bath $55, w/shared bath $50; dbl. or twin w/shared bath $40. Dep. req.: 1 night or 50%. Accepts personal checks, no credit cards. No pets. A 1797 stone farmhouse one-quarter mile off highway. Directions: on PA 34, 3 mi. S of I-81, exit 14.

Kibler Haus, 381 Longs Gap Rd., **Carlisle** 17013, (717) 243-7550. Owner: Rachel M. Kibler. Open all year. 3 rooms w/ shared bath: dbl. $40, twin $45. Dep. req.: 1 night. Accepts personal checks, no credit cards. 7-day cancellation notice for full refund. No smoking in house. Fishing, hiking trails, basketball, softball field, spacious porch. Directions: from Public Sq., go north on PA 34 for 1.4 mi. to Longs Gap Rd., turn left for 1 mi. to "J.O. Lehman Retreat" sign, turn right down hill to house.

Field & Pine Farm, RD 5, Box 161, **Shippensburg** 17257, (717) 776-7179. Owners: Allan & Mary Ellen Williams. Open all year. 3 dbl. rooms w/ shared bath $50. Dep. req.: $25. Accepts personal checks, no credit cards. No smoking indoors. 80-acre farm with 1790 restored tavern with seven fireplaces. Nearby trout fishing. Directions: on US 11, 4 mi. SW of I-81, exit 11. From I-81, go north on PA 233 to US 11, turn left to farm.

DAUPHIN CO.

Pinehurst Inn B&B, 50 Northeast Dr., **Hershey** 17033, (717) 533-2603. Owners: James & Phyllis Long. Open all year. 12 rooms: queen w/ pvt. bath $50, sgl., dbl., or queen w/ shared bath $45, queen & sgl. w/ shared bath $50, queen & dbl. w/ shared bath $55. Lower rates Oct. 15-Apr. 15. Dep. req. within 7 days after making res.: 1 night. 2-day cancellation notice for refund. Accepts V, MC, and personal checks. No smoking. The house was one of the first built as part of the Milton S. Hershey School. Within walking distance of most Hershey attractions. Accessible to handicapped. Directions: off PA 743, 0.6 mi. N of US 422.

FRANKLIN CO.

Rice's White House Inn, 10111 Lincolnway W., **St. Thomas** 17252, (717) 369-4224. Owners: Joan & M.L. Rice. Open all year. 3 rooms, all w/ pvt. bath: sgl. $49, dbl. or king $59. Dep. req.: 1 night. 3-day cancellation notice for refund. Accepts personal checks, no credit cards. No children or pets. Smoking permitted in tavern and living room only. Built as an inn and tavern before 1795, on the NRHP. Completely restored, air-conditioned, furnished with antiques. Wine, coffee, or tea served on arrival. Directions: on US 30, 12 mi. W of Chambersburg.

LANCASTER CO.

Lancaster & Environs

Buona Notte B&B, 2020 Marietta Ave., **Lancaster** 17603, (717) 295-2597. Owners: Joe & Anna Predoti. Open all year. 3 rooms: king w/ pvt. bath $45, sgl., dbl. w/ shared bath $35. Dep. req.: 1 night. Accepts personal checks for dep. only, no credit cards. No pets. No smoking or alcoholic beverages indoors. Turn-of-the-century home with large rooms and wrap-around porch. Homemade muffins, breads, and jam for breakfast. Directions: on PA 23, 1/4 mi. E of PA 741 in village of Rohrerstown, 3 mi. W of downtown Lancaster.

Hollinger House B&B, 2336 Hollinger Rd., **Lancaster** 17602, (717) 464-3050. Owner: Leon & Jean Thomas. Open all year. 5 rooms, all w/ shared bath: dbl. or twin $45, 50. Lower rates Dec. to Apr. Dep. req.: $20. Accepts personal checks, no credit cards. No smoking indoors. Originally the home of a local harness leather manufacturer and a dormitory for his employees, the 17-room house built in 1800 was remodeled in 1985 as a designer showcase home. Children of any age welcome. Directions: go south from Lancaster for 3 mi. on US 222, turn right on Hollinger Rd. for 0.7 mi. to house on right.

New Life Homestead B&B, 1400 E. King St., **Lancaster** 17602, (717) 396-8928. Owners: Carol & Bill Giersch. Open all year. 3 dbl. rooms, all w/ shared bath $50, $55. Extra person $10. Dep. req.: 1 night or 50%. Accepts personal checks, no credit cards. No children under 12 or pets. No smoking or alcoholic beverages indoors. House dates from early 1900s, features natural chestnut trim, and is decorated with antiques. Air-conditioned rooms, evening snacks. Directions: on PA 462, 1-1/2 mi. E of downtown.

Greenfield Gest Haus, 90 Greenfield Rd., **Lancaster** 17602, (717) 299-5964. Owners: Ben & Alma Landis. Open all year. 4 rooms, all w/ shared bath: sgl. $20, dbl. $24, 30. Dep. req.: 1 night. Accepts personal checks for dep. only, no credit cards. Smoking permitted on balcony only. House built in 1926 by Mennonite minister, features natural chestnut interior trim, spacious lawn, large trees. Directions: SW corner of Greenfield Rd. & Old Philadelphia Pike (PA 340), within 1/2 mi. of Greenfield Rd. & PA 340 exits of US 30.

Northern Lancaster County

Covered Bridge Inn B&B, 990 Rettew Mill Rd., **Ephrata** 17522, (717) 733-1592. Owner: Betty Lee Maxcy. Open all year. 4 rooms: queen w/ pvt. bath $65, 70; sgl. w/ shared bath $40, dbl. $50, queen $55. Dep. req.: 1 night or 50%. Accepts personal checks, no credit cards. No pets. No smoking indoors. NRHP home built in 1814 to accompany a stone mill that stood on the opposite side of the road. House has original Indian doors, handblown windowpanes, pine floors, two herb gardens. Covered bridge visible from inn. Directions: from jct. of US 322 & PA 272 in Ephrata, go south on 272 for 1.3 mi. to Rothsville Rd. (SR 1018), turn right for 0.3 mi. to Rettew Mill Rd., turn right to first house on right after covered bridge.

The Guesthouse & 1777 House at Donecker's, 318-24 N. State St., **Ephrata** 17522, (717) 733-8696. Owner: H. William Donecker. Open all year exc. Christmas. 30 rooms and suites: dbl. w/ pvt. bath $69-130, dbl. w/ shared bath $59. Dep. req.: 1 night. Accepts V, MC, AE, DC, CB, Discover, house charge, and personal checks. 2-day cancellation notice for refund. No pets. Smoking permitted. The 1777 House was built by famous clockmaker Jacob Gorgas for his family and now contains 10 guest rooms and suites. The remaining rooms are in the Guesthouse, and are air-conditioned with private phones. Buffet breakfast served to guests. Directions: in town, 4 blocks N of US 322.

The Smithton Country Inn, 900 W. Main St., **Ephrata** 17522, (717) 733-6094. Owner: Dorothy Graybill. Open all year. 8 rooms, all w/ pvt. bath: king $95, queen $95, $105, dbl. $85, $95. Weekday rates $30 less. 2 night min. Sat. & hol. Dep. req.: full payment or credit card number. Accepts V, MC, AE, and personal checks. Dinner avail. by res. Children and pets accepted. No smoking. The inn dates from pre-Revolutionary times and is adjacent to the Ephrata Cloister. Each room has canopy bed, working fireplace, sitting area, leather upholstered furniture, and writing desk. Directions: on US 322, 1 block W of PA 272 interchange.

Alden House, 62 E. Main St., **Lititz** 17543, (717) 627-3363. Owners: Jim & Lori Wilson. Open all year. 9 dbl. rooms. w/ pvt. bath $75, w/ shared bath $65, 2-room suite w/ pvt. bath $90, $95. Extra person $10. Nov. thru Mar. $10 less for min. 2 nights, exc. hol. Dep. req. within 7 days of making res.: 50% of first night. 4-day cancellation notice for full refund, 3-day notice $10 service charge, less than 3 days no refund. Accepts V, MC, and personal checks. Smoking permitted in common room only. 1850 townhouse with three porches. Directions: center of town on PA 772, 1/2 block E of PA 501.

Swiss Woods B&B, 500 Blantz Rd., **Lititz** 17543, (717) 627-3358. Owners: Werner & Debrah Mosimann. Open all year. 4 rooms, all w/ pvt. bath: dbl. or king $50-60, 1 suite $65-75. Lower rates Jan.-Mar. Dep. req.: $25. Accepts personal checks, no credit cards. No pets. Smoking permitted outside only. A Swiss-style chalet located on 30 acres of woods and meadows. Each room has private patio. Swiss breakfasts served. Directions: 3.8 mi. N of Lititz, turn left off PA 501 onto Brubaker Valley Rd. (SR 4008), go 1 mi. to Blantz Rd., turn right, then first left to house.

Herr Farmhouse Inn, RD 7, Box 587, **Manheim** 17545, (717) 653-9852. Owners: Barry & Ruth Herr. Open all year. 3 dbl. rooms: w/ pvt. bath $75, w/ shared bath $65. 1 suite w/ pvt. bath $85. Extra person $10. Nov. thru Mar. $10 less for min. 2 nights, exc. hol. Dep. req. within 7 days of making res.: 50% of first night. 4-day cancellation notice for full refund, 3-day notice $10 service charge, less than 3 days no refund. Accepts V, MC, and personal checks. Smoking permitted in common room only. The house dates from 1738 and has been restored, using the original mouldings and floors. Six working fireplaces. Directions: from PA 283 westbound, take Mt. Joy (PA 230) exit, turn right on Esbenshade Rd., then immediately right on Huber Dr. to house on left.

Eastern Lancaster County

The Osceola Mill House, 313 Osceola Mill Rd., **Gordonville** 17529, (717) 768-3758. Owners: Barry & Joy Sawyer. Open all year. 4 rooms, all w/ shared bath: dbl. $50-60, queen $60-70. Extra person $10. Rates $5 higher in Oct. Dep. req.: 1 night. Accepts personal checks for dep. only, no credit cards. No pets, not recommended for children under 12. No smoking. House built 1766 on banks of Pequea Creek. Fireplaces in some rooms, antiques and reproductions throughout. Directions: 1.6 mi. E of Intercourse on PA 772, turn right on Osceola Mill Rd. for 1/2 mi. to house.

Groff Farm Tourist Home, 766 Brackbill Rd., **Kinzers** 17535, (717) 442-8223. Owners: Harold & Mary Ellen Groff. Open all year. 4 rooms, all w/ shared bath: sgl. $26, dbl. $45. Lower rates after Nov. 1. Dep. req.: 1 night. Accepts personal checks for dep. only, no credit cards. No pets. No smoking indoors. Stone farmhouse with old-fashioned porch, spacious lawn and flower beds. Air-conditioned. Research documents date of house as 1876 but owners believe it is older. Directions: between Kinzers and Gap, turn south off US 30, or north off PA 741, on Brackbill Rd.

Turtle Hill Road B&B, 111 Turtle Hill Rd., **Leola** 17540, (717) 656-6163. Owner: Mrs. Jean W. Parmer. Open all year. 3 rooms, all w/ shared bath: sgl. $25, dbl. $40 w/o breakfast, $45 w/ breakfast. Lower rates Jan. & Feb. Dep. req.: 1 night. Accepts personal checks, no credit cards. Smoking permitted on patio only. Rural setting, along Conestoga Creek. Directions: from center of Brownstown, go E on E. Main St., which becomes Turtle Hill Rd., to house.

The Rose & Crown B&B, 44 Frogtown Rd., **Paradise** 17562, (717) 768-7684. Owners: Allan & Linde Helmbrecht. Open mid-March to early Dec. 4 queen rooms, all w/ shared bath, accommodating 3 or 4 persons $45-55. Up to 2 children free. Dep. req.: 50% of each night. Accepts personal checks, no credit cards. No smoking indoors. A family-oriented home, with volleyball, horseshoes, badminton, TV. B&B is in 19th-century carriage house; two rooms have fireplaces. One night free after six nights in same calendar year. Directions: 2 mi. S of Intercourse on Queen Rd., which becomes Frogtown Rd., or turn left off Lincoln Hwy. (US 30) 1.3 mi. E of Paradise onto Belmont Rd. (SR 2035), then immediately right on Harristown Rd. to Frogtown Rd., left to house.

Old Road Guest House, 2501 Old Philadelphia Pike, **Smoketown** 17576, (717) 393-8182. Owners: David & Marian Buckwalter. Open all year. 6 rooms: queen w/ pvt. bath $30, w/ shared bath $22-24, king w/ shared bath $24. Dep. req.: $20. Accepts personal checks, no credit cards. No alcoholic beverages or smoking indoors. Clean, suburban home, air-conditioned. Directions: intersection of PA 340 & 896.

Limestone Inn B&B, 33 E. Main St., **Strasburg** 17579, (717) 687-8392. Owners: Dick & Jan Kennell. Open all year. 4 rooms w/ shared bath: sgl. $49, dbl. $59. Dep. req.: $10 per night. Accepts AE and personal checks. No children or pets. Smoking permitted in keeping room only. A 1786 NRHP home in Historic District. Directions: center of town on PA 741/896.

Southern Lancaster County

The Walkabout Inn, 837 Village Rd., **Lampeter** 17537, (717) 464-0707. Owners: Richard & Margaret Mason. Open all year. 6 rooms w/ pvt. bath: sgl. $65, dbl. $75, apartment suite $85; sgl. w/ shared bath $50, dbl. $55, suite $85. Lower rates Dec.-Apr. Dep. req.: 1 night. Accepts V, MC, AE, and personal checks. Dinner avail. by res. Smoking permitted on porches only. Authentic British style B&B. 1925 Mennonite farmhouse with large wrap-around porches and balcony, decorated in antiques. Directions: on PA 741 in center of village.

Lime Valley Cottage, 1107 Lime Valley Rd., **Lancaster** 17602, (717) 687-6118. Owners: George & Evelyn Rohrer. Open all year. Cottage w/ 2 bedrooms, bath, sofa bed, and 2 cots, $45 for 2 persons, $4 each addl. person. Dep. req.: 1 night. Accepts personal checks for dep. only, no credit cards. No pets. No alcoholic beverages or smoking. Completely private accommodations in furnished cottage atop a hill overlooking Pequea Creek. Directions: turn left off US 222, 3.3 mi. S of intersection of PA 272 in Willow Street, onto Lime Valley Rd. (SR 2030), go approximately 1 mile to house on left.

Lake Aldred Lodge B&B, 693 Bridge Valley Rd., **Pequea** (PECK-way) 17565, (717) 284-4662. Owner: Mrs. Dolores B. Detwiler. Open all year. 3 rooms, all w/ shared bath: sgl. $35, dbl. $45-50. Dep. req.: 1 night. Accepts personal checks for dep. only, no credit cards. Smoking permitted on porch only. House built in late 1800s and overlooking Susquehanna River. Front porch with rocking chairs. Directions: PA 324 south from US 222 for 13 mi. to end at Pequea, turn left on Bridge Valley Rd. (SR 3038) to house on left.

The Decoy, 958 Eisenberger Rd., **Strasburg** 17579, (717) 687-8585. Owners: Debby & Hap Joy. Open all year. 5 dbl. rooms, all w/ pvt. bath $50. Extra person $10. Lower rates Dec. 1-Good Friday. Dep. req.: 50% of stay. Accepts personal checks, no credit cards. No pets. No smoking indoors. A former Amish home with a spectacular view of farmland. Air-conditioned. Directions: from center of Strasburg, go south on S. Decatur St./May Post Office Rd. (SR 2015) for 4 mi. to White Oak Rd., turn right for 1 mi., then right on Eisenberger Rd. for 0.2 mi. to house.

Green Gables B&B, 2532 Willow Street Pike, **Willow Street** 17584, (717) 464-5546. Owners: Karen & Mike Chiodo. Open all year. 4 rooms, all w/ shared bath: sgl. $30, dbl. $45. Dep. req.: $20 per room per night. Accepts personal checks, no credit cards. Smoking permitted in parlor and dining room only. A 1907 Victorian home with original oak woodwork and stained glass windows. Tennis on grounds. Directions: 3 mi. S of downtown Lancaster on US 222 (northbound lanes).

The Apple Bin Inn B&B, 2835 Willow Street Pike, **Willow Street** 17584, (717) 464-5881. Owners: Barry & Debbie Hershey. Open all year. 4 king rooms: w/ pvt. bath $60, w/ shared bath $45. Dep. req.: 1 night. 2-day cancellation notice for refund less 20% service charge. Accepts V, MC, and personal checks for dep. only. No smoking. A 120-year-old Colonial style home. Color cable TV in rooms, air-conditioned. Directions: in center of village, on PA 272 (northbound lanes), opposite W. Willow Rd.

Western Lancaster County

The Old Bridge Inn, 420 Chestnut St., **Columbia** 17512, (717) 684-3173. Owners: Charles & Jean Stark. Open all year. 4 rooms, all w/ shared bath: dbl. or king $45. Extra person $10. Lower rates Nov. thru Apr. Dep. req.: 1 night. Accepts V, MC, and personal checks for dep. only. No children under 13 or pets. No smoking indoors. Victorian stone home built 1889, with massive stained glass windows and large rooms. TV, VCR, and movies avail. Directions: in town on PA 462, 3 blocks from Susquehanna River bridge.

Vogt Farm B&B, RD 1, Colebrook Rd., **Marietta** 17547, (717) 653-4810. Owners: Keith & Kathy Vogt. Open all year. 3 rooms, all w/ shared bath: sgl. $25, dbl. $40, twin $45. Dep. req.: 50% of first night. Accepts personal checks, no credit cards. No smoking. House built in 1865, has fireplace in family room. Flowers and mints in rooms. Terry robes supplied to guests. Directions: from intersection of PA 441 & 772, go E on 772 for 0.5 mi., left on Colebrook Rd. to farm.

Cedar Hill Farm B&B, 305 Longenecker Rd., **Mt. Joy** 17552, (717) 653-4655. Owners: Russel & Gladys Swarr. Open all year. 3 rooms, all w/ pvt. bath: dbl. or queen $50. Dep. req.: 1 night. Accepts V, MC, AE, and personal checks. No young children or pets. No smoking indoors. The 1817 stone farmhouse overlooks Little Chiques (Chickies) Creek, has walk-in fireplace, large porch with wicker furniture, air-conditioned rooms, some furnished with family heirlooms. Directions: from PA 283 westbound, take Mt. Joy exit (PA 230), go 2.4 mi. west on PA 230, turn left at entrance of Mt. Joy on Longenecker Rd. (SR 4003), cross steel bridge, then left on drive to farm.

Chrisken Inn, 4035 Garfield Rd., **Mt. Joy** 17552, (717) 653-2717. Owners: Kenneth & Diana Hill. Open all year. 1 apartment w/ pvt. bath $50 sgl. or dbl., $10 each addl. adult, $2 addl. child to age 18. Dep. req.: 1 night. Accepts personal checks, no credit cards. No pets. No smoking indoors. A large stone home built in 1806 offering complete privacy (breakfast is not served). Electricity generated on the premises from creek water. Apartment will accommodate six. Directions: from PA 283 at Salunga-Landisville exit, go S on Prospect Rd. (SR 4001) for 2 mi. to Garfield Rd., turn right to stone home on right after bridge.

The Country Stay, RD 1, Box 312, **Mt. Joy** 17552, (717) 367-5167. Owners: Darlene & Lester Landis. Open May thru Nov. 3 king rooms w/ shared bath $45-55. Dep. req.: $20. Accepts V, MC, and personal checks. No pets. No alcoholic beverages or smoking indoors. Large Victorian farmhouse furnished from the period and accented with quilts and country crafts. Directions: go 4 mi. W of Mt. Joy on Donegal Springs Rd. (SR 4002) to Landis Rd., turn right for 1/4 mi., left on Bull Moose Rd. to house on right.

Stonebridge Farm, 745 Pinkerton Rd., **Mt. Joy** 17552, (717) 653-4866. Owners: John & Velma Brubaker. Open all year. 3 rooms, all w/ shared bath: sgl. $30, dbl. or king $45. Dep. req.: 1 night in high season only. Accepts V, MC, and personal checks. Children age 12 and up preferred. No smoking indoors. A 1730 stone house in a country setting at 3-arch stone bridge over Chiques Creek. Swimming and TV avail. Directions: turn south off PA 772 in Mt. Joy on Pinkerton Rd., go 1-1/4 mi. to farm.

Carriage House Manor, 143 W. Main St., **Mountville** 17554, (717) 285-5497. Owners: David & Patti Nace. Open all year. 3 dbl. rooms w/ shared bath $50. Extra person $10. Lower rates Jan.-May 15. Dep. req.: 50% of 1 night. Accepts personal checks, no credit cards. No pets. No smoking indoors. Built 1914 from Sears, Roebuck plans, house has large windows and unique pocket doors, Victorian decor. Yard features large maples and play area. Directions: center of town on PA 462.

Mountville Antiques B&B, 407 E, Main St., **Mountville** 17554, (717) 285-5956 or -7200. Owners: Pat & Sam Reno. Open Mar. thru Dec. 4 rooms w/ pvt. bath: sgl. $45, dbl. or twin $55, king $65; 2 dbl. rooms w/ shared bath $45. Dep. req.: 1 night. Accepts V, MC, and personal checks for dep. only. No smoking. House is also antiques shop. Air-conditioned, herb and flower garden. Directions: E end of town on PA 462.

LEBANON CO.

Swatara Creek Inn, RD 2, Box 692, **Annville** 17003, (717) 865-3259. Owners: Dick & Jeannette Hess. Open all year. 5 queen rooms, all w/ pvt. bath $50-70. Lower rates Dec. thru Mar. Dep. req.: $25. Accepts V, MC, and personal checks. No smoking indoors. 3-story Victorian brick mansion built in 1860. Owned by Milton S. Hershey from 1917-41, who used it as a boys' home. Period furnishings in rooms. Air-conditioned. Directions: From I-81 exit 29, go south on PA 934 for 1/ 2 mi. to Old Rt. 22, turn right to 3rd house on left.

LEHIGH VALLEY

Salisbury House, 910 E. Emmaus Ave., **Allentown** 18103, (215) 791-4225.Owners: Judith & Ollie Orth. Open all year. 5 dbl. rooms: w/ pvt. bath $115, w/ shared bath $100. Dep. req.: full prepayment. Accepts V, MC, AE, and personal checks. No children or pets. Smoking permitted in common areas only. 15-room house built in 1810 as a tavern, features 7 fireplaces, library, sunporch, greenhouse, boxwood garden, creek, lily pond, nature trails. Complimentary beverages served in the evening. Gourmet breakfast served by candlelight. Directions: south side of city, turn east off S. 4th St. (PA 145) onto Emmaus Ave.

Glasbern, RD 1, Box 250, **Fogelsville** 18051, (215) 285-4723. Owners: Beth & Al Granger. Open all year. 20 rooms, all w/ pvt. bath: sgl. $65, dbl. or king $80. Dep. req.: 1 night. Accepts V, MC, AE, and personal checks. Smoking permitted. Elegantly restored bank barn, features swimming and cable TV. Directions: turn north in center of village on N. Church St., go 0.6 mi. to Packhouse Rd., right for 0.8 mi. to inn.

MONTGOMERY CO.

Joseph Ambler Inn, 1005 Horsham Rd., **North Wales** 19454, (215) 362-7500. Owner: Richard Allman. Open all year. 28 rooms and suites, all w/ pvt. bath: dbl. $80-120, queen $87-127. Extra person $15. Dep. req. within 10 days of making res.: 1 night. 10-day cancellation notice for full refund. Accepts V, MC, AE, DC, CB, and personal checks. No children under 12 or pets. Smoking permitted. The fieldstone main house containing 9 rooms was built in 1734, the former tenant farmer's cottage contains 7 rooms, and the 1820 stone bank barn, 12. All are decorated with antiques and period furnishings. Inn has been featured in Colonial Homes and other country inn guidebooks. Directions: on PA 463, 1 mi. SE of intersection of PA 309, 463, and US 202.

YORK CO.

Spring House, Muddy Creek Forks, **Airville** 17302, (717) 927-6906. Owner: Ray Hearne. Open all year. 2 rooms w/ pvt. bath: sgl. $87, dbl. $95; 3 w/ shared bath: sgl. $62, dbl. $ 70. Weekday rates $10 less. Dep. req.: 1 night. Accepts personal checks, no credit cards. Pets accommodated in nearby kennel. No smoking. Dinner avail. by res. The stone house, built in 1798 by a state legislator, stands over a spring that was the main source of water for the little village that thrived while the Maryland & Pennsylvania RR was in operation. Restored over a period of 10 years by the present owner and furnished with period antiques and fabrics. Directions: 7.0 mi. SE of Red Lion at Brogue post office, turn south off PA 74 on SR 2069, go 5.0 mi. to Muddy Creek Forks.

Beechmont Inn, 315 Broadway, **Hanover** 17331, (717) 637-7796. Owners: Terry & Monna Hormel and Glenn & Maggie Hormel. Open all year. 7 rooms, all w/ pvt. bath: king $70-85, dbl. $75. Dep. req.: 1 night. Accepts V, MC, and personal checks. No children or pets. Smoking permitted in guest rooms only. Federal style house built in 1834. Air-conditioned rooms appointed with period furnishings. Directions: in town on PA 194 northbound.

C. FARM VACATION HOMES

CHESTER CO.

Elver Valley Farm, Sawmill Rd, Box 177A, **Cochranville** 19330, (717) 529-2803. Owners: Elvin & Vera Rohrer. Open Apr. thru Dec. Furnished cabin w/ full kitchen accommodating up to 12, $25 for family of four, each addl. person $3. 153-acre dairy farm in southwestern Chester County. Guests welcome to observe milking. Directions: turn north off PA 896 about 1-1/2 mi. W of PA 10.

CUMBERLAND CO.

Alwayspring Farm, RD 3, Box 480, **Carlisle** 17013, (717) 249-1455. Owners: Jeanne & Howard Fitting. Open all year. 2 rooms w/ shared bath: sgl. $25, dbl. $35. Dep. req.: 1 night. Accepts personal checks for dep. only, no credit cards. Dinner avail. by res. No smoking. Rural 45-acre farm with geese, horses, and chickens. Central air-conditioned, badminton, horseshoes, ping pong. Directions: 6 mi. NW of Carlisle, 1/2 mi. S of PA 944, on McClure's Gap Rd.

Line Limousin Farm House, 2070 Ritner Hwy., **Carlisle** 17013, (717) 243-1281. Owners: Bob & Joan Line. Open all year. 4 rooms: king w/ pvt. bath $44, sgl. w/ shared bath $32, dbl. $44. Extra person $10. Dep. req.: 1 night. Accepts personal checks, no credit cards. No pets. No smoking. Brick and stone farmhouse on 100-acre farm specializing in Limousin beef cattle and asparagus. Pastures and woodlands for hiking, fresh water trout fishing nearby. Farm is a seventh generation homestead bought in 1778 from Gen. John Armstrong. Directions: on US 11, 3.7 mi. W of Public Sq., 0.8 mi. W of PA 465 intersection.

LANCASTER CO.

Northern Lancaster County

Spahr's Century Farm, 192 Green Acre Rd., **Lititz** 17543, (717) 627-2185. Owner: Naomi Spahr. Open Apr. thru Nov. 1 king room w/ pvt. bath $50, 2 dbl. rooms w/ shared bath $40. Dep. req.: 1 night. Accepts V, MC, and personal checks. Smoking permitted. Farm in family over 125 years. Directions: 1-1/2 mi. W of town, turn south off PA 772 on Green Acre Rd.

Jonde Lane Farm, RD 7, Box 657, **Manheim** 17545, (717) 665-4231. Owners: John & Elaine Nissley. Open Mar. thru Dec. Rooms w/ shared bath: sgl. $25, dbl. or king $40. Extra adult $12.50, child $6. Dep. req.: 1 night. Accepts personal checks, no credit cards. No smoking indoors. A 90-acre farm with dairy cows, 2 large chicken houses, and large lawn and garden, operated by Mennonite family. Directions: 1-1/2 mi. S of Manheim, turn west off PA 72 on Auction Rd., go 2.2 mi. to Weaver Rd. Turn left into lane to second farm.

Stone Haus Farm, RD 7, Box 584, **Manheim** 17545, (717) 653-5819. Owners: Henry & Irene Shenk. Open all year. Rooms w/ shared bath $25-30. Dep. req.: none. Accepts personal checks, no credit cards. No alcoholic beverages or smoking. Old stone farmhouse on beef, veal, and crop farm. Picnic table and shade trees. Directions: from PA 283 westbound, take Mt. Joy (PA 230) exit, go 1/4 mi. to Esbenshade Rd., turn right to first farm on left after expressway overpass.

Eastern Lancaster County

Hershey Farm, 70 Oak Hill Dr., **Paradise** 17562, (717) 687-6037. Owners: Nevin & Ruth Hershey. Open all year. 3 rooms, 1 w/ pvt. half bath, 2 w/ shared full bath, write or call for rates. Dep. req.: 1 night. Accepts personal checks, no credit cards. No alcoholic beverages or smoking. 130-acre holstein dairy farm operated by Mennonite family. Picnic area and refrigerator avail. Free coffee. Directions: turn south off US 30 in Paradise on Black Horse Rd. for 1/3 mi., turn right on Oak Hill Dr. to farm.

Maple Lane Farm Guest House, 505 Paradise Lane, **Paradise** 17562, (717) 687-7479. Owners: Ed & Marion Rohrer. Open all year. 4 dbl. rooms: w/ pvt. bath $50-60, w/ shared bath $45-50. Extra person $8. Dep. req.: 1 night. Accepts personal checks, no credit cards. No pets. No smoking indoors. House is on 200-cow dairy farm. Each room air-conditioned and decorated with antiques, canopy, and poster beds. Free farm tours. Directions: from center of Strasburg, go E on PA 896 for 2 mi. to Paradise La., turn right to farm.

Rayba Acres Farm, 183-O Black Horse Rd., **Paradise** 17562, (717) 687-6729. Owners: J. Ray & Reba Ranck. Open all year. 6 rooms: sgl. w/ pvt bath $36, dbl. $39; sgl. w/ shared bath $28, dbl. $31, queen $28, $29. Extra person $4. Dep. req.: 1 night. Accepts personal checks, no credit cards. No smoking. Modernized 1863 farmhouse with private entrance. Air-conditioned, picnic area, refrigerator, coffee. Fifth generation dairy farm—guests welcome to observe or try milking. Directions: in center of village, turn south off US 30 on Black Horse Rd., go 2 mi. to farm.

Neffdale Farm, 604 & 610 Strasburg Rd., **Paradise** 17562, (717) 687-7837 or -9367. Owners: Roy & Ellen and Charles & Glenda Neff. Open all year. 6 rooms in two houses: king w/ pvt. bath $28-32, dbl. $30; king w/ shared bath $26, dbl. $26-28. Dep. req.: 1 night. Accepts personal checks, no credit cards. No smoking indoors. Choice of modernized 200-year-old farmhouse or modern Cape Cod, both air-conditioned. Guests may help with farm chores. No meals served. Directions: PA 741, 3 mi. E of Strasburg.

Verdant View Farm Home, 429 Strasburg Rd., **Paradise** 17562, (717) 687-7353. Owners: Don & Virginia Ranck. Open Easter-Nov. 1. 4 rooms: w/ pvt. bath $40-58, w/ shared bath $30-40. Lower rates Apr.-June. Dep. req.: 1 night. Accepts personal checks, no credit cards. No pets. No smoking indoors. 1896 house on 122-acre farm. Breakfast not served Sun. Guests may attend Mennonite church services with family. Directions: PA 741, 1 mi. E of Strasburg.

Southern Lancaster County

Winding Glen Farm Tourist Home, 107 Noble Rd., **Christiana** 17509, (215) 593-5535. Owners: Robert & Minnie Metzler. Open Apr. thru Nov. 5 rooms, all w/ shared bath: dbl. $32, children age 6-12 $9. Dep. req.: $15. Accepts personal checks, no credit cards. No smoking indoors. 250-year-old house, air-conditioned. Full breakfast included. Guests may watch cows being milked. Directions: from PA 372 in center of town, bear right on Noble Rd, pass railroad underpass. Farm is on right just beyond Lower Valley Rd.

White Rock Farm Guest House, 154 White Rock Rd., **Kirkwood** 17536, (717) 529-6744. Owners: Les & Lois Hershey. Open all year. 3 king rooms, all w/ shared bath $45. Dep. req.: 1 night. Accepts personal checks, no credit cards. No pets. No alcoholic beverages or smoking. Stone farmhouse built 1860. 100-acre farm has 150 head of beef cattle and cropland. Covered bridge, nature trails, picnic grove nearby. All-you-can-eat country breakfast $3.00 per person. Directions: turn south off PA 472 on White Rock Rd., go 1-1/2 mi. to farm.

Pleasant Grove Farm, 368 Pilottown Rd., **Peach Bottom** 17563, (717) 548-3100. Owners: Charles & Labertha Tindall. Open all year. 3 rooms w/ shared bath $40-45. Dep. req.: $10 per night. Accepts personal checks, no credit cards. No alcoholic beverages or smoking. 160-acre dairy farm built in 1814 has been in the family for 104 years, designated a Century Farm by the PA Department of Agriculture. Swimming pool and hiking on premises. Directions: Bear right off US 222, 0.5 mi. S of PA 272 intersection in Wakefield, on Pilottown Rd. (SR 3001), go 3 1/2 mi. to farm.

Tri-Spring Farm, 1048 Byerland Church Rd., **Willow Street** 17584, (717) 464-2440. Owners: Luke & Dorothy Hess. Open all year. 2 rooms w/ shared bath $12 per person per night. Dep. req.: $10 (varies). Accepts personal checks, no credit cards. No alcoholic beverages or smoking. Mennonite family 113-acre farm raising chickens, sows, piglets, and crops. Welcome to attend church with family. Directions: 3-1/2 mi. S of intersection of PA 272, US 222, and PA 741 in Willow Street, turn west off PA 272 on Byerland Church Rd. to farm.

Western Lancaster County

Olde Fogie Farm, RD 1, Box 166, **Marietta** 17547, (717) 426-3992. Owners: Tom & JoAnn "Biz" Fogie. Open Apr. thru Oct. 1 efficiency apartment w/ pvt. bath $59, 2 dbl. rooms w/ shared bath $40. Lower rates after Labor Day and for senior citizens. Dep. req.: 1 night. Accepts V and personal checks. Dinner avail. by res. No smoking indoors. Guests may help milk goat and gather eggs. Directions: 1/4 mi. W of Maytown off PA 743.

Brenneman Farm, RD 1, Box 310, **Mt. Joy** 17552, (717) 653-4213. Owners: Elvin & Marian Brenneman. 1 room w/ pvt. bath: sgl. $35, dbl. $65; 4 rooms w/ shared bath: sgl. $25, dbl. $45. Dep. req. at time of making res.: Accepts V, MC. The 14-room early 1800s log house is decorated with Victorian and country antiques and handcrafts. Directions: W of Mt. Joy on Donegal Springs Rd. (SR 4002).

Green Acres Farm, 1382 Pinkerton Rd., **Mt. Joy** 17552, (717) 653-4028. Owners: Wayne & Yvonne Miller. Open all year. Sgl. w/ pvt. bath $25, king $45; king w/ shared bath $40. Extra person: teens $10, children $6. Dep. req.: $25. Accepts personal checks, no credit cards. No alcoholic beverages or smoking indoors. 160-year-old house, featured in Winter 1988 Country Almanac. Furnished with antiques, air-conditioned. TV, trampoline, swings, pony and cart avail. Farmer's breakfast served exc. Sun. Directions: turn south off PA 772 in Mt. Joy on Pinkerton Rd.

D. HOTELS AND MOTELS

Name Mailing Address Phone	Location Description	Rates	Extra person charge	Credit cards	Lower rates avail. out of season	Surcharge for special events	Handicapped access	Restaurant	Pets	Deposit/credit card guarantee required.	Facilities	Explanations/ Comments
ADAMS CO.												
FAIRFIELD 17320 Carroll Valley Lodge 5104 Fairfield Rd. (717) 642-8245	on PA 116	S 48 D 58	0	V,M, A,DC, CB	Y	N	Y	N	Yr	Y	A,O	10% disc. at nearby rests.
GETTYSBURG 17325 Heritage Motor Lodge 64 Steinwehr Ave. (717) 334-9281	In town, Bus. US 15 South	S 48, 50 D 56 St 60, 65	5	V,M, A,DC, D	Y	2	Ys	Y	Yr	Y	A,B	Closed Thanksgiving to mid-March
Best Western Stonehenge Lodge 205 Steinwehr Ave. (717) 334-3168;(800) 528-1234	In town, Bus. US 15 South	S,D 56-66	4	All	Y	Y	N	Y	Yr	Y	A,F	
Howard Johnson Motor Lodge 301 Steinwehr Ave. (717) 334-1188;(800) 654-2000	In town, Bus. US 15 South	S 59-69 K 69-74 D 64-74	5	V,M, A,DC, CB	Y	N	Ys	Y	Yr	4PM	A,B,C,F,K,L,M,N	Cocktail lounge; AARP
Quality Inn-Gbg. Motor Lodge 380 Steinwehr Ave. (717) 334-1103;(800) 228-5151	In town, Bus. US 15 South	D,K 66 Fam 80 St 85	5	V,M A,DC, CB	Y	N	Ys	Y	Yr	4PM	A,C,D,F,N,O	Cocktail lounge; Putting green; AARP
Travelodge 10 E. Lincoln Ave. (717) 334-6235;(800) 255-3050	In town, Bus. US 15 North	S 52 D 60, 70	0	All	Y	N	Y	Y	N	Y	F,M,O	Playground, local tours; cold weather hookup
Holiday Inn 516 Baltimore St. (717) 334-6211;(800) HOLIDAY	In town	S 38-83 D 45-85	7	All	Y	Y	N	Y	N	Y	B,O	In-room whirlpool/steambath; local tours
Blue Sky Motel 2585 Biglerville Rd. (717) 677-7736	PA 34, 5 mi. N	S 38 D 44 Fam 50	3	V,M	Y	Y	N	N	N	Y	A,F	
Lincolnway East Motel 983 York Rd. (717) 334-4208	US 30, 1 mi. E	S 48 D 58 St 76	0	V,M, A,DC, CB	Y	N	Ys	N	Yr	Y	A,B,N	Weekday disc.
Quality Inn-Larson's 401 Buford Ave. (717) 334-3141;(800) 228-5151	US 30,.1 mi. W	S 44-62 D 52-62	3	All	Y	N	N	Y	N	4PM	C,D,F,O	Putting green

ADAMS CO. (cont.)

Establishment / Address / Phone	Location	Rates	No.	Cards	—	—	—	—	Time	Facilities	Remarks
GETTYSBURG 17325 (cont.)											
Sheraton Inn Gettysburg 2634 Emmitsburg Rd. (717) 334-8121;(800) 325-3535	Bus. US 15, 5 mi. S	S 73-84 D 78-84 St 149-199	5	All	Y	N	Ys	Y	4PM	A,C,E,G,K	Weekday disc.
Stuart's Motel 2520 Emmitsburg Rd. (717) 334-1339	Bus. US 15, 4 mi. S	D 48-58 St 64	0	V,M,A,DC,CB	Y	N	Y	Y	Yr	A,F,N	
Econo-Lodge 945 Baltimore Pike (717) 334-6715;(800) 55-ECONO	1 mi. N of Baltimore St. (PA 97) exit of US 15	S 33 D 40	3	All	Y	N	N	Y	Y	A,F,O	Local tours
BERKS CO.											
BETHEL 19507											
Lamplighter Motel RD 1, Box 1373 (717) 933-5675	I-78, exit 6	S 26 D 35	0	None	N	N	Y	Y	Yr	J,M	
DOUGLASSVILLE 19518											
Cedar Haven Motel 1321 Ben Franklin Hwy. (215) 385-3016; -3979	on US 422	K 25 D 30	0	V,M	N	N	N	Y	6PM		
LENHARTSVILLE 19534											
Maiden Creek Motel RD 2, Box 599 (215) 562-8413	E of town on Old US 22	D 30-35 St 35	5	None	Y	N	N	Y	8PM	A,H	
Top Motel RD 1, Box 834 (215) 756-6021	I-78, exit 12 (Krumsville)	S 30 K,D 35	4	V,M	Y	N	N	Y	6PM	A	Dep. req. summer
MORGANTOWN 19543											
Conestoga Wagon Motel RD 1, Box 2 (215) 286-5061	PA 23, 1/2 mi. from Tpk.	S 35 K 39 D 45	5	V,M	N	N	N	Y	Yr	A,H,M	
Economy Lodge PO Box 469 (215) 286-5521	PA 10, 1/4 mi. N of Tpk.	S 39 D 49, 64	5	V,M,A	Y	Y	Ys	Y	N	O	Refrig., coffee maker all rooms
READING AREA											
Luxury Budget Inn Spring St. & Paper Mill Rd.,19610 (215) 378-5105;(800) 441-4479	US 422, Paper Mill Rd. exit	S 37 K,D 46 St 48	4	V,M,A,DC,D	Y	N	Y	Y	6PM	A,B,H,J,O	Fax service
Hampton Inn 1800 Paper Mill Rd., 19610 (215) 374-8100;(800) HAMPTON	US 422, Paper Mill Rd. exit	D 46, 52 K 47, 53	0	All	Y	N	N	Y	N	B,C,H,J,O	Weekend rates available
Sheraton-Berkshire Inn Rt. 422 W & Paper Mill Rd., 19610 (215) 376-3811;(800) 325-3535	US 422, Paper Mill Rd. exit	S 80-105 D 90-115 St 140-180	0	All	N	N	Y	Y	N	B,C,E,K,O	Putting green; Kids' pool; exercise room

See **KEY TO ABBREVIATIONS** and **KEY TO FACILITIES** on page 289.

Name / Mailing Address / Phone	Location Description	Rates	Extra person charge	Credit cards	Lower rates avail. out of season	Surcharge for special events	Handicapped access	Restaurant	Pets	Deposit/credit card guarantee required.	Facilities	Explanations/ Comments
READING AREA (cont.) **BERKS CO. (cont.)**												
Penn View Motel 250 Penn Ave., W. Reading 19611 (215) 376-8011;(800) 825-PENN	1 blk. W of US 222/422 W. Reading/Penn Ave. exit	S 35-45 D 40-55	5	All	Y	N	Y	Y	Y	6PM	A,F,O	Coin laundromat
Days Inn 415 Lancaster Ave., 19607 (215) 777-7888;(800) 325-2525	US 222, 2 mi. W of US 422	S 38-57 D 41-49	5	V,M, A,DC, D	Y	Y	Y	Y	N	6PM	C,N	Govt. disc.
Econo-Lodge 2310 Fraver Dr., 19605 (215) 378-1145;(800) 55-ECONO	US 222 at Warren St. bypass interchange	S 31 D 35, 39	4	V,M	Y	N	Y	N	Y	Y	A,H	
Holiday Inn N. 5th St. Hwy., 19605 (215) 929-4741;(800) HOLIDAY	US 222 at Warren St. bypass interchange	S 62-82 D 72-97	10	All	N	Y	Y	Y	N	Y	B	
SHARTLESVILLE 19554 Dutch Motel Box 25 (215) 488-1479	I-78, exit 8	S 28-30 K 30-35 D 35-40	5	V,M, A	N	N	Ys	Y	Yr	Y	O	Free coffee
BUCKS CO.												
DOYLESTOWN 18901 Courthouse Motor Inn 625 N. Main St. (215) 348-9222	1 blk. S of PA 313	S 36 D 40 K 44	2	All	N	N	Y	Y	N	6PM	A,H,O	Free morning coffee & donuts
NEW HOPE 18938 Motel in the Woods 400 W. Bridge St. (215) 862-2800	PA 179, 3/4 mi. W	S 40 D 48-50 Q 50	9	All	N	N	Ys	N	N	Y	F	
Holiday Inn Route 202, Box 419 (215) 862-5221;(800) 222-HOPE	US 202, 2 mi. W	S 61-71 D 68-78	8	All	N	N	Y	Y	N	Y	O	Playground, shuffleboard
QUAKERTOWN 18951 Best Western Motor Inn 1446 W. Broad St. (215) 536-2500;(800) 528-1234	PA 313, 1/2 block E of PA 309/663 Intersection	S 45-50 D 47-63	8	All	N	N	Y	Y	N	Y	A,C,H,N	Govt. disc.; free coffee

BUCKS CO. (cont.)

QUAKERTOWN 18951 (cont.)

Name	Location	No.	Cards					Time	Code	Notes
Econo-Lodge Route 663 (215) 538-3000;(800) 55-ECONO	PA 663 at Turnpike exit 32	4	V,M A,DC, D	Y	Y	Y	N	Y	A	
CHESTER CO.										
EXTON 19341										
Days Inn 120 N. Pottstown Pike (215) 524-9000	PA 100, just north of US 30	5	V,M A,DC	N	Ys	Y	N	6PM	A,C,F	
Quality Inn 5 N. Pottstown Pike (215) 524-8811	NE cor. US 30 & PA 100	0	All	N	Y	Y	N	Y	B,C	
KENNETT SQUARE 19348										
Longwood Inn 815 E. Baltimore Pike (215) 444-3515	US 1, 1.5 ml. E	5	V,M A,DC, CB	N	Y	Y	N	6PM		
LIONVILLE 19353										
Hampton Inn Routes 100 & 113 (215) 363-5555;(800) HAMPTON	Jct. PA 100 & 113	0	All	N	N	Y	Y	Y	B,C,F,H,J	
Holiday Inn Box 1100 (215) 363-1100;(800) HOLIDAY	PA 100, 1/2 ml. S of Turnpike exit 23	5	All	N	N	Y	N	Y	B,C,E,O	Game room, tennis
SPRING CITY 19475										
'G' Lodge Motel Route 23 (215) 495-5103	PA 23, 2.5 ml. W of PA 724	2	V,M	N	N	Y	N	7PM	B,O	In-room coffee & refrigerators
WEST CHESTER 19382										
Beechwood Motel 1310 Wilmington Pike (215) 399-0970	PA 100, 3 ml. S	6	V,M A	Y	N	Y	N	4PM	B,M	
Brandywine Motel 1320 Wilmington Pike (215) 399-1233	PA 100, 3 ml. S	5	V,M A	N	-	Y	N	Y	O	Free morning coffee
CUMBERLAND CO.										
CAMP HILL 17011										
Hampton Inn 3721 Market St. (717) 737-6711;(800) HAMPTON	3/4 ml. W of US 11-15	5	V,M A,D, CB	N	Y	Y	N	6PM	A,C,L	
Penn Harris Inn & Convention Ctr. PO Box 839 (717) 763-7117;(800) 772-PENN	Erford Rd. exit of US 11-15	6	V,M A,DC, CB	N	N	Y	Yr	5PM	A,F,G	

See KEY TO ABBREVIATIONS and KEY TO FACILITIES on page 289.

CUMBERLAND CO. (cont.)

Name Mailing Address Phone	Location Description	Rates	Extra person charge	Credit cards	Lower rates avail. out of season	Surcharge for special events	Handicapped access	Restaurant	Pets	Deposit/credit card guarantee required.	Facilities	Explanations/Comments
CARLISLE 17013												
Harvon Motel 851 N. Hanover St. (717) 243-3113	US 11, 1 ml. N	S 32 / D 38 / Kit 35	0	V,M, A,DC, CB	Y	Y	Ys	Y	Yr	6PM	A,H,M,N	
Star Lite Motel & Restaurant 1175 Harrisburg Pike (717) 243-5504	US 11, between I-81 & Turnpike interchanges	S 28 / D 32, 34 / K 30, Q 36	2	V,M, A	Y	Y	Y	Y	Y	6PM	A,B,C,H	
Coach & Four Motor Lodge 1239 Harrisburg Pike (717) 249-2800	US 11, between I-81 & Turnpike interchanges	S 33-57 / D 43-71 / Kit 56-75	5	V,M,	N	N	Ys	Y	N	6PM	A,C,D,M,N	
Best Western Inn of the Butterfly 1245 Harrisburg Pike (717) 243-5411;(800) 528-1234	US 11, between I-81 & Turnpike interchanges	S 58 / D 63, K 66 / St 100-125	7	All	Y	Y	Ys	Y	N	6PM	B,F,N,O	Satellite TV, Efficiency units AAA, AARP
Howard Johnson Lodge 1255 Harrisburg Pike (717) 243-6000;(800) 654-2000	US 11, between I-81 & Turnpike interchanges	S 40, 50 / D 58	0	All	Y	N	Ys	Y	Y		A,C,F,O	Lounge
Holiday Inn 1450 Harrisburg Pike (717) 245-2400;(800) HOLIDAY	US 11 at I-81, exit 17	S 47-55 / D 54-62	7	All	N	N	Y	Y	N	6PM	A	
Days Inn 1460 Harrisburg Pike (717) 249-7775;(800) 55-ECONO	US 11 at I-81, exit 17	S 35 / D 39, 41	4	V,M, A,DC, D	Y	N	N	Y	N	6PM	A	
Embers Conv. Ctr./Quality Inn 1700 Harrisburg Pike (717) 243-1717;(800) 228-5151	US 11, 1/4 ml. N of I-81, exit 17	S 53 / D,K 63 / St 75	5	All	N	N	Ys	Y	Y	6PM	A,C,D,E,G,K,L,N	
ENOLA 17025												
Quality Inn Summerdale 501 N. Enola Rd. (717) 732-0785;(800) 228-5151	US 11-15, 3/4 ml. S of I-81, exit 21	S 46 / D 56	6	All	Y	N	Ys	Y	Y	6PM	A,B,C,F,J,N	AAA, Senior, Govt., Military disc.
MECHANICSBURG 17055												
Holiday Inn 5401 Carlisle Pike (717) 697-0321;(800) HOLIDAY	on US 11	S 65-82 / D 75-92	7	All	N	N	N	Y	N	6PM	B,C,O	Golf, tennis

CUMBERLAND CO. (cont.)

MECHANICSBURG 17055 (cont.)

Property	Location	No.	Credit						Time	Facilities	Remarks
Comfort Inn Mechanicsburg 6325 Carlisle Pike (717) 790-0924;(800) 228-5150	on US 11 at Lambs Gap Rd.	7	V,M, A,DC, CB	Y	Y	Ys	N	Yr	6PM	A,C,J	Off-season & spec. event rates negotiable
Best Western Plantation Inn 325 E. Winding Hill Rd. (717) 766-0238;(800) 528-1234	US 15 just S of Turnpike exit 17	5	All	Y	N	Ys	N	N	4PM	A,F,G,N,O	AAA, Senior disc. Par 3 18-hole golf course
Penn Motel 650 Old Gettysburg Rd. (717) 766-4728	1/2 mi. N of Tpk. exit 17; take Wesley Dr. exit of US 15 to Old Gettysburg Rd.	4	V,M, A,DC	Y	N	Ys	N	Yr	5PM	F	golf course

NEW CUMBERLAND 17070

Property	Location	No.	Credit						Time	Facilities	Remarks
Days Inn 353 Lewisberry Rd. (717) 774-4156;(800) 325-2525	PA 114 at I-83, exit 18	4	All	N	N	Y	Y	Y	6PM	B,C,F,N	Senior, Govt. disc.; lounge; playground
Keystone Motor Inn 353 Lewisberry Rd. (717) 774-1310	PA 114 at I-83, exit 18	4	All	N	N	Y	Y	Y	6PM	B,F,M	Lounge
Quality Inn PO Box 429 (717) 774-1100;(800) 228-5151	I-83, exit 18A, just north of Turnpike exit 18	5	All	Y	N	N	Y	N	6PM	A,F,N	Govt., military disc.
Sheraton Harrisburg West I-83 & Pa. Turnpike (717) 774-2721;(800) 325-3535	I-83, exit 18A, just north of Turnpike exit 18	0	All	N	N	N	Y	N	4PM	A,B,C,E,L,O	Hbg. Intl. Airport limo. avail.

SHIPPENSBURG 17257

Property	Location	No.	Credit						Time	Facilities	Remarks
Best Western University Lodge 720 Walnut Bottom Rd. (717) 532-7311;(800) 528-1234	N edge of town on PA 174, 1/2 mi. W of I-81, exit 10	4	All	N	N	N	N	Yr	4PM	A,C	

DAUPHIN CO.

GRANTVILLE 17028

Property	Location	No.	Credit						Time	Facilities	Remarks
Econo-Lodge RD 1, Box 5630 (717) 469-0631;(800) 55-ECONO	I-81, exit 28	5	All	N	N	Y	N	Y	6PM	A	
Holiday Inn I-81 & PA 743 (717) 469-0661;(800) HOLIDAY	I-81, exit 28	10	All	N	Y	Y	Y	N	6PM	B,E,K,N,O	Senior disc.; golf

HARRISBURG

Property	Location	No.	Credit						Time	Facilities	Remarks
Holiday Inn Center City 23 S. 2nd St., 17101 (717) 234-5021;(800) HOLIDAY	Downtown	12	All	N	N	Y	N	N	6PM	B,E,O	Racquetball
Riverfront Inn 525 S. Front St., 17104 (717) 233-1611	I-83, exit 23	5	V,M, A,DC, CB	N	Ys	Y	Y	Yr	6PM	C,F	(800) 982-6986 in PA

See KEY TO ABBREVIATIONS and KEY TO FACILITIES on page 289.

HARRISBURG (cont.)
DAUPHIN CO. (cont.)

Name Mailing Address Phone	Location Description	Rates	Extra person charge	Credit cards	Lower rates avail. out of season	Surcharge for special events	Handicapped access	Restaurant	Pets	Deposit/credit card guarantee required.	Facilities	Explanations/Comments
Howard Johnson Lodge 473 Eisenhower Blvd., 17111 (717) 564-4730;(800) 654-2000	1/4 mi. N of I-283, exit 1	S 55-85 D 60-90	0	All	N	Y	N	Y	N	6PM	B,C,F	
American Inn 495 Eisenhower Blvd., 17111 (717) 561-1885	1/4 mi. N of I-283, exit 1	S 28-70 D 35-80	5	V,M,A	Y	Y	N	Y	N	6PM	A	
Compri Hotel 765 Eisenhower Blvd., 17111 (717) 558-9500;(800) 4-COMPRI	I-283, exit 1	S 80 D,Q 90 St 150	10	V,M,A,DC,CB	Y	Y	Ys	Y	N	6PM	A,B,C,F,K,L,O	Full breakfast, 3 cocktails, 24-hr. coffee incl.
Red Roof Inn-Hbg. South 950 Eisenhower Blvd., 17111 (717) 939-1331;(800) THE-ROOF	I-283, exit 1	S 36, 38 D 42, 46	0	All	N	N	N	Y	Yr	6PM	B,C,H,N,O	Senior disc., free coffee, free USA Today.
Harrisburg Marriott 4650 Lindle Rd., 17111 (717) 564-5511;(800) 228-9290	I-283, exit 1	S 113 D,K 127 St 265	0	All	Y	N	Ys	Y	Yr	6PM	A,B,C,E,F,K,L	Lower weekend rates avail.
Holiday Inn East 4751 Lindle Rd., 17111 (717) 939-7841;(800) HOLIDAY	I-283, exit 1	S 75-80 D 85-90	5	All	N	N	N	Y	Y	6PM	A,C,E,L,O	Free Hbg. Intl. Airport trans.
Travel Master Inn 4131 Executive Park Dr., 17111 (717) 564-7790	I-283, exit 1, N on Eisenhower Blvd., L on Chambers Hill Rd.	S 25-32 D,K 32-38	3	V,M,A	N	N	N	Y	N	6PM	A,B,C,H,O	Free coffee
Sheraton Harrisburg East 800 East Park Dr., 17111 (717) 561-2800;(800) 325-3535	I-83, exit 29, 1/4 mi. E on Union Deposit Rd., R on East Park Dr.	S 75-105 D 85-115 St 135-175	10	V,M,A,DC	Y	N	Y	Y	N	4PM	A,C,E,K,L,O	13-station Nautilus
Capitol Motor Lodge 4646 Jonestown Rd., 17109 (717) 657-2650	I-83, exit 30, 1 mi. E on US 22	S 31-45 K 36-50 D 37-55	5	All	Y	Y	N	Y	N	6PM	A,D,F,M,N	AAA, Senior disc.
Quality Inn 5680 Allentown Blvd., 17112 (717) 652-3811;(800) 228-5151	I-83, exit 30, 2 mi. E on US 22; I-81, exit 26, 1/2 mi. W on US 22	S 49-57 D 57-65	6	All	N	Y	Y	Y	N	Y	B,C,F	
Greenlawn Motel 7490 Allentown Blvd., 17112 (717) 652-1530	US 22, 1 mi. W of PA 39	D 27, 37	0	V,M	N	N	Ys	Y	N	-		

DAUPHIN CO. (cont.)

Name / Address / Phone	Location	Rates	No.	Cards						Time	Codes	Notes
HARRISBURG (cont.) Days Inn-North 3919 N. Front St., 17110 (717) 233-3100;(800) 325-2525	1/4 mi. N of I-81, exit 22	K 60, 65 D 55, 63	5	All	Y	Y	Ys	Y	N	6PM	A,B,C,F,J	
Econo-Lodge 150 Nationwide Dr., 17110 (717) 545-9089	I-81, exit 24	S 37 D 41	4	All	N	N	Y	Y	Y	6PM	O	Free cribs
Inn of the Dove 2225 Kohn Rd., 17110 (717) 540-5540	I-81, exit 24, 1/4 mi. N on Progress Ave., L 1/2 mi. on Kohn Rd.	St 110, 135; 225, 275 wknds	0	V,M, A,DC	Y	N	Ys	Y	N	7PM	B,H,L,O	Steambath
Red Roof Inn-Hbg. North 400 Corporate Circle, 17110 (717) 657-1445;(800) THE-ROOF	I-81, exit 24	S 33 K 39 D 35, 41	6	All	N	N	Ys	Y	Y	6PM	B,C,H,N,O	Senior disc., free coffee, free USA Today
Best Western Harrisburg N. Mountain Rd., 17112 (717) 652-7180;(800) 528-1234	I-81, exit 26	S 65-75 D 68-78	3	All	Y	N	N	Y	Y	4PM	A	
HERSHEY 17033 Bruwin Motel 150 E. Governor Rd. (717) 533-2591	on US 322, 1/4 mi. E of PA 743	D 42, 49	4	V,M	Y	N	Y	N	N	4PM	A,H	
Cocoa Motel 914 Cocoa Ave. (717) 534-1243	intersection of US 322 & PA 743	K 58 D 68 St Kit 75, 78	5	V,M, A	Y	N	N	N	N	1PM	A,M	Kitchenettes not supplied with utensils
Hershey Colonial Motel 43 W. Areba Ave. (717) 533-7054	3 blocks S of US 422, 1/2 block W of PA 743	K 65 D 70 St 90, Eff 80	5	V,M	Y	N	N	N	N	1PM	A,C,M	Eff. & suites not supplied with dishes
Best Western Inn-Hershey Box 364 (717) 533-5665;(800) 528-1234	US 422 at Sipe Ave.	S 85-95 D 99-109	2	All	Y	N	N	Y	N	4PM	A,B,F,O	Game room
Hershey Lodge & Convention Ctr. Chocolate Ave. & University Dr. (717) 533-3344;(800) HERSHEY	US 422 W	S 68-94 D 74-104 St 155-250	0	V,M, A,DC, CB	Y	N	Y	Y	N	4PM	A,C,E,F,G,K,O	Cinema, 9-hole golf, whirlpool, bicycle rentals
Hotel Hershey PO Box BB, Hotel Rd. (717) 533-2176;(800) HERSHEY	1/2 mi. N of Hersheypark Dr.	S 98-136 D 124-154	0	All	Y	N	Ys	Y	N	Y	A,C,E,F,G,K,O	American plan packages avail.
Hometown Inn of America 115 Lucy Ave. (717) 533-2515	W end of town, between US 322 & 422	S 48 D,K 53	5	V,M	N	N	Ys	Y	N	6PM	A,C	
Simmons Motel 355 W. Chocolate Ave. (717) 533-9177	US 422, near downtown	S 60-65 D 75-85 St 100-150	5	V,M	Y	N	Ys	N	N	Y	A	

See KEY TO ABBREVIATIONS and KEY TO FACILITIES on page 289.

FRANKLIN CO.

Name / Mailing Address / Phone	Location Description	Rates	Extra person charge	Credit cards	Lower rates avail. out of season	Surcharge for special events	Handicapped access	Restaurant	Pets	Deposit/credit card guarantee required.	Facilities	Explanations/ Comments
CHAMBERSBURG 17201												
Econo-Lodge 1110 Sheller Ave. (717) 264-8005;(800) 55-ECONO		S 33 D 35, 39	3	All	Y	N	N	Y	N	6PM	A,O	Free cribs
Holiday Inn 1095 Wayne Ave. (717) 263-3400;(800) HOLIDAY		K 51, 58 D 49, 56	7	All	N	N	Yes	Y	Y	6PM	A,B,C,F	
Days Inn-Chambersburg 30 Falling Spring Rd. (717) 263-1288;(800) 325-2525		K 52 D 49 St 59	6	All	Y	N	Y	Y	N	6PM	A,B,C,N	AARP
Howard Johnson Lodge 1123 Lincolnway East (717) 263-9191;(800) 654-2000		S 49 D 61 K 68	7	All	Y	Y	Yes	Y	N	6PM	A,C,D,E,H,K,N,O	Senior, Govt. disc.; In-room refrig. coffee
Travelodge 565 Lincolnway East (717) 264-4187;(800) 255-3050	In town on US 30 W, 1 mi. W of I-81, exit 6	S 38 D 44, 49	0	All	Y	N	Y	Y	N	6PM	A,C,O	Cold weather hookups
GREENCASTLE 17225												
Travelodge-Sports Inn 50 Pine Dr. (717) 597-8164;(800) 255-3050	I-81, exit 2	S 39 D 44, 49	0	All	N	N	N	Y	N	6PM	A,C,K,O	Nautilus eqpt.; jogging tracks; racquetball
Castle Green Motor Inn 671 E. Baltimore St. (717) 597-9587	I-81, exit 3	S 26 D 34	2	V,M	N	N	Yes	Y	Y	6PM	F	
Econo-Lodge Rt. 16 & Antrim Church Rd. (717) 597-5255;(800) 55-ECONO	I-81, exit 3	S 29 D 33,37	4	V,M	N	N	N	Y	Y	6PM		
WAYNESBORO 17268												
Best Western Waynesboro 239 W. Main St. (717) 762-9113;(800) 528-1234	on PA 16, downtown	S 41 K 46 D 50	4	V,M	N	N	N	Y	Yr	Y	A,C,H,K,O	Full breakfast included in rates

LANCASTER CO.

Name / Address / Phone	Location	Rates	#	Cards						Time	Facilities	Remarks
LANCASTER & ENVIRONS												
Days Inn Lancaster, 30 Keller Ave., 17601, (717) 299-5700;(800) 325-2525	opp. Amtrak sta., cor. of PA 501 & Keller Ave.	K 78, D 72-82, St 83-90	6	V,M,A	Y	N	Ys	Y	N	4PM	A,B,C,E,F,G,K	
Holiday Inn, 1492 Lititz Pike, 17601, (717) 393-0771;(800) HOLIDAY	on PA 501, 1/4 ml. S of US 30	S 54-86, D 64-106	10	All	N	Y	N	Y	N	6PM	B	
1722 Motor Lodge, 1722 Old Phila. Pike, 17602, (717) 397-4791	on PA 340, 1/2 ml. E of PA 462, 1 ml. W of US 30	D 25-51	5	V,M,A	Y	N	Ys	N	N	4PM	A,H,J	
Travelodge, 2101 Columbia Ave., 17603, (717) 397-4201;(800) 255-3050	on PA 462, 2 ml. W of downtown, 1/4 ml. E of PA 741	S 53, D 59, 71	0	All	Y	N	Y	Y	N	Y	A,F,O	Cold weather hookups
NORTHERN LANCASTER CO.												
Ramada Lancaster Resort, Oregon Pike, Lancaster 17604, (717) 656-2101;(800) 228-2828	on PA 272, 5 ml. N of Lancaster	S 67-72, D 73-78	6	All	Y	N	Y	Y	N	4PM	E,F,K,N	Senior disc.
Holiday Inn, PO Box 129, Denver 17517, (215) 267-7541;(800) HOLIDAY	on PA 272 at Turnpike exit 21; US 222 Denver exit	S 58-68, D 68-78	6	All	N	Y	Y	Y	N	6PM	A,O	Guest laundry
Howard Johnson Lodge, PO Box 343, Denver 17517, (215) 267-7583;(800) 654-2000	on PA 272 at Turnpike exit 21, US 222 Denver exit	S 55-99, D 62-99	0	All	Y	N	Y	Y	N	6PM	B,C,D,F	Refrig. avail.; playground, picnic tables
Willow Dell Motel, RD 2, Box 717, Mohnton 19540, (215) 484-4242	just south of PA 272 on Bowmansville Rd. in Adamstown	D 33-55	5	V,M	Y	Y	Y	Y	Yr	3PM	A,O	Free coffee
EASTERN LANCASTER CO.												
Historic Strasburg Inn, Route 896, Strasburg 17579, (717) 687-7691	on PA 896 just north of Strasburg	S 70, D 90, St 125	10	V,M,A,DC,CB	Y	N	Ys	Y	Yr	6PM	F,H,N,O	Full breakfast AARP Gift shop, bakery
Timberline Lodges, 44 Summit Hill Dr., Stras. 17579, (717) 687-7472	3 ml. S of Strasburg off PA 896	D 60, Cott 80-120	5, 10	V,M,A,DC	Y	N	Ys	Y	N	Y	F,M,O	Furnished cottages sleep 4-8
Holiday Inn, Greenfield Rd., Lancaster 17601, (717) 299-2551;(800) HOLIDAY	at Greenfield Rd. exit of US 30	S 56-88, D 66-108	10	All	Y	N	Y	Y	N	6PM	B,E,F,O	Local tours; tennis; basketball; exercise room
Howard Johnson Motor Lodge, 2100 Lincoln Hwy. E., Lanc.17602, (717) 397-7781;(800) 654-2000	on US 30 just E of end of bypass	S 67-69, D 82-86	7	V,M,A,DC,CB	Y	N	Ys	Y	N	4PM	B,C,D,E,K,O	Special packages in off-season
Sheraton Golf Resort & Conf. Ctr., 2300 Lincoln Hwy. E., Lanc.17602, (717) 299-5500;(800) 325-3535	on US 30, 1/2 ml. E of end of bypass	S 89-139, D 99-149, St 170-500	0	All	Y	N	Ys	Y	Y	4PM	C,E,F,G,O	Tennis, golf, health club

See KEY TO ABBREVIATIONS and KEY TO FACILITIES on page 289.

283

LANCASTER CO. (cont.)

Name Mailing Address Phone	Location Description	Rates	Extra person charge	Credit cards	Lower rates avail. out of season	Surcharge for special events	Handicapped access	Restaurant	Pets	Deposit/credit card guarantee required.	Facilities	Explanations/ Comments
EASTERN LANCASTER CO. (cont.)												
Soudersburg Motel Box 1, Soudersburg 17577 (717) 687-7607	on US 30 in Soudersburg, 8 mi. E of Lancaster	S 52 D 66 Triple 70	0	V,M, A,DC	Y	N	N	Y	N	4PM	F	
Olde Amish Inn 33 Eastbrook Rd., Ronks 17572 (717) 393-3100	on PA 896 just S of PA 340	D,Q 46-57	5	V,M, A	Y	N	Ys	Y	N	4PM	A,C	
Cherry Lane Motor Inn 84 N. Ronks Rd., Ronks 17572 (717) 687-7646	1 mi. N of US 30, † mi. S of PA 340	S 65 D,Q, St 75	4	V,M, A	Y	N	Ys	N	N	Y	A,C,F,M	
Best Western Revere Motor Inn 3063 Linc. Hy. E., Paradise 17562 (717) 687-7683;(800) 528-1234	on US 30	S 58-68 D 60-70	4	All	Y	N	N	Y	N	4PM	A,B,E,O	Local tours
Bird-in-Hand Motor Inn Box B, Bird-in-Hand 17505 (717) 768-8271;(800) 537-2535	on PA 340 in Bird-in-Hand	D 64, 66 St 76	6	V,M, A,DC, CB	Y	N	Ys	Y	N	Y	A,E,F,G,J,L,O	Free local tours
Best Western Village Motor Inn Route 340, Intercourse 17534 (717) 768-3636;(800) 528-1234	Jct. PA 340 & 772	D 79-89	6	All	Y	N	N	Y	N	4PM	A,O	Playground; cold weather hookups
SOUTHERN LANCASTER CO.												
Staats Motel 3286 Willow Street Pike; Willow Street 17584; (717) 464-2411	on PA 272 in Willow Street, 5 mi. S of Lancaster	S 30 D 35 Kit 40	4	V,M	Y	N	N	Y	Yr	4PM	A,N,O	Weekly disc.; playground
WESTERN LANCASTER CO.												
Pleasant View Motel RD 3, Box 390, Columbia 17512 (717) 684-2833	on PA 462 at Prospect Rd. exit of US 30	S 25 D 30	5	V,M	Y	N	N	N	Yr	Y	C,H	
Westfield Motor Inn 2929 Hempland Rd., Lanc. 17601 (717) 397-9300	at Centerville Rd. exit of US 30	S 59 D,Q 69	5	All	Y	N	Ys	N	Yr	6PM	A,F,O	Game room, free coffee, washer & dryer
Quality Inn 500 Centerville Rd., 17601 (717) 898-2431;(800) 228-5151	at Centerville Rd. exit of US 30	S 61-67 D 71-80	8	All	Y	N	N	Y	N	Y	A,C,F	

284

LEBANON CO.

Establishment	Location	Rates	No.	Credit						Time	Codes	Remarks
CAMPBELLTOWN 17010 Friendly Rising Sun Motel, Main St. (717) 838-6921	US 322, 4 mi. E of Hershey	S 34 / D 38, 42	0	None	Y	Y	N	Y	N	6PM	A	Spec. event 1st week in Oct.
Village Motel, PO Box 76 (717) 838-4761	US 322, 3 mi. E of Hershey	S 44 / D 48, 56 / St 80	4	V,M	Y	N	Y	Y	Yr	6PM	A,F,G	
LEBANON 17042 Quality Inn, 625 Quentin Rd. (717) 273-8771;(800) 228-5151	PA 72, 1/2 mi. S of downtown	S 61-66 / D 75-80	5	All	Y	N	Y	Y	N	Y	F,N,O	Govt. disc.; Barber/beauty shop; game room
PALMYRA 17078 Palmyra Motel, 1071 E. Main St. (717) 838-1324	US 422, E end of town	S,K,D 72	0	V,M	Y	N	Y	Y	N	Y	A,M,O	Free coffee
QUENTIN 17083 Four Seasons Motel, PO Box 64 (717) 272-8402	Jct. PA 72 & 419	S 32 / D 38	4	V,M,A	Y	N	N	Y	Yr	6PM	A,H	

LEHIGH VALLEY

Establishment	Location	Rates	No.	Credit						Time	Codes	Remarks
ALLENTOWN Hamilton Plaza Hotel, 4th & Hamilton Sts., 18101 (215) 437-9876;(800) 728-9876	Downtown	D,K 62-72 / St 157, 219 / Theme 125	10	V,M,A,DC	N	N	Ys	Y	Yr	6PM	A,B,C,O	Valet parking; free airport transportation
Wap's Guest House, Airport Rd. & Union Blvd., 18103 (215) 435-7236	NE part of city, 1.5 mi. S of US 22	S,K 49 / St 79	0	V,M,A	N	Y	N	Y	N	Y	A,C,J	
Dorneyville Motor Inn, 3220 Hamilton Blvd., 18103 (215) 439-4000	SW part of city, 3/4 mi. E of I-78/PA 309 & US 222 Interchange	S 36-40 / D 44-48 / St 50-80	0	V,M,A,DC,D	Y	N	Y	Y	N	4PM	A,B,C,D,L,N	Senior disc.; 10% spec. event chg.
Lehigh Motor Inn, RD 11, Box 65, 18104 (215) 395-3331	Old US 22, 1/4 mi. W of Kuhnsville exit of US 22	S 34 / D 37 / K 45	5	V,M,A	N	Y	N	Y	N	6PM	A,D,M,O	Refrig. & microwaves all rooms $10 spec. events
Days Inn Conference Center, Rts. 22 & 309, 18104 (215) 395-3731;(800) 325-2525	US 22 at PA 309 Interchange	S 46-56 / D 52-62	6	V,M,A,DC,D	Y	Y	Y	Y	N	6PM	B,C,O	Airport transp. avail.
Days Inn Lehigh Valley, 15th St. & Rt. 22, 18104 (215) 435-7880;(800) 325-2525	US 22 at 15th St. Interchange	S 32-38 / D 38-44	4	V,M	N	Y	Y	N	N	6PM		
George Washington Motor Lodge, 1350 McArthur Rd., 18052 (215) 433-0131	7th St/McArthur Rd. exit of US 22	D,K 64 / St 125	6	V,M,A,DC	N	Y	Ys	Y	N	6PM	A,B,E,F,K,L,N,O	AAA, AARP disc.; fax service; free airport transp.

See KEY TO ABBREVIATIONS and KEY TO FACILITIES on page 289.

Name / Mailing Address / Phone	Location Description	Rates	Extra person charge	Credit cards	Lower rates avail. out of season	Surcharge for special events	Handicapped access	Restaurant	Pets	Deposit/credit card guarantee required.	Facilities	Explanations/ Comments
ALLENTOWN (cont.)	**LEHIGH VALLEY (cont.)**											
Sheraton Jetport Lehigh Valley 3400 Airport Rd., 18103 (215) 266-1000;(800) 325-3535	PA 987 opposite A-B-E Airport, 1 mil. N of US 22	S 75-81 D,K 83-89 St 91-107	6	All	N	N	Ys	Y	Y	4PM	C,K,L	
Red Roof Inn 1846 Catasauqua Rd., 18103 (215) 264-5404;(800) THE-ROOF	Airport Rd. S exit of US 22 to Catasauqua Rd.	S 33, 39 D 37, 41	2	All	N	N	Ys	Y	Yr	6PM	B,C,H,O	Free ice, newspaper Mon.-Fri.
McIntosh Inn Rt. 22 & Airport Rd., 18103 (215) 264-7531	Airport Rd. S exit of US 22	S 29 D 35	3	V,M, A	N	N	Y	Y	N	Y	O	Free ice; cribs avail.
BETHLEHEM												
Econo-Lodge Catasauqua & Airport Rds., 18018 (215) 867-8681;(800) 55-ECONO	Airport Rd. S exit of US 22 to Catasauqua Rd.	S 36 D 44	5	V,M, A,DC, CB	Y	N	N	Y	N	6PM	A,B,F,O	Tennis; jogging path; airport transp. avail
Holiday Inn Bethlehem Routes 22 & 512, 18017 (215) 866-5800;(800) HOLIDAY	US 22 & PA 512 Interchange	S 69 D 75 K 80	8	All	Y	N	Y	Y	N	6PM	A,C,F,L,N,O	Spec. wknd. rates Free airport transportation
Comfort Inn Bethlehem 3191 Highfield Dr., 18017 (215) 865-6300;(800) 228-5150	US 22 & PA 191 Interchange	S 35-45 D 41-52 K 45-55	6	All	N	N	Ys	Y	Yr	6PM	A,C,J,L,N	AAA, Senior disc.
EASTON 18042												
Historic Hotel Easton 140 Northampton St. (215) 253-6181	Downtown	S 56 D 56, 62 K 62, St 70, 80	6	V,M, A,DC	N	Y	Y	Y	N	6PM	A,C,J,M,O	Free parking; Comp. fruit plate
Lafayette Inn 525 W. Monroe St. (215) 253-4500	north side of city, NW corner of Monroe & Cattell Sts. nr. Lafayette College	S 70 D 80 St 90	10	V,M, A,DC	N	N	Ys	Y	N	Y	A,C,J,M,O	Rates 50% higher major college weekends
Sheraton Easton Inn 3rd St. & Larry Holmes Dr. (215) 253-9131;(800) 325-3535	Downtown	S 62, D,K 88 St 99, 105 Poolside 67, 75	6	All	N	N	Ys	Y	Yr	4PM	C,E	AAA, AARP, Govt. disc.; fax & valet service
Days Inn 25th St. Shopping Center (215) 253-0546;(800) 325-2525	25th St. exit of US 22, adj. to shopping center	S 34-40 D 42-48	0	V,M	N	Y	N	Y	N	6PM	C	

LEHIGH VALLEY (cont.)

Establishment	Location	Rates	No.	Cards					Yr	Ck-in	Facilities	Notes
FOGELSVILLE 18051												
Cloverleaf Motel, Box 213, (215) 395-3367	I-78 & PA 100 interchange	S 28-30; D,K 33-36	4	V,M, A,DC	N	N	Y	Y	N	6PM	A,O	Sunken tubs on request
Comfort Inn, 40 Penn Dr. (Allentown 18106), (215) 391-1500;(800) 228-5150	I-78 & PA 100 interchange	S 45-49; D 51-55	6	All	Y	Y	Y	Y	N	Y	A,B,C,O	Exercise room
Holiday Inn Lehigh Valley, PO Box 2226 (Lehigh Val. 18001), (215) 391-1000;(800) HOLIDAY	I-78 & PA 100 interchange	S 69-71; D 77-79	8	All	N	N	Y	Y	N	6PM	B,K,L,O	Exercise room; free airport transportation
MONTGOMERY CO.												
KING OF PRUSSIA 19406												
George Washington Lodge, Rt. 202 & Warner Rd., (215) 265-6100	US 202 between US 422 & I-76 Interchanges	S 54; D,K 62; St 134	0	V,M, A,DC	Y	N	N	Y	N	4PM	A,E,F,O	Valet service
Howard Johnson Lodge, Rt. 202 & S. Gulph Rd., (215) 265-4500;(800) 654-2000	US 202, 1/4 mi. E of I-76 Interchange	S 73; K 78, D 89; St 110	7	V,M, A,DC	N	N	Ys	Y	N	6PM	A,C,F,O	Laundry; fax, photocopy mach.; $59 wknd. spec.
Lodging Unlimited Hotel, 550 W. DeKalb Pike, (215) 962-0700;(800) 222-0222	US 202, 1 mi. E of I-76 Interchange	S 76; D 84	5	All	N	N	Ys	Y	N	6PM	A,B,C,J,O	Stocked mini-bar VCR & movie rentals
Holiday Inn, 260 Goddard Blvd., (215) 265-7500;(800) HOLIDAY	off Gulph Rd, N of US 202; adjacent to King of Prussia Plaza	S 91; D 99; K 103	0	All	N	N	Ys	Y	Y	6PM	A,C,E,K,L	
McIntosh Inn, Rt. 422 & Goddard Blvd., (215) 768-9500	US 422 & Goddard Blvd.	S 36; D 43	0	V,M,A	N	Y	Y	Y	N	Y	O	Free ice; valet service
Sheraton Valley Forge Hotel, N. Gulph Rd. & First Ave., (215) 337-2000;(800) 325-3535	US 422 at 1st Ave. Interchange	S 98-108; D 104-118; St 135-175	0	V,M, A,DC	N	N	Y	Y	N	Y	B,F,G,O	Limo. service; racquet club; travel agency
KULPSVILLE 19443												
Holiday Inn, 1750 Sumneytown Pike, (215) 368-3800;(800) HOLIDAY	Turnpike exit 31	S 68; D 73	6	All	N	N	N	Y	N	6PM	O	Phila. Intl. Airport limo service avail.
POTTSTOWN 19464												
Days Inn, 1600 Industrial Hwy., (215) 327-3300;(800) 325-2525	Armand Hammer Blvd. exit of US 422	S 52-62; D 62-72	5	V,M, A,DC, D	N	N	Y	Y	N	Y	C,F	
Econo-Lodge, 29 High St., (215) 326-7400;(800) 55-ECONO	Downtown	S 40; D 42, 50	5	V,M, A,DC, D	N	N	N	Y	N	Y		

See KEY TO ABBREVIATIONS and KEY TO FACILITIES on page 289.

MONTGOMERY CO. (cont.)

Name Mailing Address Phone	Location Description	Rates	Extra person charge	Credit cards	Lower rates avail, out of season	Surcharge for special events	Handicapped access	Restaurant	Pets	Deposit/credit card guarantee required.	Facilities	Explanations/Comments
POTTSTOWN 19464 (cont.)												
Holiday Inn Rt. 100 & King St. (215) 326-8700:(800) HOLIDAY	1/2 mi. W of downtown at Jct. PA 100 & 663	S 61-65 D 71-76	5	All	N	N	Y	Y	N	6PM	C	
YORK CO.												
ETTERS 17319 Econo-Lodge 70 Robinhood Dr. (717) 938-6200:(800) 55-ECONO	I-83, exit 14	S 40 D 46	6	All	N	N	Y	Y	N	6PM	A,O	Free cribs
GLEN ROCK 17327 Rocky Ridge Motel RD 2, Box 243 (717) 235-5646	I-83, exit 2	S 28 K 30 D 34	2	V,M	Y	N	Y	N	Yr	6PM		
YORK York Travelodge 132-40 N. George St., 17401 (717) 843-8974:(800) 255-3050	Downtown	S 35 Q 38 D 43	5	All	Y	N	Y	Y	Y	5PM	A,C	
Yorktowne Hotel 48 E. Market St., 17401 (717) 848-1111	Downtown	S 51 D 56 St 95+up	7	V,M, A,DC, D	N	N	Ys	Y	Yr	6PM	A,M,O	Valet parking (800) 233-9324 outside PA
Holiday Inn-Market St. 2600 E. Market St., 17402 (717) 755-1966:(800) HOLIDAY	PA 462, 3/4 mi. E of I-83, exit 8	S 51-70 D 61-85	10	All	N	Y	N	Y	N	6PM		
Barnhart's Motel 3021 E. Market St., 17402 (717) 755-2806	PA 462, 1 mi. E of I-83, exit 8	S 22, 25 Q 26, 29 D,Q 34	4	All	Y	N	Ys	Y	N	4PM	A,B,O	Free coffee
Flamingo Motel 3600 E. Market St., 17402 (717) 755-3901	PA 462, 2 mi. E of I-83, exit 8	S 23 K 27 D 32	4	V,M	Y	N	Y	Y	-	6PM	A,D,O	Refrig. all units
Quality Inn-York Valley 3883 E. Market St., 17402 (717) 755-2881:(800) 228-5151	PA 462, 2-1/2 mi. E of I-83, exit 8	S 46-56 D 54-64	6	All	Y	N	N	Y	N	Y	B,E,F,K,L,O	Nautilus eqpt.

YORK CO. (cont.)

YORK (cont.)		Rooms		Credit					Deposit	Facilities	
Sheraton Inn York US 30 & Rt. 74, 17404 (717) 846-9500;(800) 325-3535	PA 74 exit of US 30	S 60-87 D 60-95	0	All	N	Ys	Y	Y	4PM	C,E,F,L,O	Miniature golf
Days Inn 1415 Kenneth Rd., 17404 (717) 767-6931;(800) 325-2525	Just north of US 30, 1/2 mi. E of PA 74, 2 mi. W of I-83, exit 9W or 10	S 50 D,K 60 St 100	5	All	N	Ys	Y	N	4PM	A,C,H,M,N	Senior, Govt. disc.
Holiday Inn-Arsenal Rd. 334 Arsenal Rd., 17402 (717) 845-5671;(800) HOLIDAY	on US 30, just E of I-83, exit 9	S 51-69 D 61-84	10	All	Y	N	Y	N	6PM	B	
Howard Johnson Lodge US 30 & I-83, 17402 (717) 843-9971;(800) 654-2000	on US 30 at I-83, exit 9	S 48-64 D 54-70	0	All	Y	N	Y	N	6PM	B,C,F,O	Valet service; game room; in-room coffee
Ramada Inn US 30 & I-83, 17402 (717) 846-4940;(800) 228-2828	just N of US 30 on Toronita St.; I-83, exit 9	S 49-60 D 55-70	10	All	N	Y	Y	Y	6PM	K	
Red Roof Inn 323 Arsenal Rd., 17402 (717) 843-8181;(800) THE-ROOF	on US 30, just E of I-83, exit 9	S 35 D 43 K 46	6	All	Y	Y	Y	Y	6PM	A,B,C,H,N,O	Senior disc.; free USA Today
Snyder's Motel RD 24, 17406 (717) 252-2634; 757-6838	PA 462, 8 mi. E of York, 2 mi. W of Wrightsville	K 22	5	None	N	N	Y	N	7PM	B	

KEY TO ABBREVIATIONS

Types of Rooms: S-Single; D-Double; K-King; Q-Queen; St-Suite; Fam-Family; Kit-Kitchenette; Eff-Efficiency; Cott-Cottage;

Credit Cards: V-Visa; MC-Mastercard; A-American Express; DC-Diners Club; CB-Carte Blanche; D-Discover; All-All of these

Handicapped Access: Ys-Some rooms

Restaurant: Y if on premises or within 500 feet

Pets: Yr If permitted with restrictions--inquire about them; Yc-permitted, but at extra charge

Deposit or Credit Card Guarantee: Time shown is deadline for holding reservation without deposit or guarantee

KEY TO FACILITIES

A--Cable TV	H--Free local calls
B--Free movies	J--Free continental breakfast
C--Non-smoking rooms	K--Sauna
D--Waterbeds	L--Jacuzzi
E--Indoor pool	M--Kitchenettes
F--Outdoor pool	N--Discount plans
G--Tennis courts	O--Other (see Explanations)

E. CAMPGROUNDS

Name / Mailing Address / Phone	Location Description	Season	Number of Sites				Rates (usually for up to 4 people)	Facilities
			Basic	Elec.	Wtr.	Swr.		
ADAMS CO.								
GARDNERS 17324 Mountain Creek CG 349 Pine Grove Rd. (717) 486-7681	2 mi. W of PA 34 on Pine Grove Rd.	All year	115	105	105	0	10, 13 EW, 2.50 A/C	A,C,D,F,G,N,U,V,W
GETTYSBURG 17325 Always Welcome Traveller 1250 Baltimore Pike (717) 334-8226	1 mi. S	All year	70	70	70	5	11, 12 EW, 13 S, 1 A/C	A,B,D,M,S,U No water Nov.-Apr. 15
Artillery Ridge CG 610 Taneytown Rd. (717) 334-1288	1 mi. S on PA 134	4/1- 11/1	150	112	111	0	12, 14 EW, 1.50 A/C	A,B,D,G,K,L,M,R,S,U,V,W Pony rides, pavilion, Battlefield & Washington, DC bus tours
Drummer Boy Camping Resort 1300 Hanover Rd. (717) 334-3277	1-1/2 mi. E on PA 116 at US 15 interchange	4/1- 10/21	300	240	240	70	12.50, 14.50 E, 13.50 W, 15 S, 1 A/C	A,D,G,M,U,V,W Miniature golf
Round Top CG 180 Knight Rd. (717) 334-9565	3 mi. S at US 15 & PA 134 interchange	All year	210	200	200	133	12 EW, 14.50 S, 2.50 A/C	A,D,F,M,P,U,V,W Miniature golf
BERKS CO.								
KUTZTOWN 19530 Pine Hill CG RD 2, Box 360 (215) 285-6776	Old Rt. 22, 1-1/2 mi. W of I-78/US 22 exit 13	4/1- 11/1	56	24	34	24	Inquire	A,C,D,U,W Miniature golf
Sacony Park CG RD 3, Box 306 (215) 683-3939	3 mi. N of US 222 at Virginville on Crystal Cave Rd.	4/1- 10/31	116	101	101	0	11, 13 EW, 2 A/C	C,F,G,U,W Motorbikes
LENHARTSVILLE 19534 Blue Rocks CG RD 2, Box 548 (215) 756-6366	PA 143, 1 mi. N of I-78/US 22, exit 11	4/15- 10/30	100	50	50	15	10, 12 EW, 13 EWS	A,C,U,V
Robin Hill Camping Resort RD 1, Box 944 (215) 756-6117	E of town, off I-78/US 22, exit 11 or 12	4/1- 11/15	240	197	181	4	Inquire	A,C,D,F,G,K,M,U,V
MORGANTOWN 19520 Arcadia Farm CG RD 1, Rt. 345 (215) 286-6414	PA 345, 1 mi. N of PA 23 (in Chester Co.)	All year	46	46	46	0	12, 13 RV	B,C,D,S,U,V,W Free Sat. night children's movie

BERKS CO. (cont.)

Location	Directions	Season					Rates	Facilities
ROBESONIA 19551 Eagles Peak CG RD 1, Box 397 (215) 589-4800	2 ml. SE of Newmanstown (Lebanon Co.) via Sheridan Rd. (SR 2023), E on Eagles Peak Rd.	All year	183	156	156	73	12, 14.50 EW, 16.50 EWS, 2 A/C	A,F,G,M,T,U,V
SHARTLESVILLE 19554 Appalachian Campsites PO Box 27 (215) 488-6319	1/4 ml. NW of I-78/US 22, exit 8	All year	300	288	288	240	11, 13 EW, 14 EWS, 2 A/C	A,D,F,G,H,U,V,W Gasoline, miniature golf, snowmobiles
Hillcrest Campsite Box 367 (215) 488-1657	1 ml. W on Old Rt. 22	All year	100	45	45	55	15 EWS	F,G,U
Mountain Springs Camping Resort PO Box 365 (215) 488-6859	1 ml. N of I-78/US 22, exit 8	All year	300	260	40	30	13.50, 15.50 EW, 16.50 EWS, 3 A/C	A,D,F,G,K,U,V
Pa. Dutch Campsite Box 337 (215) 488-6268	just off I-78/US 22, exit 8	4/15-10/31	200	200	200	0	Inquire	C,F,M,U,V

BUCKS CO.

Location	Directions	Season					Rates	Facilities
OTTSVILLE 18942 Beaver Valley CG RD 2, Box 114, Clay Ridge Rd. (215) 847-5843	3 ml. E of Geigel Hill & Clay Ridge Rds.	5/1-10/31	70	70	70	0	13 EW	A,B,C,F,M,U
QUAKERTOWN 18951 Little Red Barn CG 367 Old Bethlehem Rd. (215) 536-3357	3.5 ml. E on PA 313, N on PA 563 for 2.3 ml., left on Old Bethlehem Rd. (SR 4101) for 0.7 ml.	All year	160	110	110	0	15, EW 17.50	A,B,C,D,F,M,U
Quakerwoods CG Box 456, Rosedale Rd. (215) 536-1984	2.5 ml. N of PA 663 on Old Bethlehem Pike (SR 4063), turn left on Rosedale Rd. (SR 4059)	4/1-11/30	155	155	155	99	12.50, 15 EW, 17 EWS, 2.50 A/C	A,C,F,G,M,U,V
Tohickon Family CG RD 3, Covered Bridge Rd. (215) 536-7951	1.2 ml. E on PA 663, left on Thatcher Rd. (SR 4043) for 2.8 ml. to Covered Br. Rd. (SR 4099)	All year	200	185	185	60	Inquire	A,D,F,G,K,M,U,V
UPPER BLACK EDDY 18972 Colonial Woods Family Resort RD 1, Box 82 (215) 847-5808	E from PA 611 at Revere on Marienstein Rd. 1-1/2 ml. to left on Lonely Cottage Rd.	All year	247	232	247	0	14, EW 16.50	A,C,F,G,M,P,U,V,W Snowmobiles allowed

CHESTER CO.

Location	Directions	Season					Rates	Facilities
COATESVILLE 19320 Beechwood CG 105 Beechwood Dr. (215) 384-1457	1 ml. N of US 30 on Reeceville Rd. (SR 4005) to Beechwood Dr., R to CG	4/1-11/1	350	300	300	150	10, 13.50 EW, 16.50 EWS	A,C,F,M,U,V

See KEY TO FACILITIES on page 297.

Name Mailing Address Phone	Location Description	Season	Number of Sites Basic	Elec.	Wtr.	Swr.	Rates (usually for up to 4 people)	Facilities
CHESTER CO. (cont.)								
COATESVILLE 19320 (cont.)								
Birchview Farm CG RD 2, Box 266 (215) 384-0500	From PA 340, 3 mi. W of PA 82, N on Bonsall School Rd. to Martins Corner Rd. E to CG	4/15-10/15	150	150		50	13, 14 S, 1.50 A/C	A,C,D,F,G,M,U,V
Hidden Acres CG RD 2 (215) 857-3990	on PA 340, 2-1/2 mi. E of PA 10	3/15-11/15	200	200	35		13, 16 S	A,C,M,U,V,W Gasoline
HONEY BROOK 19344								
Berry Patch CG PO Box 370, Ross Rd. (215) 273-3720	off PA 10	4/1-11/1	122	122		68	14.50, 16 S, 2 A/C	A,G,M,U,V
Brandywine Meadows Resort RD 3, Box 155 (215) 273-9753	4.2 mi. E on US 322, right on Birdell Rd. (SR 4007) 1/2 mi. to Icedale Rd. left to camp	4/1-10/31	165	165		25	15, 15 S, 3 A/C	A,C,D,G,M,U,V,W Miniature golf
LYNDELL 19354								
New Frank's Folly Family CG Box 257 (215) 942-2282	6 mi. N of Downingtown on PA 282	All year	176	77	77	7	12, 14 EW	C,G,M,T,U,V,W Motorbikes allowed
PHOENIXVILLE 19460								
Phoenixville Area YMCA CG Box 310 (215) 933-5861	just off PA 29 on Pothouse Rd.	5/1-10/31	41	24	0	0	Inquire	C,G,M,P,V
ST. PETERS 19470								
Warwick Woods CG Box 280 (215) 286-9655	N off PA 23, 2 mi. E of PA 345, on Trythall Rd. to CG	4/1-10/31	225	185	185	19	11, 14 EW, 15 EWS	A,C,D,F,L,M,T,U,V
UNIONVILLE 19375								
Phila./West Chester KOA Box 502 (215) 486-0447	8 mi. W of West Chester on PA 162	4/1-10/31	111	42	42	42	16, 18 EW, 20 EWS	A,B,D,F,G,J,K,M,U
CUMBERLAND CO.								
CARLISLE 17013								
Carlisle CG 1075 Harrisburg Pike (717) 249-4563	on US 11, 1 mi. S of Turnpike exit 16	All year	100	80	80	50	11.50, 14 EW	A,C,F,M,U
Western Village CG 200 Greenview Dr. (717) 243-1179	off Walnut Bottom Rd., 1.6 mi. SW of I-81, exit 13	All year	250	250	250	151	Inquire	A,F,M,U,V

CUMBERLAND CO. (cont.)

NEWVILLE 17241 Dogwood Acres CG RD 3, Box 1701 (717) 776-5203	on PA 944, 3 mi. E of PA 233	5/1 10/1	65	65	65	65	12, 2 A/C	G,K,N,U,V,W Frisbee golf
DAUPHIN CO.								
HERSHEY 17033 Hershey Highmeadow Camp 300 Park Blvd. (717) 566-0902	on PA 39, 1/2 mi. N of US 322/ 422 Interchange	All year	260	204	153	87	18, 19.50 E, 20.25 EW, 22.75 EWS	A,F,M,U,V
FRANKLIN CO.								
CHAMBERSBURG 17201 Twin Bridge Meadow Family CG 1345 Twin Bridge Rd. (717) 369-2216	1-1/2 mi. N of US 30, 5 mi. W of town	4/15 10/15	120	120	120	0	8, 2 A/C	C,G,L,T,U,V,W Miniature golf
NORTHERN LANCASTER CO.								
ADAMSTOWN 19501 Sill's Family CG PO Box 566 (215) 484-4806	1/4 mi. E of PA 272 on Bow- mansville Rd.	4/1 - 10/30	125	120	120	100	12, 14.50 EW, 16 EWS	A,F,M,U
BOWMANSVILLE 17507 Oak Creek Camping & Tlr. Res. Box 128-C (215) 445-6161	1-1/2 mi. E on Maple Grove Rd. (SR 1046)	3/1 - 11/30	311	292	292	136	15, 18 EW, 19 EWS	A,C,D,F,G,M,T,U,V,W Miniature golf, motorbikes
Sun Valley CG Box 238 (215) 445-6262	1-1/2 mi. E on Maple Grove Rd. (SR 1046)	All year	200	200	200	125	15, 16 EW, 17 EWS, 2 A/C	A,C,D,F,G,M,T,U,V,W Motorbikes
DENVER 17517 Cocalico Creek CG 1055 Forest Rd. (215) 267-2014	8.7 mi. N of PA 272 intersection, turn right off PA 897 on Cocalico Rd., go 1/2 mi., turn left to CG	4/8 10/23	82	74	74	51	11, 12 EW, 13 EWS, 2 A/C	G,N,U,V
Dutch Cousins Campsite, Inc. RD 3, Box 261 (215) 267-6911	1/4 mi. N of Turnpike exit 21, Turn W off PA 272 on Hill Rd., go 1 mi. to CG	All year	72	66	66	7	10.75, 12.25 EW 12.75 EWS	C,F,T,U
Hickory Run CG 285 Greenville Rd. (215) 267-5564	W end of town, turn right off W. Main St. on Greenville Rd. to CG	4/1 - 11/1	200	195	195	90	Inquire	A,D,F,G,K,M,T,U,V,W Miniature golf, motorbikes

See **KEY TO FACILITIES** on page 297.

Name Mailing Address Phone	Location Description	Season	Number of Sites Basic	Elec.	Wtr.	Swr.	Rates (usually for up to 4 people)	Facilities
NORTHERN LANCASTER CO. (cont.)								
MANHEIM 17545 Pinch Pond RD 3, Pinch Rd. (717) 665-7640	From PA 72, 0.5 mi. S of Turnpike, turn right on Cider Press Rd., go 0.4 mi. right on Pinch Rd.	4/15-10/31	96	75	75	65	Inquire	A,C,F,G,M,T,W Motorbikes
REINHOLDS 17569 Shady Grove CG RD 2, Rt. 897 (215) 484-4225	on PA 897, 1/4 mi. N of PA 272	4/1-11/1	80	72	72	72	Inquire	A,D,G,K,P,U,V,W Miniature golf
STEVENS 17578 Starlite 1500 Furnace Hill Rd. (717) 733-9655	Turn N off US 322 on Clay Rd. (SR 1035) In Clay and follow signs to CG	4/1-11/1	215	215	215	90	17, 2 A/C	A,E,F,M,P,T,U,V,W Miniature golf
EASTERN LANCASTER CO.								
GORDONVILLE 17529 Leven Acres CG & Pool 20 Leven Rd. (717) 687-8014	on US 30, 8 mi. E of Lancaster	4/1-11/1	45	24	21	0	12 S, 15 EW	DM
INTERCOURSE 17534 Beacon Camping Lodge Box 384 (717) 768-8775	just N of village on PA 772, turn right on Beacon Hill Dr.	4/1-11/1	46	36	36	26	12, 14 EWS	A,F,U
KINZERS 17535 Roamers Retreat CG 5005 Lincoln Hwy. E. (717) 442-4287	on US 30	4/1-11/1	100	100	100	96	Inquire	A,F,U,V,W
LANCASTER 17602 Old Mill Stream Camping Manor 2249 Lincoln Hwy. E. (717) 299-2314	on US 30, 3/4 mi. E of end of bypass, 4 mi. E of downtown	All year	240	222	220	0	13, 15 EW	A,G,K,T,U,W Motorbikes
NARVON 17555 Lake In Wood CG Yellow Hill Rd., Box 418 (215) 445-5525	Go E 3/4 mi. from Bowmansville on Maple Grove Rd. to Oaklyn Rd., right 1.5 mi. to Yellow Hill Rd.	4/1-11/1	220	210	210	180	15, 16 EW, 17 EWS, 4 A/C	A,G,K,M,U,V,W Golf
Pebble Rock CG RD 1, Box 199, Churchtown (215) 445-5563	2 mi. N off PA 23 in Churchtown	4/15-10/15	100	85	80	0	Inquire	A,C,G,M,T,U,V,W Motorbikes

EASTERN LANCASTER CO. (cont.)

Name / Address	Location	Dates					Facilities	Codes
NEW HOLLAND 17557 Country Haven Campsite RD 2, Box 402 (717) 354-7926	on PA 897, 4 1/2 ml. S of US 322	All year	55	55	55	52	15 WS, 16 EWS, 2 A/C	A,E,F
Spring Gulch Resort CG 475 Lynch Rd. (717) 354-3100	off PA 897 between US 322 & PA 340	4/1-11/1	250	200	200	100	16, 19 EW, 21 EWS, 2 A/C	A,C,D,G,M,U,V,W Motorbikes
RONKS 17572 Flory's Cottages/Camping Box 308 (717) 687-6670	on N. Ronks Rd. (SR 2045), 1/2 ml. N of US 30	4/1-12/1	71	71	71	71	Inquire	U,W Motorbikes
STRASBURG 17579 Mill Bridge Village Box 86 (717) 687-8181	on S. Ronks Rd., 1/2 ml. S of US 30	3/13-11/30	110	108	119	25	Inquire	A,D,G,K,U,V
SOUTHERN LANCASTER CO.								
HOLTWOOD 17532 Muddy Run Recreation Park RD 3, Box 730 (717) 284-4325	on PA 372, 3/4 ml. E of Susquehanna River bridge	Apr.-Nov.	163	136	163	0	Inquire	A,D,G,K,U,V
Olde Forge Recreation Park RD 2, Box 1545 (717) 284-2591	1/2 ml. N of PA 372 off Hilldale Rd. on McKelvey La.	4/1-11/15	65	55	55	30	Inquire	A,D,G,M,T,U,V,W Motorbikes
QUARRYVILLE 17566 White Oak CG 372 White Oak Rd. (717) 687-6207	turn E off US 222 at New Providence on White Oak Rd., go about 3-1/2 ml. to CG	All year	145	130	130	75	11, 13 E, 14.50 EWS	D,U
Woodland Acres Family CG 340 Blackburn Rd. (717) 786-3458	3 ml. S on US 222, turn E on Blackburn Rd. for 1-1/2 ml.	4/15-11/1	120	110	110	0	13.50, 16 EW, 1 A/C	A,C,F,U,V,W Motorbikes
WESTERN LANCASTER CO.								
ELIZABETHTOWN 17022 Ridge Run CG 867 Schwanger Rd. (717) 367-3454	from Rheems-E'town exit of PA 283, go W 1/2 ml., turn right on Schwanger Rd. to CG	4/1-11/1	137	120	120	90	15, 16 EW, 17 EWS, 2 A/C	A,D,F,G,M,T,U,V,W Motorbikes
LEBANON CO.								
JONESTOWN 17038 Lickdale CG RD 1, Box 1282 (717) 865-6411	from I-81, exit 30, turn left off exit ramp, go 1000 ft. to CG	All year	50	50	50	17	11, 13.50 EW	C,F,G,T,U,W Motorbikes

See KEY TO FACILITIES on page 297.

Name Mailing Address Phone	Location Description	Season	Number of Sites Basic	Elec	Wtr	Swr	Rates (usually for up to 4 people)	Facilities
LEBANON CO. (cont.)								
NEWMANSTOWN 17073 Shady Oaks Campsite RD 2, Box 579 (717) 949-3177 or 273-3817	1-1/2 ml. W on PA 419	4/1-10/31	65	65	65	65	Inquire	U,V
LEHIGH VALLEY								
MT. BETHEL 18343 Driftstone on the Delaware RD 1, Box 1728 (717) 897-6859	along Delaware R., 4 ml. S of Portland	5/13-9/18	190	151	190	0	17, 19 EW	A,C,F,G,K,M,U,V,W Motorbikes
NEW TRIPOLI 18066 Allentown-Lehigh Valley KOA RD 2, Box 138 (215) 298-2160	on PA 100, 7 ml. N of I-78/US 22	4/1-11/30	140	101	101	28	15, 17.50 EW, 21 EWS, 1 A/C	A,C,D,F,G,M,U,V,W Motorbikes
PORTLAND 18351 Shady Acres CG of Portland PO Box 417 (717) 897-6230	just S of town	5/1-10/30	110	75	75	0	Inquire	A,C,D,F,G,L,M,U,V
MONTGOMERY CO.								
HATFIELD 19440 Oak Grove Park & Sales, Inc. N. Main St. (215) 723-2007	N edge of town	All year	60	60	60	60	Inquire	A,F,M,U
SPRING MOUNT 19478 Spring Mountain Camping Area Box 42 (215) 287-7900 or -9870	1 ml. N of Schwenksville off PA 29	All year	45	15	0	0	6	
YORK CO.								
AIRVILLE 17302 Otter Creek Recreation Area RD 1, Box 243 (717) 862-3628	on PA 425 along Susquehanna River	All Year	80	80	30	0	10	A,B,D,G,H,J,K,N,S,V,W Dumping station, showers, playground, horseshoes, volleyball
DILLSBURG 17019 Harrisburg South CG Walmar Manor Office (717) 432-4523	2-1/2 ml. S of town, S off US 15 on Franklin Church Rd. (SR 4043), 1 ml. to CG	Apr.-Nov.	74	74	74	13	Inquire	A,M

YORK CO. (cont.)

DOVER 17315 Conewago Isle CG 6220 Bigmount Rd. (717) 292-1461	from US 30, 3.7 ml. W of PA 116, N on Bigmount Rd. (SR 4051) for 6-1/2 ml.	3/1-12/1	75	75	35	30	Inquire	D,G,U,V
ETTERS 17319 Park Away Park Family CG 1300 Old Trail Rd. (717) 938-1686	off I-83, exit 14	4/1-10/31	110	110	110	42	Inquire	A,F,M,U
YORK 17403 Indian Rock CG 436 Indian Rock Dam Rd. (717) 741-1764	3 ml. SW of downtown on PA 182	All year	40	40	40	30	Inquire	P,T

KEY TO FACILITIES

A--Laundry
B--Ice
C--Tank service
D--Snack bar/grocery
E--Gasoline
F--LP gas
G--Fishing
H--Hunting
J--Boat launch
K--Boat rentals
L--Horseback riding
M--Swimming pool
N--Swimming in creek or lake
P--Tennis
R--Bicycle rentals
S--Hiking trails
T--Snowmobiling
U--Game room
V--Organized recreation
W--Other (specified)

F. RESTAURANTS

Name / Address / Phone	Location Description	Type of Cuisine	Days Open	Meals Served	Prices	Non-smoking section	Handicapped accessible	Reservations	Credit Cards	Specialties/comments
ADAMS CO.										
FAIRFIELD The Historic Fairfield Inn 15 W. Main St. (717) 642-5410	center of town on PA 116	Am	Tue-Sat	LD	L 4-7.95 D 10-13	x			V,MC,AE	Baked seafood pie, chicken & biscuits, country ham steak
GETTYSBURG Herr Tavern & Publick House 900 Chambersburg Rd. (717) 334-4332	2 mi. W at US 30 & Herr's Ridge Rd.	Am	Mon-Sat	LD	L 3-6 D10-17	x	x	Rec	V,MC,AE, D	Prime rib
BERKS CO.										
BIRDSBORO Ben Franklin Inn 916 Benjamin Franklin Hwy. (215) 582-4720; 385-6031	US 422, 2 mi. E of PA 82	Am-Co	7	LD	L 4-9 D 9-32			Req	V,MC,AE, CB,DC	Beef, veal, seafood, fowl
DOUGLASSVILLE Michael's Restaurant Routes 422 & 662 (215) 385-3017; 3018	US 422 westbound at PA 662	PD, Am, Gr	7	BLD Br	B 1.50-3 L 5-9.50 D 5-9.50	x			None	Spinach pie, prime rib, seafood platter, baked goods Open 24 hrs.; brunch 3.50
LEESPORT Hess's Family Restaurant Routes 61 & 73 (215) 926-3220	Intersection of PA 61 & 73	PD, Am	7	BLD	B 1-3 L 2-4 D 3.50-8	x	x		None	Chicken, broiled crab cakes, apple dumplings; salad bar; homemade breads
NEW BERLINVILLE Country View Family Restaurant PO Box 143 (215) 367-1842	PA 100, 2 mi. N of Boyertown	PD, Am, It	7	BLD	B 2-4 L 3-5 D 5-15	x	x		None	Broiled seafood specialties; salad bar; homemade pies
OLEY Old Covered Bridge Hotel/Rest. RD 2, Box 227 (215) 689-5818	PA 73, 8 mi. W of Boyertown	PD, Am	Tue-Sun	BLD	B 4 L 5 D 6-18			Rec	V,MC	Homemade soups and desserts
READING Brass Lantern Pub 12th & Pike Sts. (215) 372-9311	NE part of city, SW corner of 12th & Pike Sts.	Am	Wed-Sun	LD	L 3.25+ D 5.95+	x		Rec	V,MC,AE, DC	Chicken Dovell, veal Ambrose, seafood, steak Ollie, gourmet skillet dishes
Joe's 450 S. 7th St. (215) 373-6794	5 blocks S of downtown, NW corner of 7th & Laurel Sts.	Am	Tue-Sat	D	D 19.50-30			Rec	V,MC,AE, CB,DC	Local veal, venison, beef, fresh fish; specializes in use of wild mushrooms

BERKS CO. (cont.)

Name / Address	Location	Res.	Days	Meals	Prices		Rec	Cards	Specialties
SHARTLESVILLE Haag's Hotel, Main St. (215) 488-6692	SW corner of 3rd & Main Sts.	PD	7	BLD	B 5 / L 2-6 / D 8-9		Rec	None	Roast chicken, fried ham, roast beef, sausage; Family style rest.
Shartlesville Hotel, Main St. (215) 488-1918	center of town on old US 22	PD	7	LD	L,D 3-5		Rec	None	Oldest PD family style rest. in PA; Complete family-style meal 8.95
TEMPLE The Vineyard, 4600 N. 5th St. Hwy. (215) 929-4266	NW corner of 5th St. Hwy. & Water St.	Am, lt	Tue-Sun	LD	L 2.95-14 / D 5.95-15	x	Rec	V,MC,AE	Veal
WYOMISSING R.J. Willoughby's, 609 Spring St. (215) 378-1131	Off US 422, behind The Inn at Reading	Am, Co	7	LD / Br	L 2.50-5 / D 7.25-13 / Br 6		Rec	All	Steak, seafood, veal, chicken; All-you-can-eat specials Tue, Thu
BUCKS CO.									
ERWINNA Golden Pheasant Inn, River Rd. (215) 294-9595	on PA 32	Fr	Tue-Sun	D	D 19-47		Rec	All	Seafood, duck, steak / All meals a la carte
LUMBERVILLE Cuttalossa Inn, River Rd. (215) 297-5082	on PA 32	Am	7	LD / Br	L 6-11 / D 16-25 / Br 6-11	x	Rec	V,MC,AE	Crab Imperial
NEW HOPE Canal House, 28 W. Mechanic St. (215) 862-2069	center of town	Co	Wed-Sun	LD / Br	L 4.50 / D 12-16	x	Rec	V,MC	
SELLERSVILLE Washington House, 136 N. Main St. (215) 257-3000	center of town	Am, Co	Mon-Sat	LD	L 5 / D 12		Rec; Req F.Sa	V,MC,AE	Fresh fish, fresh pasta
CHESTER CO.									
CHESTER SPRINGS Inn at Historic Yellow Springs, Art School Rd. (215) 827-7477	0.5 mi. N of PA 113 on Yellow Springs Rd. to Art School Rd.	Fr-Co	Tue-Sun	D / Br	D 15-22		Rec	V,MC,AE	
COVENTRYVILLE Coventry Forge Inn, Coventryville Rd. (215) 469-6222	N off PA 23, 1.5 mi. W of PA 100	Fr	Tue-Sat	D	D 15-25		Rec; Req F.Sa	V,MC,AE, CB,DC	Rack of lamb provençal, smoked veal sweetbreads; Prix fixe Sat. only 35-40

See **KEY TO ABBREVIATIONS** on page 305.

299

CHESTER CO. (cont.)

Name Address Phone	Location Description	Type of Cuisine	Days Open	Meals Served	Prices	Non-smoking section	Handicapped accessible	Reservations	Credit Cards	Specialties/comments
EXTON Ship Inn, Route 30 & Ship Rd. (215) 363-7200	corner of US 30 & Ship Rd.	Am	7	LD Br	L 3.90-9 D 12-19 Br 9.50	x		Rec	All	Roast fresh duck, seafood platter, cajun fried catfish; brunch buffet
KENNETT SQUARE Longwood Inn, 815 E. Baltimore Pike (215) 444-3515	1-1/2 mi. E on US 1, 1/2 mi. W of Longwood Gardens	Am, Co	7	BLD Br	B 3.95-6 L 3.95-11 D 15-31	x	x	Rec	V,MC,AE, DC	Mushroom & seafood specialties, Fresh Chesapeake seafood, live Maine lobster; brunch 8.95-18
LIONVILLE Vickers, 192 Welsh Pool Rd. (215) 363-6336; -7998	1 mi. S of Turnpike exit 23, off PA 113 on Gordon Dr.	Fr, Co	Mon-Sat	LD	L 5-10.50 D 15-20	x	x	Req	V,MC,AE	Filet of bison, Dover sole, sweetbreads
PHOENIXVILLE Seven Stars Inn, Route 23 (215) 495-5205	PA 23, 5 mi. W	Am	Tue-Sun	D	D 16-29	x	x	Req Sat	V,MC,AE	Western beef, fresh seafood, veal
WEST CHESTER The French Corner, 101 S. Walnut St. (215) 431-4229	downtown, SE corner of Walnut & Miner Sts.	Fr	Tue-Sat	LD	L,D 2.75-5.75				None	Chicken Veronique, mousse au chocolat, salads, pastries; take-out service only; box lunches avail

CUMBERLAND CO.

Name Address Phone	Location Description	Type of Cuisine	Days Open	Meals Served	Prices	Non-smoking section	Handicapped accessible	Reservations	Credit Cards	Specialties/comments
MECHANICSBURG B&B Crossing, 120 E. Allen St. (717) 697-9475	NE corner of Allen & Walnut Sts., 1 block N of Main St. (PA 641)	Am	Mon-Sat	LD	L 3-6.95 D 8-18	x	x	Req Fri, Sat	V,MC,AE	Crab cakes, baked oysters stuffed with crabmeat mornay
The Brothers Family Rest. 705 Gettysburg Pike (717) 697-6591	Old US 15, 1 mi. S of Turnpike exit 17	Am	7	BLD	B 2.50 L 3.50 D 5.50	x	x		None	Fancy ice cream desserts, home-made pies
Mandarin Restaurant 5101 Carlisle Pike (717) 737-7766	on US 11	Ch	7	LD	L 4.25-6 D 8-11.95		x		V,MC	Peking duck, Chow San Pan
MT. HOLLY SPRINGS The Holly Inn, 31 S. Baltimore Ave. (717) 486-5911	center of town on PA 34	Am, Co	Tue-Sun	LD	L 4.95 D 8	x	x	Rec	V,MC,AE, DC	Steak, seafood. Historic inn with rustic atmosphere

CUMBERLAND CO. (cont.)

Restaurant	Location	Cuisine	Days	Meals	Prices			Res	Cards	Specialties
NEW CUMBERLAND Pulit's Ristorante 324 Market St. (717) 774-7244	center of town on SR 2035	It, Am, Co					x	Rec	V,MC,CB, DC,D	Veal, steaks, seafood, pasta
HARRISBURG Hope Station 606 N. 2nd St. (717) 257-4480	in Capitol district, NW corner of 2nd & Liberty Sts.	Am	Mon-Sat	LD	L 5-9 D 8-18			Req	All	Original pastas, fresh seafood and veal. Casual dining 1st fl., more formal & elegant 2nd fl.
Lombardo's at Locust Court 212 Locust St. (717) 234-1691	downtown, NW corner of Locust & Court Sts.	It	7	LD Br	L 4.95 D 12.95 Br 8.95		x	Rec	V,MC,AE, DC	Shrimp scampi, lobster & crabmeat casserole, veal; Sun. all-you-can-eat brunch buffet
MIDDLETOWN The Goodville House of 1870 3268 Fulling Mill Rd. (717) 939-7194	E off Eisenhower Blvd. from I-283, exit 1	New Eng.	Tue-Sat	LD Br	L 5.50 D 11 Br 5.50	x	x	Req	None	Seafood casserole, stuffed veal roast. Home cooking

FRANKLIN CO.

Restaurant	Location	Cuisine	Days	Meals	Prices			Res	Cards	Specialties
CHAMBERSBURG The Travel Room 565 Lincolnway E. (717) 264-4187	in town on US 30 westbound, 1 mi. W of I-81, exit 6	Co	7	BLD	B 2-4 L 2.25-6 D 5-12.50	x		Rec	All	Fresh backfin crabcakes, Chicken Brittany, homemade pies
GREENCASTLE Antrim House 104 E. Baltimore St. (717) 597-8111	center of town on PA 16	Am	Mon-Sat	BLD	B 2 L 2.25-6 D 5-11	x			V,MC,AE	Fresh seafood, steaks, homemade pies; homestyle cooking

LANCASTER CO.

Restaurant	Location	Cuisine	Days	Meals	Prices			Res	Cards	Specialties
ADAMSTOWN Ed Stoudt's Black Angus Box 272, Route 272 (215) 484-4385	PA 272 just north of PA 897	Am	7	D	D 10-22		x	Rec	All	Prime rib, lobster, German specialties
LANCASTER Family Style Restaurant 2323 Lincoln Hwy. E. (717) 393-2323 or 299-7251	on US 30, 4-1/2 mi. E	PD	7	BLD	B 4.95 L 6.95 D 12.50				V,MC,AE	All meals served family style, all-you-can-eat
Friar Tuck's 1002 N. Duke St. (717) 295-2461	north edge of city, NW corner of Duke & Liberty Sts.	Am, Co	7	LD	L 4-7 D 8-15			Rec	V,MC	Homemade crab cakes, roast beef au jus, 8 oz. burgers
Golden Eagle Tavern & Rest. 170 E. King St. (717) 396-7987, -7988	downtown, SW corner of King & Lime Sts.	Ch, Thai	Mon-Sat	LD	L 4.25-6 D 3.50-10			Rec	V,MC	Ginger chicken, Vietnamese hot & sour soup, vegetable combination
Hoar House Restaurant 10 S. Prince St. (717) 397-0110	downtown, SW corner of King & Prince Sts.	Co	Tue-Sun	LD Br	L 3.50-8 D 10-16 Br 5-13		x	Rec	V,MC,AE	Duck, blackened filet mignon, seafood chemise

See **KEY TO ABBREVIATIONS** on page 305.

LANCASTER CO. (cont.)

Name / Address / Phone	Location Description	Type of Cuisine	Days Open	Meals Served	Prices	Non-smoking section	Handicapped accessible	Reservations	Credit Cards	Specialties/comments
LANCASTER (cont.)										
Jethro's Restaurant & Bar 1st & Ruby Sts. (717) 299-1700	west end of city, 1 block S of Columbia Ave. (PA 462)	Am	Mon-Sat	D	D 7-21			Rec	V,MC,AE	Steaks, fresh fish & seafood, pasta; homemade desserts
Lombardo's Amer.-Ital. Rest. 216 Harrisburg Ave. (717) 394-3749	5 blocks N of downtown, just NW of intersection of Prince & James Sts.	Am, It	Mon-Sat	LD	L to 5 D to 12.50			Rec	V,MC,AE	Homemade Italian specialties
Tom Paine's 317 N. Queen St. (717) 393-3671	just N of downtown, between Walnut & Lemon Sts.	Am	7	D	D 9-18	x	x	Rec	V,MC,AE, DC	Roast duck, prime rib, steaks
Torii Japanese Steak House 1820 Columbia Ave. (717) 299-8947	2 mi. W on PA 462, 1/2 mi. E of PA 741	Ja	Tue-Sun	D	D 10-20			Rec	V,MC,AE, CB	Steak, chicken, seafood; prices are for complete meals
Windows on Steinman Park 16-18 W. King St. (717) 295-1316	downtown, 1/2 block W of Penn Square	Fr	7	LD Br	L 2.75-10 D 15-25 Br 15.95		x	Rec, Req F.Sa	V,MC,AE, DC	Fresh Dover sole, rack of lamb, lobster soufflés, Caesar salad, tableside desserts
LEOLA										
The Log Cabin 11 Lehoy Forest Dr. (717) 626-1181	8 mi. NE of Lancaster off PA 272	Am	Mon-Sat	D	D 14-26	x	x	Req. Sat.	V,MC,AE, CB,DC	Filet mignon, sirloin, lamb chops, veal
LITITZ										
The Brickerville House 2 E. 28th Division Hwy. (717) 626-0377	SE corner of US 322 & PA 501 in Brickerville, 5 mi. N of Lititz	Am	Mon-Sat	L	L 5		x	Rec	V,MC	Homemade soup, quiche, large sandwiches, pastries
The Historic General Sutter Inn 14 E. Main St. (717) 626-2115	SE corner of the square, intersection of PA 501 & 772	Co, Am	7	BLD	B 2.76 L 2.75-7 D 11-17			Rec Req F.Sa	V,MC,AE	
Wells Warwick House 104 N. Broad St. (717) 626-8641	in town, 1 block N of square on PA 501	Am	7	LD	L 3-7.50 D 8-14	x	x		All	Seafood, steaks, chicken, veal, chocolate dessert bar
MANHEIM										
The Cat's Meow 215 S. Charlotte St. (717) 664-3370	1/2 block W of PA 72, next to railroad	Am	7	LD	L 2.95 D 7.95			Req Fri, Sat	V,MC,D	Spicy chicken wings, fillet scampi; light gourmet dinners

302

LANCASTER CO. (cont.)

Name / Address / Phone	Location	Cuisine	Days	Meals	Prices			Reserv.	Cards	Remarks
RONKS Miller's Smorgasbord 2811 Lincoln Hwy. E. (717) 687-6621	US 30, 7 mi. E of Lancaster, NE corner of Ronks Rd.	PD, Am	7	BLD	B 7.95 L 7.95 D 14.95	x	x		V,MC,AE	Prices are for complete smorgasbord meals, lower prices for children under 12

LEBANON CO.

Name / Address / Phone	Location	Cuisine	Days	Meals	Prices			Reserv.	Cards	Remarks
LEBANON Fenwick Tavern & Restaurant 2200 W. Cumberland St. (717) 272-9280	west end of city on US 422	PD, Am	Tue-Sat	LD	L 3-6 D 6-21			Rec	V,MC	Steaks, seafood, baby back ribs, pasta; prices are for complete meals
Maple Street Cafe 801 Maple St. (717) 272-0597	north edge of city on PA 343, NE corner of 8th & Maple Sts.	Am	Mon-Sat	LD	L 3-6 D 7-15				None	Home cooking

LEHIGH VALLEY

Name / Address / Phone	Location	Cuisine	Days	Meals	Prices			Reserv.	Cards	Remarks
ALLENTOWN King George Inn Hamilton & Cedar Crest Blvds. (215) 435-1723	west end of city, 1 mi. E of I-78 via Hamilton Blvd., 2 mi. S of US 22 via Cedar Crest Blvd.	Am, Co	7	LD	L 4-8 D 9-25	x		Rec	All	Veal & seafood
Parkland Restaurant 2702 Walbert Ave. (215) 432-2745	1 mi. N of US 22 via Cedar Crest Blvd., turn right on Walbert Ave. for 1 block	Am	7	BLD	B 1.30+ L 2.25+ D 3.95+	x	x	Rec	None	
Walp's Restaurant Union Blvd. & Airport Rd. (215) 437-4841	east side of city, 1.5 mi. S of US 22 Airport Rd. S exit	PD, Am	7	BLD	B 2-3.50 L 3-5	x			V,MC,AE	Fresh seafood, steaks, Pa. Dutch specialties
BALLIETSVILLE Balliettsville Inn 60 Main St. (215) 799-2435	5 mi. N of US 22 via Cedar Crest Blvd. or 15th St. exits	Co, Sw	Mon-Sat	D	D 17-30		x	Req	All	Medallions of venison St. Moritz, roast rack of lamb
BATH Lord Barrington's 7401 Airport Rd. (215) 837-1100	NW corner of PA 329 & 987, 4.5 mi. N of US 22	Am, It	7	LD	L 2-6 D 5-15		x		V,MC,AE, DC	Chicken brasciole, veal scallopini, shrimp étoufée, pasta
BETHLEHEM Aspen Inn 3301 Bath Pike (215) 865-5002	just S of US 22 Center St./PA 512 exit	Am	7	LD	L 3.50-6 D 8.50-18	x		Rec	V,MC,AE, CB,DC	Siamese chicken, cajun tuna, roast duckling, veal Johannesburg Riesling
Stefano's Restaurant 2970 Linden St. (215) 867-7775	1 mi. S of US 22 Linden St./PA 191 exit, opposite Macada Rd.	It	Tue-Sat	LD	L 5-18 D 7-18			Rec	V,AE,CB	10 varieties of veal; prices are for complete meals
EASTON Casa di Crivellaro 1690 Morgan Hill Rd. (215) 253-5245	1-1/2 mi. S of I-78 Easton exit	It	7	D	D 8-16	x		Req	V,MC	Osso buco, Sicilian seafood combination, veal marsala, shrimp scampi

See KEY TO ABBREVIATIONS on page 305.

303

LEHIGH VALLEY (cont.)

Name / Address / Phone	Location Description	Type of Cuisine	Days Open	Meals Served	Prices	Non-smoking section	Handicapped accessible	Reservations	Credit Cards	Specialties/comments
EASTON (cont.) The Windmill 769 Youngs Hill Rd. (215) 252-1541	Right off Cattell St. on Richmond Rd. (SR 2021) for 4 mi. to Ayers Rd. left to end, then right	Am	Tue-Sun	LD	L 3.25-7 D 10-20		x	Rec	All	Prime rib, fresh seafood, ice cream cocktails
EGGELSVILLE Shankweiler's Hotel PO Box 147 (215) 395-5922	NE corner of PA 100 & Old Rt. 22, 1/4 mi. N of I-78/US 22	PD	Wed-Sun	D	D 8-13			Rec	V,MC	Chicken & waffles, sauerbraten; all-you-can-eat family style meals
GUTHSVILLE Magnolia's Vineyard Main Blvd. (215) 395-1233	1 block W of PA 309, 1-1/2 mi. N of US 22	CO	Tue-Sun	D	D 10-17	x	x	Rec	V,MC,AE, CB,DC	Beef Wellington, veal Oscar, fresh seafood; extensive wine list
NEWBURG Newburg Inn Rt. 191 & Newburg Rd. (215) 759-8528	2 mi. N of US 22, 1 block S of jct. of PA 946	Am	7	LD	L 3-7 D 9-19		x		All	Prime rib, steaks, chicken, soup & salad bar
MONTGOMERY CO.										
COLLEGEVILLE Gypsy Rose Hotel Rt. 113 & Creek Rd. (215) 489-1600	1/4 mi. N of PA 29, 4 mi. N of US 422	Am, CO	7	LD Br	L 3-9 D 9-24 Br 8.95	x	x	Rec	V,MC,AE, CB,DC	Seafood, veal, prime rib
EAST GREENVILLE Judge Cooper's Restaurant Route 29 (215) 679-9928	In town, 2 mi. S of intersection of PA 29 & 663	CO	7	LD	L 1.50-8 D 10		x	Rec	V,MC,AE	
FRANCONIA Family Heritage Restaurant Route 113 (215) 723-4815	Intersection of PA 113 & Allentown Rd., between Harleysville & Souderton	PD, Am	Mon-Sat	BLD Br	B 1.75 L 3 D 5.50	x	x		V	Ham, beef, steaks; brunch 5.25 complete
HARLEYSVILLE Lord Salford Pub 712 Main St. (215) 256-8322	on PA 63 in Salford Square Shop. Center, 1/4 mi. W of PA 113	Am	7	LD	L 4-10 D 4-10		x		V,MC,AE, DC	

MONTGOMERY CO. (cont.)

Name / Address	Location	Cuisine	Days	Meals	Prices	Acc.	Reserv.	Credit Cards	Specialties / comments
KING OF PRUSSIA Kennedy-Supplee Mansion 1100 W. Valley Forge Rd. (215) 337-3777	on PA 23, 1/4 ml. N of entrance to Valley Forge Natl. Hist. Park	Am, Co	7	LD Br	L 8-15 D 18-30 Br 25	x	Req Sat	N/A	
POTTSTOWN The Depot 151 N. High St. (215) 327-4707	just W of downtown on old US 422	Am, It	Mon-Sat	LD	L 4 D 9	x	Req Fri, Sat	V,MC,AE, CB,DC	Fresh veal, barbecue spare ribs
TELFORD Rising Sun Inn 898 Allentown Rd. (215) 723-0850	on SR 1001, 2 ml. N of PA 113 at Franconia	Am	Tue-Sun	D	D 10-18	x	Rec	V,MC,AE	Prime rib, seafood
YORK CO.									
DILLSBURG Livingston Chalet 301 Route 15 S. (717) 432-3812	just outside center of town on US 15	Am	7	BLD Br	B 1+ L 2.25+ D 3.95+	x	Rec	V,MC,AE	Steaks, seafood, chicken; smorgasbord; Sun. brunch 7.95
WRIGHTSVILLE Accomac Inn River Rd. (717) 252-1521	1-1/2 ml. N of Wrightsville exit via Cool Springs, Dark Hollow, & Accomac Rds. Along Susq. River	Co	7	LD Br	L 6-10 D 17-25 Br 15.95	x	Rec Req F.Sa	All	Imported rack of baby lamb
YORK Anthony's 801 Loucks Rd. (717) 843-0063	on US 30, 1 ml. W of I-83, exit 9W	Am, It	7	LD	L 3-5 D 6+	x	Rec	V,MC,CB, DC	Italian, cajun, seafood
The Eagles Nest 2519 Mt. Rose Ave. (717) 755-2514; 2487	on PA 124, 1/2 ml. E of I-83, exit 7	Am	7	LD Br	L 2.25-5 D 7-15 Br 6.95		Rec	V,MC,AE, DC	Prime rib; brunch buffet
Meadowbrook Inn & Tavern 2816 Whiteford Rd. (717) 757-3500	just W. of Mt. Zion Rd./PA 24 exit of US 30	Am, Co	7	LD Br	L 8-13 D 12-22 Br 11.95	x	Rec Req Sat	V,MC,AE, DC	Prime rib, veal, seafood
Moser's Restaurant 1251 W. King St. (717) 854-0970	In W. York, 1 block S of PA 462	Am	7	BLD	B 1+ L 2.85+ D 5+	x	Rec	V,MC,CB, DC	Broiled seafood, homemade soups, roast turkey
San Carlos International 333 Arsenal Rd. (717) 854-2028	on US 30, 1 block E of I-83, exit 9	Co	7	LD	L (N/A) D 7.95+	x	Rec	V,MC,AE, DC	Price is for complete meal

KEY TO ABBREVIATIONS

Type of Cuisine: Am-American; Ch-Chinese; Co-Continental; Fr-French; G-German; Gr-Greek, I-Italian, PD-Pennsylvania Dutch

Prices are for entrées unless complete meal is specified in "Specialties/comments"

Non-smoking Section and **Handicapped Accessible:** x=yes

Reservations: Rec-recommended; Req-required (days specified if not required at all times)

Credit Cards: V-Visa; MC-Mastercard; AE-American Express; CB-Carte Blanche, DC-Diners Club; D-Discover; All-all of these

GENERAL INDEX

Adams County, 76
Airville, 243
Alburtis, 211
Allentown, 211
Amish, 25
Amusements, 46
Annville, 202
Antiquing, 75
Audubon, 232
Bangor, 215
Bed and breakfast inns, list of, 258
Belfast, 216
Berks County, 90
Bernville, 93
Bethlehem, 216
Bicycling, 47
Birdsboro, 93
Boating, 49
Boiling Springs, 136
Boyertown, 94
Breinigsville, 220
Brogue, 243
Bucks County, 108
Calendar of events, 57
Campgrounds, list of, 290
Camping, 50
Canoeing, 50
Carlisle, 137
Catasauqua, 220
Caves, 75
Center Point (Worcester), 233
Chadds Ford, 123
Chalfont, 111
Chambersburg, 164
Chester County, 120
Chester Springs, 124
Christiana, 188
Climate of PDC, 22
Coatesville, 124
Collegeville, 233
Columbia, 192
Cooking, regional, 35
Coplay, 221

Cornwall, 202
Covered bridges, 72
Cumberland County, 134
Dauphin County, 142
Delaware County, 121
Delaware River Towns, 111
Delta, 243
Douglassville, 94
Downingtown, 125
Doylestown, 112
Dublin, 115
East Berlin, 78
Eastern Lancaster County, 186
Easton, 221
Economy of PDC, 24
Egypt, 224
Elizabethtown, 194
Elverson, 125
Embreeville, 125
Ephrata, 182
Exton, 125
Fairfield, 78
Fairs and festivals, 51
Farm vacation homes, list of, 270
Farmers' markets, 71
Fayetteville, 168
Fleetwood, 94
Fogelsville, 224
Fort Loudon, 168
Franklin County, 162
Geography of PDC, 22
Gettysburg, 78
Green Lane, 233
Greencastle, 168
Hanover, 244
Harrisburg, 145
Hellertown, 224
Hershey, 153
Hershey, Milton S., 154
Hiking, 51
Historic districts, 73
History of PDC, 15
Hotels, list of, 274

Intercourse, 190
Jews, 34
Kayaking, 50
Kemblesville, 126
Kempton, 95
Kenilworth, 126
Kennett Square, 126
King of Prussia, 234
Kutztown, 95
Lahaska, 115
Lancaster and Environs, 176
Lancaster County, 172
Lansdale, 234
Lebanon, 203
Lebanon County, 200
Lehigh County, 209
Lehigh Valley, 208
Lenhartsville, 96
Liquor laws, 45
Lititz, 184
Manheim, 185
Map symbols, 13
Maps, sources and types, 43
    using, 12
Marietta, 194
Maytown, 194
McSherrystown, 86
Mennonites, 31
Mercersburg, 168
Middletown, 158
Millersville, 195
Mont Alto, 169
Montgomery County, 230
Moravians, 32
Morgantown, 96
Motels, list of, 274
Mount Bethel, 224
Mount Gretna, 204
Mount Joy, 195
Mount Pleasant, 87
Myerstown, 204
NRHP (National Register of Historic
    Places), 73
Nazareth, 225
Neffsville, 182
New Holland, 191

New Hope, 115
New Oxford, 87
Newmanstown, 204
Newville, 139
Norristown, 234
Northampton County, 209
Northern Lancaster County, 182
Oley Township, 96
Outlet shopping, 56
Palmyra, 205
PDC, defined, 9
    population of, 25
    traveling to, 39
    traveling within, 41
Pennsylvania, About, 45
People of PDC, 25
Phoenixvillle, 127
Places of interest, ratings of, 12
Pottstown, 235
Professional sports, 52
Quakertown, 117
Rafting, 50
Reading, 96
Recreation facilities, 46
Restaurants, list of, 298
Robesonia, 103
Sales tax, 46
Schaefferstown, 205
Schnecksville, 225
Schwenkfelders, 33
Schwenksville, 236
Shartlesville, 104
Shippensburg, 139, 169
Shopping, 55
Skiing, 53
Skippack, 236
Slateford, 226
Souderton, 236
Southern Lancaster County, 191
Speech, regional, 36
St. Peters, 128
State parks, 54, 256
Stewartstown, 245
Stouchsburg, 104
Strasburg, 186
Telephones, 46

Telford, 237
Tourist information, sources of, 14
Traffic laws, 45
Train rides, 54
Trappe, 237
Tubing, 50
Unionville, 128
Valley Forge, 237
Walking tours, 74
Waynesboro, 169
Wellsville, 245
West Chester, 128
West Shore, 139
Western Lancaster County, 192
Wineries, 74
Womelsdorf, 104
Wrightsville, 245
York, 246
York County, 240
York Springs, 87
Zoos, 47

SUBJECT INDEX

Amish
Amish Farm and House, 189
Amish Homestead, 188
Amish Village, 189
People's Place, 190

Art Museums
Allentown Art Museum, 213
Brandywine River Museum, 123
Charles Demuth House and
    Garden, 180
James A. Michener Museum, 112
Lehigh University Art Galleries, 220
Reading Public Museum and Art
    Gallery, 102

Children
Dorney Park, 226
Dutch Wonderland, 197
Hersheypark, 156
Land of Little Horses, 86
Museum of Scientific Discovery, 148
Quarry Valley Farm, 115
Toy Train Museum, 187
Weavertown One-Room School, 190

Cultural
Annie S. Kemerer Museum, 220
Founders Hall, 158
Fulton Opera House, 179
Hershey Gardens, 158
Longwood Gardens, 127
Mary Merritt Doll Museum, 94
Merritt's Museum of Childhood, 94
Pagoda, 101
Rajah Theater, 100
State Theater, 222
Swiss Pines, 128
Trumpet Museum, 126

Farm Life Museums
Alexander Schaeffer Farm Museum, 205
Folklife Museum, 96

Goschenhoppen Folklife Library and
    Museum, 233
Pennsylvania Dutch Farm Museum, 95
Pennsylvania Farm Museum, 182
Slateford Farm, 226

Farmers' Markets
Bird-in-Hand, 190
Broad Street, 151
Central (Lancaster), 179
Central (York), 250
Columbia, 193
Farmers (Hanover), 245
Farmers (York), 250

Folkcrafts
Eicher Indian Museum and Shop, 183
Folk Craft Museum, 189
Hex Sign Area, 104
Indian Steps Museum, 243

Government
Capitol Building, 149
State Museum of Pennsylvania, 149

Historic Houses
Andrew Benade House, 216
Barnett-Bobb Log House, 248
Barns-Brinton House, 124
Bonham House, 249
Brinton 1704 House, 129
Donegal Mills Plantation, 195
Fort Hunter Mansion and Park, 152
Gates House, 248
Goundie House, 219
Hans Herr House, 191
Hibernia Ironmaster's Mansion, 125
Jennie Wade House and Olde Town, 81
John Chad House, 124
John Harris Mansion, 149
John Hiester House, 98
Morgan House, 234
Peter Wentz Farmstead, 233

Historic Houses (cont.)

Renfrew Museum and Park, 169
Rock Ford Plantation, 181
Sun Inn, 219
Troxell-Steckel House and
    Farm Museum, 224
Tulpehocken Manor, 204
Wright's Ferry Mansion, 193

Historical Sites & Museums

Berks County Historical Society, 100
Bieber Farmhouse (Lenni Lenape
    Historical Society), 214
Brendle Museum, 205
Buchanan's Birthplace State Park, 169
Chester County Historical Society, 129
Codorus Furnace, 246
Cornwall Iron Furnace, 202
Ephrata Cloister, 183
Ephrata Museum, 184
Fort Zeller Museum, 204
George Neas House, 244
Golden Plough Tavern, 248
Hall of Presidents and Hall of
    First Ladies, 81
Hamilton Library (Cumberland County
    Historical Society), 138
Historical Society of Montgomery
    County, 234
Historical Society of York County, 249
Hopewell Furnace National Historic
    Site, 93
Lancaster County Historical Society, 181
Liberty Bell Shrine, 214
Mixsell House (Northampton County
    Historical Society), 222
Museum of American Life, 155
National Wax Museum, 188
Old Brown's Mill School, 168
Old Court House County Museum, 214
Old Franklin County Jail and
    Heritage Center, 165
Slate Belt Museum, 224
Star Gazer Stone, 125
Stoy Museum (Lebanon County
    Historical Society), 203

Valley Forge National Historical Park, 237
Valley Forge National Historical
    Society Museum, 238
Washington Memorial Chapel, 238
York Co. Colonial Courthouse, 247

Homes of Famous Persons

Conrad Weiser Park, 104
Daniel Boone Homestead, 93
Eisenhower National Historic Site, 84
Fonthill, 114
Frank Buckman House, 214
George Taylor House, 221
Governor's Mansion, 151
Mill Grove, 232
Pearl S. Buck Home, 115
Pennypacker Mills, 236
Pottsgrove Manor, 235
Robert Fulton's Birthplace, 192
Trout Hall, 214
Wheatland, 181

Military

Battlefield Military Museum, 85
Brandywine Battlefield State Park, 123
Carlisle Barracks, 138
Colt Heritage Museum of Fine
    Firearms, 83
"The Conflict", 83
Cyclorama, 84
Fort Loudon, 168
Gettysburg Battle Theater, 82
Gettysburg National Cemetery, 80
Gettysburg National Military Park, 78
Lee's Headquarters, 85
Lincoln Room Museum, 83
Lincoln Train Museum, 82
National Civil War Wax Museum, 82
National Tower, 82
Soldier's National Museum, 81

Natural Features

Crystal Cave, 95
Hawk Mountain Sanctuary, 95
Indian Echo Caverns, 158
Lost River Caverns, 224

SUBJECT INDEX

Religious
Conewago Chapel, 86, 244
Derry Church, 157
Donegal Church and Witness Tree, 195
Friends' Meeting House, 250
Mennonite Heritage Center, 236
Mennonite Information Center, 188
Moravian Community, 217
National Shrine of Our Lady of
Czestochowa, 114
Peace Church, 140
St. James Episcopal Church, 180
Trinity Church, 180
Warrington Meeting House, 245
Whitefield House, 225

Scenic Drives
Frontier Trail Auto Tour, 167
Scenic Valley Tour, 86
Skyline Drive, 101

Science and Technology
David O. Saylor Cement Industry
Museum, 221
Fire Museum of York County, 251
Haines Mill Museum, 215
Moravian Tile Works, 114
Museum of Natural History (Wilson
College), 167
North Museum, 181
Peach Bottom Atomic Power Station, 243
Reading Planetarium, 102
Thomas Newcomen Library and
Museum, 125
Three Mile Island Visitors Center, 158

Shopping
Hiesters Lane Outlets, 103
Kitchen Kettle Village, 190
Mill Bridge Village, 189
N. 9th St. Outlets, 102
Old Gettysburg Village of Quaint
Shops, 83
Peddlers Village, 115
Sickman's Mill, 192
Wyomissing Outlets, 103

Sports, Recreation
Bob Hoffman Weightlifting and Softball
Hall of Fame, 250
Gettysburg Game Park, 78
Middle Creek Wildlife Management
Area, 206
Trexler-Lehigh Co. Game Preserve, 225
Union Canal Towpath Tour, 102

Transportation & Industry
Berks County Heritage Center, 101
Boyertown Museum of Historic
Vehicles, 94
Canal Museum, 223
Candy Americana Museum, 185
Chocolate World, 155
18th Century Industrial Area, 218
Gast Classic Motorcars, 186
Hanover Shoe Farms, 87, 244
Kutztown Bologna Co., 204Lock 12, 243
Lock Ridge Furnace Museum, 211
Locktender's House, 223
Mercer Museum, 112
Michter's Distillery, 205
Mid-Atlantic Air Museum, 101
Palmyra Bologna Co., 205
Phillips Mushroom Place, 127
Railroad Museum of Pennsylvania, 186
Roadside America, 104
Rodney C. Gott Harley-Davidson
Motorcycle Museum, 251
Rough and Tumble Museum, 189
Skew Bridge, 100
Stroh Brewery, 224
Sturgis Pretzel Co., 185
Union Canal Tunnel, 203
Watch and Clock Museum, 194
Weaver's Bologna, 203

Wineries
Adams County Winery, 85
Allegro Vineyards, 243
Brandywine Vineyards and Winery, 126
Bucks Country Vineyards, 116
Calvaresi Winery, 93
Chadds Ford Winery, 124

Wineries (cont.)
Clover Hill Vineyards and Winery, 220
Country Creek Vineyards and Winery, 237
Fox Meadow Farm Winery, 124
Franklin Hill Vineyards, 215
Lancaster County Winery, 192
Little Vineyard and Winery, 117
Mount Hope Estate and Winery, 185
Naylor Wine Cellars, Inc., 245
Nissley Vineyards, 195
Peace Valley Winery, 111
Stephen Bahn Winery, 243
Tucquan Vineyard, 192
Victorian Wine Cellars, 181
York Springs Vineyard and Winery, 87

Zoos
Elmwood Park Zoo, 235
Zoo America, 156

NOTES